AFRIKA AND ALEMANIA

German-Speaking Women, Africa, and the African Diaspora

Edited by Priscilla Layne, Michelle James, and Lisabeth Hock

Afrika and Alemania explores the representation of Blackness in German-speaking literary, autobiographical, and cinematic texts across two centuries. By examining how different groups of women with access to German culture have depicted Africa, Africans, and the African diaspora, the book challenges the assumption that all women will tell the same story. Focusing on Black women, non-Black women of colour, and white women, it investigates how these diverse voices engage with and represent Blackness within a society shaped by racial hierarchies.

Part I analyses how Black, German-speaking women actively reshape and redefine Blackness in response to stereotypes upheld by white German society. Part II explores how non-Black women of colour navigate the complexities of othering while sometimes reproducing anti-Black stereotypes, while Part III discusses how white women's projections of fantasies about Africa often erase Black voices and render them invisible. Offering a nuanced analysis of the intersections of race, gender, ethnicity, and nationality, *Afrika and Alemania* provides a vital framework for understanding Blackness within contemporary scholarship and its broader social and cultural implications.

(German and European Studies)

PRISCILLA LAYNE is a professor of German at the University of North Carolina at Chapel Hill.

MICHELLE JAMES is an associate professor of German at Brigham Young University.

LISABETH HOCK is an associate professor of German at Wayne State University.

GERMAN AND EUROPEAN STUDIES

General Editor: James Retallack

Afrika and Alemania

German-Speaking Women, Africa, and the African Diaspora

EDITED BY PRISCILLA LAYNE,
MICHELLE JAMES, AND
LISABETH HOCK

UNIVERSITY OF TORONTO PRESS
Toronto Buffalo London

© University of Toronto Press 2025
Toronto Buffalo London
utorontopress.com
Printed in the USA

ISBN 978-1-4875-4735-6 (cloth) ISBN 978-1-4875-4775-2 (EPUB)
ISBN 978-1-4875-6073-7 (paper) ISBN 978-1-4875-4776-9 (PDF)

Library and Archives Canada Cataloguing in Publication

Title: Afrika and Alemania : German-speaking women, Africa, and the African diaspora / edited by Priscilla Layne, Michelle James, and Lisabeth Hock.
Names: Layne, Priscilla, editor | James, Michelle Stott, editor | Hock, Lisabeth M., 1963– editor
Series: German and European studies.
Description: Series statement: German and European studies. | Includes bibliographical references and index.
Identifiers: Canadiana (print) 20250144093 | Canadiana (ebook) 20250144131 | ISBN 9781487547356 (cloth) | ISBN 9781487560737 (paper) | ISBN 9781487547752 (EPUB) | ISBN 9781487547769 (PDF)
Subjects: LCSH: German literature – 20th century – History and criticism. | LCSH: German literature – 19th century – History and criticism. | LCSH: Women, Black, in literature. | LCSH: African diaspora in literature. | LCSH: Africans in literature. | LCSH: Race in literature.
Classification: LCC PT405 .A37 2025 | DDC 830.9/3522 – dc23

Cover design: Val Cooke
Cover image: Maseho, "The Return of the Fachinehae," 2024. iStock.com/blackboard1965

The German and European Studies series is funded by the DAAD with funds from the German Federal Foreign Office.

DAAD Deutscher Akademischer Austauschdienst
German Academic Exchange Service

We wish to acknowledge the land on which the University of Toronto Press operates. This land is the traditional territory of the Wendat, the Anishnaabeg, the Haudenosaunee, the Métis, and the Mississaugas of the Credit First Nation.

University of Toronto Press acknowledges the financial support of the Government of Canada, the Canada Council for the Arts, and the Ontario Arts Council, an agency of the Government of Ontario, for its publishing activities.

 Canada Council   Conseil des Arts
for the Arts   du Canada

 ONTARIO ARTS COUNCIL
CONSEIL DES ARTS DE L'ONTARIO
an Ontario government agency
un organisme du gouvernement de l'Ontario

Funded by the   Financé par le
Government   gouvernement
of Canada   du Canada

Contents

Contributors vii

Introduction: Blackness, Germany, and Representation 3
LISABETH HOCK, PRISCILLA LAYNE, AND MICHELLE JAMES

Section I: The Black Diaspora and Self-Definition

1 "They Are the Next Generation": An Interview with Sarah Blaßkiewitz 23
PRISCILLA LAYNE AND LISABETH HOCK

2 Between Autofiction and the Archive: On/Travelling Olivia Wenzel's *1,000 Coils of Fear* (2020): Touching Tale or World Refracts Nation 37
BIRGIT TAUTZ

3 Postcolonial Ghana and the Legacy of Colonial Oppression in Amma Darko's Novels 57
PRISCILLA LAYNE

Section II: Non-Black POC, Africa, and the African Diaspora

4 "Eingangstor zum Afrika" (Gateway to Africa): The Reconfigurations of Emily Ruete 81
KATE ROY

5 The Survivor as "Implicated Subject" in Stefanie Zweig's Autobiographical Africa Novels *Nirgendwo in Afrika* (*Nowhere in Africa*) and *Nirgendwo war Heimat. Mein Leben auf zwei Kontinenten* (*Nowhere Was Home: My Life on Two Continents*) 112
SARAH HENNEBÖHL

6 Making the Invisible Visible? Representations of Black Masculinity in Texts by Yoko Tawada 132
LISABETH HOCK

Section III: White Settler Colonialism and Its Legacies

7 German Cultural Superiority and Racial Hierarchy in Gabriele Reuter's *Glück und Geld* 153
DAVID TINGEY

8 The Black Slave Martyr Re-imagined for Christian Missions in Colonial Africa: Maria Theresa Ledóchowska's *Zaïda* (1889) 171
CINDY PATEY BREWER AND ELIZABETH MOYE-WEAVER

9 Rethinking the Periphery: Blackness in Eugenie Marlitt's *Im Schillingshof* (1879) 191
BETH MUELLNER

10 White Feminism and the Colonial Gaze: Frieda von Bülow's Diaries from German East Africa 210
CAROLA DAFFNER

11 Single White Female: Independent Women and Colonial Knowledge Production in German Colonial Fiction 227
MAUREEN O. GALLAGHER

12 Colonial Propaganda Fiction: Else Steup's *Backfisch* Novels from the 1930s 246
JULIA K. GRUBER

13 Perspectives on Namibia by Contemporary White German-Speaking Women Authors 266
LORELY FRENCH

Index 285

Contributors

Sarah Blaßkiewitz studied film at the Beuth University in Berlin and worked at the same time in the directing and camera department for film productions. From 2016 she attended Thomas Heise's film class at the Academy of Arts Vienna. Her first feature film, *Precious Ivie*, celebrated its premiere at the Munich Film Festival in 2021 and received the rating "Particularly Valuable." Among other things, it was awarded Best Film at the German Film Festival and received the Guild Film Prize of the Art Cinemas 2021. At the same time, Blaßkiewitz directed four episodes of the web series *Druck*. In 2022, she directed the series *Sam – a Saxon* for Disney+, based on true events, for which she was awarded the Grimme Prize 2024. Her comedy series *Oh Hell* (Season 2) is currently running on HBO MAX in the USA. Blaßkiewitz is currently preparing her second feature film.

Carola Daffner received her PhD from Vanderbilt University and is currently Associate Professor of German and Chair of the Department of Global Languages and Cultures at the University of Dayton. Her teaching interests include the history of human rights and advocacy, National Socialist cinema, and gender and sexuality in German literature. In her research, she focuses on gender and the politics of space in German literature and film. Her work has been published as a monograph and in several academic journals, including *German Studies Review*, *Journal of Austrian Studies*, and *Women in German Yearbook*.

Lorely French is Professor of German at Pacific University in Oregon and author of *Roma Voices in the German-Speaking World* (2015). She has published on German women writers and on Romani authors, specifically Ceija Stojka, survivor of three concentration camps. French co-edited a

2020 special issue on Romani literatures for *Romani Studies*, and her annotated English translation of Stojka's memoirs appeared in 2022 with Camden House. She has received grants from the Fulbright Commission, Deutscher Akademischer Austauschdienst, American Council of Learned Societies, and the National Endowment for the Humanities. She is the recipient of the Confederation in Oregon for Language Teaching Professor of the Year award and the Pacific Ancient and Modern Language Association Distinguished Service Award.

Maureen O. Gallagher is a Lecturer in German Studies at Australian National University. She holds a PhD in German Studies from the University of Massachusetts Amherst. Her research interests are in the areas of gender studies, critical race theory and critical whiteness studies, and postcolonialism and decolonization. Recent publications have focused on inclusive and decolonial pedagogy, race and gender in German colonial literature, and First World War literature; she is currently working on a book manuscript on whiteness in Wilhelmine German youth literature and culture. She is also on the authoring team of the online open-access German curriculum Grenzenlos Deutsch, which has been supported by an NEH grant.

Julia K. Gruber is Associate Professor of German at Tennessee Tech University, where she teaches beginning, intermediate, and advanced German classes in the undergraduate program. Her research has focused on Jewish child exiles and the Kindertransport, works by Eva Menasse, and the Austrian family novel. Gruber is currently editing a collection of essays on feminist anger, which includes her own article on Stefanie Sargnagel, the Austrian fraternity Hysteria, and radical rudeness as a form of female empowerment.

Sarah Henneböhl received her PhD in German Studies from the University of Illinois Urbana-Champaign. She is Associate Teaching Professor of German at the Pennsylvania State University, University Park. Henneböhl directs the Basic German Language Sequence and is the TA Coordinator for the German program. She teaches all levels of German language, literature, and culture, as well as introductory classes on foreign language pedagogy at the college level. Her research interest lies in critical whiteness and gender studies with a geographical focus on the African continent.

Lisabeth Hock received her PhD from Washington University in St. Louis and is Associate Professor of German at Wayne State University and Program Director of the Junior Year in Munich Program. She teaches all levels of German language, literature, and culture and in her department's Global Studies program. Her research focuses on women writers, literature and psychiatry, and the scholarship of teaching and learning. Her work has been published as a monograph and in academic journals, including *The German Quarterly*, *German Studies Review*, *History of Psychiatry*, *Die Unterrichtspraxis*, and *Women in German Yearbook*.

Priscilla Layne is Associate Professor of German and Adjunct Associate Professor of African Diaspora Studies at the University of North Carolina at Chapel Hill. Her book, *White Rebels in Black: German Appropriation of Black Popular Culture*, was published in 2018 by the University of Michigan Press. She has also published essays on Turkish German culture, translation, punk, and film. Her translation of Olivia Wenzel's debut novel, *1000 Serpentinen Angst*, appeared in 2022 and was longlisted for the 2023 National Translation Award. She is currently finishing a manuscript on Afro-German Afrofuturism and a critical guide to Fassbinder's *The Marriage of Maria Braun*.

Elizabeth Moye-Weaver teaches beginning and intermediate German courses as an adjunct instructor at Utah Valley University. She has a master's degree in Second Language Teaching from Brigham Young University, where she developed a course on Women's Studies topics in the German-speaking world. Her research focuses on mission literature, motivational course design, and blended language learning.

Beth Ann Muellner is Professor of German at the College of Wooster, where she teaches all levels of language and culture. Her research focuses on nineteenth- and twentieth-century travel writing, women's writing, visual culture, graphic novels, food studies, and interdisciplinary approaches to literature. Muellner earned her PhD (2003) from the University of Minnesota. She has published articles on Malwida von Meysenbug, Clärenore Stinnes, Lou Andreas-Salomé, Annemarie Schwarzenbach, the Empress Elisabeth of Austria, and the Poet-Queen Carmen Sylva (Elisabeth of Romania). Her current book project is entitled "Working the Gilded Cage: The Life and Writing of Poet-Queen Carmen Sylva aka Queen Elisabeth of Romania (1843–1916)."

Cindy Patey Brewer holds a doctorate in German Literature from the University of Utah. She is currently Associate Professor at Brigham Young University. Past research focused on German literature by women writers of the eighteenth and nineteenth centuries. She is an associate director of Sophie: Digital Library of Works by German-Speaking Women (http://sophie.byu.edu/). Current research focuses on German-language colonial literature with a particular emphasis on Christian mission narratives about Africa, India, China, and South America.

Kate Roy is an Adjunct Professor in Languages, Literatures, and Cultures at Franklin University Switzerland. She holds a PhD in German and French Studies from the University of Manchester, UK. Her research interests include diasporic writing, Deleuzian theory, and comparative studies in postcolonial literatures and cultures. She has published journal articles and contributions to edited volumes on German-language writers Emine Sevgi Özdamar, Yadé Kara, and Emily Ruete, and on French writer Leïla Sebbar, and has edited and co-edited volumes in Border Studies, Academic Travel, and contemporary German-language literature. Her current research project explores the many incarnations of Emily Ruete's *Memoiren einer arabischen Prinzessin* (1886).

Michelle Stott James is an Associate Professor of German at Brigham Young University. After the publication of her first book, *Behind the Mask: Kierkegaard's Pseudonymic Treatment of Lessing in the "Concluding Unscientific Postscript,"* Dr. James turned her research interests to early German-language women writers. Through the Sophie Mentored Research Project, she and her colleagues Rob McFarland and Cindy Brewer developed the extensive online Sophie Digital Library (now the Sophie Scholars Archive: https://scholarsarchive.byu.edu/sophie/), and have engaged numerous students in textual preparation, editing, and research. The first volume of her digital four-volume *Critically Annotated Collected Works of Elisa von der Recke* will appear with Peter Lang in 2025. In 2016, with Rob McFarland she published the edited collection *Sophie Discovers Amerika: German-Speaking Women Write the New World*. A book chapter, "'Collaborating with Spirits': Cagliostro, Elisa von der Recke, and the Phantoms of Unmündigkeit," written in collaboration with Rob McFarland, appeared in 2019 in the volume *Gender, Collaboration, and Authorship in German Culture: Literary Joint Ventures, 1750–1850*.

Birgit Tautz is the George Taylor Files Professor of Modern Languages and Professor of German at Bowdoin College. She is the author or editor of four books, most recently of *Translating the World: Toward a New Literature of German Literature around 1800* (2018) and the co-edited *Social Capital, Material Culture, Reading: European Networks at 1800*. She has written many articles on eighteenth-century German literature, philosophy, and culture, almost all of them engaging with questions of cultural alterity and exchange, race and ethnic difference, as well as legacies of the past. Occasionally, Tautz has ventured into the area of post-1945 literature and film, and she is currently at work on a book manuscript, "The Ethics of the Image," devoted to film of the past thirty years, as well as a new project on "Small Things, Narrative Episodes," tracking their fate in the Transatlantic rim.

David Tingey is Associate Professor of German and Comparative Literature at the University of Tulsa, where he teaches German, honours, and humanities courses. His teaching and research interests include Gabriele Reuter, Uwe Timm, *Faust*, the German Märchen, and foreign language teaching. He is the author of *Seeing Jaakob: The Poetics of Visuality in Thomas Mann's "Die Geschichten Jaakobs"* (2009). He is the creator and director of the International Engineering/Science and Language dual degree program at the University of Tulsa. He is the president of the University of Tulsa's Faculty Senate and chair of the College of Arts and Sciences Curriculum Committee.

AFRIKA AND ALEMANIA

Introduction: Blackness, Germany, and Representation

LISABETH HOCK, PRISCILLA LAYNE,
AND MICHELLE JAMES

It has been clear since the 1977 publication of the *Combahee River Collective Statement*,[1] and the 1986 publication of *Farbe bekennen* (*Showing Our Colors*),[2] that neither women nor feminists speak with one voice, and that intersecting categories of identity – among them race and gender – grant some women more and other women less access to power and to personal and societal authority and influence. More recently, the issue of privilege among white feminists came up in the writings of Nigerian American Luvvie Ajayi Jones,[3] University of Pennsylvania Provost Mamta Motwani Accapadi,[4] and German Nigerian journalist and podcast host Malcolm Ohanwe,[5] all of whom criticize white women's weaponizing of tears – crying in response to, and as a way of deflecting, criticism of bias or racism – in an effort to wield social power. Not only as individuals, but also as groups, different women occupy different positionalities in the societies in which they live, and vis-à-vis one another.

Our understanding of the concepts of positionality and intersectionality gives rise to our volume's hypothesis that, when their writing engages with race and ethnicity, women from different racial and ethnic groups will tell different stories. The essays in this volume test this hypothesis by turning to German-speaking women – a category we use to broaden the authors and texts we study beyond national boundaries and citizenship – and asking how they represent Africa, Africans, and the African Diaspora. The fields of Feminist German Studies, Black German Studies,[6] and Postcolonial German Studies[7] have produced much valuable scholarship, and especially recently, much has been written on the ways in which white women help to perpetuate racism and the structures of white power. Yet no volume to date has taken a comparative approach to the ways that different groups of women with linguistic access to German culture represent Blackness across a broad spectrum of time. Our volume explores the way German-speaking women of different racial and ethnic backgrounds represent Africa, Africans, and peoples of the African Diaspora in their artistic production. It then demonstrates in its three sections that, while Black women struggle to define and represent Blackness, Black peoples, and Africa in their own terms, the representations of Africa and people of the African Diaspora in texts by white women – and also by non-Black People of Colour – continue to the present day to fall back on stereotypes or serve as surfaces for identity projection.

We emphasize here that, in formulating our hypothesis, test case, and conclusion, we do not consider race and ethnicity to be essential, biologically determined categories. Rather, we recognize the historical reality that a woman's sense of belonging to a particular racial or ethnic majority or minority in the German-speaking world – and the ways that she is defined by that world as belonging to a given group – shape her experiences and therefore her artistic production and representations.

To understand the artistic production of German-speaking women and the ways in which they represent race and ethnicity, one must understand the broader context in which they produce their work. As the website Black Central Europe[8] so well documents, connections between African and European peoples can be traced back to the Middle Ages. The left panel of Nikolaus von Verdun's Klosterneuburg Altarpiece (1181)[9] features a depiction of the meeting between the Queen of Sheba and King Solomon. In Wolfram von Eschenbach's thirteenth-century epic, *Parzival*, the phenotypically black-and-white Prince Feirefiz is the mixed-race son of the Black queen Belacane of Zazamanc and the white knight Gahmuret. Yet we must move forward in time five centuries to find intellectual and artistic production by German-speaking women that engages with Africa and persons of African descent.[10]

The first German-speaking woman to publish a text related to Africa was the Jewish writer and salon hostess Henriette Herz (1764–1847), who translated into German the Scottish explorer Mungo Park's *Journey to the Interior of Africa in the Years 1795 and 1797*.[11] While Park's best-seller introduced Europeans to Africa, its resources, and their potential for exploitation, Herz's translation marks the first engagement of a modern, German-speaking woman writer with the continent and its landscapes, peoples, and regions.

Despite her close ties to Romantic intellectual circles, Herz's Sephardic Jewish roots marked her as an outsider within German society and culture, a distinction she shared with the Zanzibari Muslim princess, Salama bint Said (1884–1944). After growing up speaking Arabic and Swahili in the royal house of Zanzibar, Salama bint Said conceived a child fathered by a white German merchant, married the father, changed her name to Emily Ruete, and moved to Hamburg where she learned German and taught Arabic. Accounts of Ruete's life between Europe and Africa can be found in her published correspondence[12] and her two-volume *Memoiren einer arabischen Prinzessin* (1866).[13]

Notably, access to wealth for at least some part of their lives gave Herz and Ruete a public voice that most other nineteenth-century women, particularly Women of Colour, did not have. This was the case, for example, with a group of Sudanese and Ethiopian girls whom an Italian monk freed from slavery in Egypt in the mid-nineteenth century. These girls were forced to assimilate to European culture and become nuns in a Dominican monastery in the Vorarlberg region of Austria, where they were viewed as "wild" and "uncivilized." Most of these girls died of European diseases while still in their teens.[14] They have no voices other than the ones that historians have given to them.

Well into the twentieth century, most German-speaking women with the education and authority to produce accounts of Africa and African-descended peoples were white Europeans, who, beginning with Germany's colonial period, had increasing opportunities for encounters with Black people. German unification in 1872 and the Berlin Conference of 1884 formalized the so-called "scramble for Africa": the rush of western European countries to lay claim to territories in the Americas, Africa, and Asia. Germany invaded and gained control of German East Africa, German South West Africa, German Cameroon, Togoland, and territories in the Pacific. From this point until the loss of those colonies at the end of the First World War, an increasing number of white women, including farmer's wives such as Clara Brockmann (c. 1910),[15] travelled abroad and wrote accounts in support of Germany's colonial project.

As professional opportunities for white women increased in the wake of the nineteenth-century women's movement, so did the ways in which they engaged with Africa. German member of the Basel Mission Society, Johanna (Hanna) Bohner (1853–1935), not only recorded her memories of her missionary work in Cameroon[16] but also collected local flora and fauna to send back to Germany for research. Jewish-born Helene Bresslau (1879–1957) married Albert Schweitzer and worked as nurse, Protestant missionary, and social worker in Gabon. Polish noblewoman Maria Theresia Ledóchowska (1863–1922) took up Catholic missionary work and wrote about, among other topics, the anti-slavery work of the Catholic missions in Africa.[17] Annemarie Schwarzenbach (1908–42) of Switzerland worked in Africa as a journalist and photographer.[18] German pilot Elly Beinhorn (1907–2007) began with acrobatic feats in Europe before turning to long-distance flying that took her to Africa.[19]

Into the twentieth century, most Black People and People of Colour living in German territories arrived there either forcibly or via immigration from the German colonies. When they found representation, it was often through the words and images of others. Kira Thurman has shown that in the final third of the nineteenth century, Black musicians began to travel to and perform in Central Europe, challenging myths and assumptions about Black people.[20] Nevertheless, most nineteenth-century white women addressing the topic of our volume did not consider Black people or People of Colour to be in any way German or to have access to German culture.

When white German soldiers began fathering children with African women in the colonies, German politicians became intent on maintaining the structure of white supremacy by prohibiting these Black German children from acquiring German citizenship. Thus, in 1905 a law was passed in German South West Africa (present-day Namibia) that banned marriages between German men and African women. An amended law not only retroactively voided previously legal marriages, but also "stripped wives and children of their German citizenship, making all children of these unions 'bastards' and subject to the laws governing the native population."[21] It was, however, the births of mixed-race children in Germany in the aftermath of the First and Second World Wars that began to challenge the stereotypical association of Blackness with Africa and whiteness with Europe.

Following the First World War and the Treaty of Versailles, France employed troops from its African colonies to occupy the Rhineland. As was the case with British and American occupation troops, some of these men had relationships with German women that resulted in pregnancies and births. Julia Roos cites a German government report that counted just over 4,500 *Besatzungskinder* (occupation children) in the Rhineland in 1930, 41 per cent of whom were fathered by Americans, 24 per cent of whom were fathered by British troops, and 19 per cent of whom were fathered by French troops.[22] Doubly insulted by the outcome of the Treaty of Versailles and the stationing of Black troops on German soil, German nationalists chose to focus their attention on the Black French troops. Despite a dearth of evidence in support of their claims,[23] they alleged that French colonial troops were committing rapes and other sexual crimes, and throughout the 1920s they employed "pseudo-Darwinism and sexual stereotypes"[24] in public discussions and published articles about the "Black shame" or "Black horror" on the Rhine: *die schwarze Schmach am Rhein*.

Because their mothers held German citizenship, these children born in the Rhineland were German citizens at birth. Yet with the rise of National

Socialism, this first significant group of Black Germans was considered a threat to the German nation and the "purity of the race."²⁵ As Tina Campt writes, public officials began towards the end of the Weimar Republic to consider the sterilization or deportation of these children but were hindered from doing so by German law. Under National Socialism, hundreds of these individuals were nevertheless illegally sterilized.²⁶

The Allied occupation of West Germany following the Second World War, the travel boom made possible by the *Wirtschaftswunder*, and Cold War cultural politics in East and West Germany led to expanded opportunities for people from African countries to study or work in or migrate to German-speaking countries, as well as to the birth of a significant number of biracial German children with one white German parent and one parent from Africa or the African Diaspora. Coming to adulthood in the late 1960s and early 1970s and resisting the racist terminology that white Germans used to describe and address them, these individuals consciously and intentionally began to refer to themselves in the 1980s as Black Germans, *Schwarze Deutsche*, or *Afrodeutsche*.

In the watershed year of 1986, the German poet, educator, and activist May Ayim (1960–96) wrote as her dissertation the first study of African-German history. She then used her dissertation as the basis of the volume *Farbe bekennen*,²⁷ which she co-edited with Katharina Oguntoye (b. 1959) and Dagmar Schultz (b. 1941); Ayim also helped to found the Initiative Schwarze Deutsche (Initiative of Black Germans). In addition to testimonies of Black German women born in the postwar period, *Farbe bekennen* included the accounts of German women whose lineages reflected African ties to Germany going back to Weimar Germany and the Kaiserreich. Since then, an increasing number of German and German-speaking women writers and film-makers have examined in their art the experience and meaning of growing up Black in Germany, among them Ika Hügel-Marshall (b. 1947)²⁸ and Abini Zöllner (b. 1967),²⁹ who explore their identities through autobiography.

As the writing and films of German-speaking Black women and Women of Colour have increasingly gained authority in the German discourse on Africa and the African Diaspora, texts and films by contemporary white writers and directors have often revealed what Dirk Göttsche³⁰ describes as a tension between stereotypical exoticization of Africa, a critical postcolonial gaze, and the search for an intercultural poetics. Among these are Swiss author Corinna Hoffman's (b. 1960) accounts of her experiences in Kenya, including *Die weisse Massai*,³¹ which German director Hermine Huntgeburth (b. 1957) turned into a hit film.³² Brigitte Beil (1941–2016) offers an example of white women's engagement with Germany's colonial past in her fictionalization of the story of Berlin architect Carl Haertel in Ethiopia in the early twentieth century.[33] Fictional accounts of the lives of Frida von Bülow and Emily Ruete appear in novels by Austrian Monika Czernin (b. 1965)[34] and German Nicole Vossler (b. 1972),[35] respectively.

Globalization and concomitant changes in migration and travel patterns have added further dimensions to the stories told by German-speaking women about Africa and the African Diaspora. Lucia Engombe (b. 1972)[36] and Stefanie-Lahya Aukongo (b. 1978)[37] are two Black women who write in separate accounts of being brought from Namibia to East Germany in 1979, and then being sent back to Africa after the fall of the Berlin Wall. Born to Ghanaian parents who migrated to Germany, model, actress, and activist Dayan Kodua (b. 1980) published a collection of essays about the lives of prominent Black Germans.[38] Exophonic Japanese writer Yoko Tawada (b. 1960) has reflected in her fiction on Anton Wilhelm Amo (c. 1703–c. 1759), a German Enlightenment philosopher originally from the Gold Coast before he was enslaved and brought to Germany as a child, and the African American singer Michael Jackson (1958–2009).[39] Exophonic Nigerian Welsh film-maker Branwen Okpako (b. 1969) studied at the Berlin Film Academy and produced a documentary[40] and a television film[41] about the Black experience in East Germany; Christa Wolf's *Medea*;[42] and her fellow film-school student, Auma Obama (b. 1960),[43] who was born in Kenya and lived as a student in Germany in the 1980s and 1990s. These names and titles are important, because they remain largely invisible in the cultural mainstream. However, they merely scratch the surface of the rich cultural production of German and German-speaking Black women.

Representation of Black voices in art and literature is no substitute for political representation, but it does support political calls for and efforts in the interest of that representation. Unlike the United States, the Federal Republic of Germany still does not collect data on its citizens and inhabitants regarding race and ethnicity. On the one hand, the term *Rasse* (race) was so tainted by the Nazis that it remains a taboo term. On the other hand, despite the lessons of the Second World War – and despite changes in the citizenship laws at the turn of the millennium that allow for some people born on German soil to automatically become German citizens – the country has had great difficulty moving beyond the idea of itself as ethnically German, and thus as white. Because Germany officially collects no data on discrimination against groups from specific racial and ethnic backgrounds, the country has no way to account for institutional biases in areas such as policing.[44]

The United Nations Secretariat's "Report of the UN Working Group of Experts on People of African Descent on its Mission to Germany," issued in September 2017, took the Federal Republic of Germany to task for its "lack of disaggregated data on people of African descent without a migrant background."⁴⁵ It notes that people of African descent remain structurally indiscernible in Germany because they are "collectively grouped under the all-embracing concept of 'people from a migrant background,' thereby rendering invisible German citizens of African descent beyond the second generation. This approach does not specifically address the challenges faced by people of African descent in Germany, and indeed reflects the general lack of attention paid to their socioeconomic and political welfare."⁴⁶ The report goes on to recommend that "People of African descent in Germany should be legally recognized by the Government as a minority group that has made and continues to make profound economic, political, social and cultural contributions to Germany."⁴⁷

This has yet to happen, however. Instead, to the present day, Black German women have played a central role in the "articulation and representation of the Black community in Germany."⁴⁸ We see this in Black German activism: women made up nineteen of the twenty-four scholars, artists, and intellectuals who signed a petition criticizing the "organization and management of the Creative Unit: *New Black Diaspora Studies*" at the University of Bremen because it consisted "solely of white professors, white post-doctoral fellows, and white graduate students."⁴⁹ Black German women have also made the most widely cited contributions to the development of the scholarly field of Black German studies, which as a result, particularly in conjunction with the US paradigm on which it was based, has long been dominated by a "feminist/womanist" focus.⁵⁰ Their contributions include the publication of the volume *Farbe bekennen (Showing Our Colors)*⁵¹ and the founding of ADEFRA (The Organization for Black German Women),⁵² both in 1986, as well as the founding of the Black German Heritage and Research Association by Rosemarie Peña.⁵³

It would thus appear that Black women are in the forefront of moving and writing Black people into the German nation, thus making them visible. This perspective, however, does not account for the fact that the First Black German Movement, which was active during the Weimar period, was largely dominated by men. Moreover, Black German men have always been involved in the community building and activism that has taken place since the 1980s. As Tiffany Florvil notes in *Mobilizing Black Germany*, from the very beginning, the Initiative Schwarzer Menschen in Deutschland "mobilized against all forms of discrimination and encouraged Black German solidarity between women and men."⁵⁴

The present volume considers explicitly the intersection of gender with race and ethnicity. To this end, we organize the volume into three sections: 1) The Black Diaspora and Self-Definition; 2) Non-Black POC, Africa, and the African Diaspora; and 3) White Settler Colonialism and Its Legacies. This allows us to compare the ways that German-speaking women of different racial and ethnic backgrounds represent Africa, Blackness, and the African Diaspora. Certainly, artists work in the realm of the imagination, where it is possible to sensitively represent the other and attempt to speak in their voice. Yet because of the wide-ranging impacts of colonialism and global racism, this requires much thought and discipline and is not always accomplished successfully.

Afrika und Alemania spans the period of the mid-nineteenth through the twenty-first century, and while we aim for chronological breadth, we do not organize our articles in ascending chronological order. To do so would inevitably privilege white narratives about Africa and the African Diaspora by allowing them to become the lens through which subsequent articles are read. Instead, we begin by looking at the ways in which Black women have chosen to represent themselves, Africa, and the African Diaspora. We then use this lens of self-representation to examine representations in texts by non-Black Women of Colour and white women.

Our volume is concerned with intersectionality, and particularly with how the intersections of race, ethnicity, and gender influence one's representation of racial and geographical difference. Section one consists of studies of Black, German-speaking women who redefine Blackness in the face of the stereotypes held by white German society and who expand our understanding of the Black German canon. Our first piece, "They Are the Next Generation," is an interview with television and film director, Sarah Blaßkiewitz. Born in Leipzig in 1986, Blaßkiewitz's East German citizenship became German citizenship four years later. Not only did she grow up both German and Black, she represented this identity in her long-running role (from 2000 to 2005) as Josephine Langmann in the German television series *Castle Einstein*. In the interview, she reflects on what it means to be a director who focuses on Black themes in her work, as well as on her desire not to be defined by or limited to a single thematic focus and a single identity marker. Birgit Tautz's article, "Between Autofiction and the Archive," shows how Olivia Wenzel's 2020 novel, *1000 Serpentinen Angst*, challenges the boundaries we draw around German literary history and the history of Africa and the African Diaspora. The novel achieves this by allowing the narrator to draw on a personal archive that relates the local and the global in the history of Wenzel's biracial family and by chronicling the changing status of objects in order to represent the lingering, constitutive presence of literary forms of the past (it-narratives) in the present. Priscilla Layne's "Postcolonial Ghana and the Legacy of Colonial Oppression" situates two novels by the Ghanaian author, Amma Darko, in the Black German canon. Both novels, *Der verkaufte Traum* (*Beyond the Horizon*, 1991) and *Spinnweben* (Webs, 1996), offer a damaging look at what it is like to be an African woman in Germany in the 1980s. Although African immigrant women are subjected to intersectional oppression similar to that of Black German women (along the lines of race, gender, and sexuality), there are additional identity categories that may situate them in a less powerful position, categories like citizenship, residency status, and language competency. By discussing Darko's depictions of Germany, Layne introduces a postcolonial perspective to the topics explored in this volume.

The middle section of our volume looks at representations of Africa and the African Diaspora by non-Black Women of Colour who write in German. Here, we ask what happens when women from groups that are themselves stereotyped and Othered in white, Christian, German society, represent Blackness and the notions of Africa and the African Diaspora in their texts. We find that despite such experiences, the authors are not immune to replicating anti-Black stereotypes or to using Africa and Blackness as projection surfaces for their own imagined identities. Kate Roy's article, "Eingangstor zum Afrika" (Gateway to Africa) engages with the complex question: who and what do we define as African, Africa, and the African Diaspora when discussing the planet's second largest continent, its three thousand different ethnic groups, and the significant geographical, ethnic, and cultural differences between North and Sub-Saharan Africa. This contribution engages with the multiple identifications of Emily Ruete as "African woman." It begins with Ruete's self-fashioning in her *Memoiren einer arabischen Prinzessin* (1886) and the collection of her letters, *Briefe nach der Heimat* (first published in 1999), and then turns to recent reconfigurations of Ruete in literary texts and by the Sayyida Salme Foundation in Zanzibar itself. Roy argues that the characterization of Ruete as African is less an accurate representation and more a commentary on German-African interactions past and present. Sarah Henneböhl's "The Survivor as 'Implicated Subject' in Stephanie Zweig's Autobiographical Africa Novels" examines Stefanie Zweig's *Nirgedwo in Afrika* and *Nirgendwo war Heimat*, both of which draw on the author's experience in the British Kenya Colony as a child survivor of the Holocaust. It shows how Jewish victims of Nazi Germany can simultaneously be victims of Nazi Germany and what Michael Rothberg describes as "implicated subjects" in a colonial system in which they occupy a position of white privilege over Black colonial subjects. As the chapter demonstrates, racist attitudes and stereotypes infiltrate both of Zweig's autobiographical novels. Lisabeth Hock's "Making the Invisible Visible?" turns to Yoko Tawada's short story, "The Shadow Man" (1998), her novel *Etüden im Schnee* (2014), and their representations of Black Enlightenment philosopher Anton Wilhelm Amo (c. 1703–c. 1759) and African American pop star Michael Jackson (1958–2009). It unpacks the strategies that "The Shadow Man" employs to make Amo visible as a Black man and a unique human being and to simultaneously dissect the societal processes by which he was emasculated, made invisible, and erased from history through various racist practices. The paper goes on to show how "The Shadow Man" and *Etüden im Schnee* nonetheless participate in what Ronald Jackson refers to as "scripting the Black body" by assigning racialized discourses to the Black male body in ways that prevent the texts from completely breaking away from stereotypes about Black men.

Section Three of this volume turns to the legacies of settler colonialism in the writing of white, German-speaking women. We see how white women project their own fantasies onto their depictions of Africa and the African Diaspora, thereby rendering persons from Africa or of African descent mute and invisible. These authors also tend to reject or undermine the notion that Black people can have full membership as citizens of the German nation.

The nineteenth-century writers in this section are Gabriele Reuter, Maria Theresia Ledóchowska, and Eugenie Marlitt. David Tingey's "German Cultural Superiority and Racial Hierarchy in Gabriele Reuter's *Glück und Geld*" argues that Reuter's 1888 *Roman aus dem heutigen Egypten* engages in a Eurocentric manner with the ideas of Egypt and Africa. Notably, by depicting North Africa as part of a diverse Africa, the novel challenges monolithic notions of the continent. At the same time, both the author's culturally chauvinistic and nationalist message and her adoption of contemporary beliefs in racial hierarchies are unmistakable. Reuter uses Egypt as an ideological vehicle, as a foil to Germany, and champions German culture as superior to the Ottoman Pasha's mid-nineteenth-century Egypt. In "The Black Slave Martyr Re-imagined for Christian Missions in Colonial Africa," Cindy Patey Brewer and Elizabeth Moye-Weaver demonstrate how Ledóchowska's 1889 hagiographic drama, *Zaïda*, recalls the prototypical Black slave martyr depicted in Harriet Beecher Stowe's 1852 *Uncle Tom's Cabin*. In the play, Zaïda appears as a gendered reimagining of the heroic Christian slave of antebellum America, now projected onto Africa as a modern mission fantasy. Unique among colonial writers of her day,

Ledóchowska humanized her Black characters, challenged dominant discourses on race and gender, and created a role model for Christian women's activism. Yet, despite her dedication to the abolitionist cause, Ledóchowska never fully escaped the project of whiteness, measuring the worthiness of her Black heroes and heroines based on European cultural standards. Beth Muellner's "Rethinking the Periphery" analyses the representation of Blackness in Eugenie Marlitt's *Im Schillingshof*. With the arrival of Spanish American heroine Mercedes de Valmaseda and her liberated African American slaves, Deborah and Jack, at the eponymous Schillingshof in Germany, readers are offered a clear reminder of the narrative of the Lost Cause: the myth according to which enlightened masters and their contented slaves together build a civilization far superior to that which had existed in the Northern US. This article builds on the insights of Toni Morrison and Zakiyyah Iman Jackson to push back against the idea that the novel's Black characters occupy a marginal status. It compares the Black female characters, Mercedes and Deborah, to reveal that Mercedes's mixed-race identity shifts from its initial association with Blackness to a gradual and complete whitewashing, while Deborah's Blackness remains unchanged. At the same time, we see that Deborah's central role as nursemaid, with access to coveted spaces in which she often remains unseen, offers opportunities for resistance, particularly in the context of her spoken and unspoken communication.

Carola Daffner, Maureen Gallagher, and Julia K. Gruber examine texts from the first half of the twentieth century by Frida von Bülow, Lena Haase and Lydia Höpker, and Else Steup, respectively. Daffner reminds us in "White Feminism and the Colonial Gaze" that discussions around colonialism and human rights violations raise questions of how and why white European women participated in the exploitation of Black African women and men. As she demonstrates, the journal entries of Frida von Bülow, which represent the first white female voice coming out of the German East African colonies, advance the very specific struggles of white feminism against conventional gender constraints in Wilhelmine Germany by demeaning both the East African space and its local inhabitants. In "Single White Female: Independent Women and Colonial Knowledge Production in German Colonial Fiction," Gallagher examines two colonial novels – *Raggys Fahrt nach Südwest* by Lena Haase (1910) and *Um Scholle und Leben* by Lydia Höpker (1927) – both of which feature unmarried protagonists who travel to Namibia under German colonial rule. The authors write heroines who defy traditional gender norms, enacting white female authority in colonial spaces and going beyond the relatively narrow possibilities envisioned for them by colonial authorities who sought to recruit white women to serve primarily as wives, mothers, and housekeepers in Namibia. Travelling to a colonial space thus grants white German women a kind of precarious privilege, freeing them from the rigid gender roles of the German metropole while giving them status over Indigenous men and women. Julia K. Gruber's "Colonial Propaganda Fiction: Else Steup's *Backfisch* Novels from the 1930s" turns to depictions of the single, ethnic German woman living in Africa in the post–First World War period after Germany relinquished its colonies. Like other postcolonial texts about German colonialism that were written during the Nazi period, Steup's (1881–1942) novels for young girls, *Wiete will nach Afrika* (1936) and *Wiete erlebt Afrika* (1938) reveal a wish to reverse the Treaty of Versailles. At the same time, the idea of female independence that the novels promote differs from the independence represented by the (mythical) New Woman of the Weimar Republic: by not having their female protagonists marry at the end of their adventures, the novels strongly contradict the Nazi dictum of the German woman as wife and mother.

The final article in this volume, Lorely French's "Perspectives on Namibia by Contemporary White German-Speaking Women Authors" moves us to the present. French analyses texts by white German-speaking women who have grown up or lived extensively in Namibia: the collection *Hauptsache Windhoek*, edited by Silvia Schlettwein and Erika von Wietersheim (2013); Anna Mandus's *Licht und Schatten in Namibia: Alltag in einem Traumland* (2016); and Hannah Schreckenbach's *Sehnsuchsland Namibia* (2017). Employing what Peggy Piesche calls a "critical white perspective," the article asks how the authors recognize and assess the colonial power's lingering impact. As much as the authors appreciate the beauty, diversity, and complexity of Namibia's history, geography, and peoples, they ultimately focus on whites as harbingers of those positive aspects. They rarely look critically at how colonial history still determines economic, social, and cultural divides.

This project has been some time in the making. It began as a conversation between Michelle and Lisa at the 2017 Women in German Conference in Banff, Alberta. The idea was picked up again when Lisa and Priscilla organized a seminar at the Conference of the German Studies Association (GSA) in Portland, OR, in 2019, in which most of the contributors to this volume participated. We thank the GSA for the hard work that went into the development and that continues to go into the organization of this productive format. We are also grateful for the contributions and inspiration of those seminar participants who chose not to be involved in this volume: Monika Hohbein-Deegen, Kristina Pilz, and especially Kira Thurman, whose insights at the GSA found their way into many of the present articles. The COVID pandemic brought many of our lives to a standstill, while the murder of George Floyd directed our attention towards political concerns and the needs of our BIPOC students and colleagues. Children were born, and children fell gravely ill. Russia invaded Ukraine. Hamas and Israel went to war with one another, providing a tragic reminder of the need to continually reflect on our flawed nature as implicated subjects. Through this long process, we had the generous support of the University of Toronto Press. We are particularly grateful to acquisitions editor Stephen Shapiro and to the anonymous readers for their thoughtful criticisms and suggestions.

We wish to note, finally, that participants at the GSA seminar and the contributors to this volume agreed to a set of guidelines for dealing with racism or racist language that we encounter in the texts we discuss. We decided to allow troubling terms, such as those that have been used historically to denigrate Black people, to stand when used in quotations, because not doing so would deny their use and the harm caused by this language. At the same time, we have agreed to limit our citation of such terms as much as possible, and when we do cite them, not to let those terms stand without commentary and analysis. Two resources that helped us here, recommended by Priscilla Layne, were Susan Arndt, Antje Hornscheidt, and Marlene Bauer's 2018 *Afrika und die deutsche Sprache: ein Kritisches Nachschlagewerk*[55] and Susan Arndt and Nadja Ofuatey-Alazard's 2015 *Wie Rassismus aus Wörtern spricht: (K)Erben des Kolonialismus im Wissensarchiv der deutschen Sprache*.[56] While aware of divergence among Black intellectuals regarding the capitalization of the colours black and white to refer to race – Kwame Appiah makes a case for capitalizing both,[57] John McWhorter does not find the capitalization of Black to be helpful,[58] we adhere to the publishing convention of our professional organization, the Coalition of Women in German which, in its commitment to anti-racism, "uses Black (capitalized), Brown (capitalized), and white (lowercase) when referring to race."[59]

NOTES

1 The Combahee River Collective, *The Combahee River Collective Statement*, by Zillah Eisenstein Demita Frazier, Beverly Smith, and Barbara Smith, 1978.
2 Katharina Oguntoye, May Ayim, and Dagmar Schultz, *Farbe bekennen: afro-deutsche Frauen auf den Spuren ihrer Geschichte* (Berlin: Orlanda, 1986).
3 Luvvie Ajayi Jones, "About the Weary Weaponizing of White Women Tears," Awesomely Luvvie, 17 April 2018, https://awesomelyluvvie.com/2018/04/weaponizing-white-women-tears.html.

4 Mamta Motwani Accapadi, "When White Women Cry: How White Women's Tears Oppress Women of Color," *College Student Affairs Journal* 26, no. 2 (Spring 2007): 208–15.
5 Marcel Aburakia und Malcolm Ohanwe, "Weiße Zerbrechlichkeit und Weiße Tränen," 20 February 2020, in *Kanackische Welle*, podcast, 00:64, https://podcasts.apple.com/us/podcast/kanackische-welle/id1438144361?i=1000466145176.
6 See Fatima El-Tayeb, *Schwarze Deutsche: der Diskurs um "Rasse" und nationale Identität 1890–1933* (Frankfurt am Main: Campus, 2001); Tiffany N. Florvil and Vanessa D. Plumly, eds., *Rethinking Black German Studies: Approaches, Interventions and Histories* (Oxford: Peter Lang, 2018); Priscilla Layne, *White Rebels in Black: German Appropriation of Black Popular Culture* (Ann Arbor: University of Michigan Press, 2018); Asoka Esuruoso and Philipp Khabo Koepsell, *Arriving in the Future: Stories of Home and Exile. An Anthology of Poetry and Creative Writing by Black Writers in Germany* (Berlin: Epubli, 2014); Sara Lennox, *Remapping Black Germany: New Perspectives on Afro-German History, Politics, and Culture* (Amherst: University of Massachusetts Press, 2016).
7 See Gabriele Dürbeck and Axel Dunker, eds. *Postkoloniale Germanistik: Bestandsaufnahme, theoretische Perspektiven, Lektüren* (Bielefeld: Aisthesis Verlag, 2014); Friederike Habermann, *Der unsichtbare Tropenhelm: wie koloniales Denken noch immer unsere Köpfe beherrscht* (Klein Jasedow: ThinkOya, 2013).
8 Jeff Bowersox, ed., Black Central Europe, accessed 21 February 2022, https://blackcentraleurope.com.
9 Jeff Bowersox, "Solomon and the Queen of Sheba (1181)," Black Central Europe, accessed 21 February 2022, https://blackcentraleurope.com/sources/1000-1500/solomon-and-the-queen-of-sheba-1181/.
10 Studies focusing on the intertwined histories of Europe and the Black Diaspora include Hans Werner Debrunner, *Presence and Prestige: Africans in Europe. A History of Africans in Europe before 1918* (Basel: Basler Afrika Bibliographien, 1979); and Mischa Honeck, Martin Klimke, and Anne Kuhlmann-Smirnov, *Germany and the Black Diaspora: Points of Contact, 1250–1914* (New York: Berghahn, 2013).
11 Henriette Herz and Friedrich Schleiermacher, trans. *Reisen im Inneren von Afrika*, by Mungo Park (Berlin: Haude and Spener, 1799).
12 Emily Ruete, *Briefe nach der Heimat*, ed. Heinz Schneppen (Berlin: Philo, 1999).
13 Emily Ruete, *Leben im Sultanspalast: Memoiren aus dem 19. Jahrhundert*, ed. Annegret Nippa (Frankfurt: Athenäum, 1989).
14 Walter Sauer, "'Mohrenmädchen' in Bludenz, 1855–1858. Ein Beitrag zur Geschichte der afrikanischen Diaspora in Österreich," *Vierteljahresschrift für Geschichte und Gegenwartskunde Vorarlbergs* 56, no. 4 (2004): 293–300.

15 Clara Brockmann, *Die deutsche Frau in Südwestafrika: ein Beitrag zur Frauenfrage in unseren Kolonien* (Berlin: Mittler, 1910).
16 Johanna Bohner, *In Sturm und Wetter: eine gefahrvolle Fahrt nach Kamerun* (Basel: Verlag der Basler Missionsbuchhandlung, 1913).
17 Maria Theresia Ledóchowska and Anton Schöpfleuthner, *Was geht das uns an? Gedanken und Erwägungen über das Werk der Antisclaverei und die katholische Missionsthätigkeit in Afrika* (Salzburg: Druck und Verlag von Anto Pustet, 1892).
18 Annemarie Schwarzenbach, *Afrikanische Schriften: Reportagen, Lyrik, Autobiographisches* (Zurich: Chronos, 2012).
19 Elly Beinhorn, *Flying Girl* (New York: Holt, 1935).
20 Kira Thurman, *Singing Like Germans: Black Musicians in the Land of Bach, Beethoven, and Brahms* (Ithaca, NY: Cornell University Press, 2021).
21 Kathleen J. Reich, "Racially Mixed Marriages in Colonial Namibia," in *Crosscurrents: African Americans, Africa, and Germany in the Modern World*, edited by David McBride, Leroy Hopkins, and Carol Blackshire-Belay (Columbia, SC: Camden House, 1998), 160.
22 Heinrich Webler, "Besatzungskinder," *Zentralblatt für Jugendrecht und Jugendwohlfahrt* 22, no. 4 (July 1930): 126–8, quoted in Julia Roos, "Racist Hysteria to Pragmatic Rapprochement? The German Debate about Rhenish 'Occupation Children,' 1920–30," *Contemporary European History* 22, no. 2 (May 2013): 162.
23 Iris Wigger, *The "Black Horror on the Rhine": Intersections of Race, Nation, Gender and Class in 1920s Germany* (London: Macmillan, 2017).
24 Roos, "Racist Hysteria," 479.
25 Tina Campt, *Other Germans: Black Germans and the Politics of Race, Gender, and Memory in the Third Reich* (Ann Arbor: University of Michigan Press, 2004), 64.
26 Campt, *Other Germans*, 69.
27 Katharina Oguntoye, May Opitz/Ayim, and Dagmar Schultz, eds., *Farbe bekennen: afro-deutsche Frauen auf den Spuren ihrer Geschichte* (Berlin: Orlanda Frauenverlag, 1986).
28 Ika Hügel-Marshall, *Daheim unterwegs: ein deutsches Leben*, 2nd ed. (Berlin: Unrast, 2020).
29 Abini Zöllner, *Schokoladenkind: meine Familie und andere Wunder* (Reinbek: Rowohlt, 2013).
30 Dirk Göttsche, *Remembering Africa: The Rediscovery of Colonialism in Contemporary German Literature* (Rochester, NY: Camden House, 2013).
31 Corinne Hofmann, *Die weiße Massai* (Munich: A1 Verlag, 1998).
32 *Die weiße Massai*, directed by Hermine Huntgeburth (Munich: Bayrischer Banken-Fonds and Constantin Film, 2005).
33 Brigitte Beil, *Maskal oder das Ende der Regenzeit* (Lübbe: Bergisch Gladbach, 2003).

34 Monika Czernin, *"Jenes herrliche Gefühl der Freiheit": Frieda von Bülow und die Sehnsucht nach Afrika* (Berlin: List, 2008).
35 Nicole C. Vosseler, *Sterne über Sansibar* (Cologne: Lübbe, 2010).
36 Lucia Engombe, *Kind Nr. 95: meine Jugend zwischen Namibia und der DDR* (Berlin: Ullstein Taschenbuchverlag, 2004).
37 Stefanie-Layha Aukongo, *Kalungas Kind: wie die DDR mein Leben rettete* (Reinbek bei Hamburg: Rowohlt, 2009).
38 Dayan Kodua, Thomas Leidig, Susanne Dorn, and Günter Wallraff, *My Black Skin: Schwarz. Erfolgreich. Deutsch* (Lüdenscheid: Seltmann, 2014).
39 Yoko Tawada, "The Shadow Man," in *Facing the Bridge*, trans. Margaret Mitsutani (New York: New Directions, 2007); and *Etüden im Schnee* (Tübingen: Konkursbuch, 2014).
40 *Dreckfresser*, directed by Branwen Okpako (Berlin: Deutsche Film- und Fernsehakademie Berlin, 2000).
41 *Tal der Ahnungslosen*, directed by Branwen Okpako (Berlin: TeamWorx Television & Film, 2003).
42 *Fluch der Medea*, directed by Branwen Okpako (Berlin: Branwen Okpako and JPgotMangos, 2014).
43 *Die Geschichte der Auma Obama*, directed by Branwen Okpako (Berlin: Branwen Okpako and Das Kleine Fernsehspiel [ZDF] and Filmkantine UG, 2011).
44 Eddie Bruce-Jones, "German Policing at the Intersection: Race, Gender, Migrant Status and Mental Health," *Race & Class* 56, no. 3 (2015): 36–49.
45 United Nations Human Rights Council, "Report of the Working Group of Experts on People of African Descent on Its Mission to Germany," United Nations Digital Library, 2017, p. 13, digitallibrary.un.org/record/1304263.
46 United Nations Human Rights Council, "Report of the Working Group," 12. In 2020, the Back German organization, Each One, Teach One, took it upon themselves to do a survey of the Black German community to address some of these questions and concerns. See Afrozensus, accessed 13 April 2021, https://afrozensus.de.
47 United Nations Human Rights Council, "Report of the Working Group," 14.
48 See Stefanie Kron, "Afrikanische Diaspora und Literatur Schwarzer Frauen in Deutschland," *Heinrich Böll Stiftung*, accessed 14 August 2020, https://heimatkunde.boell.de/de/2009/02/18/afrikanische-diaspora-und-literatur-schwarzer-frauen-deutschland; Tiffany Nicole Florvil, *Mobilizing Black Germany: Afro-German Women and the Making of a Transnational Movement* (Urbana: University of Illinois Press, 2020).
49 "Community Statement: 'Black' Studies at the University of Bremen," January 2015, http://www.fb10.uni-bremen.de/inputs/pdf/Communitystatement_BlackStudiesBremen_engl_Undersgnd415.pdf.

50 Nancy P. Nenno, "Reading the 'Schwarz' in the 'Schwarz-Rot-Gold': Black German Studies in the 21st Century," *Transit: A Journal of Travel, Migration, and Multiculturalism in the German-Speaking World* 10, no. 2 (2016): 3.
51 Oguntoye, Ayim, and Schulz, *Farbe bekennen*.
52 "Welcome," Generation ADEFRA, 2024, http://www.adefra.com.
53 "About Us," Black German Heritage and Research Association, 2024, http://bghra.org.
54 Florvil, *Mobilizing Black Germany*, 122.
55 Susan Arndt, Antje Hornscheidt, and Marlene Bauer, eds., *Afrika und die deutsche Sprache: ein kritisches Nachschlagewerk* (Münster: Unrast, 2004).
56 Susan Arndt and Nadja Ofuatey-Alazard, *Wie Rassismus aus Wörtern spricht: (K)Erben des Kolonialismus im Wissensarchiv deutscher Sprache: ein kritisches Nachschlagewerk*, 2nd ed. (Münster: Unrast, 2015).
57 Kwame Anthony Appiah, "The Case for Capitalizing the B in Black," *The Atlantic*, 18 June 2020, https://www.theatlantic.com/ideas/archive/2020/06/time-to-capitalize-blackand-white/613159/.
58 John McWhorter, "Capitalizing 'Black' Isn't Wrong. But It Isn't That Helpful, Either," *The New York Times*, 4 March 2022, https://www.nytimes.com/2022/03/04/opinion/capitalizing-black.html.
59 "Feminist German Studies Style Guide," Coalition of Women in German, updated October 2021, https://www.womeningerman.org/feminist-german-studies-style-guide/.

SECTION I

The Black Diaspora and Self-Definition

1 "They Are the Next Generation": An Interview with Sarah Blaßkiewitz

PRISCILLA LAYNE AND LISABETH HOCK

We begin this volume with an interview with the Afro-German television and film director Sarah Blaßkiewitz. After centuries of invisibility, or of being written about by others, in the 1980s and 1990s Black Germans began writing about their experiences, in edited volumes like Showing Our Colors *(1986), autobiographies like Ika Hügel's* Invisible Woman *(1998) and in aesthetic works like May Ayim's volume of poetry* Blues in Black and White *(1995). Today they continue to tell their own stories, but are increasingly doing so in venues that give far more visibility and influence than in the past.*

Blaßkiewitz was born in Leipzig in 1986, grew up in Potsdam, and now lives in Berlin. She started her film career playing the role of Josephine Langmann in the long- running television series for young people, Schloss Einstein *(Einstein castle); in this interview she discusses the groundbreaking nature of this series due to its depiction of a diverse set of students at a fictional boarding school. She studied at the Beuth Hochschule in Berlin and the Akademie der Künste in Vienna, and after her studies she directed four short films and a 2016 music video for the song "Christel von der Post" by the Berlin-based Bruno Nagel Band.*[1] *The colour palette of the video anticipates that of Greta Gerwig's 2023* Barbie, *but it is employed to more macabre ends. Blaßkiewitz then turned her attention to larger projects. In 2018, she filmed a pilot for the television series* Supercrew, *and in 2020 she worked as one of the directors of the popular television series* DRUCK *(English title:* Shame). *Like* Schloss Einstein, DRUCK *tells the stories of a diverse group of teenagers, but like the Norwegian television series that inspired it,* Skam, *it is situated firmly in the digital age. The series is initially broadcast as daily clips on YouTube, its characters have real Instagram accounts, and the broadcast clips are compiled into full episodes at the end of the week.*

Sarah Blaßkiewitz's first feature film, Ivie wie Ivie *(Precious Ivie),*[2] *premiered at the 2021 Munich Film Festival. Thanks to this film's breakthrough success, the director received an invitation to work as co-director, alongside*

Soleen Yusef, on the first German-language miniseries made for Disney+, Sam – Ein Sachse (Sam – A Saxon), *which is based on the true story of the first Black policeman in East Germany, Samuel Meffire.*³ *The Nigerian Welsh filmmaker, Branwen Okpako, created a television documentary based on Meffire's life that was released in 2000,* Dreckfresser (Dirt for dinner).⁴ *While Okpako incorporated into her documentary mostly interview material and while she adhered closely to Meffire's biography, Yusuf and Blaßkiewitz worked with the writers of* Sam – Ein Sachse *to tell a broader tale about Black Germans in Germany in the 1980s and 1990s. The film can thus be read as an account of the fall of the Berlin Wall and German unification relayed from a Black perspective.*

The following interview focuses on Ivie wie Ivie, *a film about two Black German women: Ivie who lives in Leipzig and Naomi who lives in Berlin. The two get to know each other after learning, upon his death, that they have the same father. Filmed in lush colours and with clear affection for its main and supporting characters – including Haley Louise Jones as Ivie, Lorna Ishema as Naomi, and Sheri Hagen as Naomi's mother, Miriam –* Ivie *takes a different approach to Black German storytelling than does* Sam. *Whereas* Sam – Ein Sachse *uses a historical figure as a foil for a much broader story of the mistreatment of and disregard for Black Germans in German society leading up to and after the fall of the Berlin Wall,* Ivie *zooms in on two women to tell a difficult but hopeful story of both family and of diversity within Blackness.*

Priscilla Layne and Lisabeth Hock interviewed Sarah Blaßkiewitz on Zoom on 8 July 2022, asking questions that relate to the themes of this volume on German-speaking women representing Blackness, Africa, and the Black Diaspora. The three discuss the director's understanding of herself as a Black female filmmaker and the motivations behind the creative decisions that went into making Precious Ivie.

PRISCILLA LAYNE (PL): This interview will be published in a volume entitled *German-Speaking Women, Africa, and the African Diaspora*. What do these terms mean to you personally and to your film and television work?

SARAH BLASSKIEWITZ (SB): At first, as an outsider to this discourse, I thought it was an intriguing topic: German-speaking women, Africa. These are broad terms, however, and I wondered what was so interesting about German-speaking women…. I do deal with these topics in my work, but they were never important for me as a child, or rather, they were important, but I didn't really think about them. "Africa" was Africa, and the word "diaspora" didn't exist for me. I wouldn't have known what it meant. I have noticed, though, that my more recent work has given me a way to engage with these issues, especially in *Ivie wie Ivie* or *Precious Ivie*, and my series,

DRUCK, which has an Afro-German protagonist, and now also in *Sam – A Saxon*. These projects give me a way to address history and topics that ... affect me *personally* without having to focus on myself or think about my personal relationship with the African Diaspora. We all know that working through personal issues takes time, and I don't want to focus in my work on psychoanalysing my biography. At some point, that just becomes tedious navel-gazing. These concepts have, of course, made me who I am, but mainly because of my work, or because of the way that others see and perceive me. I am interested in many *other* topics, however, so while this is currently my focus, I don't want to make it my life's work ... But I have been closely engaged with these topics for the past two years, and I will always be attuned to them. I can't escape them.

PL: A lot has changed for Black people over the past couple of years, especially since the murder of George Floyd in 2020 and the protests and debate in Germany about the problem of racism. What would you say it's like to be Black in Germany now, in 2022?

SB: We're perceived and seen differently. That is different from before. As a Black filmmaker, for example, people who previously weren't so interested in me or my story suddenly find me interesting. That wasn't the case ten years ago. Things have also changed in the past two years, through Black Lives Matter and what we see on the street. Advertising is changing. These days you see Black women in such great numbers that you have to ask yourself whether having an afro on every billboard isn't overkill. That's not how things really are. We are not England or France or America. Still, there have been positive changes. In television series like *DRUCK*, Black people are finally visible. You see people who previously weren't in German films. Or if they were, they appeared as foreigners, not as Germans. That has changed a lot.

PL: Who are the role models and inspirations for your work?

SB: That's a good question because it's so hard to answer. I'm always on the lookout for inspiration in everything: music, art, literature. These things *nourish* me. I need to consume and incorporate them to *live*. I couldn't say exactly where my inspiration comes from, though. Probably more from visual sources. There are, however, many female musicians who give me strength, who have something to say to us, and who do their own thing. There are people like M.I.A., and of course Beyoncé, who is so political, and Anohni. I listen to this kind of music a lot, and I find it exciting when someone takes something like pop, which is supposed to be about good mood and entertainment and dance and *yeah*, in order to *criticize* or *thematize* it. My favorite films are also sources of inspiration. I watch them again and again to understand how they were made and what kind of strategy the filmmaker used to develop a language. In this regard, I would say I find my role models in French and American independent cinema. Both can be *very dramatic* and down to earth, or very sad. I don't take that kind of approach at all in *Ivie* – I tend to take things in a humorous direction – but those are the films that move me.

PL: The next question is very personal and has something to do with my biography as well. At the meeting of the Black German Heritage Association [in February 2022], you talked about your father's experience, telling us that he had relatives, siblings whom he didn't know, who would come forward out of the blue. My own family is from the Caribbean. Both of my parents immigrated to America, and this kind of thing happens to me all the time. I have so many relatives I've never met. So, I was wondering, how did your father react when these relatives came forward? Do you think there's something unique in the African Diaspora in terms of the experience of family?

SB: First of all, my father often reacted at the same time we did. He has three children, and we have a lot in common. He was always open and interested because he was so surprised. So, I'd say he reacted positively: surprised, curious, and then interested in finding out what our relationship means now. Three sisters were born over time, with such different stories that they don't immediately cohere. But that's the special thing: because you know you're family, you then immediately fit together, or there is a distance, but an interesting one. There were many different variations of that in my father's life. If the meeting takes place later, everyone already has their own life, and it is more difficult because you have to integrate this new aspect into your life ... and who has the time to travel? That's why, in *Ivie*, I deliberately decided that Naomi has to travel only two hours to the next city to meet her sister, so that the two have time to get to know each other. Naomi actually *moves in*, and this was intentional. Things weren't like that in real life. People always think, oh, the film is autobiographical, but I've left it intentionally abstract. I wanted to convey a *feeling*: what does it mean if someone is there, knocking on the door or calling? That way, the story becomes special and above all universal. It's no longer related to one individual but can happen to anyone. In other words, the stories that I tell, about everyday racism and all the other issues, they are parallel stories for me. I situated what's private and family in an external context. I wanted to tell a story about two Black women because I knew that it wouldn't be done in Germany if someone didn't do it. Recently, when I was in Johannesburg, I gave a copy of the film to a South African actress, and after she saw it, she said "Oh my God, I can really relate to that." That was *beautiful* for me because it was a kind of test at the other end of the world: what does a South African woman think if she sees the film? Can she *understand* the East German story that I tell there? Her reaction was the one I had hoped for. That is why I like independent cinema so much. It allows you to get to know a place you may never travel to, and you believe what you see and become acquainted with something new. That's why I never wanted to make a film that tried to explain East Germany. Instead, I try to tell a universal story that could take place anywhere. Of course, it can't, and the particularities are presented through the characters.

PL: Yes, I can imagine that – even if people don't know about East German history – they have an idea of what it's like to be Black in a place where there aren't a lot of Black people. I'm encountering that more and more in America. I grew up in Chicago, which was very multicultural, but occasionally, I see a story about Black people from, say, South Dakota or Montana, somewhere out west with cowboys, where there are very few People of Colour and I always wonder, "Gee, what was that like, growing up there as a Black person?" And that brings me to my next question about your experiences in East Germany. What was it like for you growing up there? Do you think that the way people in the New German states deal with Black Germans has changed since 1989?

SB: The Wall came down when I was three or four. That was more my parents' experience, not my own. They certainly experienced hostility because they had a Black child. I've heard stories about how people reacted to me. I was quite protected, though, so I can't remember much now. As far as how things changed in the East German states, that is difficult to say because of the claim that there was no racism in the GDR. Then, when the Wall came down, people thought: "Oops, there is that racism again. Oh, you mean to tell me it was never gone?" I'm no expert, but since *Sam – A Saxon* is clearly about an East German Black man, we were dealing with the topic as we made the film in cities like Magdeburg, Gera, and Dresden. We of course informed ourselves in advance about the situation on the ground. Especially in Magdeburg I felt quite frightened. I was there for a few hours, didn't see much, and then I saw the *worst* Nazi you can imagine. He walked towards me with an attack dog and tattoos and his wife and a *German imperial flag*. Then it became obvious that he was over fifty, and that he had been the same person in the 1990s and 80s. He has *never* changed and *never* moved away. I was afraid when I met him and had to step out of his way. I knew he wouldn't do anything in broad daylight, but I wondered: "What if he continues to watch me and what I'm doing? I'm really *foreign* in this city." It was my first time in Magdeburg, and … I came away very disillusioned about how little has changed: the image we encountered was like the one we were filming. Of course, we also filmed in Magdeburg because we wanted to show prefab buildings, and a film that took place in the East. You need to see each place on its own terms, though. Leipzig has a very different reputation as a diverse, left-wing city. I don't want to presume to be able to speak about East Germany or to say, "that's how it is." Things change quite a bit. I think I can do film work there because I was socialized in East Germany, and because I'm prepared to ask the tough questions about how this or the other group identity arose, or why is and was there a higher number of racist attacks in the East.

PL: In the film, *Precious Ivie*, you portray a preschool in Leipzig that has a great diversity of children. Was that intentional? Does it reflect reality in Leipzig today?

SB: Yes, it was totally intentional. I wanted to make a point. I exaggerated the scene, of course. I told the costume designer that everyone should wear a different colour. So, it's provocative because it is not reality, but fiction. Clearly not all children would be wearing bright colours on a given day, but the interesting thing is that all the kids did come from the same preschool. I didn't research what preschools were like in Leipzig and then try to reproduce that. Rather, we went to a preschool as part of the pre-production work and asked if we could shoot there with the children. The children were how they were, and I was happy about that.

LISABETH HOCK (LH): The first time I was in Germany was 1982, and Germany has changed radically since then.

SB: Yes, I would agree with that. I grew up in Potsdam and there I was, with my father and my little brother, and two or three other Afro-German people, but that was it. Things today are completely different. That has changed for the better, that one is no longer so alone. And that's what I brought into *Ivie*: Ivie grew up more like me, while Naomi is a bit younger and grows up in a more diverse context and is therefore socialized very differently.

LH: Let's go back to when you were in the children's television series, *Schloss Einstein*. How did you get that role, and did you see yourself then as a Black actress?

SB: When I was a young girl, I was in this fabulous theatre group and wanted to become an actress. And this series for young people came along. I went to the casting by chance because my father knew that I wanted to be in film and that I wanted to participate in castings – we have the connection in Babelsberg to Studio Babelsberg. We went to an agency to sign up and someone asked if I wanted to take part in the casting that was going on at the time. It was actually by chance that I heard about *Castle Einstein*, and I started there. Teenagers between thirteen and sixteen have a lot of personal stuff going on. I was more preoccupied with meeting boys and my best friend and shopping and *Castle Einstein* than with who I was. I also grew up in a small town, which is perhaps safer than a big city. I was sheltered. When I noticed differences, it was in very simple things, like … the other characters, who were blond, got to use hair products. Hairstyles were very important in *Schloss Einstein*, and with me it was like, "Oh, you're already pretty enough. Go on, you can go straight down to the studio." There was the sense that they didn't have to do much. I don't want to criticize anyone now, but at that time, my skin and my hair weren't so common, and there was no make-up available. They would have had to order it from America. So, while the others were being powdered and made up at the age of thirteen or fourteen, nothing was done for me. That was a different time, over twenty years ago. We don't have to criticize the make-up artists, but that was when it became clear to me that I am Black and different. At the same time, the series itself was a kind of forerunner. Back then, there were no other series with a Black actor. In the series, there was someone in every grade with a migrant background. Before me, there was the kid from India on the series, and then I came along. With each new generation of children, one or two would have a different background, and sometimes that would become a part of the show's theme. We were treated like the other German children, though. I liked that. I didn't have the feeling that I had been "bought" as a Black person. My first casting, for example, was for a role that a white girl got, and it involved dancing. They wanted me to dance, but they really wanted a ballerina or a ballet dancer, and I couldn't deliver that. Then I got another role, or it was written for me. I don't know exactly.

LH: How did your career develop from there? Did you still want to be an actress at the end of *Castle Einstein*, or did you know that you wanted to go in a different direction?

SB: By that point I knew I wanted to be behind the camera. I did my *Abitur*, and it was clear that I wanted to work in film. I started with internships and applied to study cinematography. I had many different jobs and at some point, I realized: Okay, assistant directing is nice, but I want to do my own thing. Then it took me a few more years to make *Ivie*.

LH: What do you consider special about your work as a director? How would you describe your style?

SB: I don't come from the camera the way other filmmakers do. Although I studied cinematography, I'm always very fixated on acting and interested in creating scenes that range from the fantastic to the authentic. As a director, I have several tools for bringing people together. That's what I enjoy the most. That's why I put so many characters into *Ivie*, and that was what was difficult with the script – the characters all had to make sense. I wanted to show more rather than condensing everything. In my next project, though, I'd like to concentrate on one or two people. So, the acting is what I enjoy the most and where I take the most risks. I'm not sure what I consider special about my style. I think it is about following my instincts and not following a pattern or thinking that there is one way to make or shoot a film, but rather seeing what I can do differently.

LH: Priscilla and I both noticed in *Precious Ivie* that you worked with very intense colours. What's the meaning of colour and how consciously do you work with it?

SB: It was clear the film would make use of colour, in part because it was such a summer film. And of course, the viewer was supposed to enjoy it. I remember my camerawoman saying before the shoot: "Coloured light on Black skin is just much more beautiful than on white skin," so you can do more beautiful things. That's why the solarium and the club scene are somewhat exaggerated. We let loose with the costume design and our use of accents with Naomi. With Ivie, it was important to me that she have a bit of a small-town feel to her. She wears normal clothes, if you can describe them that way. It was also important to me that [both characters] sometimes just wear T-shirts. When the two sisters meet, for example, they are wearing T-shirts like the one I have on. Then, when Ivie puts on the dress with the African motif, it was clear that it had to pop. Clothing matters for costume design, and also for how you are perceived and what gets projected onto you. It's an important topic, especially in the case of racism, and leads to daily attacks. If I go out onto the street in an African dress, someone who doesn't know me will view me completely differently than if I were wearing an everyday outfit. The use of intense colour was important, but it was project specific.

I wouldn't say that every film will be that way, but I think a certain style will be recognizable in the camera work and the acting work. I would *really* like to make a black-and-white film next. Maybe everyone dreams of this when they start. But it must suit the story.... That's also how I decide whether to use a handheld camera. In *Ivie*, there is very little handheld camera, although I think everyone who read the script thought at the beginning that the film would make use of handheld camera. But the film was completely staged, with framing and CinemaScope, and the pace starts quietly and then becomes faster.

LH: Now you're working on a series about Sam Meffire with Disney. Branwen Okpako made a black-and-white documentary film about him. How did you come to the topic? – And to Disney?

SB: The series was developed by others, and I was brought in as a director. The project already existed and was being developed. There was already a lead director, and I became second director because it is a Black, East German story, and I came to their attention because of *Ivie*. It was quite sweet: the other director, Soleen Yusef, had just seen my film and had the feeling, "ah, the women I see there could be the children of Sam, they are the next generation." I felt drawn to the project because it is about the generation before mine. It also takes place in Dresden, and I come from Leipzig. There were a lot of connecting points. Of course, I also watched Okpako's *Dreckfresser* (Dirt for dinner) ... , and I then got to know Sam ... I didn't have a lot to do with Sam directly. There wasn't an exchange, or anything, but of course I researched everything, I had interview material. One of the producers, Tyron Ricketts, met Sam many years ago and thought this story was worth telling. There were a lot of recordings of him, where the questions were already asked, and I got to know him that way. It's a puzzle. At the same time, it is fiction. They changed the story and used it for their own purposes. The shooting ended only a week and a half ago. It's now in the editing phase. But there are quite a lot of people involved. It's not *my* project.

LH: I don't know if you can or want to say this, but are you working on other projects? And do you now prefer film or television?

SB: I definitely prefer film, which is becoming more and more difficult to make. Series increasingly dominate the market in Germany right now. *Sam* involved a year of work. It was important and interesting for me, but I can also say that, in doing the series, I've again found my love of film. That's always the case, isn't it? ... I need change. I worked on a series, and I now want to go back to cinema. Probably, if I'd just done a cinema film, I'd want to shoot an episode of some series again, just shoot without the other responsibilities. I'm excited about what will come next. Once you've done such a *big* project, invitations start to come in. Now I can see what interests me, what topics are coming my way. I'm even more interested in working abroad. Those are my two wishes: I'd like to do another small project now. Small in the sense of effort and money. But I'd like to do it in London, New York, or South Africa, or West Africa. That's why film is my priority.

LH: How do you arrive at your topics? How did you get to *Ivie*?

SB: There are many ideas slumbering in me, but they're usually not plot-ready. I might know what the main character has to be able to do, and where it should take place and who meets whom and so on. Then the theme will be clear, say: *world politics* as experienced through a love story. That might be clear, but then I don't immediately have the plot, or I couldn't say how the film ends. I just know that I have to make it. It was the same with *Ivie*. In that case, I knew what the ending would be, but I didn't know how to get there. I had to go through the process first. There is also the question of how I navigate between commissioned work and my own ideas. How do I find a balance and not torture myself?

PL: I have three more questions. The first is about Ivie and Naomi's different perspectives on racism or dealing with racism. Naomi seems to be better informed about racial politics. She knows about positive racism, for example. Do you think Naomi is more political because she grew up in Berlin, or is it because Naomi's mother is Black and taught her from a young age how to deal with racism? Or is this difference due to something else?

SB: No, that is the difference. But I wouldn't say that Ivie doesn't know what positive racism is. She does. But Naomi insinuates in front of the friend that Ivie doesn't. It's an insinuation and a provocation. I deliberately chose that. Perhaps Ivie isn't yet using the terminology, but she knows very well what positive racism is. Sometimes I have the feeling that Ivie is a bit like I was. You don't want to address certain topics because it hurts too much. And if you want to focus on other things, and if the people you hang out with don't make it an issue, or you are not confronted with it ... Ivie created her daily life in the solarium. She just wants to be a teacher and is interested in mathematics. If she had grown up in Berlin, she hypothetically might have chosen a completely different course of study and focused on something completely different. I addressed this issue of socialization by giving Naomi a dark-skinned, Black mother.

With Ivie that's not the case. That explains why one person is more informed and is *interested* in informing herself: she needs that more in her context, as the doorwoman in a club. Ivie only begins to deal with this through the encounter with Naomi. But she is a very smart person, she already knows about these things.

PL: The next question is related. Were you interested in portraying the problem of colourism? Is the film telling us that Naomi has different experiences in Germany or has different experiences with racism because she has a darker skin colour than Ivie?

SB: That was important, but it was addressed subtly. I tend to be like Ivie. I didn't think: oh, I'm going to make a film about positive racism. That wasn't the case. Rather, I was studying *people*, from a sociological perspective. So, I decided to use two different skin tones for my protagonists – and that was a conscious decision, that one had an afro and was dark skinned ... It also had to do with the cast: it was clear that Lorna [Ishema] would play Naomi, and in this way, Naomi had to become dark skinned. I then found it interesting that I am the one with light skin, and I have the experience with the [white] mother – that is more like Ivie. It was, so to speak, a *gift* for me to be able to address many things, to make clear the variety and the differences, that there isn't just one version of racism that people experience, but rather many different forms. Having two different women let me emphasize that. It was important to show these different kinds of racism, both of which are hurtful. It's clear that physical violence is associated with more pain, but speech can also be painful. It was important to show that even a light-skinned woman, who has probably had different experiences from a dark-skinned woman, also suffers pain. They don't have to be *compared* to one another. You don't have to say one is worse and the other better. Rather, I wanted to show that they are, in general ... shitty (*laughs*).

PL: My last question about the film also has to do with this issue. Ivie and Naomi have specific physical, or rather health, issues. Ivie has a skin rash and Naomi suffers from sleeplessness. Did you want to show the physical effects of racism?

SB: The subconscious and its impact were very important to me, although, speaking honestly, the insomnia and the skin rash have more to do with the family ambiguity, the void that the father left behind. This affects them in different ways. For Ivie, the rash is a part of her process. I chose this deliberately, the effect on the skin. Someone else might have stomach cramps or a stomach ulcer. With her, it's the skin. Even in the dream, or when she's lying under the covers and has a nightmare, the blankets are like a skin that she wants to tear open, or one that's lying on top of her. I wanted to use a concrete image to show how she is caught in a kind of skin that is projected onto her. How can Ivie free herself? That's her journey in the film: How can she stand there at the end and say, "I am *new*, I am someone else and you have to see me as I am and not as you would like to see me." Of course, skin and hair play a big role there.

LH: There is also a terrible scene where Naomi is spat upon and threatened, and then Emma comes. Is it important that this happens to Naomi and not Ivie, and that it is a white woman – Emma – who helps her?

SB: To my mind, the fact that this happens to Naomi has nothing to do with the colour of her skin or with colourism. She's a stranger in the city, she gets lost, and that's an issue you face as a Black woman in Germany: which city can you go to and where can you spend a night on your own? There are places you simply wouldn't go alone as a Black woman. That was the issue. Naomi had that experience because she came to Leipzig. Ivie goes to Berlin, but there are other issues there. Maybe the same thing would happen to her in Berlin, as well. Yes, that is of course one of the key scenes, also for me. It was also one of the most discussed and interesting scenes as the film was being made: that Emma is a white woman. I know one could view this critically. People who don't know me or haven't had the chance to talk to me might have their own opinion and think it was stupid. That's fine. I wanted to show a positive example of civil courage and show a role model. Moreover, to get a white audience, I had to have a white figure who does this. It was important for me. I thought about it a million times. Because if it had been an Afro-German woman, that also would have said a lot and would have been so complicated. It was important to me to let the film look into the future and show good things. The decision was to show something good in the worst scene of the film. And the actress I chose is herself a committed activist and great woman. There are people in Leipzig and other cities who are committed, who stand up against racism and engage in different activities, like driving into small towns to do educational work. I wanted to show this role model.

LH: I think that also shows that this is the responsibility of all of us, that it is not only the responsibility of Black people or of minorities to defend themselves against racism, but it is important for all of us. I think you showed that well. I also found that the film was not only about racism, but also about the relationships that sustain us. We see this at the end when Ivie and her good friends, Ingo and Anne, get matching tattoos, a scene you see already in the opening credits.

SB: Yes, the tattoo business got a bit short-changed. But I too found the friendship symbol important. It's a bit kitschy but it's also sweet somehow.

LH: And somehow this friendship continues despite the difficulties. The end of the film is also quite interesting. Ivie does not go to her father's funeral. Naomi does, and we see the scene through her camera as she is making a video. Her camera then pans over the body of the father, and we feel like we're going to see the father, but then at the end we see Ivie's face. Why did you end the film like that, with this big question mark?

SB: Because I wanted to say that the story continues and of course it's not over. The two women had to make a lot of decisions over the course of two hours, which was about a week in their lives ... or two weeks. But things are not finished. They aren't thinking: "Ah yes. Now I have a sister, and our father is dead, and that's how things are, and life goes on." There is clearly a longer process, beyond the film, beyond the part of the story about the two women that I told, that one travels to the funeral and the other doesn't. It's self-determined action, that one woman says, "I can't yet. I can't do this yet; I may NEVER be ready." The other hesitates but takes the step and flies there alone. That's such a big step, isn't it? And then she also takes a step in telling her sister about it, who then takes her own step in saying: "Okay, I have gotten to know *you*. I won't let *you* out of my life now. Even if it is so difficult with us. I'll look at what you've given me." There are a lot of little steps that they still have to take to maybe become sisters who are cool with each other. By having Ivie look into the camera, I wanted her to look to the future but also towards the viewers, telling them: "Now, think about it."

LH: Her gaze is also a challenge....

SB: Yes: "What would you do now if you were in my situation?" The film is structured in such a way that more and more happens. It's not the classic dramaturgical arc, but rather, Ivie had to *really* go through something, and she also hurt others along the way. I wanted to make it possible to experience that. That you as a viewer are together with her at such an intimate moment and she is still looking at you. I found that somehow quite exciting.

LH: As you probably saw, we still have many, many questions

SB: You asked good questions.

LH: Well, the most important ones. It also means that this is a very rich film. There is so much in the film, and when we watch the film again, there will be more questions ...

PL: I have a better understanding of the film: especially what you said about moral courage and that Ivie and her friends still have a friendship. I think that's very important because in America now we have so many problems with racism and we're so divided. One feels like there's so much hostility, that non-Black people think that racism is none of their business, that they don't have to do anything about it. Or, if you say something against racism, it means you're the enemy or you're trying to disturb the peace. It makes one very tired, the atmosphere. What you said is really important.

NOTES

1 Bruno Nagel Studio, "Christel von der Post," directed by Sarah Blaßkiewitz, 12 August 2016, video, 3:42, https://www.youtube.com/watch?v=YXqnLi_zoZc.
2 *Ivie wie Ivie* (Precious Ivie), directed by Sarah Blaßkiewitz (Weydemann Bros., 2021).
3 *Sam – Ein Sachse* (Sam – A Saxon), directed by Soleen Yusef and Sarah Blaßkiewitz (Disney, 2023).
4 *Dreckfresser* (Dirt for dinner), directed by Branwen Okpako (Berlin: Deutsche Film- und Fernsehakademie Berlin, 2000).

2 Between Autofiction and the Archive: On/Travelling Olivia Wenzel's *1,000 Coils of Fear* (2020): Touching Tale or World Refracts Nation

BIRGIT TAUTZ

Manchmal denke ich es wäre gut, sich nicht bloß über Erzählungen und Bilder zu erinnern, sondern über Berührungen.

Ein Archiv in sich zu tragen, das alle Berührungen der Haut gespeichert hätte und das jederzeit abrufbar wäre.

Sometimes I think it would be nice to remember not just narratives and images, but also touches.

To carry an archive within yourself that has saved all the touches your skin has felt, and that can be recalled at any moment.

Olivia Wenzel, *1000 Serpentinen Angst (1,000 Coils of Fear)*[1]

Olivia Wenzel's *1000 Serpentinen Angst (1,000 Coils of Fear)* represents what Leslie Adelson called a "touching tale" in German literature – one of a new generation, that is. By oscillating between autofiction and the archive, Wenzel's text ends up exemplifying what Adelson pondered more than twenty years ago when she described the then-new German literary landscape that was taking on pervasive contours after the fall of the Wall (1989) and unification (1990). Adelson outlined a forever altered narrative of contemporary German literature by examining the many ways in which Turkish German literature challenged the domineering mode of reading post-1945 German literature solely in the shadow of the Holocaust while still forcing us to read against the atrocities and culpabilities of the twentieth century. Wenzel's novel shows how we may think about the African Diaspora entering this constellation.

Since 1989/1990, scholars have found themselves on rugged territory marked, on one hand, by a narrative that thrived on the tension between the telos of national reunification (purportedly now achieved) and the formative presence of the recent past, namely the Third Reich and Holocaust, which continued to serve as a constant reference point by fueling a binary that pitted German against Jewish identity. This image of national literature failed to incorporate other social and cultural forces, for example a long-standing Turkish presence that, though largely depicted in sociopolitical or historical rather than literary or cultural terms, generated Turkish and Turkish-German narratives. While "touching" themes of Jewish identity in a shared residual Othering in the eyes of a German mainstream tradition, these new stories unsettled the domineering – sometimes called a "grand" or "historical" – narrative[2] of literary historiography without undoing the preoccupation with working through the recent, national past. But the transforming impact of these stories was everywhere – and positively disrupting. Adelson's message is clear: German literary history includes literary works that are void of overt reference to a historical caesura like 1945 or 1990.

Wenzel's debut novel, *1000 Serpentinen Angst*, or in the title of Priscilla Layne's translation, *1,000 Coils of Fear*, is one of these works. The novel provides a new version of German literature's engagement with its own historiography. It alludes to some well-worn narratives central to the post-1945 German literary canon, while exhibiting many of the thematic and identity-inflected uptakes that drive contemporary literary production. The novel resonates with Wenzel's biography, for example. The narrator's life and her family's story recall and refract the still-looming textual and historical presence of a Germany divided into East and West. Migrant and diasporic patterns of identification thus play a constitutive role in the novel. The latter thread moves to the fore in my discussion of *1000 Serpentinen Angst*, seeking to engage with the centuries-long presence of Black Germans and the laden and complex role that the African continent, in all its heterogeneity, plays in German history and imagination.[3]

The novel creates formal points of reference to an archive that Adelson described as a "riddle of referentiality, modernity, temporality"[4] and thus to the "touching tales" that she unearthed. But Wenzel's text exceeds this framework as well as what I would call "the strictures of representation" that contemporary critics, writing in news media and popular blogs, apply to the novel. I propose a reading that transcends Adelson's original impetus as well as allusions to both biographical and geographical markers in the protagonist's and the author's lives. Although the book is uniquely Olivia Wenzel's – who by the customary classifications is an East German, Black, queer, female author – it is not an example of literature that succeeds by thriving solely on these markers of identity. The novel tracks the protagonist's musings about both the Black Diaspora and migration out of Germany to non-European countries, while challenging the narrative of German literary historiography, thematically as well as structurally. By emphasizing space over temporality, the novel leaves telos-driven stories behind. The text pivots towards a global frame of reference, as it resonates with the traits of "novels in the age of Black Lives Matter" by exposing whiteness, making it visible as physical force, while "reveal[ing] Black vulnerability."[5] Wenzel thus enacts new parameters of thinking, speaking, and engaging with literary fiction; they are delineated perceptually, representationally, and referentially. Modes of remembering matter, just as intersecting history and historiography matter, but so do other frameworks for thinking and writing about literature.

One of these frameworks is race. Priscilla Layne reads the novel as autofiction that moves its readers to affectively recognize, even if they do not experience, the race relations of the present and past. The text exposes quotidian white violence, to paraphrase Layne, and makes whiteness visible. Simultaneously, rather than constructing Blackness as something to be contained, relegated, managed and thus, ultimately, depicted as disturbing "Other," the novel sutures Black vulnerability into its pages as a relatable and integral part of text and reading. Sarah Colvin's recent attempt to read the novel through the different temporalities (that she sees at work in the text) relies on yoking together Wenzel's working habits as dramatist (which, in Colvin's reading, loom in the background) and the looping images of the coils. Colvin traces along the latter winding, non-teleological, even encapsulated, accounts of past and future.[6] Somewhat at odds with this reading, Wenzel situates her roots as dramatist not as a pivot to alternative temporalities but as one defining affective *style*; to her, the use of multivocality signals *presence*. What all three approaches share is a resistance to replicating racialized *paradigms that centre whiteness*.

By uprooting or at least destabilizing such paradigms, Layne, Colvin, and Wenzel herself delineate an interpretive terrain of openness that allows for what I propose in this chapter. By revisiting perception, representation, and reference, I will attempt to chart interpretive frameworks for reading Wenzel's novel beyond the national (past), while still accounting for the archives of literary history. *1000 Serpentinen Angst* constructs Africa and the African Diaspora in a manner that asserts the novel's place in a broader, global working of literary representation, while nevertheless teaching us to read German literature differently and, ultimately, to reframe the writing of its history. We shall see that part of the novel's affective success is its complex revisitation of proclaimed foundations of literary history, while appearing on the surface to disengage from national roots.

The Turn to the World: Senses, Snack Machines, and the Role of the African Diaspora

The novel interrogates the visual as a domineering form of perception and representation. On the one hand, it deconstructs, reconstructs, and turns the gaze through recurrences of *Augen/AUGEN* (eyes/EYES) as an organizing structure of the narrative. Indeed, in a promotional video for the novel, Wenzel reiterates the complex role of eyes as confining, defining, and exposing organs. On the other hand, it leaves us wondering whether visual perception and representation can be undone by other sensual registers. *1000 Serpentinen Angst* seeks to elevate touch and hearing as modes of remembering, by expanding common understandings of "archival media." They enable alternative modes of "seeing," as handed-down tales and photographs force us to embrace the past while still privileging a view in the present. Routine but painful chatter (aka undefined, almost stereotypical and/or ingrained beliefs, motives, and behaviour) engulfs the protagonist/narrator, inflicting what Layne sums up as latent microaggressions.

All the while, as the novel articulates such complex sensual perception, its narrative runs up against the stubborn, raw physicality of an inanimate object, a snack machine. The snack machine not only equates symbols of sensuality in the novel's very first sentence – "Mein Herz ist ein Automat aus Blech" (My heart is a snack machine made of tin)[7] – but it also evolves as a narrative-generating force. Becoming a subject-in-its-own-right, not just an objectifying captor of the protagonist's imagination, it steers us towards the legacy of global eighteenth-century stories, namely it-narratives that projected narrative agency emanating from objects. By cycling through these alternate narrative origins and competing archives of the past, Wenzel's novel situates itself in the world and ends up suggesting that national literature might in truth be the historical blip that eclipsed more enduring, all-encompassing literary styles, periods, and legacies. The (imaginary) nation structured literary projects, albeit for a limited period. Today, loosely defined ideas of world and person become a gravitational force of identification.

It is in this suggestive moment that the protagonist's experiences in Africa move to centre stage. Recollections of her experiences end up effectively dislodging the narration from oscillating between, and reproducing dialectically, a Western Self and its Other, and towards an alternate modernity. For example, this alternative does not project

Angola, the birth country of the protagonist's father, as a sole aim of the narrative's telos which would have fallen into the trap of projecting Self and Other as narrative poles. Instead, the binary recedes into the background as the historical underpinning in the Western world, namely dialectical modernity, appears increasingly fragile in light of multitasking or of what may be called a flattening of world amid globalized production and consumption, social relations and media. What seemed historically certain (e.g., social-dialectical progress) and individually desirable (e.g., personal development or progress) is under siege. The protagonist experiences this fragility as she accumulates disordered, and contradictory, impressions of her surroundings. Destinations of her travel slip away as desired points of arrival at identity: none of the countries she visits (United States, Angola, Morocco, Vietnam) make the protagonist whole. Nor does she reach stability. As a fragile multidirectionality generates her (and our) present moment, it is the object, the "it," the snack automaton, that recurs. It finds its historical place in the construction of subjectivity, only to eventually crumble.

Travel as Method, But Not as Genre: Adjusting the View

To explore the relationships between senses, a looming inanimate object, and the role of the African Diaspora further, I turn to travel. Its perpetual movement defines the text, foreclosing the possibility of pinpointing the novel's content or purpose. Travel conjures up an associative link to the book's German title and its invocation of the hairpin turns of mountain roads, which are transposed formally into the book as speed and rhythm of narration. It relates to the English title by exploring the unnamed narrator and thus working psychologically. While hairpin turns convey deceleration and acceleration of physical movement, the coils of anxiety, stress, and trepidation stand for this inner side of the narrator and evoke the density and elasticity of mind or Self.

Travel – and debunking its promise – allows the protagonist to get a new hold on Self or personal identity along the vectors of race, gender, and sexuality. Yet travelling, or rather the unfulfilled yearning for travel, had also unified her family across at least two generations, connecting as well as separating the protagonist and other family members. The narrative juxtaposes, for example, "Aber ich will ja unbedingt hinaus in die so genannte weite Welt" (But I want to go out in the so-called wide world, by all means);[8] with "Ich komme aus einer Familie, in der das Reisen immer eine unerfüllte Sehnsucht war" (I come from a family that's always unduly romanticized the idea of getting as far away from yourself as possible).[9] In this way the motif of travel births a subtext that sustains the jarring qualities of the narrative, ultimately making for new parameters of storytelling and remembering.

Though far from writing a travelogue,[10] Wenzel works with the genre's core ingredient, namely movement: "REISEN ALS GRUNDTHEMA" (TRAVELLING IS THE SUBJECT).[11] Stylistic elements further resonate with the metaphoric discovery of the narrator's inside, transforming pathways into fragile perceptions and emotions. If conjured at all a faint image of roads dissolves, or rather breaks, into voices. Multivocal dialogues transpose perspectives, replicating paths within the Self and impacts from the outside. Typography of letters and lines transfers, misaligns, and realigns subject positions. Multilayered transpositions, into other languages as well as labels, stereotypes, and other discursive shortcuts, articulate what seemingly defies linguistic representation but nevertheless creates meaning. What established literary criticism and scholarship, at one point, may have simply called "stream of consciousness," emerges in current criticism as "prismatic," focused on "inner dialogue," or expressing "multivocality."

Travel as textual movement further resonates with Wenzel's statements about writing the novel. She laboured to emphasize free flow and to embrace an inner voice, while disregarding critics' interpretive models as well as her own and others' research.[12] For Wenzel, autobiography is not the key to her fiction. Instead, she resists calls for explication and personal representation by turning to other art forms, for example by promoting the novel through the short film I mentioned before. She boldly introduces film as a substitution amid requests to represent herself and a broader, racially inflected social context. In deflecting representation, Wenzel seeks to "match aesthetically" her attempt to avoid being reduced to the role of a "messenger in white spaces, there to explain racism."[13] She establishes film as the medium influencing her writing, while forcefully pointing audiences to the overblown, simultaneously abstracted and surreally magical play-eyes (my term) that feature prominently in the short feature. Through the film Wenzel articulates her firm belief in the insufficiency of language and, more broadly, representation (while tipping us off, somewhat ironically, to the figurative role that eyes, seeing, and visuality/visibility play in the novel). Her intention, it seems, is to defy unequivocal semantics and representation, while simultaneously commanding and subverting the power of the written word.

The Eyes Have It

Travel can distort the gaze, dilate the view, and bother – figuratively and literally – the eyes. It re-engineers visuality. In *1000 Serpentinen*

Angst, it amplifies visual perception as a mode of spatial organization of text, injecting eyes and seeing, like directions, into the narrative. Consequently, any random observation may trigger a reorganization of message and form of the text. While eyes serve as a hook or cliffhanger for Wenzel to position herself vis-à-vis her writing *beyond this text*, and to serve throughout the book as an anchor for both protagonist and narrator *within the text*, they also express the complexities and contradictions of gazes and seeing in constructing a person's identity in German/Western societies. The novel's many eyes inhabit what John Berger, the author of second section's epigraph, elsewhere calls *Ways of Seeing*. There are "active" eyes in pain from being strained and tired, as well as those that were hurt by a surplus of unwelcome impressions from their surroundings, by other people's gazes and the stereotypes they inflict. Eyes capture the stories with which protagonist/narrator live and force the narrator to see those stories. Latently, they appear as personified, metonymic creatures standing in for protagonist/narrator and seemingly relegating all their sensual perceptions to domineering vision. Finally, there are eyes that simply cannot fully function: "WAS IST MIT DEINEN AUGEN?" (WHAT'S UP WITH YOUR EYES?) asks a narrative voice at various, non-arbitrary junctures, always pointing to impaired eyes and/or forcing – us, the protagonist, or somebody else entirely – to see.[14]

As eyes are everywhere, they turn their role – to discern and identify – upside down, obscuring, blurring, and mangling what they see instead. Ultimately they also recall the literary historian's textual memory looming in the background: eyes do not only reference the technologically mediated, visual paradigm defining the twentieth century that is being "felt" by all of us, they also offer an allusion to Ingeborg Bachmann's short story "Ihr glücklichen Augen" (Your happy eyes),[15] in which the narrator cycles through the perspectives of defective eyes, glasses-wearing eyes, double vision and distorted vision to expose the fraught and vulnerable position of women, and image, in the 1950s and beyond. The hibernating presence of the textual past, while not embraced by Wenzel, opens a reader's perspective that innovates, multiplies, and amplifies the narrative dimensions of *1000 Serpentinen Angst*. Wenzel's English-language subheading of part one, "(points of view)," ends up endorsing this interpretation, underscoring the turn towards pre-semantic signification merely hinted at in non-capitalization, non-narrative, and non-visual modes of remembering through a motto that quotes Missy Elliott, again in English, to "give you a taste."[16] The text opens towards the full spectrum of sensual experiences, while interacting with "knowledge" of history.

Travel also encapsulates the protagonist's actual journeys to the United States, Morocco, Angola, and Vietnam, helping her articulate her narrative present and future while recalling, if not digesting, her past. Here travel splinters rather than unifies. For example, engaging with contemporaneous political and historical processes through travel – the protagonist travels to the United States on the day of the 2016 presidential election and experiences the election's aftermath – breaks open the narration's tale(s) of German history, diversifies its focus, and triggers personal introspection. The statement, "Seit ich in den USA bin, sehe ich zuallerest die Hautfarbe der Menschen" (Ever since I got to the US, the first thing I notice about people is their skin colour),[17] engenders presence and arrests the narrative flow by establishing predominantly visual modes of perception and representation. Skin colour as widely posited marker of racialized identity joins the novel's discursive repertoire. In its local reference and resonance to the United States' public realm, the sentence names the hypocrisy of claims of a postracial society. More importantly, still, the presence of Blackness as a discursive force – or as Wenzel has repeatedly stated, her coming out as a Black person – makes whiteness visible, both in the United States and in Germany. Germany's overbearing whiteness shaped the author's perception, unconscious suppression, domineering models of identity formation, and sense of Self – all of which erased, eclipsed, or rendered "meaningless" what was still there: being perceived and represented as Other in everyday life. Racialized "naming" adds to the protagonist's family roots and her self-positioning within the African Diaspora. It impacted Wenzel's acts of translation as she created fictional selves. The role of whiteness as the organizing centre of narration, at least in the predominant modes that had defined German literary historiography and its reception, is exposed. All too long, this unarticulated centre had imbued narration with articulations of national and historical consciousness, producing and replicating alternative expressions of racial identity as marginalized, or Other.

The full stop gives the narrator pause and creates space for metadiscursive elements, like sociopolitical discourse and frame of reference, and enables the protagonist to reveal, finally, how other, mostly white, people see her. It is perhaps in wrestling with Blackness that the narrator's and author's positions align most, while underscoring their difference. We sense traces of Wenzel's growing up in East Germany, where the legacy of a "racial Chromatism" and its thinking about "Race without Racism"[18] remains palpable well beyond the country's demise. In fact, the East German government's pronounced, and often pre-emptive, international thinking propels the protagonist to acknowledge what she sees as her privileged position as a German citizen. This perspective consequently augments her insight that she is not the descendant of slaves, leading her to conclude that she therefore cannot find models of identification among the African American community in the United States. In Wenzel's explanatory comments, this reads like the author herself could only ever imagine being a "tourist in Blackness."[19] Similarly, while the narrator carefully delineates the ways in which the protagonist is read in Angola, namely "AUSSEN BRAUN, INNEN WEISS" (BROWN ON THE OUTSIDE, WHITE ON THE INSIDE [13,9]), and ponders the status of Africa in African American and German history, the same protagonist rejects, early on, persistent requests to talk about racism.

Global Prisms – Spectral Africa

Mein afrikanischer Vater ist in Marocco mehr wert.

My African father is worth more in Morocco.[20]

Der Verdacht, ich könnte eine Geflüchtete sein, *eine maximal Andere* also, lässt sich nicht länger aufrechterhalten, sobald ich meinen deutschen Pass vorzeige. Die Tatsache, dass Afroamerikaner an den Nachwehen der Slaverei leiden, mittels deren sie *zu maximal Anderen* degradiert wurden, löst sich vielleicht nie auf. (emphases added)

The suspicion that I could be a refugee, the utmost subaltern, can no longer be maintained, as soon as I produce my German passport. The fact that African Americans are still suffering the aftermath of slavery, during which they were degraded most inhumanely, may never be resolved.[21]

Travel unveils hidden and suppressed layers of identity construction, namely those manifesting latent Otherness. This observation extends to the protagonist's perception of the ways in which she is constructed by other people, as well as their expectations of how she should identify herself. She, in contrast, seeks to avoid any identification that would "arrest" identity. In addition to creating mundane experiences of being seen by others, however, travel also reveals remnants of history, to the protagonist but also to readers. The remnants inflect how we imagine identity constructions among political and national communities across the globe as well as race discourse in Germany. Legacies of German colonialism in Africa, internationalism as a state doctrine in East Germany, and ever-present legacy of slavery in the USA[22] intersect the protagonist's Blackness, mingling how she is perceived by herself and others. Through cross-cultural comparison, *1000 Serpentinen Angst* lifts these remnants of history into the narrative present, while clearly delineating national differences between the United States and Germany.

Upon arriving in the United States with its many majority-minority cultures, the protagonist begins to grapple with a radical alterity at the core of race, while acknowledging, eventually, the altering if not mitigating effects of national and personal histories. Such effects may include privilege. While she may be ostracized as being Black in a predominantly white world, she readily acknowledges that which distinguishes her from many African Americans. Not only is she not the descendant of slaves, but she is also a privileged holder of a German passport. Its possession distinguishes her from refugees and Black migrants, most notably those from the African continent, and thus dissolves any misreading of her as an absolute Other à la Hegel, who had excluded Africa (and by extension Africans) from the historical process.[23] But national privilege and personal standpoint also impair her narration, preventing the protagonist from experiencing, and the author from conveying, the generational trauma among African Americans. Consequently, the narrator resorts to alternating narrative standstill and movement by intersecting *narrative snapshots* with her intellectual awareness of the ever-present legacy of slavery. While she renders the latter through a persistent feeling of helplessness, which signals the limits of rational understanding when it comes to translating historically different experiences and feelings, the snapshots produce different effects. Detached from the protagonist's actual experience, they resemble almost factual statements unearthing Germany's colonial past or identifying Black individuals (e.g., Anton Wilhelm Amo, whose representation by Yoko Tawada Lisabeth Hock discusses in this volume) who have been forgotten in the country's historiography of national identity. The snapshots resemble fossilized remnants in an archaeologist's field or found objects in an archive.

Not surprisingly, resurrected, multiple voices cave in upon the narrator; they are trying to ascertain the *affective impact* that the narrative abundance of the German forest has upon the protagonist, compared to the barely existing reckoning with German colonialism. At the same time, the narrator rejects being reduced to her advocacy for Africa and the expectation that, simply by pointing out incongruencies in memory and historiography, she is considered an expert on all things African. On an individual level, however, history translates into narratives of personal situatedness. As her belonging remains elusive, a stable identity evades the protagonist. The national facets of her existence come to the fore, not just in her attitude towards the German passport, but also as an inheritance of political bygones. For in a post-unification context, nationalized "Othering" of East Germans appears transposed into her East German family, a gesture that ignores older, racialized public discourses in Germany.

The narrator's travel thus winnows our view of German history, while exploring new modes of articulating her personal narrative present as well as her past and future. Thus reconceived, travel boldly brings to the fore German colonial legacies, notably in Africa. Most importantly and in furthering new narrative centres, travel makes accessible the diversity of Africa, transporting the reader into the social, historical, and cultural realities of a continent that encompasses many countries, peoples, and traditions. Challenging the synecdochic use of "Africa" as reductive, the book thrives on a multiplicity of African locations that enables a spectrality of view (or prismatic representation) that extend to the African Diaspora.

Wenzel represents Angola, where the protagonist's father is from, predominantly in terms of kinship, family, and economic constellations, while creating a subtext through entwined individual and national aspiration, in education as well as in neoliberal capitalist economies in which different members of her family have arrived (or not). Her father had come to East Germany as a young student embracing socialist ideals; upon his return to Angola, he became wealthy through investments in oil and fully embraced the neoliberal, globalized economy after initially trying to reconcile ideology with economic reality. We learn that the protagonist visited Angola more than once, first in 2006, while reading and reintegrating her experiences across the narrative that takes us onto her inner and outer journeys. Here, the entire African continent gains some prominence, with steady reminders of its internal, cultural, and national diversity and a geographical expanse that is rarely accounted for in the Western view. On the winding paths of travel and imagination, Sub-Saharan Angola occupies a different narrative space than Northern Africa. The protagonist's "African father" enjoys higher social prestige in Morocco than her white mother, be it because of his station, ethnicity, or gender. But idealized whiteness – and internalized, racialized hierarchies that derive from it – structure the protagonist's everyday experiences in the North African country. There is more than proverbial distance between her and her father when she messages him from Morocco, suggesting that they meet "in der Mitte der Strecke, die zwischen uns lieg[t]" (halfway between here and there).[24] After all, she is *"in Afrika."*[25] Only afterwards does she realize the enormous geographical distance and expense such a plan would entail, noting:

"[D]ie Reisekosten übersteigen mein monatliches Einkommen um ein Vielfaches" (The travel costs exceed my monthly income significantly).²⁶

Similarly, and somewhat paradoxically, one of her experiences in Angola relates the privilege of white skin, as the narrator draws comparisons between the widespread use of whitening creams in Angola and Western obsessions with suntanned skin, clearly demarcating the latter as a choice with bifurcated effects. Whereas Germans can cover their whiteness with another layer that signifies the same privilege aesthetically, Africans have only the choice to symbolically "accept," namely by using skin bleach, or not to accept white privilege. Their Black skin gets erased from the Western beauty regime and only re-coded as an exoticizing ideal that only white people can appropriate. If they embrace this beauty regime at all, Angolans read and treat it only as a surface act, while the same regime reminds the protagonist that she has been socialized into white privilege.

While this observation transposes structural racism onto a visual realm, this reading does not extend to Morocco. Although the protagonist implies that Moroccans respected her father in class terms, and for his socio-economic success, her initial expectations upon arrival – namely to come as a tourist and digital nomad – are refracted through the cab driver's reading of skin colour and the economic conditions of "Sub-Saharan" workers domiciled in Morocco. He misunderstands her intention *to work from the resort* as her wanting *to work in the resort* and offers recommendations for jobs available to "Sub-Saharan" workers.²⁷ As racial hierarchies embedded in the global labour market of neoliberal economies thus extend to Morocco, a correction is necessary, eventually liberating the protagonist from being misread and allowing her to enter the space as a privileged tourist. By affixing to Morocco clichés and qualities of an exotic tourist destination that can harbour the protagonist's individualized idealism about the future and by then refracting the country through a socio-economic and sociopolitical lens, Wenzel ends up constructing the North African country in distinct ways – and in a very different manner (and temporality) than she depicts Angola.

As a geographical and imaginary space akin to a tabula rasa, Morocco provides the protagonist with transformative experiences *of the present*; they resonate only superficially with those she had had earlier in Vietnam. While she comes as a tourist to both countries, she develops different imaginary ties. Because she had explored Vietnam with her partner Kim, her journey became inevitably entangled with a romantic relationship. At the same time, her decision to stay in a resort catapults her into the tourist mindset. The protagonist stays in a Vietnamese vacation resort that is developed and managed by a German and his Vietnamese wife; their behaviour and values replicate tourists' stereotypical attitudes and tastes for linguistic and cultural islands of Germanness in far-flung destinations. Meeting this German ex-pat enwraps her experience in old paradigms of narrating Otherness, namely exoticism, and makes visible the trope's endurance in today's imagination. Communal, neocolonialist practices, not to say national and class fantasies, survive in the locale.

In contrast, Morocco arises as a realm that she can traverse unencumbered by familiar, local, or national memories: unlike the Vietnamese nail artists, whose shop her grandmother frequents back in the East German province, no Moroccan nationals appear in this novel's Germany. In the perhaps naive way of the tourist, the protagonist explores Moroccan beach resorts, while also assuming an observing and attentive role. This self-assured positionality frees her to imagine alternative spaces of community and provides a reprieve from the spiraling experience of latent fear, arresting gazes, and the oscillation between facets of identity. Here the narrator reinvents an actual travel destination, through meandering tales, in the hope of securing the protagonist's inner quest for alternative modes of identity construction. She projects alternatives to seeing and being seen, as she rummages around in history, only to extricate and ultimately liberate herself from the confining nature of old archival histories and objects.

The strategy of diffusing the image of a monolithic Africa runs counter to the narrator's quest for stability, unfolding particularly effective representations when narration connects the fate of individual members of the protagonist's family to geopolitical constellations. It resonates with the juxtaposing of global and local frames of reference: there are recurring international travel locations coexisting with others that denote an increasingly narrow locale (the grandmother's *Schrebergarten* and the hometown's train station). These places serve to articulate the double quest for stability and personal congruity (for *eine Stelle*/a spot), which the protagonist embraces, while simultaneously delineating the profound Otherness of some characters: "DEINE MUTTER HAT SICH AN KEINE STELLE GESETZT" (YOUR MOTHER NEVER SAT IN ANY SPOT).[28] For the narrator's mother, there is ultimately no room in the harmonious but contrived family picture, once she begins to dream of extricating herself from the life of confinement that she sees herself as having in East, and later unified, Germany. She had fantasized about non-belonging (e.g., absolute freedom) as existence, but her dream of emigrating to Angola was quashed. Her own return to a place on the Moroccan beach, marked by mandarin peels, is shot through with memories of casually meeting a young Moroccan man, but ultimately signifies a transient stage. Observing the mother's character insinuates, on one hand, a model for the daughter, but undercuts the utopian motif of motherhood on the other. While still expressed here through the protagonist's own future child, the motif has stood for continuity, reproduction, and renewal throughout literary history but remains a fragile spectre in *1000 Serpentinen Angst*.

The protagonist's search for closure and stability also recalls the ideal outcome of psychoanalysis and its holistically driven representation through narrative. Hoping to have such affirming experiences, the protagonist only encounters their failure. Her efforts reveal therapy situations that historicize psychoanalysis as method while situating it culturally in terms of white privilege. Whereas her friend Burhan infuses his migrant experiences into the therapy situation – and thus transposes a feeling of non-belonging into a fraught objectivity – her German-born therapist goes through psychoanalytic motions (e.g., exploring her extended family background) while rejecting alternative cultural or national interpretations from the outset: "*Ich denke, Sie haben alles richtig gemacht.//Aber sie sind in unserem Land eben eine Minderheit*" (*I think you did everything right.//But you are indeed a minority in this country*).[29] And he proceeds to "read" her in spatial, not to say racial, terms, observing a conflict with the outside world. He concedes that he may be ill-equipped to help: "*Mein Therapienagebot richtet sich ja eher an Menschen, die von der Vergangenheit belastet sind ...* " (*My therapy is directed more toward people who are burdened by the past ...*).[30] Another therapist relates a story that shares the internalization of racist patterns, even among people affected by racism, launching into an episode in which its narrator confesses to having told racist jokes herself. But the narrator does not leave it up to the reader to draw interpretive conclusions. Encouraged by a persistent Burhan, she searches the phonebook for other therapists. Structurally dominant whiteness then becomes self-evident, translated typographically in the most obvious way on screen and the novel's page: "~~Es fehlt: of colour~~" is eloquently translated, and in an equally expressive way as "Missing: ~~of Color.~~"[31] In other words: German national history's obsession with the (Nazi) past is transformed into a present that cannot shed the signs of racism, while leaving colonial legacies and personal African heritage unnamed.

An Archive of Inanimate Objects, Including a Snack Machine

Undoing stereotypes about African heritage is part of archival work, something that the protagonist herself embarks upon. It is also work that unearths the complicated status of race in the GDR which, in turn, helps us bring a new approach to understanding the intersection of visuality and racial thinking in *1000 Serpentinen Angst*. GDR history, in the apt language of Slobodian, traces "socialist chromatism," and has perpetuated a paradox: East Germany – in official policy as well as lived practice – denounced race as determinant but relied on a "folkloristic difference" to advance its own narratives of internationalism (e.g., solidarity, camaraderie). Particularly in the first years of the GDR's existence, East German politicians were heavily invested in denouncing racism while preserving the category of race and simplified visual forms of expressing skin colour as property of race.[32] In the novel, the protagonist's father had come to East Germany as a young man, a *Genosse* (comrade) open to socialist ideas. He was embraced by her grandparents who, devoted to the party line but nevertheless petit bourgeois, saw her father as the person who would reign in Susanne, the protagonist's restless punk mother, while upholding the family's hollow political convictions. Petit bourgeois ideas and ideals of social rise trumped race and a latent bias, even racist thinking on part of the grandmother; it surfaced in a full-fledged way once the bourgeoisie became the "official" social ideal to which she aspired after unification. But in keeping with socialist ideology, the father had been viewed without race, merely a part of the internationalist solidarity movement. Only later, as a young adult, does the protagonist see the father as a human being (with or without "race"?) living his own, mundane existence.

Such personalized (and at times nationalized) narratives hinge on "objects" that only become animate once extricated from the archive. They therefore help to untangle and "unmake" the confinement imposed by images, either literally through other images (e.g., family photographs) or metaphorically in the snapshots encapsulating history. The second part of the novel picks as its central theme the "arresting" function that photography has and ponders ways "out." Family sadness and trauma, embodied by the protagonist's mother, can be read through the power of (Black) family photography within a domineering, overwhelming archive of visuality that follows the rules of whiteness to take full effect. Photography oscillates between passivity, namely the code brought to bear on the image constructed for us, and activity, the seeming flaws and lapses that made their way into the image but that speak to the subject's agency. Black family photography sustains alternative histories, while tracing both logic and subversion of domineering representation.[33] Once the protagonist "reads" these pieces of memory through her new-found insights and experiences, she more clearly discerns who was rendered "stuck" and who grew personally.

Yet another "object" looms large, the ominous snack machine. Directing the narrative, it signifies (access to) movement and, quite literally, arrest. The perhaps most surreal element in the text, the machine unleashes a truly generative force, serving as more than simply a marker of where the brother had died and where departing and arriving trains mark the stable station, and thus paradoxically stand for a spot, a *Stelle*, despite constantly moving. The machine represents more than the dead object that holds the narrator's heart, and eventually her person, captive. Angelica Fenner elaborates on the complicated relationship between subject and object, reversing positions and suggesting that the machine becomes the subject in the text, organizing the entire narrative.[34] The snack automaton recalls a lost, somewhat tedious textual tradition, that of it-narratives, which inhabited, even possessed, stories a few hundred years ago.[35] But where it-narratives circulate their object and tell stories from the perspective of this object, the snack machine circulates, or revisits, the narrator's position amid a captive memory of the erstwhile same train platform, to dissolve her trauma and loss after her brother died. Simultaneously, the machine implodes a historical position that had locked the protagonist in place. At first, by embracing the object, the protagonist slips on its inanimate role, but tries to shed it, retake it, destroy it for good. The soulless machine engenders the protagonist-narrator's difficulty constructing, let alone finding, a Self.[36] The machine must disappear, or be thoroughly relegated to the past, for the narrator to move on and take agency – by escaping the binary constellation of subject and object, or Self and Other. In Wenzel's text, the constituting presence of it-narratives' resonance innovates the novel form. It is indeed a form that moves beyond "ritualized approaches"[37] in narrating identity-driven experiences in German literature, which Adelson had criticized thirty years ago and that make Wenzel's work part of a broadly – historically and globally – circulating genre. This formal intervention finds its parallel in the elusiveness of destination guiding the protagonist's travel. Her aim cannot be to arrive at a fixed place, be it in an African country or anywhere in the Diaspora. She exists in movement.

Images, Objects, Unlocking the Archive: A Conclusion

Though the narrator wants to escape confining gazes, visuality dominates the narrative. The protagonist's appreciation of being visible in the United States – as an individual, a Self, a Black woman – fades as the narration examines the stronghold that images, specifically photographs, have over our lives: *Was sind Bilder von uns, wenn sie uns in uns selbst einschließen? (What are photos of us when they lock us inside ourselves?*).[38] The embedded criticism is pronounced. Acknowledging the importance of representation, the narrator reveals static and constricting qualities of the image. But she also attempts to animate the image by confronting it with "archival pasts," which at first glance support well-worn narratives thriving on exclusion and silence: "Ich vermute, alles soll versiegelt bleiben."[39] This radiates beyond its original contextual reference, in which the grandmother refuses to re-establish contact with the protagonist's father, and which the translation renders accordingly: "I suspect she wants everything to stay sealed."[40] But the German original extends towards treatments of history, challenging the protagonist's agency more than once. Prevailing, she ably unlocks the archive eventually.

Travel, once more, holds the key, *parsed memories* of actual travel – as well as of genre – intersect with astute, *momentary* observations to construct an autopoetic Self – expressed in accelerating speech and a manner that feels fragmented, anxious, and eventually noting that "IRGENDETWAS STIMMT AN ALL DIESEN ERZÄHLUNGEN NICHT" (SOMETHING IS NOT RIGHT ABOUT ALL THESE STORIES).[41] This statement, made by an inner voice that channels the perspective of other, often publicly sanctioned discourses, or even legal, political, or journalistic speech, is constitutive of "autofiction."[42] It channels the elusiveness of autofiction vis-à-vis authorial sovereignty. Unlike the moments of personal authenticity, or what I would call "congruity," autofiction enwraps readers while also deploying distance strategically, as Layne has repeatedly argued. Autofiction enables importation of diasporic experiences. What sets Wenzel's narrator apart, I believe, is the unique way in which her personal archive relates the local and the global through family history; it incorporates the African Diaspora. Moving towards a promising, global existence in alternate communities of friends and lovers erases a hypocritical East German narrative of an internationalized past that posited community above all else. The narrator charts an individual path of identification that readily acknowledges gaps and incongruities and in which community is but one form of existence. Furthermore, the narrator unearths, against Wenzel's intention, a complex, transnational, and indeed global archive of literary and other media genres that resonates in readers' minds. We therefore engage with the novel through a history of *reading in multiple registers*, using alternative archives of literary historiography and in spaces that allow readers to join emotionally rather than searching for sociobiographical references.

The novel aids our reading of recent German literary texts as part of tradition and an emerging canon, while underscoring Wenzel's self-understanding as a writer. She not only resists sympathetic, if overwrought, interpretations by scholars, but also people's expectation that she will speak as a representative of a racialized group. This dual resistance creates context, and it has hovered over my larger argument. Mindful of the author's refusal to speak about her own authorial intentions and falling into a "trap,"[43] I attempted to not let go of my task to read, interpret, and understand. As I set out to detect any resonances that embed this novel in literary tradition and do so in novel ways, I hopefully provided a meaningful supplement to the far-reaching approaches offered to date. In fact, my claim is – and this is similar to Layne's – that the novel showcases the hooks that the text offers for dialogue among readers, but also that it continues to tell its story as integral part of literary historiography, in Germany and beyond. On a more modest level, the novel's archive is interwoven with or recalling texts in the mind of this reader, and it integrates this chapter, in a particular form of intertextuality, with the overarching thematic reach of this volume. Semantically and metaphorically, travel as method then resonates with autofiction, which Layne has introduced as a method to liberate contemporary Black German writing without being beholden to the authentic. But whereas Layne teases out the relations among author, narrator, and reader in our historical moment of heightened political awareness, I have tried to integrate the text in the texture of literary historiography, exposing its "baggage," and the ethical complicities this historiography carries. But I also see myself as a reader in Layne's sense, indulging the animations that Wenzel's text offers and that are breaking apart any remnants of an absolute Other, a status that Women, Blackness, and Africa – though never exchangeable for one another – have occupied for too long in the stories we tell in and about German historical and cultural narratives. This touching tale therefore morphs into one of transformation, leaving us to puzzle and debate – and be it about a scrambled, broken snack machine as a subject of literary studies.

NOTES

1 Olivia Wenzel, *1000 Serpentinen Angst* (Frankfurt: Fischer, 2020), Kindle e-book, 200; *1,000 Coils of Fear*, trans. Priscilla Layne (New York: Catapult, 2022), Kindle e-book, 161.
2 Leslie A. Adelson, "Touching Tales of Turks, Germans, and Jews: Cultural Alterity, Historical Narrative, and Literary Riddles for the 1990s," *New German Critique* 80 (Summer 2000): 93–124.

3. See Priscilla Layne, "Suspicious Spiral: Autofiction and Black German Subjectivity in Olivia Wenzel's *1000 Serpentinen Angst*," Center for German and European Studies, Braideis University, 26 October 2020, Zoom webinar, 1:13:46, https://www.brandeis.edu/cges/news-events/fall-2020/201026_layne_priscilla.html; see also Philipp Khabo Koepsell, ed., *The Afropean Contemporary: Literatur-und Gesellschaftsmagazin* (Berlin: epubli, 2015), esp. "Editorial," 5–7.
4. Adelson, "Touching Tales," 103.
5. Priscilla Layne, "'That's How It Is': Quotidian Violence and Resistance in Olivia Wenzel's *1000 Coils of Fear*," *Novel: A Forum on Fiction* 55, no. 1 (Spring 2022): 38 and 40, respectively.
6. Sarah Colvin, "Freedom Time: Temporal Insurrections in Olivia Wenzel's *1000 Serpentinen Angst* and Sharon Dodua Otoo's *Adas Raum*," *German Life and Letters* 75, no. 1 (January 2022): 138–65.
7. Wenzel, *1000 Serpentinen Angst*, 9; *1,000 Coils of Fear*, 5.
8. Wenzel, *1000 Serpeninen Angst*, 11; *1,000 Coils of Fear*, 7.
9. Wenzel, *1000 Serpeninen Angst*, 41; *1,000 Coils of Fear*, 30.
10. See Karin Baumgartner and Monika Shafi, eds., *Anxious Journeys: Twenty-First-Century Travel Writing in German* (Woodbridge, UK: Boydell and Brewer, 2019).
11. Wenzel, *1000 Serpentinen Angst*, 46; *1,000 Coils of Fear*, 33.
12. See "A Conversation with Olivia Wenzel," BGHRA: Black German Heritage and Research Assocation, 17 January 2022, video, 1:24:16, https://www.youtube.com/watch?v=grmcDHZImiY; Layne, "That's How It Is," 49.
13. See "A Conversation with Olivia Wenzel," and recurring in all of her public commentary and the novel itself. See, for example, Wenzel, *1000 Serpentinen Angst*, 13; *1,000 Coils of Fear*, 9.
14. For example, Wenzel, *1000 Serpentinen Angst*, 15; *1,000 Coils of Fear*, 10. See also Layne, "Suspicious Spiral."
15. Ingeborg Bachmann, *Werke, Bd. 2: Erzählungen*, ed. Christine Koschel (Munich: Piper, 1984), 354–72.
16. Wenzel, *1000 Serpentinen Angst*, 5; *1,000 Coils of Fear*, 3.
17. Wenzel, *1000 Serpentinen Angst*, 13; *1,000 Coils of Fear*, 9.
18. Quinn Slobodian, ed., *Comrades of Color: East Germany in the Cold War* (New York: Berghahn, 2015), 22.
19. Olivia Wenzel, "Es war selbstverständlich, jeden Tag Angst zu haben," *Deutschlandfunk Kultur*, 7 July 2020, https://www.deutschlandfunkkultur.de/autorin-olivia-wenzel-es-war-selbstverstaendlich-jeden-tag-100.html.
20. Wenzel, *1000 Serpentinen Angst*, 87; *1,000 Coils of Fear*, 66.
21. Wenzel, *1000 Serpentinen Angst*, 178; *1,000 Coils of Fear*, 141.
22. Wenzel, *1000 Serpentinen Angst*, 178–9; *1,000 Coils of Fear*, 142.

23 See Birgit Tautz, *Reading and Seeing Ethnic Differences in the Enlightenment: From China to Africa* (New York: Palgrave, 2007), 1–30.
24 Wenzel, *1000 Serpentinen Angst*, 87; *1,000 Coils of Fear*, 67.
25 Wenzel, *1000 Serpentinen Angst*, 87; *1,000 Coils of Fear*, 67.
26 Wenzel, *1000 Serpentinen Angst*, 88; *1,000 Coils of Fear*, 67.
27 Wenzel, *1000 Serpentinen Angst*, 87; *1,000 Coils of Fear*, 67.
28 Wenzel, *1000 Serpentinen Angst*, 93; *1,000 Coils of Fear*, 72.
29 Wenzel, *1000 Serpentinen Angst*, 189; *1,000 Coils of Fear*, 150. All paragraph breaks are in the original.
30 Wenzel, *1000 Serpentinen Angst*, 189; *1,000 Coils of Fear*, 150.
31 Wenzel, *1000 Serpentinen Angst*, 198; *1,000 Coils of Fear*, 159. Original and translation use strikethroughs in different ways. The quotations exactly replicate usage in original and translation.
32 Quinn Slobodian, "Socialist Chromatism: Race, Racism, and the Racial Rainbow in East Germany," in Slobodian, *Comrades of Color*, 23–40.
33 Tina M. Campt, *Image Matters: Archive, Photography, and the African Diaspora in Europe* (Durham, NC: Duke University Press, 2012), Kindle e-book, 431.
34 BGHRA seminar, "A Conversation with Olivia Wenzel."
35 See Lorraine Daston, ed., *Things That Talk: Object Lessons from Art and Science* (New York: Zone Books, 2004); Mark Blackwell, ed., *The Secret Life of Things: Animals, Objects, and It-Narratives in Eighteenth-Century England* (Lewisburg, PA: Bucknell University Press, 2007).
36 See Barbara Benedict, "The Spirit of Things," in Blackwell, *The Secret Life of Things*, 19.
37 Adelson, "Touching Tales," 109.
38 Wenzel, *1000 Serpentinen Angst*, 165; *1,000 Coils of Fear*, 132.
39 Wenzel, *1000 Serpentinen Angst*, 185.
40 Wenzel, *1000 Coils of Fear*, 146.
41 Wenzel, *1000 Serpentinen Angst*, 339; *1,000 Coils of Fear*, 270.
42 Serge Doubrovsky's term, used in his novel *Fils* (1977). For usage by Doubrovsky and genesis of the term, see Hywel Dix, "Autofiction: The Forgotten Face of French Theory," *Word and Text* 7 (2017): 69. See, among others, Layne, "That's How It Is," and Siddharth Srikanth, "Fictionality and Autofiction" *Style* 53, no. 3 (2019) 344–63.
43 For my use of language to describe Wenzel's positionality, see also Ismail Muhammed, "Can Black Literature Escape the Representation Trap?," *NYTimes Magazine*, 13 October 2022, https://www.nytimes.com/2022/10/13/magazine/black-literature-representation-trap.html?searchResultPosition=1.

3 Postcolonial Ghana and the Legacy of Colonial Oppression in Amma Darko's Novels

PRISCILLA LAYNE

In the past three decades, much of the focus within the field of Black German Studies has been placed on analysing autobiographies and very little scholarship has dealt with the works of fiction by Black German authors, with a primary focus on the late poet May Ayim (d. 1996), who is arguably the most well-known and easily identifiable Black German literary figure and after whom a literature prize was established in 2004.[1]

If we were to consider what scholarship has looked at the fictional writing of Black Germans *other than* May Ayim, the pool is relatively small.[2] Birgit Tautz's essay on Olivia Wenzel's *1,000 Coils of Fear* in this volume is one of a handful of essays to engage with more recent Black German fiction.[3] The narrow focus on autobiography is, in part, a logistical problem. While autobiographies have been in abundance since the 1990s,[4] it is often difficult to access the fictional work produced by Black Germans either because the texts were never published, were self-published, or printed in small quantities. That is why when scholars *do* address fictional works, they tend to focus on Ayim, not only because of the exceptional quality of her work, but also because it is more widely available in both German *and* English.[5] Thus, because the Black German cultural archive tends to be ephemeral and inaccessible, this poses a problem for expanding the field of Black German Studies.

An excellent example of an author whose work has perhaps not received much attention due to its limited publishing is Amma Darko, an author who has been largely overlooked in the context of Black German literary history. Ophelia Amma Darko was born in 1956 in the northern part of Ghana and belongs to the Fanti ethnic group. She was raised by her aunt and uncle and at the age of ten, the family moved to the capital city of Accra because her uncle's job was transferred.[6] Darko initially wished to pursue a career in industrial design, for which she studied at the University of Science and Technology in Kumasi. However, after graduation in 1980, she decided to seek out a pen pal in Germany, hoping to find work there: "Darko was shocked when she arrived in Germany and found that the only jobs available to African women were in menial service and prostitution. She took a job as a domestic and made very little money."[7] Though Darko is usually described as having been an asylum seeker in Germany,[8] Louise Allen Zak claims that after earning too little money with domestic work, she simply returned to Ghana in 1987 where she found work as a tax inspector.[9]

Zak points out that while Darko had dabbled in creative writing while working with a theatre group at university, it was the experience of living in Germany that really made writing creatively a viable option for her: "Time abroad provides not only time and psychic distance but also the emotional impetus to begin to write."[10] Darko is the author of two novels that have been translated into German: her first, *Der verkaufte Traum* (*Beyond the Horizon*, 1991), and her second, *Spinnweben* (Webs, 1996). While János Riesz describes Darko as one of the "most read *African* authors" (my italics), Black German author and scholar Philipp Khabo Köpsell writes, "These publications deserve to be mentioned in the context of *Black German literature production*."[11] And yet, despite the important influence Germany had on Darko's writing, scholarship on her novels doesn't really discuss in depth how Darko portrays Germany nor how her characters' view of and relationship to Germany impacts their lives in Ghana.

Interestingly, despite the fact that she writes in English, several of Darko's novel were first published in German and two of them, *Spinnweben* (Webs, 1996) and *Verirrtes Herze* (Confused hearts, 2000), are not even available in English. As Zak notes in her outline of Darko's path to becoming an author, Darko's manuscript happened to grab the attention of a specific publisher in Germany, Schmetterling Verlag in Stuttgart, and thanks to their support she was able to garner an audience there even before her work was published in English. This German interest in her writing generated new opportunities for Darko; she spent several months writing in Stuttgart in 1999, thanks to a fellowship from the Akademie Schloss Solitude, she went on several reading tours in Germany, and she subsequently won a scholarship for the Iowa International Writers' Workshop.[12] Despite these successes, like many African women writers, Darko's work suffers from "inadequate supply and distribution" and a "lack of critical attention at home and in the West."[13] Zak lays the blame on problems among publishing markets on the continent: "small, under-capitalized houses; expensive materials in an inflationary economy; underpaid staff; printing irregularities;

cultural expectations that the author herself should subsidize publication; and lack of means of wide distribution, which means that her work may be difficult to find and soon go out of print."[14]

I suspect that because Darko originally wrote her novels in English, even if they were first published in German translation, literary critics wouldn't consider them a part of a potential Black German literary canon. It is certainly not the case that the content of Darko's novels isn't comparable to the kinds of themes being discussed in the works of more contemporary Black German writers who have been receiving increasing attention from major publishers. Both Sharon Dodua Otoo and Olivia Wenzel recently published novels with Fischer Verlag (Frankfurt am Main): *Adas Raum* (*Ada's Realm*, 2021) and *1000 Serpentinen Angst* (*1,000 Coils of Fear*, 2000), respectively. An equally well-known publisher, Rowohlt Verlag (Hamburg) published Jasmina Kuhnke's novel *Ein Schwarzes Herz* (A black heart, 2021). And more recently, Black Germans organized the literary festival Resonanzen (Resonances), which in part came about because Kuhnke was not feeling supported by the Frankfurt Book Fair when she expressed concerns about her safety due to the presence of right-wing publishers at the fair in 2021. It is remarkable that all of these Black German authors receiving attention from major publishers are women; women who address issues like sexism, motherhood, and gendered violence in their novels – all themes that are prominently discussed in Darko's work as well.[15] This is perhaps why scholars and artists like Köpsell have argued that supporting Black authorship in Germany does not only mean creating spaces for current authors, but also uncovering older writing by Black people in German that hasn't received more attention.

In the essay "The Invisible Archive: A Historical Overview of Black Literature Production in Germany," Köpsell intentionally expands the archive to include " ... the literature of Black people who settled or lived for a limited period in Germany as well as Black Germans who grew up in Germany."[16] He criticizes literature studies scholars for trying to

> separate those groups for a clean structural approach, ignoring that in many cases the former are the parents or grandparents of the German-born generations. Hence, this clear-cut separation is oftentimes obscuring the bigger picture. In order to fully understand the interconnections of Black literature production in Germany, it is important to focus on Germany as a geographic contact zone, where people meet, exchange ideas, and put these ideas into writing. This perspective allows us to put publications coming from seemingly different Black communities in relation to each other.[17]

In this quote, Köpsell is primarily talking about the restraints of structures limited by time and generation. However, later on his essay further expands the archive in additional ways, such as including literature written by African immigrants in Germany that has been published in German, whether or not the texts were originally written in German or later translated. Köpsell points out that in the 1970s, '80s, and '90s, there were several African writers living and writing in Germany, but their work is simply not seen as contributing to a Black German canon, for whatever arbitrary reason. By utilizing the word "contact zone," Köpsell is perhaps drawing on Mary Louise Pratt's definition of the term as a "space and time where subjects previously separated by geography and history are co-present, the point at which their trajectories now intersect."[18] Thinking of Germany as a contact zone for Black authors allows us to include authors who may have spent a limited amount of time in Germany. Besides, when it comes to thinking about Black German literature, a national paradigm is not necessarily helpful, since people of the Black Diaspora do not need a "literal homeland" to which they wish to return. Instead, what unites them is "shared narratives of experiences of racialized oppression" in the form of slavery, colonialism, and white supremacy.[19]

If we let go of a national framework when thinking about Black German literature, it allows us to incorporate authors born or living outside of Germany and authors writing in languages other than German. In the foreword to the publication following Resonanzen, Sharon Dodua Otoo and Jeannette Oholi emphasize that "the heterogeneity of the African diaspora is reflected by Black German literature, because it [Black German literature] consists of a plurality of languages, aesthetics and genres."[20] And Jamele Watkins points out that in the foreword to the May Ayim Award collection, "Michael Küppers and Angela Alagiyawanna-Kadalie explain the importance of accepting artistic contributions in other languages besides German," particularly because English is one of the main languages of the African Diaspora.[21]

In this chapter, I'd like to consider how Black German Studies specifically and German Studies more broadly can be enriched by rediscovering, teaching, and writing about Darko's novels by looking at the two novels that thematize migration to Germany: *Der verkaufte Traum* and *Spinnweben*. Darko's novels are perhaps best described as "racial realism," which Gene Andrew Jarrett briefly defines as literature that "supposedly portray[s] the black race in accurate or truthful ways."[22] In *Deans and Truants*, Jarrett traces the debates among African American authors regarding to what extent a realistic portrayal of race and the Black experience is more useful to the community than texts which engage with fantasy. He argues that for years, a preference was given for Black artists who produce "racial realism," while those who "avoid[ed] or complicat[ed] racial realism suffered public criticism for shirking the political responsibilities inevitably bestowed on them as identifiable members of the *black race*."[23] While Jarrett focuses specifically on these debates within an *African American* context, one can find similar opinions about the importance of realism in literature throughout the African Diaspora. According to Tsitsi Jaji and Lily Saint, African literary scholars have long been concerned with the so-called "split between aesthetic formalist approaches (where form is taken to be a primary concern) and historicist and materialist approaches (where form is viewed as suspect and quietist)."[24] Darko's novels conform both to "racial-realism" and a historicist/materialist approach, because in them she is primarily concerned with offering a realistic, damaging look at what it's like to be an African woman in Germany in the 1980s, a topic that is important to explore considering the focus of this volume. But she does not just indict Germany for its racism, rather she attempts to convey the racist, sexist, and colonial structures responsible for why African women are so mistreated both in Ghana and abroad. But even though Darko herself spent time in Germany, her novels should not be read as autobiographical. In each case, she creates fictional, female Ghanaian characters to help her make a political argument about Black women's disenfranchised and oppressed existence both in Ghana and in Germany. This is why I will first focus on what Darko's novels convey about Ghana, then on how this in turn sheds a light on African female immigrants' experience of Germany.

I argue that Darko's novels, in particular *Spinnweben*, complicate otherwise simplified, black-and-white understandings of Africa, whether positive or negative. Contextualizing Darko's novels vis-á-vis the writing of other African authors, Zak describes Darko's work as addressing themes "that have long occupied writers from the African continent: the psychological and economic impact of colonialism on women, the injustices of patriarchal society, the conflict between the traditional values of the village and the pressures of urban life, and recently, critiques of pressing social problems."[25] But Darko does so with a critical eye, trying not to simply reproduce negative stereotypes about Africa. In a keynote address to the African Literature Association in 2006, Darko declared that the need to abolish certain customary practices in Africa " ... should be no basis to reduce our culture in its entirety to those few negatives ones and use it to justifying [*sic*] branding it as inferior and primitive."[26] In her keynote, she makes very clear that though the "physical enslavement of Black people is over," mental and financial oppression continues due to how Africa is financially exploited by Europe and the US, and Western (white) culture is upheld as superior.[27]

Darko also addresses these problems in her novels as the root cause for why her female protagonists ultimately leave for Germany, which contributes to a more complex image of Africa(ns) that doesn't succumb to the image of " ... fly infested children and their mothers with long dangling breasts, [who] sprawl daily on a desert land somewhere, starving and waiting for free food from the U.N."[28] First of all, despite its setting in a postcolonial, pro-Nkrumah Ghana, rather than a country where Black is beautiful, in *Spinnweben*, we are faced with a society that has spent so much time subjected to white supremacy that whiteness, even in its absence, continues to reign supreme. Secondly, Darko offers us an array of Black female characters whose different intersections demonstrate the true diversity among Black, African women. For example, the female protagonists in each novel are wildly different. Sefa in *Spinnweben* is educated and from an urban, middle-class family and Mara in *Der verkaufte Traum* is uneducated and from a poor, rural village. Nevertheless, both women are subjected to a patriarchal society that leaves little room for female agency. Darko expresses her frustration with Africans' depiction as a monolith when she declares "This continent is made up of over fifty (50) countries. South of the Sahara alone is composed of over eight hundred (800) ethnic groups. Yet Africa is always treated like just one big country."[29] Finally, despite the many negative portrayals of life in Ghana, there is a glimpse of hope provided through female community: in *Der verkaufte Traum* it's the friendship between Mara and Mama Kiosk, a female entrepreneur who employs her but who also gives her advice. In *Spinnweben* this community emerges during Sefa's time at a girls' boarding school where she discovers her sexuality with her fellow classmates. Thus, in the next few pages I will focus on four categories to explore how Darko's portrayal of postcolonial Ghana would help complicate and diversify Germans' understanding of at least one African country: whiteness, intersectionality, gender relations, and female community.

Whiteness

Spinnweben opens with the protagonist, Sefa, a young girl who was given to her aunt and uncle to be raised, along with another sister, because after her parents' separation, her mother could no longer care for her. Sefa comes of age in Ghana at a volatile time. The newly independent country (independent since 1957) is struggling to find its identity and decide whether to align itself with the West or with the Soviets and ultimately decide whether to accept foreign aid or "tighten their belts" and get by with less in exchange for being "truly independent." One of the core struggles in this society is how to deal with old belief systems that might seem "silly" or "uneducated" according to a Western framework. Sefa expresses that her aunt and uncle tried hard to shield her from older, superstitious beliefs:

> Onkel Quaye war so sehr damit beschäftigt, uns zu entafriknaisieren, daß er sich nicht riskieren konnte, uns solche Geschichten zu erzählen. Zu seinen Vorstellungen von anständiger Erziehung und Disziplin gehörte das Lesen jener Geschichten, von denen man sagte, daß auch britische Kinder sie lasen, desweiteren der korrekte Umgang mit Messer und Gabel, vor allem das konsequente Ausklammern des Themas Sex.[30]

> (Uncle Quaye was so busy de-Africanizing us that he couldn't risk telling us such stories. His notions of proper upbringing and discipline included reading the kind of stories that British children were said to read, the proper use of knife and fork, and, above all, consistently ignoring the subject of sex.)

Despite her uncle's efforts to shield her from unscientific beliefs, it is still clear that in Sefa's day-to-day reality, tradition and modernity, old and new, exist side by side. For example, although she doesn't believe a childhood friend's superstitions about pregnancy, she tells us that there is a boy in her town with Down's syndrome, whom everyone calls *Schlangenjunge* (snake boy), and of whom people assume " ... seine Mutter während der Schwangerschaft entgegen der Warnung des Medizinmanns, eine Schlange angeschaut hatte" (... his mother had looked at a snake while pregnant, contrary to the medicine man's warning) and this is allegedly what caused him to be born with Down's syndrome.[31] Darko's portrayal of how some old beliefs are subsiding to science, while some superstitions remain, indicates the dynamic nature of culture to which she refers in her keynote. In Darko's portrayal of Ghanaian society, rather than creating a black-and-white image of Africa being Other than the West, or even aspiring to be *like* the West, instead she shows the complexities of culture.

But even though Darko depicts a country where superstition, traditional medicine, and science coexist despite years of colonialism, there are still lasting effects on Ghanaians who have started using the colonizers' standards against one another, fueling interethnic prejudices. In an interview quoted by Louise Allen Zak, Darko stated "Because colonialism degraded our traditions, we now find ourselves too protective of them. We stubbornly refuse to look objectively at our culture."[32] In *Spinnweben*, Sefa states, "Während nämlich der Rest der Welt Afrika als Ganzes als wild und primitiv erachtet, werden innerhalb Afrikas jene Volksgruppen als Wilde betrachtet, die weiterhin sehr ursprünglich traditionell leben, unverfälscht durch 'Zivilisation.' Und in Ghana sind das die Völker des Nordens" (while the rest of the world considers Africa as a whole to be wild and primitive, within Africa those groups of people, who continue to live very traditional lives, undistorted by "civilization," are considered to be savages. And in Ghana these are the peoples of the north).[33] This split between what her relatives consider to be the cultivated, modern South and the primitive, traditional North places Sefa in a difficult position as she was born in the North, where her mother still lives, but she is a Fanti, an ethnic group not typically from the North and she has grown up in the South, in Accra, with her aunt and uncle, making Sefa even more of a transitory figure, which is intensified when she moves to Germany.

This position on the threshold perhaps gives Sefa an unusual perspective on Ghana and its different ethnicities and traditions, because she is constantly seen as an interloper. Occasionally her mixed background puts her in an underprivileged position, such as when her elementary school headmaster believes she is disobedient because she's from the North, which leads Sefa to think that "Ich hätte mich niemals so ungeschlacht benehmen können, wäre ich nicht im Norden zur Welt gekommen!" (I could never have behaved so rudely if I hadn't been born in the North).[34] But when she is older, and a student at university, she is able to use the privilege of her Southern upbringing and her education to her advantage vis-à-vis women in the North, something I will explore more later on.

Through Sefa's awkward adolescent conversations about sex and childbirth we see how misled young girls and women can be if they do not receive the proper information that allows them to take control of their reproductive health.[35] And no doubt, Sefa's aunt and uncle's aspirations of being more Western and appealing to science above anything else have benefited her in this respect. But on the other hand, this same respect for Western ways can easily shift to a belief in white supremacy that has had detrimental economic and cultural effects on the country. Sometimes this obsession with whiteness is expressed in banal idiosyncratic habits that Ghanaians have picked up either from copying the behaviours of their former colonial leaders or picked up overseas in Europe. Sefa often quips about some of these idiosyncrasies, which range from serving schoolchildren tea and bread for breakfast to the tendency to buy socks that are much too warm for the climate:

Jeden Morgen ging ich durch die heiße Sonne, in meinen Achimota-Schuhen und in den gleichen dicken Socken, die ich die Leute in Deutschland nur im Winter habe getragen sehen. Aber eben diese Socken wurden bei uns in den Geschäften verkauft. Und dort wurden sie verkauft, weil die Kolonialherren inzwischen fort waren und mit ihnen all ihr Geld, und wir uns nur leisten konnten, das aus dem Land der Kolonialherren einzuführen, was dort nicht mehr gebraucht war – ihre Ladenhüter also. Und diese Ladenhüter bestanden aus Kleidung für alle vier Jahreszeiten: Winter in England, Sommer in England, Frühling in England und Herbst in England. Und was glauben Sie, was Ghanamann tat? Weil er die Socken bevorzugte, die am längsten hielten, griff er immer zu den Wintersocken. Daß diese für den englischen Winter produziert worden waren, nun, woher hätten wir das wissen sollen? Schließlich hatten die meisten von uns nicht die leiseste Vorstellung davon, was Winter bedeutet.[36]

(Every morning I walked in the hot sun, in my Achimota shoes and in the same thick socks that I only saw people in Germany wear in winter. But these socks were sold in our shops. And they were sold there, because the colonial masters were gone in the meantime and all their money with them, and we could only afford to import from the colonial masters' land what was no longer needed there – in other words, their slow-moving goods. And these slow sellers consisted of clothes for all four seasons: winter in England, summer in England, spring in England, and autumn in England. And what do you think Ghanaman did? Because he preferred the socks that lasted the longest, he always grabbed the winter socks. Well, how should we have known that these had been produced for the English winter? After all, most of us didn't have the faintest idea what winter meant.)

This quote demonstrates that although the British colonizers have left, the Ghanaian people still associate Britishness and *whiteness* with quality, which is why they prefer to buy winter socks from England, even though they are impractical for Ghana's climate. Furthermore, in reality these socks are available in abundance in Ghana, because this is what the colonizers had imported and Ghanaian shopkeepers can't afford to import any new wares, so Ghanaians are left with the leftovers of the former colonial power.

While this example of a colonial mindset is quite humorous, in subsequent passages Sefa reflects more seriously on how colonial rule has influenced people's thinking and robbed them of agency. She remarks how now that the British have left, immigrants have come from other countries – Syria, India, and Lebanon for example. And because these newcomers have also been conditioned in a white supremacist colonial system, they view themselves as better than the Ghanaians. As such, they walk around arrogantly and dominate the Ghanaian economy. Sefa laments that Ghanaians don't realize that the countries from which these new immigrants stem are not "paradise on earth." But the Ghanaians don't question their behaviour because

> Ghanamann hat einen schwachen Punkt: Jeden, dessen Haut heller ist als seine, betrachtet er als einen Weißen. Und für Ghanamann ist jeder Weiße ein Master, ein Herr, so daß jeder heruntergekommene Inder, der seine letzten Rupien zusammengeratzt hat, um seinem vergammelten Ghetto gen Afrika zu entfliehen zu seiner eigenen Verblüffung feststellte, daß er schon innerhalb weniger Tage sich als großer Herr aufspielen konnte, daß man sich vor ihm verneigte, als sei er Lord Champion persönlich.[37]

> (Ghanaman has a weakness: he considers anyone whose skin is lighter than his as white. And for Ghanaman, every white man is a master, a lord, so that every shabby Indian who scraped together his last rupees to flee his rotten ghetto for Africa found to his own amazement, that within a few days he could pretend to be a great lord, whom one must bow before, as if he were Lord Champion himself.)

And according to Sefa, because of the internalized racism in Ghana, rather than recognizing the parasitic nature of these newcomers, Ghanaians see themselves as in desperate need of help and aid, which these immigrants are graciously bringing to them. In reality, Sefa states, "Sie beherrschten uns, sie machten uns zu Bürgern zweiter Klasse in unserem eigenen Land und behandelten uns wie Hunde" (They ruled us, they made us second-class citizens in our own country and treated us like dogs).[38]

This cult of whiteness also has a negative effect on Ghanaian women, as the problem of colourism is a constant reminder that having darker skin makes one less attractive. Even the country's revolutionary leader, Kwame Nkrumah (1909–72), who vows to cleanse the country of its colonial ways chooses a foreign, Egyptian wife. Sefa wonders, "Warum zum Teufel hatte er sein Leben eingesezt, um die weißen Kolonialherren loszuwerden, nur um sich dann eine Frau zu suchen, die ja praktisch so etwas wie die Kopie einer weißen Frau war?" (Why the hell had he risked his life getting rid of the white colonizers only to find a wife who was practically a copy of a white woman?).[39] For Sefa the message is that what the revolutionary leaders say about promoting gender equality and supporting Black women is all talk and they are not actually backing this rhetoric up with action. Jeffrey S. Ahlman confirms, in his history of Ghana under Nkrumah rule, that while the government strived for gender equality, in reality Black women were often either seen as "disembodied, faceless victims of capitalist imperialism or caricatured threats to the anticolonial cause."[40]

Intersectionality in Ghana

Although Darko spends ample time addressing the effects of white supremacy and colonialism on Ghanaian life, she still articulates how identity categories among Ghanaians result in different forms of privilege, which is often based on religion, region, ethnicity, education, and class. Sefa decides to gain the attention of a male love interest who is a documentary film-maker by working on a documentary on female genital mutilation (FGM), which in Ghana is only practised in the North, in Muslim communities, and is a practice which non-Muslim Ghanaians condemn.[41] When Sefa travels to the North, in part to track down her mother, it becomes clear what kind of privilege she has as an educated, middle-class Southerner, which is the reason she would even consider she has the right to intrude on women's lives to question them about female circumcision. Her mother warns her: "Verrate bitte nicht, worum es dir wirklich geht. Die Leute dürfen nicht das Gefühl haben, daß du gekommen bist, um ihnen zu erzählen, wie sie zu leben haben" (Please don't reveal what you're really about. People must not feel that you have come to tell them how to live).[42] Sefa is also shocked to discover that simply for the purpose of her documentary, her mother has arranged for the circumcision of her prepubescent female servant to be moved up several days. Her mother admits, "'Normaleweisen werden die Mädchen nicht einzeln beschnitten,' fuhr sie fort, 'denn zusammen können sie sich gegenseitig Mut zusprechen, damit sie die Schmerzen in Würde ertragen. Aber die nächste Beschneidungszeremonie findet erst in drei Monaten statt. Ich nahm an, das sei zu spat für dich'" ("Girls are not usually circumcised individually," she continued, "because together they can encourage each other to endure the pain with dignity. But the next circumcision ceremony is three months from now. I assumed that was too late for you").[43]

On the one hand, Sefa is excited about the opportunity to experience the ritual first-hand, but on the other hand, she feels guilty that Salima will now have to endure pain alone, without the support of her friends, just for the sake of Sefa's research.[44] Sefa's mother has the power to make this decision, because Salima is her slave or indentured servant for the time being: "Salimas Muter schuldete meine Mutter einen Sack Mehl, den sie ihr wohl auf keinen Fall würde zurückzahlen können. Um diese Schuld zu begleichen, wurde Salima zur Mutter gebracht, um bei ihr für eine vorher vereinbarte Zeit zu arbeiten" (Salima's mother owed my mother a sack of flour, which there was no way she could pay back. To settle this debt, Salima was brought to my mother to work for a prearranged time).[45] This practice recalls the history of the slave trade, in which many Ghanaians were involved, both as slavers and the enslaved.[46] Learning about this history reveals to Sefa that her past association between the slave trade and "bösen Weißen in Europa und Amerika" (evil whites in Europe and America) was an incomplete picture.[47]

Her mother tries to defend the practice by insisting that she is helping Salima's family, not only with flour but by taking away an additional mouth to feed, but rather than the labour Salima performs for her mother, what really troubles Sefa is that Salima has been transformed into a piece of property. Nevertheless, Sefa agrees to witness the act for selfish reasons: "Meine Diplomarbeit 'Klitorisbeschneidung – Folter unter dem Deckmantel der Tradition' wurde als beste Arbeit des Jahres an meiner Fakultät ausgezeichnet" (My diploma thesis "Circumcision of the Clitoris – Torture under the Guise of Tradition" was awarded as the best work of the year at my faculty).[48] In that moment Sefa privileged her academic career over Salima's dignity. Only later, when she is in Germany fighting for the right to stay as an asylum seeker and faced with the prospect of going into sex work does it dawn on Sefa that she was foolish to believe her academic career would shield her from being treated as someone's property. At the conclusion of the novel, in a letter to a white German girlfriend she writes that there isn't much that differentiates between those Africans starving on the continent and those performing sex work in Europe:

> Erstere [die Hungrigen] sind ausgezerrt, nur noch Haut und Knochen, in Fetzen gekleidet, wenn überhaupt. In krassem Gegensatz dazu stehen letztere [die Sexarbeiter*innen], die normalerweise gesund, wohlgenährt und schick gekleidet erscheinen. Doch beider Augen blicken verloren umher, denn beide sind sehr hungrig; erstere hungern nach Nahrung und Wasser, letztere nach Würde und Selbstachtung. Irgendwo in den Windungen des Schicksals kreuzen sich die Wege der Hungernden.[49]

(The former [the hungry] are emaciated, reduced to skin and bones, clad in rags if anything. In stark contrast are the latter [the sex workers], who usually appear healthy, well-fed, and smartly dressed. But both eyes look around lost, because both are very hungry; the former starve for food and water, the latter for dignity and self-respect. Somewhere in the meanders of fate, the paths of the starving cross.)

Thus, it is Sefa's experience in Germany that has made it clearer to her, that despite the privileges of her education, anti-Blackness and sexism dehumanize *all* Black women. And she has been made particularly vulnerable to these structures when living in Germany without her support network.

Gender Relations

Darko's depiction of gender relations in her novel has led several scholars to describe her work as feminist, even if she herself has never identified with the term.[50] Nevertheless, Gervase Angsotinge, Kari Dako, Aloysius Denkabe, and Helen Yitah still argue that "Darko's portrayal of the Ghanaian female seems to belie the idealized image of the African woman, especially in the Negritude tradition, as guardian of mythical and ancestral values and nurturing mother of Africa's male sons," an observation with which I disagree.[51] Neither Mara in *Der verkaufte Traum* nor Sefa in *Spinnweben* resolve to simply be the caretaker for a man. Sefa's thoughts on sex work in Germany offer an opportunity to transition to the problem of gender relations in both novels. The second part of *Der verkaufte Traum* and the second part of *Spinnweben* shift the focus from Ghana to Germany, as both Mara and Sefa end up emigrating there, with the help of the men in their lives. In Sefa's case, her affair with Ben, a married man, allows her the opportunity to travel to Munich, because Ben arranges to get her a temporary visa to visit an old pen pal of hers, with the hopes of eventually acquiring a residency and work permit. In *Der verkaufte Traum*, Mara travels to Germany by following her abusive husband Akobi (in Germany he goes by Cobby), who summons her to join him there after a few years of living apart. Sean P. O'Connell and Vincent O. Odamtten write of Akobi that he and Mara may be motivated by similar desires, "however, the privilege afforded by his gender, coupled with his lack of understanding of how such desires might unfold in the neocolonial context of the world in which they live, make his actions all the more disastrous."[52]

Despite the women's wildly different upbringings and circumstances – Sefa is educated, from a city, and unmarried; Mara is uneducated, from a rural village, and married to an abusive husband – both of them have very similar destinies when they reach Germany. Sefa is shocked to discover that despite her education, the best job she can get in Germany is working illegally as a cleaning woman and the most secure job is sex work, something Sefa refuses to do, instead opting to return to Ghana a failed "been-to." Mara's destiny is even more tragic. She believes her husband calls for her to join him in Germany because he wishes to share his prosperity with her and will eventually bring their two sons over. However, upon arrival she realizes that not only is her husband Cobby married to a white German woman – in an effort to secure residency – but he has only brought Mara over with the intention of blackmailing her into doing sex work, from which he and a friend could then profit.

Angsotinge, Dako, Denkabe, and Yitah describe Darko's feminism as "unconscious" because her proposed resolutions to women's suffering are "descriptive, rather than prescriptive."[53] Both women's experiences reveal a very dark reality for African women in Germany who, despite their education and ambitions, are seen only as sexual objects.[54] As Angsotinge, Dako, Denkabe, and Yitah write, in Darko's novels, " ... everything, including all human relationships, is commodified."[55] In the novels, as opposed to the Ghanaian men who are able to seduce white German women into marriage within a matter of months – which recalls Damani Partridge's investigation of the interactions between Black immigrant men and white German women in nightclubs in *Hypersexuality and Headscarves* – Ghanaian women can only find a white German husband if they pay them.[56] Thus, in this case Germany is not an enlightened society free of gender inequality; in Germany's patriarchal society system Black men's capital as hypermasculine is worth more than Black women's capital. The tragic ending to both Mara's and Sefa's lives in Germany and their negative experiences with men back in Ghana suggest that in its patriarchal system, women have little agency. As wives in a culture of polygamy, they can possibly marry men who treat them as property; as servants who exist to care for them and have their children. As unmarried women they have to be wary of dishonest boyfriends who may have a wife at home or who may not take responsibility for a pregnancy resulting from their affairs.

Female Community and Same-Sex Desire

In both *Spinnweben* and *Der verkaufte Traum*, female community plays an important role in helping the female protagonists through difficult times in their lives. In *Der verkaufte Traum*, after Cobby leaves for Germany and Mara is left alone to care for their first son, she befriends an older woman, Mama Kiosk, who, like her name indicates, runs a kiosk in their neighbourhood. Mama Kiosk provides Mara with work so she can support her son, but she also offers Mara advice on her relationship with Cobby. While their friendship is an excellent example of intergenerational female community, I find the issue of same-sex female desire in *Spinnweben* even more thought-provoking because it makes Darko's novel stand out not just because of her acknowledgment of same-sex practices in what is known as an otherwise religious, patriarchal, and heteronormative society, but also because of how it's normalized.

Considering how negatively heteronormative sexuality is portrayed from a female perspective in both novels, what is remarkable about *Spinnweben* is Sefa's experience of same-sex unions at her secondary boarding school. It is at boarding school that Sefa introduces us to the term *Supi*:

> Wir mußten mit dem Defizit an Männern auf unserem Campus zurechtkommen. Wir suchten die Lösung bei uns selbst. Und das Stichwort hieß 'Supi.' Erklären wir am Beispiel: Agnes wollte Monica als Liebhaberin und Monica akzeptierte Agnes Antrag, dann bezeichnete man Agnes und Monica als jeweils deren Supi. Und man konnte durchaus zwei, drei oder sogar noch mehr Supis haben und erweckte dabei keinerlei Eifersucht. In diesem System hatte Eifersucht keinen Platz.[57]

> (We had to make do with the lack of males on our campus. We looked for the solution in ourselves. And the keyword was *Supi*. Let's explain using an example: Agnes wanted Monica as a lover and Monica accepted Agnes's proposal, then Agnes and Monica were each called each other's *Supi*. And you could have two, three, or even more *Supis* and not arouse any jealousy. Jealousy had no place in this system.)

Thus, these schoolgirls were able to create a system of same-sex exploration which depended on consent and desire and rejected negative behaviours like jealousy. This space could only exist behind the walls of the school, creating a kind of utopian space outside of the heteronormative patriarchy into which the girls would be thrown upon leaving school.

There were some forms of hierarchy within the system that depended on age; the older, more experienced girls introduced the younger girls to the culture, but this practice isn't uncommon to same-sex communities:

> Es existierte lediglich ein ziemlich einfacher Leitsatz, nach dem eine Juniorschülerin einer Seniorschülerin keinen Antrag machen durfte. Das war strikt tabu. Wenn eine Supi ihr Bett verlassen hatte, um in das einer anderen zu hüpfen, hieß es, sie sei wandern gegangen. Wir Kleinen durften nur jemandem aus unserem Kreis auswählen und auch niemanden in unser Bett einladen.[58]

> (There was just a fairly simple rule that a junior student could not propose to a senior student. That was strictly taboo. If a *Supi* had left her bed to hop into another's, it was said that she had gone wandering. We younger ones were only allowed to choose someone from our circle and didn't invite anyone to our bed.)

What is also remarkable about *Supi* culture is that it is not necessarily sexual, but can revolve around non-sexual, romantic companionship. Sefa has her first experience with a *Supi* before she has begun to experiment sexually, although she does report "ich spürte ein Prickeln da unten, immer wenn ich mich wusch. Und auch wenn ich noch nicht ganz verstand, wie ich gebaut war, wußte ich doch, daß das Ding da unten zwischen meinen Schenkeln mehr war als nur eine Öffnung für den Urin" (I felt a tingle down there whenever I washed. And even if I didn't quite understand how I was built, I knew that the thing down there between my thighs was more than just an opening for urine).[59] Her first sexual experience ends up being with a girl named Jennifer, whom she accidentally catches masturbating in a hidden corner of the school and who subsequently teaches Sefa not only how to masturbate but also how to please others as well.

All of these experiences happen to Sefa without her ever using the words "lesbian," "homosexual," or "same-sex." She doesn't feel the need to categorize her experience, nor does she indicate that there is anything deviant about it. This recalls arguments made in Queer of Colour Studies, by scholars such as Roderick Ferguson and Fatima El-Tayeb, that when queers of Colour engage in same-sex behaviour or express same-sex desire, they don't necessarily use the same language as those of their white peers. Sefa's experiences, though queer, clearly exist outside of a queer/straight dichotomy imposed by colonialism and therefore perhaps suggest that this is either an older practice or a practice that has developed out of necessity due to the girls' living conditions in the boarding school. The final thing that is remarkable about Sefa's same-sex experiences is that when it comes time for her to choose a *Supi*, she is willing to take on a girl whom several other girls have rejected and whom all others seem to avoid: Fula. The rumor circulating at the school is that Fula does not have a vagina. Initially, Sefa is simply curious to find out whether or not this is true. But eventually she learns that this exaggerated rumor is based on the fact that Fula, who comes from a Muslim village in the North, has been circumcised. And Sefa and Fula develop a relationship based on camaraderie and not centred around sex, which allows Fula to be Sefa's *Supi* and therefore no longer an outcast.

The same-sex relationships Darko portrays are one example of a moment that opposes stereotypes of Africa as homophobic, lacking in any female agency, and therefore non-modern. Nevertheless, these same-sex experiences do not set Sefa on a path different from her straight female Ghanaian peers. She eventually has boyfriends and has fantasies of marriage; the fact that her dream is to marry a white German man and have "zwei Mulattenkinder" (two mulatto children) is a further indication of how a colonial mindset has left lasting impressions on her. Despite her openness to having sexual and romantic relationships with (Black) women, she knows that her access to power ultimately depends on her increasing her proximity to white masculinity.

Conclusion

Darko's experience of the German publishing market is indeed curious. On the one hand, she has found perhaps her greatest success in Germany. Riesz claims that Darko is one of the most read African writers in Germany.[60] And as Zak writes, "The first print run [of *Der verkaufte Traum*] was sold out within three months, and a second edition came out in 1994, before it had yet appeared in English."[61] Zak suggests that "being known first as a German writer may not have been to Darko's disadvantage after all. Schmetterling has made sure that Germans have access to all her works and sponsored annual reading tours, helping to position Darko in the West as the politically astute and committed writer she is."[62] But if Darko has had such popularity in Germany, why is she unknown in *German Studies* circles? Is it perhaps because Darko has been marketed as an *African* writer rather than a German writer? After all, Darko's first reading tour of Germany "was organized by a three-year campaign called 'Afrikanissimo' to organize readings of African literature," which gave the work "a ready-made forum." But why does presenting Darko's text within the context of African literature have to exclude it from German literature? These novels should not be excluded because they weren't originally written in German, because they offer priceless information about the lives of African women in Germany and also tell us something about the construction of German identity and whiteness in Germany, as well as how the legacy of colonialism has affected Africa(ns).

NOTES

1 A more recent publication on Black German fiction writing is Jeannette Oholi's *Afropäische Ästhetiken: plurale Schwarze Identitätsentwürfe in literarischen Texten des 21. Jahrhunderts* (Bielefeld: Transcript, 2024). For scholarship on Ayim, see for example Michelle Wright, *Becoming Black: Creating Identity in the African Diaspora* (Durham, NC: Duke University Press, 2004); Ela Gezen, "May Ayim und der Blues," *Monatshefte* 108, no. 2 (Summer 2016): 247–58; Arina Rotaru, "May Ayim and Diasporic Poetics,"

The Germanic Review: Literature, Culture, Theory 92, no. 1 (2017): 86–107; and Natasha Kelly, *Afrokultur: "der Raum zwischen gestern und morgen"* (Münster: Unrast, 2021).

2 In addition to Oholi's recent monograph, some older examples are Leroy Hopkins's "Expanding the Canon: Afro-German Studies," *Die Unterrichtspraxis/Teaching German* 25, no. 2 (Autumn 1992): 121–6, and Aija Poikane-Daumke's monograph *African Diasporas: Afro-German Literature in the Context of the African American Experience* (Berlin: Transaction, 2006). Additionally, there is increasing work being done on Black German theatre and performance. See Jamele Watkins, "The Drama of Race: Contemporary Afro-German Theater" (PhD diss., University of Massachusetts – Amherst, 2017) and Vanessa Plumly, "Black-Red-Gold in 'der bunten Republik': Constructions and Performances of Heimat/en in Post-Wende Afro-/Black German Cultural Productions" (PhD diss., University of Cincinnati, 2015). More recently, Leslie Adelson published on Michael Götting's novel *Contrapunctus* in "Future Narrative as Contested Ground: Emine Sevgi Özdamar's 'Bahnfahrt' and Michael Götting's *Contrapunctus*," *Gegenwartsliteratur: A German Studies Yearbook* 17 (2018): 41–67. And Evan Torner and Sarah Colvin have each published on Sharon Dodua Otoo's work: see Sarah Colvin "Talking Back: Sharon Dodua Otoo's *Herr Gröttrup setzt sich hin* and the Epistemology of Resistance," *German Life and Letters* 73, no. 4 (2020): 659–79, and Evan Torner, "Posthumanism and Object-Oriented Ontology in Sharon Dodua Otoo's *Synchronicity* and 'Herr Gröttrup setzt sich hin,'" in *Minority Discourses in Germany since 1990*, ed. Ela Gezen, Priscilla Layne, and Jonathan Skolnik (New York: Berghahn, 2022), 228–46. See also my monograph, *Out of this World: Afro-German Afrofuturism* (Evanston: Northwestern University Press, 2025).

3 I also published an essay on this novel. See Priscilla Layne, "'That's How It Is': Quotidian Violence and Resistance in Olivia Wenzel's *1000 Coils of Fear*," *Novel: A Forum on Fiction* 55, no. 1 (Spring 2022): 38–60.

4 Dirk Göttsche, "Self-Assertion, Intervention and Achievement: Black German Writing in Postcolonial Perspective," *Orbis Litterarum* 67, no. 2 (2012): 83–135.

5 Luckily, in the past few years, there have been some Black German works of fiction published in English translation, including Olivia Wenzel, *1,000 Coils of Fear*, trans. Priscilla Layne (New York: Catapult, 2022), and Sharon Dodua Otoo, *Ada's Room*, trans. Jon Cho-Polizzi (London: MacLehose, 2023).

6 Louise Allen Zak, "Amma Darko: Writing Her Way, Creating a Writing Life," in *Broadening the Horizon: Critical Introductions to Amma Darko*, ed. Vincent O. Odamtten (Banbury, UK: Ayebia Clarke Publishing, 2007), 12.

7 Zak, "Amma Darko," 13.

8 János Riesz, "Autor/innen aus dem schwarzafrikanischen Kulturraum," in *Interkulturelle Literatur in Deutschland: ein Handbuch*, ed. Carmine Chiellino (Stuttgart: Metzler Verlag, 2000), 257.

9 Zak, "Amma Darko," 13–14.
10 Zak, "Amma Darko," 13.
11 Philipp Khabo Köpsell, "The Invisible Archive: A Historical Overview of Black Literature Production in Germany," in *AfroFictional In[ter]ventions: Revisiting the BIGSAS Festival of African(-Diasporic) Literatures, Bayreuth 2011–2013*, ed. Susan Arndt and Nadja Ofuatey-Alazard (Münster: Edition Assemblage, 2014), 131.
12 According to Zak, despite having the opportunity to dedicate her time solely to writing at Schloss Solitude, Darko had a difficult time concentrating due to the fact that she was ripped out of the everyday context of being a working mother in Ghana that offered her so much inspiration. Zak, "Amma Darko," 18.
13 Zak, "Amma Darko," 12.
14 Zak, "Amma Darko," 19.
15 There are also male Black German writers who have published books in the past twenty years: take for example Philipp Khabo Köpsell's collection of poetry, *Die Akte James Knopf: afrodeutsch Wort- und Streitkunst* (Münster: Unrast, 2010), and Michael Götting's debut novel *Contrapunctus* (Münster: Unrast, 2015). However, both of those texts were published by Unrast, which is a largely academic press that occasionally publishes literature. And Köpsell's subsequent publication of his poetry, *Afro Shop* (Berlin: epubli, 2014), was published by print-on-demand publisher, epubli.
16 Köpsell, "The Invisible Archive," 121.
17 Köpsell, "The Invisible Archive," 121.
18 Mary Louise Pratt, *Imperial Eyes: Travel Writing and Transculturation* (London: Routledge, 2008), 8.
19 Erica Still, *Prophetic Remembrance: Black Subjectivity in African American and South African Trauma Narratives* (Charlottesville: University of Virginia Press, 2014), 15.
20 Sharon Dodua Otoo and Jeannette Oholi, "Vorwort," in *Resonanzen: Schwarzes Literaturfestival, Ruhrfestspiele Recklinghausen, 19.–21. Mai 2022, eine Dokumentation*, ed. Sharon Dodua Otoo and Jeannette Oholi (Berlin: Spector Books, 2023), 9. All German to English translations by Priscilla Layne.
21 Watkins, "The Drama of Race," 147.
22 Gene Andrew Jarrett, *Deans and Truants: Race and Realism in African American Literature* (Philadelphia: University of Pennsylvania Press, 2007), 1.
23 Jarrett, *Deans and Truants*, 9.
24 Tsitsi Jaji and Lily Saint, "Introduction: Genre in Africa," *Cambridge Journal of Postcolonial Literary Inquiry* 4, no. 2 (2017), 152.
25 Jaji and Saint, "Introduction," 12. Gervase Angsotinge, Kari Dako, Aloysius Denkabe, and Helen Yitah claim there are several themes that Darko's

novels share with Ghanaian popular fiction, for example "the story of bad marriages, female deviance, and romantic love." Angsotinge, Dako, Denkabe, and Yitah, "Exploitation, Negligence and Violence: Gendered Interrelationships in Amma Darko's Novels," in Odamtten, *Broadening the Horizon*, 84.

26 Amma Darko, "Rethinking Pan-Africanism: Keynote Address, Women's Caucus Luncheon," in Odamtten, *Broadening the Horizon*, 137.
27 Darko, "Rethinking Pan-Africanism," 137.
28 Darko, "Rethinking Pan-Africanism," 137.
29 Darko, "Rethinking Pan-Africanism," 137.
30 Amma Darko, *Spinnweben*, trans. Anita Jörges-Djafari (Stuttgart: Schmetterling-Verlag, 1996), 21–2.
31 Darko, *Spinnweben*, 22.
32 Zak, "Amma Darko," 15.
33 Darko, *Spinnweben*, 35.
34 Darko, *Spinnweben*, 36.
35 In fact, a focus of Darko's keynote is the need to stop female genital mutilation (FGM).
36 Darko, *Spinnweben*, 27–8.
37 Darko, *Spinnweben*, 107.
38 Darko, *Spinnweben*, 107.
39 Darko, *Spinnweben*, 47.
40 Jeffrey S. Ahlman, *Living with Nkrumahism: Nation, State, and Pan-Africanism in Ghana* (Athens: Ohio University Press, 2017), 165.
41 For more on female circumcision, see Awa Thiam, *Speak Out, Black Sisters: Feminism and Oppression in Black Africa* (London: Pluto Press, 1978), 57–87.
42 Darko, *Spinnweben*, 205.
43 Darko, *Spinnweben*, 205.
44 Darko, *Spinnweben*, 206.
45 Darko, *Spinnweben*, 206.
46 See Sadiya V. Hartman, *Lose Your Mother: A Journey along the Atlantic Slave Route* (New York: Farrar, Straus and Giroux, 2007).
47 Darko, *Spinnweben*, 206.
48 Darko, *Spinnweben*, 206.
49 Darko, *Spinnweben*, 281.
50 Angsotinge, Dako, Denkabe, and Yitah, "Exploitation," 81. While Angsotinge, Dako, Denkabe, and Yitah view Darko's feminism as a positive development in Ghanian literature, Odamtten views feminism as something negative, the equivalent to "male-bashing" and he actually praises Darko for depicting the "plight of African women in Europe" and "the abuse of women in modern-day Africa" without "male-bashing." I should note that Odamtten's reading of *Der verkaufte Traum* is written from a very

patriarchal perspective. Despite his sympathy for Mara, the language he uses to describe the narrative – her as being "trapped into permitting him [her husband] to sell her into prostitution" (101), describing her as being "like a well-trained puppy" (106), and describing the readers' position as a "john" (109) who also "eye[s] both the curve of the woman's [Mara's] back and the reflection of her face and naked torso" (108) – demonstrate an analysis of the novel from a position of male privilege and from the position of a male gaze. This demonstrates the need for more intersectional scholarship on Darko's work. Vincent Odamtten, "Amma Darko's *Beyond the Horizon*: Vending the Dream and Other Traumas for the Obedient Daughter," in Odamtten, *Broadening the Horizon*, 100–110.

51 Angsotinge, Dako, Denkabe, and Yitah, "Exploitation," 98.
52 Sean P. O'Connell and Vincent O. Odamtten, "Licit Desires, Alien Bodies and the Economics of Invisibility in Amma Darko's *Beyond the Horizon* and Stephen Frears' *Dirty Pretty Things*," in Odamtten, *Broadening the Horizon*, 50.
53 Angsotinge, Dako, Denkabe, and Yitah, "Exploitation, Negligence and Violence," 81.
54 Darko also explores this issue in the short story "Die Farbe der Armut," which depicts an African woman taking a train in Germany to her job, only to be propositioned by a white German man on the train platform who believes she is a sex worker. "Die Farbe der Armut" in *Aller Menschen Würde: ein Lesebuch für amnesty international*, ed. Reiner Engelmann and Urs M. Flechtner, 112–119 (Sauerländer: Aarau, 2001).
55 Angsotinge, Dako, Denkabe, and Yitah, "Exploitation," 81.
56 Damani Partridge, *Hypersexuality and Headscarves: Race, Sex, and Citizenship in the New Germany* (Bloomington: Indiana University Press, 2012).
57 Darko, *Spinnweben*, 67.
58 Darko, *Spinnweben*, 67.
59 Darko, *Spinnweben*, 67.
60 Riesz, "Autor/innen," 257.
61 Zak, "Amma Darko," 20.
62 Zak, "Amma Darko," 23.

SECTION II

Non-Black POC, Africa, and the African Diaspora

4 "Eingangstor zum Afrika" (Gateway to Africa): The Reconfigurations of Emily Ruete

KATE ROY

Emily Ruete was born in Zanzibar in 1844 as Sayyida Salme, the daughter of the sultan of Oman and Zanzibar. She later penned the first extant published autobiography by an Arab woman, which appeared in German with Friedrich Luckhardt (Berlin) in 1886. Writing about Ruete in the context of German-*African* exchanges and subject positions requires a number of challenging considerations of positionalities: hers, my own as author of this essay, and those of modes of construction of modern-day Zanzibari identity – or identities – especially in relation to that island's recent history.[1] Both Ruete's subject position and the position of Zanzibar in relation to the African continent challenge us to think about the complexity of categories and to interrogate, within the framework of the (cultural) texts presented here, who is considered "African," by whom, and how, and in what context this "Africanness" is represented.

On the face of it, Ruete's identification as African writer might seem straightforward. Zanzibar, a semi-autonomous region of modern-day Tanzania, lies off the East African coast. Ruete was born there, and lived there until she was in her early twenties, when she left for Hamburg to pursue her relationship with a German trader. Her *Briefe nach der Heimat* (*Letters Home*) are addressed to a recipient she has self-consciously constructed as being in her *homeland*, and as receiving, there, her critiques of German society in the 1860s–1880s as viewed through the lens of comparisons with this Zanzibari *Heimat*. At the same time, however, Ruete was enmeshed in not one, but two colonial projects: her own memory is tied up with the legacy of enslavement in the Indian Ocean, and she herself has long been read and arguably largely constructs herself as an Arab and "Oriental" woman from Zanzibar.

My approach to and sense of connection with Ruete and her works comes from my positional reading – as a white academic from a settler culture now living in Europe (I am a Pākehā from Aotearoa–New Zealand) – of the dynamics of Ruete's constructions of belonging to the *place* of her birth, as well as grappling with what she is and what she is not in relation to that place. Given Ruete's POC identity and experiences of racism in Europe, which I lay out below, this connection is problematic, as is my always already compromised ability to critically process the discomforts of the layered nature of postcolonial society, the privilege of the settler position, and complicity with the colonial project, what Regine Criser and Ervin Malakaj identify as an "irreconcilable tension."[2] Further, my own (post)colonial subject positioning necessarily also renders me incapable of "speaking about" (*darstellen*) or "speaking for" (*vertreten*) contemporary notions of Zanzibari identities and where Ruete might fit here.[3] I do not possess the authority to comment on or draw conclusions about this topic. This essay seeks instead to bring to light through descriptive observation the modes of construction employed by various groups to represent Emily Ruete, born Sayyida Salme of Oman and Zanzibar, as "African" or as belonging to an "African" context. In their many incarnations (her own, and subsequent depictions in fiction, performance, and exhibitions) I seek to understand how characterizations of Emily Ruete are used to comment on German-African interactions past and present.

This essay addresses multiple constructions of Emily Ruetes: the author figure, the self-created persona, the fictional character, the historical archival figure, and the tourist creation. Ruete's own "personhood"[4] is multidimensional and beset with contradictions. She is Arab, Zanzibari, from a ruling colonial family, a plantation owner, and defender in her writing of Arab enslavement practices. She is also a migrant and POC in Germany who experiences racism and microaggressions and tracks them in her *Briefe nach der Heimat*. Our understanding of Ruete as an author is complicated by representations of her in the work of other authors and artists and in the contemporary Zanzibari tourist landscape. Some of the most recent "reconfigurations" of Emily Ruete re-enact the ambivalence of Ruete's own self-positioning: as a German African character "writing back" or being "written back to," asking questions, or herself being put in question. Finally, both Ruete's self-representations and the artistic renderings of her seem to shape-shift as they interact with the "larger structure" of (German) colonialism in East Africa and Zanzibar's postcolonial, post-revolutionary memory and collective identity.

Such complexity begs further investigation through Gayatri Chakravorty Spivak's reading of the equally ambivalent figure of the "native informant": an "imagined, (im)possible perspective," a manipulatable "blank" data-provider whose "generat[ion] of a text of cultural identity," to enable its recognition, must be "inscribed," "interpreted," "read," and "mediated" by the Global North(erner), and, ideally, always already "mouth[s ...] the answers that [...] confirm [... this] view of the world."[5] At various moments in the life cycle of her story, Emily Ruete as author both plays into and expresses discomfort with the apparent "native informant" role she finds herself in, while in later texts, in particular by contemporary German-language writers, she is employed in this role precisely to enable what Binyavanga Wainaina calls a "writing about Africa," a confirmation of stereotypical tropes affirming a Global Northern view of the world.[6] Spivak's native informant is not only data-provider, but also, in a more symbolic function, a "trace," a "reminder of alterity." The native informant assumes this role despite

> ha(ving) rather little to say about the oppressed minorities *in* the [...] nation as such, except, at best, as an especially well-prepared investigator. Yet the aura of identification with those distant objects of oppression clings to these informants as, again at best, they identify with the other racial and ethnic minorities in metropolitan space. At worst, they take advantage of the aura and play the native informant uncontaminated by disavowed involvement with the machinery of the production of knowledge[, ...] piecing together great legitimizing narratives of cultural and ethnic specificity and continuity, and of national identity – a species of "retrospective hallucination."[7]

Ruete's direct critical engagement with the German colonial machine and its production of knowledge in an African context is most often routed through her own biography, and in this context, an "aura of identification" must be generated. And yet, as we will see, especially in her later writing, both Ruete-as-author and Ruete-as-self-created-persona call into question some outputs of the "machinery of the production of knowledge," resisting mouthing only what her implied reader would want to hear, writing back to certain colonial definitions (while leaving others hanging) by including and challenging them within phrasing that leaves space for reader reflection on their function and meaning. What she largely omits, however, is a voicing of the "contamination" and complicity of her role, and an indication of whom she is speaking over.

Situated between Spivak's "at best" and "at worst" is the arguably similar notion of "complex personhood" as it intersects with representation. Avery Gordon writes that the way that something is remembered –

as in Spivak's "retrospective hallucination" – allows us to create stories of selves and stories of others:

> Complex personhood means that all people […] remember and forget, are beset by contradiction, and recognize and misrecognize themselves and others. Complex personhood means that even those who haunt our dominant institutions and their systems of value are haunted too by things they sometimes have names for and sometimes do not.[8]

Thinking, concurrently, that "the truth about stories is that that's all we are,"[9] it makes sense to emphasize that Ruete frames her writing impetus as a desire "aus meinem Leben einiges für meine Kinder niederzuschreiben, welche bis dahin von meiner Herkunft weiter nichts wußten, als daß ich Araberin sei und aus Zanzibar komme" (to write down something of my life for my children, who until then had known only that I was of Arab descent and hailed from Zanzibar). She further states she was inspired to publish her autobiography "in Folge einer Reise nach Zanzibar, meiner alten Heimath" (as a consequence of a trip to Zanzibar, my old homeland).[10] Yet H. Porter Abbott reminds us that "autobiographies are performative. They always are doing something (either well or ill) for the writer at the time of the writing," and we should watch for "the kind of act we are reading and the context it fits into."[11] Ruete, writing back to the versions of her story her children have implicitly heard from others, simultaneously performs the acts of writing herself into German and Zanzibari history.

Akbar Keshodkar has written about pre-revolutionary Arab/African binaries of expression in Zanzibar and their return in contemporary political discourse.[12] These labels, he observes, are entwined with debates about the Africanization vs Arabization of Zanzibar, where the latter is actually termed Zanzibarization, but understood as becoming Arab.[13] Ruete's language in constructing herself and her subject position plays into this binary, yet without denying herself (and Zanzibar) a place as African. These complex identitarian dynamics move throughout all the versions of Emily Ruete we encounter here – the author figure, the self-created persona, the fictional character, the historical archival figure and the tourist creation – as they collide or clash with the (dis)appropriation of the role of the native informant.

"Eine (…) leibhaftige Afrikanerin"?

Ruete's own representation of herself in relation to the African continent is always already tied to notions of place, and of that place as

"Heimat" – a "Heimat" almost always explicitly named as "Zanzibar." And yet, within her "Zanzibar," Ruete evokes ethnicities and hierarchies in a complex layering of identities that are conveyed in a vocabulary utterly complicit with that of the colonial project: "Es hat meinen Mann auch oft genug Mühe gekostet, den biederen Nordländern begreiflich zu machen, daß zwischen Arabern und Negern ein großer Unterschied besteht und daß im großen Afrika auch andere Völker als die letzteren wohnten" (My husband often had to go to a lot of trouble to make the worthy Northerners understand that there is a great difference between Arabs and N* and that people besides the latter also lived on the great African continent).[14]

Ruete's colonial vocabulary is consistent across her written work. As well as N*, she initially attempts to resist, but ultimately employs "Mohammedaner" (Mohammedan), even to refer to her earlier self, what Susan Arnt identifies as derogatory terminology used by "weiße Christ_innen[, um] Muslim_innen auf eine bloße Anhängerschaft des Propheten Muhammed [zu reduzieren]" (white Christians, to reduce Muslims to mere adherence to the Prophet Muhammed).[15] The very first mention of the term in her memoirs expresses this tension: "Zum Beten braucht jeder Muslim (Mohammedaner) ein besonderes, vollkommen reines Gewand" (For praying, every Muslim (Mohammedan) needs a special, completely clean garment).[16] Ruete employs the term "Naturvölker" ("natural peoples," usually translated as "primitive peoples") to refer to all inhabitants of Zanzibar, where this notion of "primitive peoples" functions as a vehicle of the construction of white superiority in the colonial context, pitting "weiße[], sich selbst falscherweise als 'Kulturvölker' bezeichnende[] Gruppen" (white groups who falsely designate themselves as "peoples of culture") against "Gruppen, die nicht industrialisiert und deswegen logischerweise ohne Kultur leben" (groups who are not industrialized and therefore, according to the logic of the former, live without culture).[17]

There are suggestions that Ruete understands the workings of this vocabulary: she recognizes, ironizes, and writes back to it in the cases of the terms "Oriental,"[18] and "Naturvölker" and their derivatives, yet not in those of other hierarchical, racialized, and racist terminology. In the "Nachtrag zu meinen Memoiren" ("Afterword to my Memoirs"), for example, Ruete phrases her critique of German colonialism through an engagement with its terminology: "sowohl die Meinen als auch die Bevölkerung von Zansibar glaubten, dass die Ankunft des Geschwaders zu dem Zwecke erfolgt sei, mich – die deutsche Untertanin – bei der Geltendmachung ihrer Ansprüche zu unterstützen. Die Naturvölker, denen es an Verständnis für die so meisterhaft geschulte Diplomatie des

Abendlandes und ihrer Schachzüge mangelt, nahmen diese Erzählung für bare Münze" (Both my relatives and the population of Zanzibar believed that the arrival of the fleet was for the purposes of supporting me – the German subject – in the assertion of my claims. These natural people, who lack understanding of the expertly schooled diplomacy of the Occident and its gambits, took this version at face value).[19] Here, the Naturvölker/Kulturvölker dichotomy is employed to undercut the hypocrisies of the German colonial project, where "Kultur" is directly aligned with the machinations of colonialism.

Alongside her use of racist colonial terminology to distinguish herself from other Zanzibaris, Ruete also places herself outside of the marker "white" when she describes her arrival in Germany: "Anfänglich war mir ganz komisch zumute. Ausschließlich nur mit lauter weißer Menschen zu verkehren, dazu noch mit so vielen Blondhaarigen! Es dauerte auch lange, bis ich mich daran gewöhnen konnte. Die Menschen überhaupt voneinander zu unterscheiden, war für mich auch keine Kleinigkeit, denn alle kamen meiner ungeübten Augen so sehr ähnlich vor" (In the beginning I felt very strange. Interacting with none but white people, and with so many blondes besides! It took a long time before I was able to get used to that. Just telling people apart was no small thing for me either, since they all looked so alike to my untrained eye).[20]

The following key passage from Ruete's *Briefe nach der Heimat* details a visit to the theatre in Hamburg to see Giacomo Meyerbeer's opera *Die Afrikanerin* (L'Africaine/The African Woman), first performed in 1865 and partly set on an East African island. It encapsulates the complexities of Ruete's identity positioning of her self-constructed persona through the use of ethnic markers:

> Als mein Mann mich fragte, ob mir das Spiel gefiele, konnte ich nur mit "Nein" antworten. Darauf fragte ich ihn, ob die Spielenden [...] verrückt seien. Oh, bewahre, erwiderte er lachend. – Aber warum tun sie denn so, wenn sie wirklich nicht verrückt sein sollen, war meine ungebildete Frage. "Damit wollen die Leute ja das Leben in Afrika nachahmen." Was war dabei noch meinerseits zu erwidern? Gar nichts! Afrika ist bekanntlich sehr groß; noch größer aber schien mir die europäische Phantasie zu sein. Dem seligen Meyerbeer ist vielleicht zu Lebzeiten der Kummer glücklich erspart worden, eine solche leibhaftige Afrikanerin als Zuschauerin seines Stückes zu erleben, welche doch so wenig Verständnis für seine Kunst besitzt. Gewiß schaute sein Geist mit großer Betrübnis auf meine Unbildung herab, und noch weniger erbaulich würde er es gefunden haben, mich schon – um neun Uhr auf dem Heimweg zu sehen. [...] Auf uns Orientalen wirken die Schauspiele lange nicht so wie auf die Europäer;

offenbar fehlt uns das nötige Verständnis für die hier so hochgeschätzten Kunstleistungen.[21]

(When my husband asked me if I liked the play, I could only answer with "no." I then asked him if the actors were mad. Oh, on no account, he replied, laughing. – But why do they act like that if they are not really supposed to be mad, was my uneducated question. "Well, with that, the people want to mimic life in Africa." What could I possibly respond to that? Nothing at all! It is well known that Africa is very big; the European imagination, however, seemed still bigger to me. The late Meyerbeer was perhaps lucky to be spared, in his lifetime, beholding a living and breathing African woman in the audience of his play who possessed so little understanding of his art. Doubtless his ghost was looking down with great distress at my lack of education, and he would have found it even less edifying to see me on the way home – at nine o'clock already. [...] Plays have much less effect on us Orientals than they do on Europeans; clearly we are lacking in the necessary understanding for the artistic achievements that are so prized here.)

There are three identitarian categories in this passage (African, "Oriental," and European), and Ruete slips between two of them. The ironic self-depiction portrays Ruete as "ungebildet" (uneducated), "eine [...] leibhaftige Afrikanerin" (a living and breathing African woman) with "wenig Verständnis" (little understanding) of Meyerbeer's art, whose aversion to artistic performance is attributed to this "lack" of culture and understanding. The ideas of "Unbildung" (lack of education) and this lacking "Verständnis" are repeated here so often that they overload the passage. These repetitions, which are characteristic of Ruete's narrative style, thus work to direct our attention to the subversion of content through the narrative idiom inherent in the passage, a pushing back against native informant-complicity, in a conscious manipulation of what her readership would "want to hear." In this way, the idea of a superior European "knowledge" about Africa is fundamentally questioned by this ironic commentary on Meyerbeer's opera, namely by this self-styled "leibhaftige Afrikanerin" in her supposedly "completely uneducated," but self-consciously ironic question: "Aber warum tun sie denn so, wenn sie wirklich nicht verrückt sein sollen?" (But why do they act like that if they are not really supposed to be mad?). Yet, while the challenge to European modes of expression in this highlighting of their false and fantastical "allegorical appropriation" may suggest an impetus of "African" solidarity, what the concluding words of the passage *also* demonstrate to us is Ruete slipping back into the role of the Arab, the middlewoman, the "Orientalin" (Oriental woman), the tension that informs both her own work and its modern-day reception and adaptation, reminiscent of Abdul Sheriff's comments on ethnicity in East Africa not as a "biological category" but as a "sociological dimension."[22]

What Ruete is obviously tackling here is the question of the power of representation in the production of "knowledge," who is doing it and for whom, while simultaneously making clear for whom it is not: namely, ironically, those it depicts. Secondly, the passage emphasizes the question of identity construction, and the slips between "Afrikanerin" and "Orientalin." This changing identification has shaped the literary life of Emily Ruete and empowers both the *Thousand and One Nights*–style "inner life of the Muslim woman" reviews it received and the few early reviews that also emphasized the practical, social, and historical value of the narrative for German interests in Africa at the time. With its declaration that "When these memoirs appeared, [...] Germany's colonial ambitions were newly fledged [...] Briefly, to the world at large the Black Continent [sic] and its peoples then meant less than today,"[23] Lionel Strachey's translator's introduction justifies the need for a second English translation in the context of the early twentieth century by making explicit the connection of the memoirs with colonial history, and Germany's entry into colonial politics in the African continent.

This direct, German colonial interlude in Ruete's life followed her husband's death in an accident in 1870, after which Ruete herself, now mother to three small children, made the difficult decision to remain in Germany. Struggling financially, and desperate to claim her inheritance, she became involved in Bismarck's colonial politics, and in 1885, travelled with her children as a German and under the German flag to Zanzibar, hoping to reconcile with her brother, the sultan, and receive her share of the family inheritance. The pressure that Germany was able to exert through the presence of Emily Ruete ultimately led to Sultan Barghash's recognition of the German annexation of his East African territories, emphasizing Zanzibar's always significant interconnectedness with the African mainland – for which it famously serves as an entry point[24] – in a colonial context. On her return to Germany, Ruete included a chapter about this episode in her memoirs that also seemed to explicitly voice her (authorial) support for Germany's colonial projects, while her constructed persona in this section simultaneously attempts to downplay a direct native informant role and provide advice to would-be German colonists:[25]

> Von Anfang an habe ich zu dem kleinen Häuflein von Menschen gehört, welche mit warmen Interesse die Kolonialbestrebungen Deutschlands verfolgten, mochten diesselben nun Angra Pequena oder dem Kaiser-

Wilhelms-Land gelten. So war es auch der Fall bei der Usugara-Gesellschaft. Als dieselbe auftrat, wurde ich vielfach von Vertretern der siebenten Großmacht, die meinen Beziehungen zu Afrika und meiner Kenntniß mehr Werth beilegten, als gerechfertigt war, über das Land ausgeforscht.[26]

(From the beginning I have belonged to the handful of people who follow Germany's colonial endeavours with warm interest, be these in Angra Pequena or Kaiser-Wilhelmsland. This was also the case for the Usugara Society.[27] When this society came into being, I was often called upon for information on the land by representatives of the seventh Great Power, who attached more value to my connections with Africa and my knowledge than was justified.)

After Ruete's death in 1924, *Briefe nach der Heimat*, a text also clearly intended for publication, was discovered among her papers. It is this text that contains the passage on Meyerbeer's opera, and in this text, Ruete is highly critical of Germany and open about her negative experiences in a German society she characterizes as fundamentally racist. These experiences are often centred on others' representations of her as an "Afrikanerin." Considering that it is precisely in spaces such as the opera that Ruete experiences this Othering gaze most frequently, it is not insignificant that the Meyerbeer interlude is the only time that she directly describes herself as African in her published writings. Ruete's subsequent testimony, in her *Briefe*, about her experiences of racism, continues to intertwine with the perception of her as "African": "Schließlich erlebte ich noch diese Genugtuung, daß eine sehr naïve Dame es zuwege brachte, sich in meine angeblichen Negerhaare zu vertiefen und sich die sonderbare Freiheit nahm, diese sogar zu befühlen!" (Ultimately I experienced the pleasure of a very naive woman succeeding in digging her hands into my supposed N* hair and taking the curious liberty of even fingering it!),[28] and similarly "man [hatte] schon die tollsten Geschichten von der Araberin zu erzählen gewußt [...] Ich hätte die Haare und Gesichtsfarbe einer Negerin. Meine Füße sollten so klein sein wie die Füße einer Chinesin [...]" (the most fantastic stories had been told about the Arab woman [...] I supposedly had the hair and complexion of a N*. My feet were said to be as small as the feet of a Chinese woman).[29]

Further, Ruete's "Nachtrag zu meinen Memoiren," also among the papers discovered after her death, is both openly critical of the German colonial project and explicitly acknowledges her belief that she was used in German colonial politics. On German colonialism, Ruete-as-author writes here, "heute nach Ablauf von fast 20 Jahren ist es selbst den der kolonialen Bewegung Nahestehenden ausser Zweifel, dass unsere Politik Zansibar gegenüber, die einleitende trügerische Machtentfaltung inbegriffen, eine Kette aussergewöhnlichen Ungeschickes darstellt" (today, after nearly twenty years, it is beyond doubt even to those close to the colonial movement that our politics in relation to Zanzibar, including the initial treacherous display of power, represent a string of exceptionally clumsy manoeuvres).[30] Contrary to the chapter she added to her memoirs before publication, she now makes clear: "Mit meiner Abberufung wurde es mir klar, dass man mich von deutscher Seite nur als Mittel zum Zweck benutzt hatte" (with my dismissal it became clear to me that I had been used by the Germans only as a means to an end).[31]

In the interaction between the above passages, the tensions between iterations of Ruete's story become apparent – in the latter chapters of her memoirs, Ruete performs a persona that is enmeshed with the colonial project and that colludes with the function of the "generalized native informant [… ,] appear[ing] in the Sunday supplements of national journals, mouthing for us the answers that we want to hear as confirmation of our view of the world."[32] In the "Nachtrag," on the other hand, she explicitly undoes all of this mouthing to upend that worldview and speak unmediated. At every point it is important to remember that Ruete's writing about Zanzibar and about her life is conducted explicitly and significantly through the medium of the German language and for a German audience, not only in her published memoirs, but also in her *Briefe nach der Heimat* (unpublished in her lifetime and first appearing in its original German in 1999) and in her as yet unpublished (in German)[33] "Nachtrag zu meinen Memoiren" and "Syrische Sitten und Gebräuche" (Syrian habits and customs). Addressing the language of Ruete's writing is significant, because it tracks her construction of her persona ("Arab" and "African") within the German colonial framework in all of its ambivalences, colluding and challenging. In this sense, it also paves the way for the rewritings of Ruete I will discuss here, all of which have German involvement and/or are engaging in some way with the memory of the intertwined histories of Zanzibar and Germany in the age of colonialism.

The Native Informant as Trace

The Meyerbeer passage from *Briefe* explored above serves as an effective "foreword" to a discussion of the literary life of Emily Ruete in the German-"African" (post)colonial context. The challenge to the intersection of (European) knowledge and representation that the Ruete persona undertakes there could equally well remind us of the situation that a (re)constructed Emily Ruete faces in the fantastic retellings by others of her life story, in particular her "flight" from Zanzibar, which have preceded and postdated the publication of her memoirs, and about which I have written elsewhere.[34] In the intervening years, not much has changed in the constant, unproblematized pendulum swing between "Oriental" and "African," as expressed by the fictional Ruete character in Hans Christoph Buch's *Sansibar Blues* (Zanzibar blues) – "zwar liegt Sansibar vor der Küste Afrikas, aber ich habe mir angewöhnt, meine Heimat aus deutscher Perspektive zu sehen" (It's true that Zanzibar is located on the African coast, but I have become used to seeing my homeland from the German perspective)[35] – and the ever-present exoticism. It is interesting to note, however, that the way in which Ruete is referred to or constructed in the multiple German rewritings of and engagements with her life story, has, in recent times, taken a strongly "African" turn, using Ruete, as Dirk Göttsche would put it, as a figure that enables a creative engagement with the "shared history" of Tanzania and Germany.[36] This "African" turn often rests on Ruete's relationship with language (Kiswahili) rather than with place, perhaps because the multi-ethnic, multicultural, "cosmopolitan" Zanzibar poses challenges to any straightforward reading of "African," as does Ruete's own double-layered colonial history as Omani and German.

The following section will explore the construction of this female African identity by "German-German" writers through two recent German-language depictions of Ruete and adaptations of her story. One is an *Afrikaroman* (Africa novel): Rolf Ackermann's *Die weiße Jägerin* (The white hunter), and the other is a romance novel that seeks to style itself as postcolonial: Nicole C. Vosseler's *Sterne über Sansibar* (Stars over Zanzibar). I will explore how these authors choose to write Ruete as African woman, what they set her in opposition to, and what these reworkings might suggest about contemporary German representations of German colonialism in East Africa. Rather than functioning as a medium to critically comment on and reread the German-African past, for example through the "Verwendung [ihrer] transkultureller Stimme" (use of her transcultural voice) as Dirk Göttsche would argue,[37] I put forward that the manipulation and inscription of Ruete as fictional character in these texts in fact seems to evoke Spivak's "[im]possible perspective of the native informant as a reminder of alterity, rather than [... an] identity,"[38] a figure written into the text to be "reconstituted for [epistemic] exploitation."[39]

Ackermann's and Vosseler's texts both arguably need the figure of Ruete to function as "native informant" to support their different projects, and yet she presents an imperfect figure in this regard because of the Orientalist discourse that typically surrounds her and because of her own resultant complex personhood. Vosseler repeatedly demonstrates that she is not prepared to accept Ruete-as-author's contention that she was not an oppressed Muslim woman in danger of her life for her relationship with a German, and returns to the Arab/African dichotomy to support her reading and justify her (re)mediation of an existing autobiography. Ackermann makes use of a reference in the *Briefe* to Ruete teaching Kiswahili to construct Ruete as African and his own protagonist, white German colonist Margarete Trappe (1884–1957), her star Kiswahili student, thereby, as a "good" colonist who "cares."[40]

Spivak emphasizes the "possibility" of the native informant as a figure that enables "European knowledge of the culture of others,"[41] but she also argues that this knowledge is processed within the workings of the dominant (here, German) discourse to take away voice and expression, leaving only "the appropriation of (a) trace."[42] It is clear that what makes Ruete appealing in these two adaptations of her as "African" is her "aura of identification with those distant objects of oppression"[43] – the African *Untertanen* (subjects) of German colonialism, in the case of Ackermann, and in the case of Vosseler, those perceived as oppressed under Arab rule: "Africans" and women. As Spivak recognizes in similar contexts, this identification is dangerous precisely because of its conflation, it "undermines the struggle" to simply an "effect," and silences many "small" voices in the interests of "coherence and focus" into one, more easily digestible (and less marginalized) position.[44] In this vein, the figure of Ruete enables a palatable, accessible character whose implicit or constructed explicit endorsement mouths, grants, and legitimizes the "impeccable liberalism"[45] of protagonist, writer, or both in the representation of (German colonialism in) Africa.

The fictional Ruete character thereby constructed in the texts of Ackermann and Vosseler becomes an "'allegorical' appropriation […] recognizably ['African'] without 'real' [African] specificity."[46] These two narratives hinge on the unproblematized configuration "Kiswahili speaker/teacher = African" and draw on the language in different ways to support their identity constructions. Ackermann's novel uses its Ruete character to "justify" and support the motivations of its own historical figure, Margarete Trappe, as in the following passage:

Emily Ruete […] erwartete eine Sprachschülerin für Kisuaheli, eine junge Frau, die mit ihrem Mann nach Ostafrika gehen wollte und ihr vom Sekretariat der Deutsch-Ostafrikanischen Gesellschaft vermittelt worden war. […] Sie hatte eine Aversion gegen diese Deutschen, diese Siedler, die

"Eingangstor zum Afrika" (Gateway to Africa) 93

sich irgendwo am Kilimandscharo auf afrikanischem Land niederlassen wollten, Deutschland verließen, weil sie keine Arbeit fanden. Aber sie benötigte dringend Geld. [...]
"Jambo, Frau Zehe?," begrüßte sie die Frau, wissend, dass diese Höflichkeitsfloskel in Kisuaheli die meisten ihrer Schüler zunächst völlig verunsicherte.
Aber die junge Frau reagierte völlig unerwartet: "Jambo, Mama Ruete!," sprudelte es flüssig aus ihrem Mund. [...] Emily Ruete schaute ihrer neuen Schülerin in die Augen. Intuitiv spürte sie, dass diese junge Frau anders war als all jene, die sie bislang unterrichtet hatte. "*Karibu* ... " hieß sie Margarete Zehe willkommen und ließ sie eintreten [...].[47]

(Emily Ruete [...] was expecting a language student for Kiswahili, a young woman, who wanted to go with her husband to East Africa and who had been sent on to her by the secretary's office of the German East African Society. [...] She had an aversion to these Germans, these settlers, who wanted to take up residence somewhere on Kilimanjaro on African land, leaving Germany because they couldn't get any work. But she desperately needed money. [...]
"Jambo, Mrs. Zehe?" she greeted the woman, knowing that this polite phrase in Kiswahili completely unsettled most of her students at the outset.
But the young woman reacted completely unexpectedly: "Jambo, Mama Ruete!" bubbled fluently out of her mouth. [...] Emily Ruete looked her new student in the eyes. Intuitively she felt that this young woman was different to all the others she had taught before. "*Karibu* ... " she welcomed Margarete Zehe, letting her in [...].)

Ruete's praise for Trappe's language skills and its implied endorsement of her character in this passage performs a symbolic legitimization of Trappe's "entry into Africa" (through the fictional Ruete character's door) and her settlement of "afrikanischem Land" (African land): here, she is quite literally, through the medium of Kiswahili, "welcomed in" by the figure of Ruete as Spivakian native informant.

Vosseler's process is more insidious. Spivak underlines that the native informant is not supposed to write themselves, but rather act as "generative of a text of cultural identity that only the West [...] could inscribe[, to] provide data, to be interpreted by the knowing subject for reading."[48] In her justification for her rewriting of an existing autobiographical voice (and, as per Abbott, an existing identity performance) Vosseler records that she has done her best "Widersprüchen zwischen [Ruetes] eigenen Erinnerungen und anderen zeitgenössischen Quellen Rechnung zu tragen – vor dem Hintergrund, dass persönliche Erinnerungen nie falsch sind, oftmals aber eine ganz andere Wahrheit tragen" (to do justice to contradictions between Ruete's own memories and other contemporary sources – given the fact that personal memories are never wrong, but often hold another truth entirely).[49] Further, in a reader-complicit "*sotto* voice" expression of what Wainaina would surely term her "impeccable liberalism" in writing about (an) Africa(n), Vosseler announces that she has promised this to Ruete at her grave.[50] The fictional story, character, and space that result from this interpretation, reading, and mediation are "generative of" and "inscribed with" a troubling binary where Arab/Muslim identity performs oppression and Kiswahili, carrier of the "African" incarnation of the Ruete character, is projected as the language of liberation and love, associated with the New Year festival under cover of which Ruete escapes Zanzibar, and with her relationship with Heinrich Ruete (the [only] context in which Kiswahili appears in Ruete-as-author's *Briefe*).

Vosseler's novel is increasingly structured by chapter sections with Kiswahili epigraphs in translation, epigraphs that, interestingly, also seem to focus on Vosseler's depiction of her fictional Ruete character as a victim in the face of Arab and German power play. Each of these epigraphs is supplemented with the subtext "Sprichwort aus Sansibar" (Saying from Zanzibar). The particular chapter that follows the header "Das Feuer hinterlässt Asche, Sprichwort aus Sansibar" (Fire leaves ashes, Saying from Zanzibar),[51] for example, opens with a scene of Kiswahili speaking, as Vosseler's "Salmé" interacts with a group of women wearing the printed fabric cloth known as kanga. She lives on the land, wrapping her own hair with a kanga, and dispensing with hierarchies in her joyous interaction with women and children, enjoying the "Swahilization" of her name:

> Das Leben auf Kisimbani war deutlich afrikanisch geprägt; bezeichnend, dass man sie hier nur mit *Bibi* betitelte, "Herrin" oder einfach "Frau," nicht mit *Sayyida*, "Prinzessin," und dass man sie ausschließlich mit *Salmé* ansprach, einer runderen Version ihres Namens, die das Suaheli aus den arabischen Lauten schliff. In Haus und Hof, unter Frauen und Kindern, ließ sie *schele* und Maske einfach weg und begnügte sich, mehr zum Schutz gegen die Sonne denn aus Sittsamkeit, mit einer *kanga*, unter der sie ihr Haar verbarg.[52]

> (Life on Kisimbani had a distinct African influence; as demonstrated by the fact that she was only called by the title *Bibi* here, "Mistress," or just "Madam," not *Sayyida*, "Princess," and that people only ever called her *Salmé*, a rounder version of her name, that the Swahili had smoothed out of the Arabic sounds. In her household, among the women and children, she left off her *shayla* and mask and made do, more for protection against the sun than for modesty, with a *kanga* to cover her hair.)

This egalitarian interaction, via the medium of Kiswahili and the East African kanga, elides the problematic aspects of the setting in an African context (aspects now pushed onto the identity "Arab" via title, language, and "*shayla*," the equivalent outer garment), namely, that this interlude takes place on Ruete's plantation, where her enslaved workers harvest cloves. Vosseler similarly emphasizes that the vehicle for the love story with the German Heinrich Ruete is also Kiswahili,[53] thereby arguably positivizing this interaction with the German colonist in a manner reminiscent of Ackermann's linguistic treatment of Trappe.

The momentous chapter that reimagines Ruete's departure from Zanzibar is headed "Liebe ist wie ein Husten – sie kann nicht verheimlicht werden, Sprichwort aus Sansibar" (Love is like a cough – it cannot be hidden, Saying from Zanzibar).[54] This section details the festival under cover of which the pregnant Ruete "escapes" Zanzibar. Again surrounded by women in kanga, she is depicted as an enthusiastic participant: "'*Pumbavu likipumbaa p'umbe*,' sang Salima aus voller Kehle mit, '*fit'u usilo nadhari n'gombe*. Wenn der Narr ganz närrisch wird, ist er ein großer Narr, dumm gar wie ein Ochs!' Die altvertrauten Verse lösten ihre Anspannung" ("*Pumbavu likipumbaa p'umbe*," Salima sang along at the top of her lungs, "*fit'u usilo nadhari n'gombe*." When the fool becomes totally foolish he is a great fool, as dumb as an oaf! The familiar verses soothed her tension).[55] In a passage that allegorically appropriates contemporary prejudice in a situation where the native informant (Ruete-as-author *and* her self-constructed persona) has been noncompliant and Ruete's autobiographical "provided data" is deemed insufficient,[56] Vosseler further projects her binary to suggest that Ruete is "singing against" the fear of being followed and killed by her brother Sultan Majid's henchmen.

Equally problematically, this time in terms of the unreflected conflation of native informant and colonized, the section instrumentalizing Ruete's apparent victimization in the context of German colonial politics in Africa is significantly headed "Wenn zwei Elefanten kämpfen, ist es das Gras, das darunter leidet, Sprichtwort aus Sansibar" (When two elephants fight, it is the grass underneath that suffers, Saying from Zanzibar).[57] The use of this saying generates a direct, unambiguously African postcolonial connection for both the fictional Ruete character and, resultantly, for Vosseler's text: it was famously uttered on the world stage by Julius Nyerere, the first president of independent Tanzania.

Kiswahili, in Vosseler's *Sterne über Sansibar*, is thus seen to enable the Ruete character's emancipation, her love, and her departure from an "oppressive" Arab milieu. For both protagonist and text, the constructed binary it fosters ("modern" and "zeitgemäß" [contemporary] in ways Vosseler was perhaps not even intending)[58] also legitimizes the fictional Ruete character constructed here as "recognizably [African] without 'real' [African] specificity," a palimpsestic trace of the overwritten data of Ruete-as-author that paves the way for a "speaking for" in a troublingly unproblematized postcolonial projection.

In the expropriation (and in Vosseler's case clumsy politicization) of Kiswahili as rendered through German in the construction of Ruete as "African" in these two texts by Ackermann and Vosseler, both the italicized, and thus (ironically) made-foreign words[59] in the German text and the cipher of Ruete are arguably quite literally a "reminder of alterity, rather than [... an] identity." The utilization of the accessible "possibility" of Ruete to let Ackermann and Vosseler into a "writing about (German colonialism in) Africa," however, enacts a problematic conflation of subject positions: it is thus precisely through language that other voices are silenced.

The Subaltern Penumbra

In Spivakian terms the publishing of Ruete's autobiography in a colonially inclined Germany of the 1880s could be considered to "confin(e) the destabilization of the metropole" to the idea that there are non-German-Germans in it who can write and be read (even if they are to be [re]mediated), an "emergent discourse" that we must remember is the benefit of the native informant role, enabled by Ruete's societal status marker as (albeit Arab) princess. The flipside of this, Spivak would assert, is that "the racial underclass and the subaltern South step back into the penumbra," for, as we have seen in the examples above, the "accessible" native informant always already trumps the subaltern, and sets up for a dangerous conflation of subject positions.[60]

Exploring the concept of voice, and especially of who speaks and who listens, HMJokinen's problematizing modern incarnation of Ruete exposes her native informant position and performs the silences of her "African" life story. At its outset, the performance feeds on the opposition of two portraits.

The photo engraving of Emily Ruete (from a Hamburg photo studio) forms the cover picture of the memoirs and adorns the covers of almost all contemporary versions. The image of Maria Ernestina, whose biographical portrait I give below in context, functions in its elbow positioning, folds of clothing, and direct gaze at the audience as a mirror.

The Finnish-German visual artist HMJokinen gave the performance *An Maria Ernestina* at the opening of the exhibition "Hinter dem Schleier der Geschichte – eine arabische Prinzessin in Sansibar,

"Eingangstor zum Afrika" (Gateway to Africa) 97

Figure 4.1. Frontispiece of the *Memoiren einer arabischen Prinzessin* (Memoirs of an Arabian Princess), Berlin, Friedrich Luckhardt, 1886 (Author's collection), and "An Maria Ernestina" © HMJokinen. The author is grateful to Hannimari Jokinen for her kind permission to reproduce this work here.

Oman, Deutschland und Tscherkessien" (Behind the veil of history – an Arabian princess in Zanzibar, Oman, Germany, and Cherkessia) at Hamburg's City Hall during "Sansibar-Woche" (Zanzibar Week), 2009.[61] In the exhibition Sayyida Salme/Emily Ruete was celebrated as a symbolic representative figure for Hamburg's city-twinning with Dar es Salaam. With the counterpart of Maria Ernestina (d. 1974), the last-surviving formerly enslaved woman from Bagamoyo on the Tanzanian coast, the performance also serves to remember Ruete's identity as a slave-owner and defender of the institution of slavery, an aspect of her memoirs not featured in the exhibition at the Hamburg City Hall and that creative and historical work has only recently begun to give due attention.

As part of the performance, Maria Ernestina's biography was conceived as a sign of the silences and sidelinings of history and of the archive, especially significant because of a contemporary emphasis on the use of Ruete-as-author's memoirs by historians, and the emphasis on her writing as recording (also in a Zanzibari context, as in the Princess Salme Museum, for example). HMJokinen explains that Maria Ernestina left few biographical traces and only one photo portrait. Thirty-five screen-printed reproductions of this portrait (denoting the number of years since the death of Maria Ernestina in 1974) were provided by the artist during the performance for viewers to take away.

HMJokinen's portrait frames Maria Ernestina's image with gold-coloured Kiswahili texts and she has stated[62] that this gold colour – as in the icon tradition – symbolizes eternity and "exalts" Maria Ernestina's image. This portrait of Maria Ernestina, performed as a "forgotten sign" of history, reminds us that the Emily Ruete who authored the memoirs and the Ruete persona who speaks in them are complex in Gordon's sense, characters with "mehreren Seiten" (many sides),[63] figures doubled in the context of positions of power and in the history of East Africa as victims and perpetrators simultaneously. The texts that frame the image of Maria Ernestina, and arguably her biography in turn, reproduce proverbs given in German translation by the artist on the "Denk-Zettel" (lesson, here, literally "Thought-Program"). These proverbs both symbolize the practice of their inscription on the kanga worn by Tanzanian women, and, the artist argues, in their nature evoke the positioning of those forgotten by (German colonial) history:

HABA NA HABA, HUJAZA KIBABA – "Steter Tropfen höhlt den Stein" (Constant dripping wears the stone; usually translated from Kiswahili to English as "little by little fills the pot")
  MTENDA WEMA KIJUKI, MWISHOWE HUTIMA MOTO – "Die Biene, die den Honig bringt, verbrennt" (The bee that brings the honey burns)
    HATA UKINICHUKIA LA KWELI NITAKWAMBIA – "Auch wenn Du mich nicht magst, werde ich die Wahrheit erzählen" (Even if you don't like me, I will tell you the truth)[64]

The use of Kiswahili (and kanga) in this context has a very different function to the use of language in Vosseler's text. Operating in opposition to Ruete, rather than spoken by her, it promotes the idea of language as a vehicle of remembrance, via an understanding of Maria Ernestina as a "subaltern" who does not have a (recorded) voice of her own in comparison to the published Emily Ruete, but comes visually to voice here.[65]

Spivak, in "Can the Subaltern Speak?," objects to the reliance of subaltern studies on a "buffer" class of "native informants," which was also a colonial practice, pointing out that the subaltern is neither discussed nor heard, but rather constituted by what they are not. In contrast with all the previous figures of Emily Ruete we have encountered, all very much constructed in the native informant nexus, Maria Ernestina is

"Eingangstor zum Afrika" (Gateway to Africa) 99

arguably constituted by what she is not. As Robert J.C. Young would argue of Spivak's subaltern, "to write her history has to involve a particular effort of retrieval."[66] This notion of "retrieval" is also, following Ranajit Guha, illustrative of the choices we have in listening to the past, a challenge to accept a complex historiography pushing against "coherence and focus" on one subject position to ensure that "small voices [...] are [not] drowned in the noise of statist commands."[67]

By juxtaposing Maria Ernestina with and simultaneously questioning contemporary identity constructions of Emily Ruete, who, we must remember, *did* get to publish one version and leave a written record of another about her story as a woman manipulated in the service of German colonialism, *An Maria Ernestina* challenges Ruete's "ability" to speak for a nation and its colonial experience.

Epilogue: Performing Ruete in Zanzibar

In the Zanzibari context, always already involving external participation, and still often with a German hand, we encounter again and differently the idea of how Ruete is presented and in what context her personhood is employed in terms of its relationship with Zanzibari history. Here, the involvement of local actors in the role of Ruete makes an arguably significant representational statement in the sense of "darstellen" (representation as "depiction"), incorporating her into a perceived "contemporary" (twenty-first century) Zanzibari identity, a Ruete "as she might look in Zanzibar now," implicitly less "Arab."

In Zanzibar itself, remembering Ruete as a Zanzibari (writer or otherwise) seems always already enmeshed in painful memories of seeking to understand – from both sides – the legacies of Omani Arab colonization on the island and the 1964 revolution, which unseated the sultanate and established the socialist People's Republic of Zanzibar and Pemba, led by the Afro-Shirazi Party. The figure of Ruete, like that of Queen lead singer Freddie Mercury, another complex presence in the context of contemporary Zanzibari identities, has been functioning for some years as a tourist attraction for visitors to the island. Tours, sites, and experiences related to the historical figure of Ruete are largely run by people, both Zanzibari and European, who, by their own admission (in conversation with the author), feel a connection to the figure of the princess-writer, perhaps because she seems to enact their own (often lived) conceptions of Zanzibari identity and cosmopolitanism. This portrayal, given the relative lack of material in Kiswahili, the main language of the island,[68] could, as I will discuss, largely be seen as outward-facing (to European tourists, often with European funding,[69] and to Oman, often with Omani funding): the crossover to local heritage and education projects is only now beginning, for example with the Zanzibar Heritage Walks project and its "Princess Salme Promenade."

As a final reflection on the figure of Emily Ruete in a German-"African" context, therefore, I evoke constructions of Ruete in contemporary Zanzibari public space. Given Ruete's Arab heritage and resulting complicity in the history of Omani Arab rule, her place in fractured collective memory is always already fraught, political, and arguably not obviously "performable" in any notion of an "African" identity, especially post-1964.

Commentators here agree that, in the Zanzibari context, "change of state identity" always already has an effect on the perception and "re-categorization of individual identities."[70] Lupa Ramadhani writes that "Zanzibar's long and troubled history['s] enduring effects that haunt the islands" impact identity construction, splitting it in two directions, namely the building of individual identities alongside the "politicization of collective identities in the making of state identity."[71] Particularly any notion of "African identity" is resultantly enmeshed with memories of the Revolution, leading into a "contemporary political battle" that "rekindles" the labels Arab and African, and that opposes the ideas of "Africanization" and "Zanzibarization" of Zanzibari space, where "Zanzibarization" carries echoes of the Arab colonial past.[72] William Cunningham Bissell and Marie-Aude Fouéré underline that it is the *way* that Zanzibari stories are told that is as interesting and significant as what actually happened, providing a commentary on spaces of social memory, where "personal or individual memory is [...] always tied to one's perspective, subject position, and place," constantly generating what Keshodkar would term the "embedding (of) new meanings."[73]

When this storytelling is turned towards the past, multiple commentators identify ironies in terms of collective memorialization, where the challenges of feeding the tourism industry and the "lure of the Arabian Nights" present complications for a "properly revolutionary" post-1964 identity in the public space.[74] In this context, the Omani past of the islands must necessarily be targeted by government promotion in the hopes of attracting "high class cultural tourists" despite its conflict with contemporary Zanzibari political values and replacement of a memorialization of the revolutionary past.[75]

In view of all of these contemporary identitarian complexities, what do Zanzibaris do with the figure of Ruete now? How has she returned, how is she performed, and where? The "German" element of identity constructions of Ruete, unsurprisingly, is implicit rather than explicit – what

Figure 4.2. Poster advertising performances at Emily Ruete's birthplace, Mtoni Palace, Zanzibar. The author warmly thanks Said Magofu for the poster and Daniel Twumasi for the photographic image.

seems paramount is the window her memoirs give on a substantial period of Zanzibar's past. Three contemporary projects use Emily Ruete – or Princess Salme, as she is constructed in Zanzibar itself – and her writings to revisit (and arguably reconstruct) a "cosmopolitan" Zanzibari past always already infused with complexities and ghosts.

Significantly, all of these three projects face outward rather than inward. Rafael Marks describes a situation in Zanzibar's Stone Town where "cultural and economic change [is] generated by the tourist trade and economic liberalisation" and impacts the decision of what buildings to restore and preserve, leading to a prioritization of "servicing the needs of visitors rather than the local residents."[76] The same skewed emphasis is seen in cultural production, where "[t]he history of the Sultan's rule is summarised in a few rooms of furniture and household wares in the 'People's Palace,' while Europeans organise 'traditional' African dance shows in the concrete auditorium in the Old Fort for a few dozen tourists. Ticket prices are generally beyond the means of residents and the dancers imported from the mainland."[77] In this situation, the ways in which heritage preservation and heritage fostering are determined and celebrated are always already "politically charged."[78]

One such contested space is Ruete's childhood home, Mtoni, which, while not in Stone Town itself, is considered a heritage building. Dutch and Italian funding was behind the initial stages of the rebuilding. Prior to 2019, performances were organized for tourists that presented Ruete and her life story through the medium of taarab. This music form, for which Zanzibar is now known globally, was introduced by Ruete's brother Sultan Barghash, who sent Zanzibari musicians to train in Egypt.[79] The developing fusion with Kiswahili lyrics and melodies (since the time of Siti Binti Saad, whom Rosabelle Boswell describes as "an ex-slave African woman," in the early twentieth century) produced this new and characteristic form that could also function as social and political commentary.[80] The Arab (and elitist) roots of taarab led it to be labelled as "subversive" in post-revolutionary Zanzibar, and in the contemporary period, European and American funding, via the Zanzibar International Film Festival (ZIFF), is both encouraging and preserving the form and, Boswell argues, sparking "fears about such investment [by largely Western-inspired regimes of heritage preservation] shaping the art form and delivery of artists, leading to the de-authentication of indigenous music."[81] At the Mtoni concerts, leading taarab musicians would perform alongside an actor representing Ruete narrating from her memoirs (in English) and singing about palace life, followed by African dance that she would have "actually experienced."[82]

"Eingangstor zum Afrika" (Gateway to Africa)   103

Significantly, this is not the only tie-up of Ruete and Zanzibar's not uncontested "national music."[83] In 2014 the Munich production studio Winter & Winter released the CD *Memoirs of an Arabian Princess – Sounds of Zanzibar*. The CD cover functions to create a distinct impression of Zanzibar that is very much located in the past, drawing as it does explicitly on iconography from the cover art of the original German publication of Ruete's memoirs, as well as from that of the 1907 English translation.

The DEMAX production company collaborated with the Omani cultural magazine *Nizwa* and Zanzibari partners to produce *Sons of Sinbad – A History of Oman* in 2018 ("Monsoon Empire," "Route to India," "The Call of Zanzibar"). Like Winter & Winter, the company is sited in Munich and professes that "We prefer projects that also convince us in terms of content: How do we improve coexistence, how can we contribute to maintain social consensus? What can we learn from history? What is relevant for our lives in a global world? We are interested in what connects people and overcomes borders!"[84] Ruete's story is part of the documentary series' third episode "The Call of Zanzibar," which tracks Omani rule and the struggles with the (other) colonial powers in the Indian Ocean in the nineteenth and twentieth centuries, "Oman's foremost competitors."[85] The episode ends with reflections on the 1964 revolution and contemporary Omani-Zanzibari collaboration projects, particularly in education. The segment on Ruete contains contributions from historian Abdul Sheriff and Princess Salme Museum curator Said el-Gheithy (also the location consultant) as well as re-enactments of significant moments from Ruete's life story – her childhood in Mtoni, where "elements of Arab and African cultures converge to form something unique," producing "new forms" in architecture, music, and language;[86] the palace revolution for which "the young, literate Salma" functioned as scribe;[87] her first encounters with Heinrich Ruete; her departure from the island; and her return as part of the German colonial project. The episode characterizes the story of Ruete and her siblings as that of a family "entangled […] in web of European politics."[88]

Featuring local Zanzibari actors in the role of Ruete at various stages of her life (child, young woman, and middle-aged woman), the Ruete character looks like a contemporary Zanzibari and speaks only (subtitled) Kiswahili. These modes of depiction, not only in visual representation, but also in terms of the politics of language use, seem deeply significant, given that questions of the representation of Omani rule infuse the episode, which ends with a reflection on the path to the revolution (termed an "invasion […] launched from Tanganyika"[89]) and the challenges of the post-revolutionary period in a cultural space

Figure 4.3. Film stills from 27.20 and 36.21 of the Omani-German co-production *Sons of Sinbad: The History of Oman – The Call of Zanzibar*, depicting local Zanzibari actors Safia Khalifa Salum as "Young Salme bint Said Al Said" and Fatma Khalifa Salum as "Salme bint Said Al Said."

that Sheriff characterizes as "based on Arabic-Omani tradition," "politically divided," and "failing" to create a unified identity because of the "history, memory of slavery."[90] The documentary episode ends with the words of the Omani sand artist whose art is used as a framing device: "the shroud of silence, once lifted, […] makes room for new stories."[91]

The "Princess Salme Promenade," officially inaugurated in 2019, maps locations (including former German sites) from Ruete's memoirs onto the face of Zanzibar's Stone Town, with plaques on buildings of significance in Ruete's life story. Part of the Heritage Walks project, it sites Ruete and her history alongside six other tours of the Stone Town space. The Heritage Walks Facebook post explains the impetus of the project in the context of a 2018 workshop for tour guides:

> Developed through the collaboration of Professor Abdul Sheriff, the Walks have been taught to 33 tour guides during two Heritage and Preservation Trainings previously carried out by (Kawa Training Center) KTC. During these training, the Walks have been further developed through the feedbacks of the tour guides.
> Our joint efforts have produced the following Walks:
> 1. Dhow Culture
> 2. Cosmopolitan Architecture
> 3. Modern Architecture
> 4. Imani na Amini – Faith and Peace
> 5. Doors and other Handicrafts
> 6. Sights, Sounds and Scents of Zanzibar
> 7. Princess Salme Promenade
>
> At the end of the workshop, the idea is, that tour operators will officially include these new tours in their offers. This would mean new and culturally valid tourism opportunities for international and national tourists, business opportunities for tour operators, as well as job and improvement opportunities for tour guides.[92]

While the KTC emphasizes the training, development, and support of tour guides from the local community in the conducting of these tours, which also implies a cost, theoretically it is also possible to walk the route alone, or indeed to encounter a bilingual English-Kiswahili plaque as a part of everyday movement around the space. The "Farewell to Zanzibar" plaque of the Princess Salme Promenade, for example, happens to be at the site of a popular restaurant, the former Hansing House, site of the trading company Heinrich Ruete worked for, is now the Lands Commission Building, and "Salme's last abode" is now the People's Bank. Unlike the Mtoni taarab concerts, the German-produced CD and the Omani-German "The Call of Zanzibar," the language and siting of these plaques enable their "national" accessibility (as the Heritage Walks team terms it). While the choice of themes and routes are certain to be "politically charged," and the size of the English titles suggests that English remains the main language of these plaques, the contemporary lived and everyday nature of the sites themselves (in the case of the Princess Salme Promenade at least) and the vehicle of language (these are, significantly, the only accessible excerpts from Ruete's memoirs translated into Kiswahili) offer Ruete's story two major entry

Figure 4.4. "Princess Salme Promenade" plaques "Hansing House" and "Salme's Last Abode" *in situ* in Stone Town, Zanzibar.

"Eingangstor zum Afrika" (Gateway to Africa) 107

points into Zanzibari spaces that both enable a conversation about the multiplicity of "embedded meanings" and "re-negotiated public spaces," and, importantly, also offer up to those actually living in these spaces the option of engaging with this reading and mediation of history and this conversation or not.

The multiplicity of different contexts and interactions that characterize Emily Ruete's complex personhood both inside and outside of narrated space as *Eingangstor* to "Africa" for a variety of different players – herself, as autobiographical "performer," contemporary German-language writers and artists engaging with the colonial legacy, and actors in the contemporary Zanzibari (tourist) landscape – makes for an (im)possible cultural identity construction. Throughout, as we have seen, questions of language – both Ruete's own German and the instrumentalization of Kiswahili in later texts – terminology and voice arise in (often problematic) characterizations, while from the beginning to their contemporary "rekindling" the identitarian categories "Arab" and "African" are manipulated or thrown into relief. In the German-African context, the figure of Ruete, swinging between "generalized native informant" and glimpses of something more critical in her pushing of her own "data," seems always in some way or other (not least for herself) a malleable trace, a continually reconfigured allegorical act of writing or act of reading.

NOTES

1 The author thanks Franklin University Switzerland's Faculty Development Fund for its 2019 support for research in Zanzibar and attendance at the GSA conference in Portland, Oregon, without which her participation in this volume would not have been possible. She is also grateful to the FUS LLLS program for funding her research assistants Destiny Brown (2021–3) and Daniela Perezchica-Trancoso (Summer 2022), and to Destiny and Daniela themselves for their enthusiastic and collaborative assistance. Finally, she extends her warm thanks to the editors of this volume, and her heartfelt gratitude to Lisabeth Hock in particular for her exceptional support and encouragement to bring this contribution to completion.
2 Regine Criser and Ervin Malakaj, "Introduction: Diversity and Decolonization in German Studies," in *Diversity and Decolonization in German Studies*, ed. Regine Criser and Ervin Malakaj (Cham, Switzerland: Palgrave Macmillan, 2020), 1.
3 Gayatri Chakravorty Spivak, "Can the Subaltern Speak?," in *Marxism and the Interpretation of Culture*, ed. Cary Nelson and Lawrence Grossburg (Urbana: University of Illinois Press, 1988), 271–313.

4 Avery F. Gordon, *Ghostly Matters: Haunting and the Sociological Imagination* (Minneapolis: University of Minnesota Press, 2008), 4–5.
5 Gayatri Chakravorty Spivak, *A Critique of Postcolonial Reason: Toward a History of the Vanishing Present* (Cambridge, MA: Harvard University Press, 1999), 6, 9, 153, 342.
6 Binyavanga Wainaina, "How to Write about Africa," *Granta* 92 (2005), https://granta.com/how-to-write-about-africa/.
7 Spivak, *Critique*, 342, 352, 360.
8 Gordon, *Ghostly Matters*, 4–5.
9 Thomas King, *The Truth about Stories: A Native Narrative* (Toronto: House of Anansi Press, 2003), 2.
10 Emily Ruete, *Memoiren einer arabischen Prinzessin* (Berlin: Friedrich Luckhardt, 1886), 1:i-ii. All translations from the German are by the author.
11 H. Porter Abbott, *The Cambridge Introduction to Narrative*, 2nd ed. (Cambridge: Cambridge University Press, 2008), 141.
12 Akbar Keshodkar, *Tourism and Social Change in Post-Socialist Zanzibar: Struggles for Identity, Movement, and Civilization* (Lanham, MD: Lexington Books, 2013), 65.
13 Keshodkar, *Tourism*, 69.
14 Emily Ruete, *Briefe nach der Heimat* (Berlin: Philo, 1999), 28.
15 Susan Arndt, "Mohammedaner," in *Wie Rassismus aus Wörtern spricht: (K)Erben des Kolonialismus im Wissensarchiv deutsche Sprache: ein kritisches Nachschlagewerk*, ed. Susan Arndt and Nadja Ofuatey-Alazard (Münster: Unrast, 2019), 693.
16 Ruete, *Memoiren*, 1:2.
17 Noah Sow, "Naturvolk," in Arndt and Ofuatey-Alazard, *Wie Rassismus aus Wörtern spricht*, 694.
18 As I have discussed elsewhere: see for example, Kate Roy, "German-Islamic Literary Interperceptions in Works by Emily Ruete and Emine Sevgi Özdamar," in *Encounters with Islam in German Literature and Culture*, ed. James Hodkinson and Jeffrey Morrison (Rochester, NY: Camden House, 2009), 166–80.
19 Emily Ruete, "Nachtrag zu meinen Memoiren" (unpublished manuscript, 11 September 1929), typescript.
20 Ruete, *Briefe*, 18.
21 Ruete, *Briefe*, 34–5.
22 Abdul Sheriff, "Race and Class in the Politics of Zanzibar," *Africa Spectrum* 36, no. 3 (2001): 307.
23 Lionel Strachey, "Authenticity of These Memoirs," in *Memoirs of an Arabian Princess*, trans. Lionel Strachey (New York: Doubleday, Page and Company, 1907), v.
24 See for example, Heinz Schneppen, "Nachwort," in Emily Ruete, *Briefe*, 176.

25 Ruete, *Memoiren*, 2:189.
26 Ruete, *Memoiren*, 2:188.
27 A society founded to promote the colonization of German East Africa.
28 Ruete, *Briefe*, 28.
29 Ruete, *Briefe*, 28.
30 Ruete, "Nachtrag."
31 Ruete, "Nachtrag."
32 Spivak, *Critique*, 342.
33 An academic-style English-language translation has been provided by E.J. van Donzel in Sayyida Salme/Emily Ruete, *An Arabian Princess Between Two Worlds: Memoirs, Letters Home, Sequels to the Memoirs, Syrian Customs and Usages*, ed. and introd. E.J. van Donzel (Leiden: Brill, 1993), 511–26.
34 For example, Kate Roy, "Only the 'Outward Appearance' of a Harem? Reading the *Memoirs of an Arabian Princess* as Material Text," *Belphégor. Littératures populaires et culture médiatique* 13, no.1 (2015); Kate Roy, "'So ähnlich könnte es gewesen sein, aber (…)': Unethical Narrations of Emily Ruete's 'Große Wandlungen,'" *Edinburgh German Yearbook* 7 (2013): 115–38.
35 Hans Christoph Buch, *Sansibar Blues, oder, Wie ich Livingstone fand* (Frankfurt am Main: Eichborn, 2008), 54.
36 Dirk Göttsche, "Rekonstruktion und Remythisierung der kolonialen Welt. Neue historische Romane über den deutschen Kolonialismus in Afrika" in *Deutsch-afrikanische Diskurse in Geschichte und Gegenwart. Literatur- und kulturwissenschaftliche Perspektiven*, ed. Michael Hofmann and Rita Morrien (Amsterdam: Rodopi, 2012), 171–95.
37 Göttsche, "Rekonstruktion."
38 Spivak, *Critique*, 352.
39 Spivak, *Critique*, 370n78.
40 Binyavanga Wainaina, in his famous, ironic essay "How to Write about Africa," details just such a process of establishing "caring credentials" through the strategic employment of tropes.
41 Spivak, *Critique*, 66–7.
42 Spivak, *Critique*, 342.
43 Spivak, *Critique*, 66.
44 Spivak, *Critique*, 66; Ranajit Guha, "The Small Voice of History," in *Subaltern Studies IX: Writings on South Asian History and Society*, ed. Shahid Amin and Dipesh Chakrabarty (Delhi: Oxford University Press, 1996), 8.
45 Wainaina, "Africa."
46 Spivak, *Critique*, 346.
47 Rolf Ackermann, *Die weiße Jägerin* (Munich: Knaur, 2006), 100–1.
48 Spivak, *Critique*, 6, 49.
49 Nicole C. Vosseler, "Nachwort," in *Sterne über Sansibar* (Augsburg: Weltbild, 2010), 533.

50 Wainaina, "Africa"; Vosseler, "Nachwort," 534.
51 Vosseler, *Sterne über Sansibar*, 143.
52 Vosseler, *Sterne*, 149.
53 Vosseler, *Sterne*, 184, 189.
54 Vosseler, *Sterne*, 213.
55 Vosseler, *Sterne*, 243.
56 See also Roy, "So ähnlich könnte es gewesen sein."
57 Vosseler, *Sterne*, 419.
58 Vosseler, "Nachwort," 533.
59 Here I reference Aotearoa–New Zealand writer Alice Te Punga Somerville's magnificent *Always Italicise: How to Write While Colonised* (Auckland: Auckland University Press, 2022), 5, which pushes back against this typographical trend.
60 Spivak, *Critique*, 360–1.
61 This was an early version of the exhibition text now sited at the Princess Salme Museum in Zanzibar. The present museum text does now attempt to address many of the points HMJokinen touched on in her performance, *An Maria Ernestina*.
62 HMJokinen, *An Maria Ernestina* (unpublished performance text, 16 February 2009), typescript.
63 HMJokinen, *An Maria Ernestina*.
64 HMJokinen, *An Maria Ernestina*.
65 Spivak, "Subaltern."
66 Robert J.C. Young, *Colonial Desire: Hybridity in Theory, Culture, and Race* (London: Routledge, 1995), 162.
67 Guha, "Voice," 3.
68 This is also noted at the Princess Salme Museum within the text of the museum exhibition (as observed on visits in 2015 and 2019). Said el-Gheithy, curator of the Princess Salme Museum, is also instrumental in the Heritage Walks project and in their Kiswahili language translations. I am grateful to Said el-Gheithy for useful discussions about this project, as well as about the *Sons of Sinbad* – "The Call of Zanzibar" project which I discuss and for which he was the location coordinator.
69 For example, the Italian and Dutch funding for the reconstruction of the Mtoni Palace, Emily Ruete's childhood home, see Antoni Folkers, Anne-Katrien Denissen, Abdul Sheriff, Gerrit Smienk, and Frank Koopman, *Mtoni: Palace, Sultan and Princess of Zanzibar* (Utrecht: ArchiAfrika, 2010).
70 Lupa Ramadhani, "Identity Politics and Conflicts in Zanzibar," *The African Review: A Journal of African Politics, Development and International Affairs* 44, no. 2 (December 2017): 172; see also Keshodkhar, *Tourism*, 9.
71 Ramadhani, "Identity Politics," 172.

72 Ramadhani, "Identity Politics," 176–7; Keshodkar, *Tourism*, 65, 69.
73 William Cunningham Bissell and Marie-Aude Fouéré, *Social Memory, Silenced Voices, and Political Struggle: Remembering the Revolution in Zanzibar* (Dar es Salaam: Mkuki na Nyota Publishers, 2018), 7–8; Keshodkar, *Tourism*, 205.
74 Bissell and Fouéré, *Social Memory*, 15.
75 Keshodkar, *Tourism*, 71–2.
76 Rafael Marks, "Conservation and Community: The Contradictions and Ambiguities of Tourism in the Stone Town of Zanzibar," *Habitat International* 20, no. 2 (June 1996): 271.
77 Marks, "Conservation and Community," 274.
78 Marks, "Conservation and Community," 271–2, 275.
79 Rosabelle Boswell, *Challenges to Identifying and Managing Intangible Cultural Heritage in Mauritius, Zanzibar, and Seychelles* (Dakar: CODESRIA, 2008), 62–3.
80 Boswell, *Challenges*, 63–4.
81 Boswell, *Challenges*, 64, 69.
82 Said Magofu, a guide at Mtoni, conversation with the author, 17 June 2019.
83 Boswell, *Challenges*, 62.
84 "About DEMAX," DEMAX, accessed 31 March 2023, https://www.demaxtv.de/en/about-us/.
85 *Sons of Sinbad – A History of Oman:* "The Call of Zanzibar," DEMAX GmbH, 2018, documentary, 45:55, https://vimeo.com/ondemand/sonsofsinbad/321193450.
86 "Call of Zanzibar," 12:11.
87 "Call of Zanzibar," 12:44.
88 "Call of Zanzibar," c. 36:00.
89 "Call of Zanzibar," 39:00.
90 "Call of Zanzibar," 40:00.
91 "Call of Zanzibar," 44:00.
92 Zanzibar Walks, "Zanzibar Built Heritage Group: Tour Operators Workshop – Heritage Marketing and Customer Journey," Facebook, 16 June 2017, https://www.facebook.com/people/Zanzibar-Walks/100064033893534/.

5 The Survivor as "Implicated Subject"[1] in Stefanie Zweig's Autobiographical Africa Novels *Nirgendwo in Afrika* (*Nowhere in Africa*) and *Nirgendwo war Heimat. Mein Leben auf zwei Kontinenten* (*Nowhere Was Home: My Life on Two Continents*)

SARAH HENNEBÖHL

Intertitle: Introduction

In 1938, German Jewish writer Stefanie Regina Zweig (1932–2014) and her mother fled Nazi persecution and followed Zweig's father into exile in Kenya. At that time, Kenya was officially the Kenya Colony and part of the British Empire.[2] After starting her writing career as a feuilleton writer and author of children's books, Zweig published numerous books which drew on her experience in Kenya,[3] among them *Nirgendwo in Afrika* (1995; *Nowhere in Africa*, 2004)[4] which marked her beginning as a writer for an adult readership and formed the basis for the feature film *Nirgendwo in Afrika* (2002; *Nowhere in Africa*, 2003),[5] and *Nirgendwo war Heimat. Mein Leben auf zwei Kontinenten* (*Nowhere Was Home: My Life on Two Continents*, 2013),[6] which was to be her last novel.

The two novels can be considered autobiographical fiction. *Nirgendwo in Afrika* is an autobiographical novel in which the characters' names have only been partially fictionalized. The story follows the life of an exiled German Jewish refugee family, the Redlichs, who survive the Holocaust in British Kenya during the years 1938–47. Privileges that the upper-class family enjoyed in Germany before the rise of National Socialism are no longer a given; in Kenya, the refugees are poor and the family struggles to make a living. The father, Walter, a former lawyer, finds work as a farm manager even though he has no knowledge of farming, and later, he enlists as a soldier in the British Army, which opens the opportunity to return to Germany after the war. The mother, Jettel, runs the household and occasionally works as a nanny or waitress. Yet, despite being poor, the white family enjoys privileges as both parents rely heavily on their Black Kenyan farm aids and household servants.

In contrast, *Nirgendwo war Heimat* is an autobiographical epistolary novel. Unlike in *Nirgendwo in Afrika*, Zweig refrains here from the use of any fictional aliases for her characters. The novel lacks a narrator, and the story is told entirely through letters which comprise the correspondence between father, mother, and daughter, as well as between friends and relatives and the Zweig family, diary entries taken from Stefanie Zweig's childhood diary, and twenty-five black-and-white photographs. The included material documents the life of the Zweigs from 1932 until the present. Although their exile in Kenya is part of the story, almost a third of the novel is dedicated to the family's life in pre-war Germany, beginning with Stefanie Zweig's birth, and a sizeable portion of the book is dedicated to the family's return to Germany in 1947, as well as the post-war years. The novel ends with an epilogue that gives a brief summary of the life of every member of the immediate Zweig family up until the present. In *Nirgendwo war Heimat*, Black Kenyans remain at the margins of the story. They are rarely mentioned and when they are, it is only in brief comments.

Why did Zweig write a second autobiographical novel? We might find an answer in the preface to the English translation of *Nirgendwo in Afrika, Nowhere in Africa*. Here, Zweig gives voice to her frustration with the reception of both her first novel and Caroline Link's film:

> When I started writing the story of my life I had only one ambition – to honor the father who had lost everything that makes a man a man, his hope, dignity and future, his fatherland and his family … It was in memory of this remarkable father that I wrote my life-story. When I started remembering and writing I never fathomed that *Nowhere in Africa* would be the bestseller it immediately was … It saddened me to think that my parents, who both died young, could not read it. And it distressed me even more that people were all too eager to feed their minds with the alleged romanticism of colonial Africa. To most German readers Owuor … was of far greater interest than the refugees who had to leave their home country to escape death. …Whoever had seen the film had an even greater urge to talk about Owuor. The day that the news came out that *Nowhere in Africa* had won the Oscar for the best foreign film, one fax reached me saying "well done, Owuor!" and another one asking "does Owuor know?"[7]

The above quote suggests that Zweig saddles her readers with the responsibility not only for critically understanding the colonial context of the novel and refraining from an attitude of colonial nostalgia, but also for prioritizing what motivated her to write: she wanted to author the story of her Jewish family's escape from the Nazis and their survival in the Kenyan colony. Hence, Zweig's second novel is best understood as a reappropriation of her family history. But the quote further demonstrates that Zweig avoids any responsibility as a writer in the reception of her novels by her readers. In a similar vein, Natalie Eppelsheimer defends *Nirgendwo in Afrika* against allegations of colonial nostalgia when she claims that "the setting of the story reveals a deeply colonized society and mentality through the interactions between characters and offers this society to the reader for critical contemplation."[8]

Zweig's autobiographical writings have a therapeutic function, allowing the author to process her traumatic experience as a child survivor of the Holocaust and bearing witness to the fate of her family. The use of the adverb "nirgendwo" (nowhere) in both titles indicates that for Zweig, her family occupies a liminal space. According to Victor Turner, "the subject ... is, in the liminal period, structurally, if not physically, 'invisible.'"[9] In this liminal space of the colony, Zweig portrays her family as victims only: they are victims of the Nazi regime, but also of the British colonialists who discriminate against them for being Jewish and refugees. Yet, the case of the Zweig/Redlich family is more complex: certainly, they are victims, but they are also, in terms of the phrase coined by Michael Rothberg, "implicated subjects":

> Implicated subjects occupy positions aligned with power and privilege without being themselves direct agents of harm; they contribute to, inhabit, inherit, or benefit from regimes of domination but do not originate or control such regimes. An implicated subject is neither a victim nor a perpetrator, but rather a participant in histories and social formations that generate the positions of victim and perpetrator, and yet in which most people do not occupy such clear-cut roles ... [10]

Whiteness, which I define with Noah Sow as "a socio-political marker that means: this person belongs to the group of whites and is treated accordingly,"[11] was denied to the family in Hitler's racial state. The situation was different in the Kenyan colony, however: here, "whiteness determines a historically created social position that exists independent of self-perception."[12] It grants the family the status of *Bwana* ("master" or "boss"),[13] *Memsahib* ("white foreign woman of high social status ... "),[14] and *Memsahib Kidogo* (kidogo = Swahili for "little, small").[15]

Racism as "the connection between prejudice and institutional power"[16] lies at the core of colonial societies, and European colonial states gained their hegemony from a "codification and institutionalization of white privilege."[17] In the Kenyan colony, the family's "liminality" and self-perceived invisibility are only possible from a place of white privilege which in turn makes them "implicated" in a system of racist oppression. As white Europeans they are passively and actively supporting a colonial system that operates through a racist policy against Black Kenyans.

Racist attitudes and stereotypes infiltrate both of Zweig's autobiographical novels. In *Nirgendwo in Afrika*, Black Kenyans are one-dimensional characters who remain trapped in the colonial setting of a novel that is dictated by a privileged white gaze. In the novel, the characters as well as the visual descriptions of Black Kenyans align with racist colonial stereotypes of Black people: Black people are naturally happy to serve their white masters and do not question or resist their authority. In contrast, *Nirgendwo war Heimat* tries to do away with the issue of the representation of Blackness altogether: Kenya and its Black inhabitants are pushed to the periphery of the story, they "cannot speak"[18] and are merely referenced in the letters written by the Zweigs.

Zweig was a victim of racism herself: she was forced into exile by the manifestation of hatred against Jews under National Socialist rule in Germany. And it is no sophisticated guess that she had to face anti-Semitism throughout her life after relocating to Germany, where hate crimes against Jews did not end with the collapse of the Third Reich. The most recent increase in anti-Semitic attacks bears sad witness to that.

Yet, in the same way that "antipathy"[19] and "malevolence"[20] are not preconditions for racism, as Noah Sow points out, being the victim of one form of racism does not make a person immune to adopting other forms of racism. It is my belief that a respectful, historically nuanced, and often uncomfortable approach towards texts is a productive way to dismantle writing practices of racial discrimination. While Zweig had every right to prioritize her own history as the victim of racism and genocide in her autobiographical writings, she not only fails to provide a critical reflection on the history of colonial racist oppression and violence that the Black Kenyans she encountered as a child had to face, but ignores her family's status as *implicated subjects* in the British colonial system. My point is to show how through her writing Zweig became complicit in reproducing racist stereotypes about Black people. The two memory discourses – the Holocaust and the history of colonialism – seem "at war with each other [and] only one side can prevail."[21]

Intertitle: *Nirgendwo in Afrika (Nowhere in Africa)*

Nirgendwo in Afrika gained wide popularity and was a huge commercial success. For weeks, it stayed on German bestseller lists, over six million copies were sold, and it was translated into numerous languages.[22] In the mid-1990s, a rising number of literary productions engaging with the history of German colonialism – both novels in which the historical background of European colonialism serves as a setting for their plots, and novels set in contemporary Africa that feature "strong" white women who fall in love with Africa and/or an African – flooded the German book market. Instead of offering a new perspective on Africa, most of these books "[exploited] a continuing exoticist cross-cultural fascination of the African theme."[23] The German book covers for *Nirgendwo in Afrika* resemble those of other popular German Africa novels. The title evokes an "Idea of Africa"[24] that is circulated throughout the media: an established discourse that presents Africa as a country and not a continent that comprises fifty-four states. In this discourse, writes Cameroonian philosopher Achille Mbembe, Africa remains a metaphor "through which the west represents the origin of its own norms, develops a self-image, and integrates this image into the set of signifiers asserting what it supposes to be its identity."[25]

Potentially, a more fitting title for the novel would have been "Nirgendwo in Kenia" (Nowhere in Kenya). After all, the novel is set in Kenya. However, the actual title positions the novel within a discourse about Africa that is all too familiar to a white Western audience. Natalie Eppelsheimer claims that "Africa ... does not stand in the center of the narrative."[26] Yet, judging the book by its covers, there is no indication that the novel tells the story of a Jewish refugee family. In fact, the successful marketing of the novel as part of an "Afrika Boom"[27] in the German book market promoted its commercial success.

In 2002, the film adaptation of *Nirgendwo in Afrika* by director Caroline Link was released under the same title as the book. That same year, it won the Bavarian Film Award as well as the German Film Award, and, in 2003, the Academy Award for best foreign-language film. The film emphasizes the *white* colonial element of the story by making two radical changes to the plot: it is the mother, Jettel Redlich, not the father, Walter Redlich, who becomes the central character of Link's narrative. In the exposition, the mother is introduced as survivor and victim of the Holocaust. But as the plot evolves, the story of Jettel's emancipation from patriarchal gender norms and her transformation into a successful, white female colonialist becomes increasingly central and undermines a critical view of the history of colonialism.

Although written for an adult readership, *Nirgendwo in Afrika*[28] is still very much at home in the genre of children's literature. An omniscient narrator guides the reader through the story, but the narrator frequently adopts the point of view of Regina, Zweig's alter ego. Regina's childlike and naive perspective mystifies and romanticizes Kenya and its Black inhabitants. Zweig's narrating voice mirrors a colonialist "commanding gaze"[29] that reproduces racist stereotypes about Black people and engages the reader in exoticist fantasies about Black Kenyans.

A passage from the beginning of the second chapter, when mother and daughter arrive at the farm in Kenya, demonstrates this:

> "Toto," Owuor laughed as he lifted Regina out of the car. He threw her a little way up into the air, caught her again, and pressed her close to his body. His arms were soft and warm, his teeth were very white. The big pupils in his round eyes lit up his face, and he wore a high, dark-red hat that looked like one of those upside-down pails that, before the big journey, Regina used to take outside [to bake][30] cakes in the sandbox. A black tassel with fine fringes was swinging from the hat; [tiny][31] black curls crept out from under the rim. Owuor was wearing a long, white shirt over his trousers, just like the cheerful angels in the picture books for good children. Owuor had a flat nose and thick lips, and his head looked like a black moon. As soon as the sun shone on the droplets of sweat on his forehead, the droplets changed into multi-colored beads ... Owuor's skin smelled delightful like honey, chased away any fear, and made a big person out of a little girl. Regina opened her mouth wide so that she would be able to swallow the magic that drove all the [pain][32] and tiredness from her body. First, she felt herself getting strong in Owuor's arms, and then she realized that her tongue had learned to fly.[33]

In this passage, Owuor's body is visualized in isolated parts. His "white teeth," his hair, his "flat nose," his "thick lips," his head, and finally his Blackness ("dark moon") are singled out. His Black body is what Ronald L. Jackson describes as "scripted":

> Scripting as a discursive act, is ideologically driven. The peculiar arrangement of prescribed identities is, alone, an institution without which there would be no need to preserve the stifling disease of racism and the hierarchy that accompanies it.[34]

The child-narrator "scripts" Owuor as racially different but simultaneously tries to reconcile his Otherness by comparing his clothes to items and images that are familiar to her: Owuor's hat is compared to a pail she pretended to bake in, and his shirt looks like the garment worn by "cheerful angels" in picture books. Still, physical markers of his difference remain and cause a seemingly irreconcilable barrier between the racialized Other and the white spectator. Jackson argues that "within the interplay of race relations, corporeal zones such as that of skin color and hair texture automatically evoke feelings, thoughts, perhaps anxieties, if they are already resident or dormant."[35] In the above passage, the reader is invited to adopt the narrator's gaze, and hence invited to engage in in colonial fantasies about the Black man Owuor.

The description of Owuor is an example of how Zweig introduces all the Black Kenyan characters in *Nirgendwo in Afrika*: the emphasis lies on their visual description. The family's nanny, Aja, whose real name remains unknown to the reader, has eyes that are "gentle, and coffee-brown, and large like Suara's [the fawn],"[36] her hands are "delicate,"[37] and the inside of her hands "white"[38] – even whiter than the fur of the family's dog, Rummler. Aja's appearance is compared to that of the family's pets. In addition, Aya's breasts are described in precise visual detail: "When the wind tore at the yellow wrap that was fastened with a big knot on Aya's right shoulder, her firm, small breasts moved like small spheres on a string."[39] The visual descriptions of Black Kenyans stand out because nowhere in the novel do we find similar visual descriptions of whites. Neither Walter Redlich's skin colour nor that of his wife is compared to the snow-covered peak of Mount Kenya or the fur of the family's dog, and Jettel Redlich's breasts are not assessed based on texture, size, and movement.

> [T]he structure of racial difference is founded on a master signifier – Whiteness – that produces a logic of differential relations. Each term in the structure establishes its reference by referring back to the original signifier … which itself remains outside the play of signification even as it enables the system.[40]

The parents' visual appearance is neither exoticized nor eroticized because they are white, and their skin colour constitutes the "master signifier" in the colony. In contrast, Black Kenyan bodies are "racially inscribed,"[41] which immediately marks them as Other in both the colonial world of the novel and the imaginary of a white readership.

An ekphrastic passage from the novel further emphasizes the novel's underlying racism: Walter Redlich observes a scene between Owuor, the family's new nanny, Chebeti, and his own children, Regina and Max:

> His son was lying sheltered in the folds of Chebeti's light blue dress. Only the child's tiny white linen cap was visible. It touched the woman's chin

and appeared in the light wind like a ship in a quiet ocean. Regina crouched with crossed legs in the grass, a wreath of leaves from the lemon tree in her hair ... Owuor was sitting under a cedar with dark leaves and watching the smallest move of the baby with close attention. Next to him lay the stick with the carved lion's head on the handle that he had acquired on the first day of Chebeti's employment ... In its harmony and abundance, the scene reminded Walter of pictures in the books of his childhood. He smiled a little when he realized that people in the European midsummer are not black and do not sit under cedars and lemon trees.[42]

Just as the above quoted passage where Owuor's appearance reminds Regina of "cheerful angels in the picture books for good children,"[43] Walter is reminded of "pictures in the books of his childhood" until the reality of Owuor's and Chebeti's skin colour and the non-European landscape disturbs and ultimately destroys the imagined picture. Ronald L. Jackson argues that the "intent of scripting is frequently to create harmony via homogeneity, the resultant effect in interracial scripting is often social polarization."[44] Although Walter is pleased that his children are well taken care of, clearly, his scripting of the Black bodies creates a disharmony, and his fantasy reveals his racist bias: he imagines a white family idyll for his children in which there is no place for Blackness.

The only photograph that is included in *Nirgendwo in Afrika* illustrates the Redlich's/Zweig's position as whites within the colony.

The photograph has no caption, but it anchors the story in a historical reality by giving visual evidence of Walter Zweig's presence in Kenya. The Zweig's/Redlich's dog, Rummler, who sits on a sack of corn in front of Walter Zweig helps the viewer identify the family patriarch. The other subjects of the photograph remain anonymous. The camera focus lies on the three white men in the front who are dressed in typical farm outfits. They contrast sharply with the eight Black men on the truck who are moved to the background and who except for one are dressed in dark-coloured sarongs only. The eight Black men on the truck seem uncomfortable: they stand stiff, most of them hold their arms straight at their sides, only one has his hands folded behind his back, and only four of them look straight into the camera. The white man in the middle of the white trio in the foreground leans casually with one hand against a farm machine and puts the other hand assertively on his waist. The white man on the left is holding on to a farm tool, giving the air of a person of action. The relaxed postures of the two anonymous white men form a stark contrast to the stiff postures of the Black men on the truck. The white men convey an air of dominance and authority over the Black men. Despite being unified with the two other white men through skin

Figure 5.1. Photograph of Walter Zweig with anonymous people in Kenya.
By courtesy of Langen Müller Verlag. From Stefanie Zweig, *Nirgendwo in Afrika* (*Nowhere in Africa*). © 1995, Langen Müller Verlag, München

colour and dressing style, Walter Zweig's body language disconnects him from them. He is turning sideways and has his hands in his pockets which gives the impression that he is uncomfortable or even insecure.

Although the quality of the photograph is poor, upon closer inspection, the viewer detects another reason for Walter's disconnect from the other white men: a Black man who is almost unrecognizable stands between Walter Zweig and the two other white men. He is wearing a white shirt which is almost entirely covered by a black jacket. The viewer can only see part of a white collar and an inch of a white sleeve. The visual presence of the ninth Black man is further complicated by the unhappy folding of the book: the photograph spreads over two entire pages and the Black man vanishes in the "natural" gap that the binding of the novel creates. The fact that the Black man next to Walter Zweig is not part of the group of eight Black men on the truck but is moved to the foreground suggests that there might be a closer relationship between him and Walter Zweig, or that he might hold a superior position over the other Black men.

The photograph is clearly taken in the colonial fashion of the time and creates a contrast in dressing style, colour, and location between white men and Black men. It demonstrates the racial divide between colonizer and colonial subject and celebrates the colonial endeavour. The photograph was not taken with an "innocent eye" but a "colonial eye," and the photographer not only chose the location, objects, and people, but arranged them deliberately. What we are supposed to see is an image of colonial farm life with white men in charge of the land and the Black men. What we are not supposed to see is a Black man in a white shirt standing on an equal level with the three white men, which would take the focus of the photograph away from the white men and blur the racial hierarchy between colonizer and colonized. It is only with further knowledge of Walter Zweig's biography that the viewer could potentially sense another dividing force in the photograph: the one between the two white men on the left and the one Jewish but visibly white man and the nine Black men on the right. Overall, the photograph is a rather poor visual choice for an "innocent" portrait of Zweig's father.

In *Nirgendwo in Afrika*, the family's contact with the Indigenous inhabitants is described as harmonious, and Zweig avoids placing them in proximity with the colonizers. Yet, the family simultaneously aligns with both colonizers and colonized. The above-mentioned photograph of Walter Zweig has been removed from later editions of the novel. One might speculate that Zweig felt uncomfortable with providing visual proof of her father's implied connection with the colonizers. However, the "African" book cover and title remain.

Intertitle: *Nirgendwo war Heimat. Mein Leben auf zwei Kontinenten (Nowhere Was Home: My Life on Two Continents)*[45]

In contrast, *Nirgendwo war Heimat* consciously resists a categorization as popular Africa novel and positions itself as Holocaust memoir. The book cover clearly sets it apart from other popular Africa novels. The red and orange tones of stereotypical African scenery have been switched out with more discreet colours: beige and a faint green. We can see a stamp, a locket that contains a photograph of Zweig with her parents and part of another photograph that shows a ship. The book cover hints at a journey. While the personal objects of the family are featured in the foreground, the stereotypical "African" elements – a giraffe and the prototypical flat-topped tree (*burkea Africana*) are moved to the background. The viewer's gaze is directed towards the personal objects that visually emphasize the focus of the book.

In *Nirgendwo war Heimat*, Zweig tries to step out of the fictional world of *Nirgendwo in Afrika*. With the inclusion of black-and-white photographs, the author aims to lead the reader's imagination to historical images of real people and away from "colonial fantasies."[46] Thus, the publication of Zweig's last novel is best understood as an act of reappropriation of her family's survivor story. The novel encourages the reader to accept the authenticity of the included material. But in an article published in the *Frankfurter Allgemeine* on Zweig's eightieth birthday, Hans Riebsamen mentions in passing that although many letters might ("vermochten"[47]) have been saved, others were lost over the years ("im Laufe der Jahre verloren gegangen"[48]), forcing the author to reconstruct them from memory. It is not obvious to the reader which letters in the book are fictional and which ones are authentic. Hence, *Nirgendwo war Heimat* is not merely a collection and arrangement of historical documents but still contains elements of a work of fiction.

We also find visual descriptions of and racist stereotypes about Black people in Zweig's second autobiographical novel. For example, in a letter that Jettel Zweig writes to her husband while on her journey via ship to Kenya, she reports her daughter "wurde von einem pechschwarzen Riesen mit einem roten Bommelhut getragen" (was carried by a pitch-black giant with a red fez).[49] We can speculate that the welcoming scene between Owuor and Regina in *Nirgendwo in Afrika* was inspired by this letter, but in contrast to Regina's lengthy description of Owuor, Jettel Zweig's description of the anonymous Black man is a mere commentary that is part of a much lengthier letter in which Jettel Zweig talks about many other encounters that happened during her passage to Kenya.

The daughter's positive encounter with the Black man is Jettel Zweig's way of communicating to her husband that the child is fine with her new surroundings. Still, the comment about the Black man focuses on his skin colour, his height, and his dressing style. It reflects a fascination with the Black man but also communicates anxiety when Jettel Zweig resorts to the language of fairy tales to describe him: his striking height makes him appear like mystical creature, a "giant." The perceived threat of the Black man is a racial stereotype that has a long history and its manifestation in the form of the fear of the tall Black man has proven to have a long durability. A recent article by Neil Hester and Kurt Gray, "For Black Men, Being Tall Increases Threat Stereotyping and Police Stops," shows that "Being tall is often discussed as a wholly good trait,"[50] but the authors conclude that "height means something different for Black men: height amplifies already problematic perceptions of threat, which can lead to harassment and even injury."[51]

In *Nirgendwo war Afrika*, the cook Owuor is an essential character, but in *Nirgendwo war Heimat*, Owuor is mentioned only twice, in two letters written by Jettel Zweig. In her letters, Jettel Zweig, in a patronizing tone, refers to Owuor as "our Owuor."[52] The use of the possessive pronoun hints at the master-servant relationship between the cook and the family. In another letter, Jettel Zweig expresses her satisfaction with her daughter's assimilation process, including Stefanie's uninhibited attitude towards Black people:

> Hier auf der Farm erscheint uns [Steffi] glücklich wie in ihrem ganzen Leben nicht. Wenn wir sehen, wie sie auf die Menschen zurennt (die Schwarzen sind unglaublich kinderlieb und immer fröhlich) und vor keinem Tier mehr Angst hat, vergessen wir für Momente sogar, wie unglücklich wir sind. Wenn die Frauen mit den nackten Brüsten und den Bananenstauden auf dem Rücken auf die Farm kommen, lacht sie mit ihnen, als hätte sie nie etwas anderes getan.[53]

> (Here, on the farm, Steffi seems happier than ever before. When we see how she runs towards Black people here (Black people are incredibly fond of children and always cheerful) and how she has completely lost her fear of animals, we momentarily forget how unhappy we really are. When the bare-breasted women with the banana bunches on their backs arrive at the farm, she laughs with them as if she had done nothing else in all her life.)

Jettel Zweig's racist mentality becomes apparent in her generalizations about Black Kenyans. To her, all of them are "extremely fond of children" and "always cheerful." She also "scripts," in Jackson's terms, Black women as visibly different from herself by mentioning their "bare breasts." Characteristics like being "fond of children" and "cheerful" become racist in this context because Jettel Zweig attributes them to an entire ethnic group of people who for her display these characteristics all the time.

More generalizations about Black people follow in a letter to her sister, in which she utters her frustration about the monotonous life at the farm: "Bestimmt habt ihr in New York Menschen, mit denen ihr reden könnt. Auf der Farm gibt es ja nur die Schwarzen, die keine Ahnung von dem haben, was uns bewegt" (In New York, you probably have people to talk to. On the farm, there are only Black people who have no idea what is going on with us).[54] The use of the personal pronoun "us" makes it clear that Jettel Zweig draws a barrier between her family and the Black people on the farm. For her, Black people have their limitations and can certainly not become her confidants. She seems oblivious to the fact that she herself "has no idea" what is going on with the Black people on the farm either, and that she does not know anything about their personal lives and their family histories. It is her status as *Memsahib* and her family's white privilege that drive the racial division between Blacks and whites.

Walter Zweig displays similar attitudes towards Black people. In a letter to Helen Groag who has "lost" her golden snake-shaped bracelet at a New Year's party at the Zweig's, Walter writes:

> Liebe Leni! Heute früh geschah wieder eines der vielen Wunder, mit denen uns Afrika so beglückt. Der Schamaboy Kimani trug an seinem rechten Handgelenk das goldene Schlangenarmband, das Du zu Silvester getragen und bei deiner Abfahrt vermisst hast. Nach Kimanis unvereidigt gebliebener Aussage wickelte sich das Armband um sein Handgelenk, während er schlief. Beim Erwachen hielt er die Schlange für lebendig und wagte nicht, sie zu entfernen.[55]

> (Dear Leni! This morning, one of the many wonders happened with which Africa always favors us. Kimani, the shamaboy, carried the golden snake bracelet that you were wearing at New Year's and that you were missing when you left. According to Kimani's unsworn statement, the bracelet wrapped itself around his wrists while he was sleeping. When he woke up, he thought the snake was alive and did not dare to remove it.)

Instead of informing Helen Groag in a factual manner that the "Schamaboy" Kimani stole her bracelet, Walter Zweig ridicules Kimani's fantastic and exaggerated account in which Kimani explains how the bracelet came into his possession. Although Walter Zweig refrains from criminalizing Kimani by avoiding the word "theft," he implies that Kimani's statement is not worthy of being taken seriously ("unsworn statement") and displays the attitude of a gracious parent towards his child who played a silly prank.

In another letter to his wife on her birthday, Walter Zweig mentions Chebeti, the family's nanny, and cautions Jettel to watch her carefully:

> Chebeti hat mir beim Einpacken zugeschaut und war äußerst interessiert. Wir sollten mit vereinten Kräften dafür sorgen, dass die Kette nicht um ihren Giraffenhals zu hängen kommt. Vielleicht könntest Du zum Anlass deines Geburtstags heute auch verstärkt darauf achten, dass Maxens geliebte Aja nicht allzu viel von dem teuren Wodka aus der NAAFI säuft und die Flasche, wie am vorigen Sonntag mit Wasser auffüllt.[56]

> (Chebeti watched me packing and seemed very interested. We should combine our efforts to make sure that the necklace will not hang around

her giraffe's neck at some point. On your birthday, maybe you should also make sure that Max's beloved Aja does not swig too much of the expensive vodka from NAAFI and does not refill the bottle with water like she did last Sunday.)

This letter highlights a visual aspect of the Black nanny's appearance: he dehumanizes Chebeti by comparing her neck to that of a giraffe. In addition, he refers to a previous incident of alcohol theft. Oddly, Walter Zweig is mostly worried about Chebeti stealing the expensive vodka. It does not seem to occur to him that the nanny might have an alcohol addiction, which might put his son in danger. He is least of all interested in the reasons for Chebeti's potential alcohol abuse.

Unlike in *Nirgendwo in Africa* where, for instance, the Black farmer Kimani is a confidant and a source of farming knowledge for Walter Redlich, Walter's Zweig's letters in *Nirgendwo war Heimat* address issues of theft and alcohol abuse and indicate a strained relationship between the Zweigs and their Black servants. *Nirgendwo war Heimat* gives a more realistic insight into the Zweig's life in Kenya by exposing their racist attitudes towards Black people. In the letters, the described relationships between the Zweigs and Black Kenyans follow the social and racial code of the colony with the Zweigs being the masters and the Black Kenyans being the servants.

The black-and-white photographs that are included in the novel show mostly family members. Two photographs depict Black Kenyans, however: in the first photograph (Fig. 5.2), we see nine-year-old Stefanie Zweig holding a Kenyan baby named Warimu.

The caption reads: "My father crafted a rattle made of wood, metal and little stones for the little one."[57] In the second photograph (Fig. 5.3), we see Max Zweig, Stefanie Zweig's brother, as a baby sitting on a blanket next to a Kenyan baby whose name is not mentioned.

The caption reads: "Max, eleven months old, with his favorite playmate at the garden of the Hove Court in Nairobi."[58] The German National Library's German Exile Archive, which hosts part of Zweig's literary and personal estate holds an entire family photo album with snapshots from the Zweig's life in Kenya. A whole page of this album is dedicated to Owuor.[59] The question is why Zweig decided to include only the two above-mentioned images. None of the children displayed in the photographs is referenced in the letters or diary entries, but as mentioned before, other Black Kenyans are. If we have a closer look at the photograph of Max and his playmate, we can see that a Black arm reaches into the picture to support the little Black boy, and that part of a shoulder is revealed. We can speculate that arm and shoulder belong to the little boy's

Figure 5.2. Stefanie Zweig with Warimu. *Nirgendwo war Heimat* (*Nowhere Was Home*), 170.
By courtesy of Langen Müller Verlag. From: Stefanie Zweig, *Nirgendwo war Heimat – Mein Leben auf zwei Kontinenten* (*Nowhere Was Home: My Life on Two Continents*). © 2012, Langen Müller Verlag, München.

Figure 5.3. Max Zweig with an anonymous playmate. *Nirgendwo war Heimat* (*Nowhere Was Home*), 256.
By courtesy of Langen Müller Verlag. From: Stefanie Zweig, *Nirgendwo war Heimat – Mein Leben auf zwei Kontinenten* (*Nowhere Was Home: My Life on Two Continents*). © 2012, Langen Müller Verlag, München.

mother or the family's nanny. The photograph has either been cropped for editorial reasons, or the adult Black person was never part of the image in the first place. What is clear is that Zweig deliberately avoids photographs with adult Black Kenyans or those that display Black Kenyans only. Instead, she presents two photographs that display Kenyan children together with the Zweig children. The photographs display an idyll of a childhood in which the children's innocence hides racial hierarchies and Black and white children appear to live harmoniously together.

The lack of colonial nostalgia, the absence of romanticized descriptions of Black Kenyans, and the less "African" title and book cover, might be the reasons *Nirgendwo war Heimat* did not become a bestseller like *Nirgendwo in Africa*. For a Holocaust memoir– saturated German readership it might have been "just" another Holocaust memoir. The shift in genres in *Nirgendwo war Heimat* demonstrates Zweig's attempt at a more accurate portrayal of her family's story. The latter novel does not follow the traditional conventions of a novelistic plot. Authentic materials – letters, diary entries, and photographs – document the family's life and allow Zweig to tell her story in a fragmented way that leaves room for things untold. The letters and diary entries do not contain lengthy descriptive passages; instead, their authors communicate in a shorter format what they consider the most noteworthy aspects of their lives.

As mentioned previously, we do not know how many of the letters and diary entries were reconstructed from memory. But it is obvious that these documents – reconstructed or not – are Zweig's personal testimony and an attempt to let the survivors speak for themselves. However, Zweig's act of reappropriation comes at the expense of Black Kenyans who seem neither important to her family's life story anymore nor essential for the narrative. Kenya is rendered to a mere station in the life of the family. The family's status as Holocaust survivors and their life as refugees are the focus of the novel and conceal their position as *implicated* white *subjects* of the British Empire.

Intertitle: Conclusion

Zweig's autobiographical novels lack a balanced account of the historical reality of the life of the Jewish refugee family in the Kenyan colony. The author leaves out the Black characters' personal backgrounds and thus denies her readers an insight into the Black experience under colonial rule. Black characters become copies of stereotypical portrayals of Black servants serving their masters in a colonial society. In his satirical 2005 essay "How to Write about Africa," Kenyan author Binyavanga Wainaina notes sarcastically that in a successful text about Africa "African characters should be colourful, exotic, larger than life – but empty inside, with no dialogue, no conflicts or resolutions in their stories, no depth or quirks to confuse the cause,"[60] and Zweig seems to do exactly that. In her texts, a white privileged–gaze presents loyal and devoted Black Kenyan characters, an all too familiar figure for a white readership. The novels do not account critically for the family's white privileged–position in the British colony which makes them "implicated" in a system of racial oppression, and therefore Zweig's autobiographical Africa novels reinforce the legacy of racism against Black people.

NOTES

1 Michael Rothberg, *The Implicated Subject: Beyond Victims and Perpetrators* (Stanford: Stanford University Press, 2019), 1.
2 Simeon Hongo Ominde, Kenneth Ingham, and Mwenda Ntarangwi, *Encyclopedia Britannica*, s.v. "Kenya," accessed 5 January 2024, https://www.britannica.com/place/Kenya/The-British-East-Africa-Company.
3 ... *doch die Träume blieben in Afrika* (1998); *Karibu heißt willkommen* (2000); *Vivian und ein Mund voll Erde* (2001); *Wiedersehen mit Afrika* (2002), *Owuors Heimkehr: Erzählungen aus Afrika* (2003); *Es begann damals in Afrika* (2004); *Nur die Liebe bleibt* (2006); *Und das Glück ist anderswo* (2007).
4 Stefanie Zweig, *Nirgendwo in Afrika – Irgendwo in Deutschland* (Munich: Heyne Verlag, 2000).
5 *Nowhere in Africa*, directed by Caroline Link (Columbia – Tristar Home Entertainment, 2003).
6 Stefanie Zweig, *Nirgendwo war Heimat. Mein Leben auf Zwei Kontinenten* (Munich: Heyne Verlag, 2014).
7 Stefanie Zweig, *Nowhere in Africa: An Autobiographical Novel*, trans. Marlies Comejean (Madison: University of Wisconsin Presss/Terrace Books, 2004), viii–ix.
8 Natalie Eppelsheimer, "Homecomings and Homemakings: Stefanie Zweig and the. Exile Experience in, Out of, and Nowhere in Africa" (PhD diss., University of California, Irvine, 2008), 91.
9 Victor Turner, "Betwixt and Between: The Liminal Period of Rites of Passage," in *Betwixt and Between: Patterns of Masculine and Feminine Initiation*, ed. Louise Carus Mahdi, Steven Foster, and Meredith Little (La Salle, IL: Open Court, 1987), 6.
10 Rothberg, *Implicated Subject*, 1–2.
11 Noah Sow, "Rassismus," in *Wie Rassismus aus Wörtern spricht: (K)Erben des Kolonialismus im Wissensarchiv deutsche Sprache: ein kritisches Nachschlagewerk*, ed. Susan Arndt and Nadja Ofuatey-Alazard (Münster: Unrast, 2019), 37.
12 Peggy Piesche and Susan Arndt, "Weißsein: Die Notwendigkeit Kritischer Weißheitsforschung," in Arndt and Ofuatey-Alazard, *Wie Rassismus aus Wörtern spricht*, 193.
13 *Merriam-Webster*, s.v. "Bwana," accessed 5 January 2024, https://www.merriam-webster.com/dictionary/bwana.
14 *Merriam-Webster*, s.v. "Memsahib," accessed 5 January 2024, https://www.merriam-webster.com/dictionary/memsahib. The exact entry reads

"white foreign woman of high social status living in India." Interestingly, the entry seems to limit the use of *Memsahib* to colonial India, although the term was also used in other colonies of the British Empire.
15. *Online Swahili-English Dictionary*, s.v. "kidogo," accessed 5 January 2024, https://africanlanguages.com/swahili/.
16. Sow, "Rassismus," 37.
17. Caroline Elkins, "Race, Citizenship, and Governance: Settler Tyranny and the End of Empire," in *Settler Colonialism in the Twentieth Century: Projects, Practices, Legacies*, ed. Caroline Elkins and Susan Pedersen (New York: Routledge, 2005), 204.
18. Gayatri Chakravorty Spivak and Rosalind C. Morris, eds., *Can The Subaltern Speak?: Reflections on the History of an Idea* (New York: Columbia University Press, 2010), 128.
19. Sow, "Rassismus," 37.
20. Sow, "Rassismus," 37.
21. Michael Rothberg, *Multidirectional Memory: Remembering the Holocaust in the Age of Decolonization* (Stanford: Stanford University Press, 2009), 3.
22. Hans Riebsamen, "Noch einmal zurück nach Afrika. Die Schriftstellerin Stefanie Zweig wird achtzig und legt eine Biographie in Briefform vor. Die Liebe zur Literatur entstand im Internat," *Frankfurter Allgemeine*, 15 September 2012, https://www.faz.net/aktuell/rhein-main/stefanie-zweig-im-portraet-noch-einmal-zurueck-nach-afrika-11891558.html.
23. Dirk Göttsche, *Remembering Africa: The Rediscovery of Colonialism in Contemporary German Literature* (Rochester, NY: Camden House, 2013), 60.
24. V.Y. Mudimbe, *The Idea of Africa* (London: Indiana University Press, 1994).
25. Achille Mbembe, *On the Postcolony* (Berkley: University of California Press, 2001), 2.
26. Eppelsheimer, "Homecomings," 91.
27. Jürgen Zimmerer, review of *"Das Afrika. Lexikon [Stuttgart: Metzler, 2001],"* *Literaturen* (June 2002), 91.
28. For my analysis of text passages from the novel, I quote from the English translation of the novel which I find close to the original.
29. David Spurr, *The Rhetoric of Empire: Colonial Discourse in Journalism, Travel Writing, and Imperial Administration* (Durham, NC: Duke University Press, 1993), 15.
30. I exchanged "for baking" for "to bake."
31. I exchanged "very small" for "tiny."
32. I exchanged "pains" for "pain."
33. Zweig, *Nowhere in Africa*, 19.
34. Ronald L. Jackson, *Scripting the Black Masculine Body: Identity, Discourse, and Racial Politics in Popular Media* (Albany: State University of New York Press, 2006), 55.

35 Jackson, *Scripting the Black Masculine Body*, 10.
36 Zweig, *Nowhere in Africa*, 23.
37 Zweig, *Nowhere in Africa*, 23.
38 Zweig, *Nowhere in Africa*, 23.
39 Zweig, *Nowhere in Africa*, 23.
40 Kalpana Seshadri-Crooks, *Desiring Whiteness: A Lacanian Analysis of Race* (London: Routledge, 2000), 20.
41 Jackson, *Scripting the Black Male Body*, 44.
42 Zweig, *Nowhere in Africa*, 229.
43 Zweig, *Nowhere in Africa*, 19.
44 Jackson, *Scripting the Black Male Body*, 54.
45 For readability purposes, I will use the abbreviated form of the title *Nirgendwo war Heimat* in my analysis of the novel.
46 Susanne Zantop, *Colonial Fantasies: Conquest, Family, and Nation in Precolonial Germany, 1770–1870* (Durham, NC: Duke University Press, 1997).
47 Riebsamen, "Noch einmal zurück nach Afrika." Unless indicated otherwise, all English translations of German quotations are my own.
48 Riebsamen, "Noch einmal zurück nach Afrika."
49 Zweig, *Nirgendwo war Heimat*, 100.
50 Neil Hester and Kurt Gray, "For Black Men, Being Tall Increases Threat Stereotyping and Police Stops," *Proceedings of the National Academy of Sciences* 115, no.11 (2018), 2714.
51 Hester and Gray, "For Black Men," 2714.
52 Zweig, *Nirgendwo war Heimat*, 104, 107.
53 Zweig, *Nirgendwo war Heimat*, 109.
54 Zweig, *Nirgendwo war Heimat*, 161.
55 Zweig, *Nirgendwo war Heimat*, 132.
56 Zweig, *Nirgendwo war Heimat*, 257–8.
57 Zweig, *Nirgendwo war Heimat*, 170.
58 Zweig, *Nirgendwo war Heimat*, 265.
59 "Foto Album der Familie Zweig, Rongai/Kenia, 1938," Deutsches Exilarchiv 1933–1945, Deutschen Nationalbibliothek, accessed 5 January 2024, https://exilarchiv.dnb.de/DEA/Web/DE/Navigation/MenschenImExil/zweig-stefanie/zweig-stefanie.htm.
60 Binyavanga Wainaina, "How to Write about Africa," *Granta* 92 (2005), https://granta.com/how-to-write-about-africa/.

6 Making the Invisible Visible? Representations of Black Masculinity in Texts by Yoko Tawada

LISABETH HOCK

Ralph Ellison's *Invisible Man* explores the paradox of Black invisibility in the United States in the first half part of the twentieth century, with a primary focus on the invisibility of Black men. The unnamed narrator tells us already in the first paragraph of the prologue, "I am invisible, understand, simply because people refuse to see me."[1] The novel then takes the reader through what amounts to an encyclopedia of the explicit racism and implicit biases of white people in the United States, examining in microscopic detail how they, and the social structures and institutions they create, reduce the narrator to a set of stereotypes and thus render him invisible in multiple senses of the word. Invisibility means both not being seen by the society in which the narrator lives,[2] as well as being hypervisible as a racially marked "Other" in ways that lead to a loss of individuality and humanity, discrimination, and exploitation. It also means being invisible to oneself and thereby experiencing the "double-consciousness" described by W.E.B. Du Bois as "this sense of always looking at one's self through the eyes of others, of measuring one's soul by the tape of a world that looks on in amused contempt and pity."[3]

German-speaking lands offer a different history of the exploitation of persons of African descent and different constructs of racism. Common to the US and German contexts, however, are a colonialist history, widespread racism, and long-standing stereotypes that have coalesced to make Black people invisible. This paper will focus on representations of men and masculinity, and there is a long history in German-speaking lands of Black men being reduced to their bodies as tools of labour and as objects of both threat and attraction. Silke Hackenesch describes how postcards and other images from the German colonies in Africa equated "masculine Blackness ... with physical labor and masculine whiteness with control and power," thereby expressing "the hierarchical structure of colonial rule: the white body commands and disciplines, whereas Black bodies toil and sweat."[4] In the aftermath of the First World War, France employed troops from its own African colonies for its occupation of the Rhineland. Julia Roos examines how Germans employed pseudo Darwinism and sexual stereotypes[5] to justify their allegations that colonial troops were committing rapes and other sexual crimes. Tina Campt estimates there were two hundred thousand Black troops stationed in Germany in the winter of 1919 alone,[6] and she describes depictions of the children born of their relationships with German women as "the first representation[s] of a domestic, German-born Black native."[7]

These stereotypes have persisted throughout the twentieth century and into our own. Damani James Partridge studies how, in the wake of German unification in 1990, Black diasporic men gained access to German society through hypersexual performance for white women who sometimes married them, paving a way to citizenship. Partridge describes this kind of inclusivity as a form of "exclusionary incorporation"[8] that grants Black migrants citizenship but does not allow them to move beyond the stereotypes that confined them for centuries.

We find additional examples of this kind of stereotyping in journalistic reports about assaults on women in several German cities on 31 December 2015. According to the Federal Criminal Police Office, around 1,200 women were victims of sexual assaults committed by what were estimated to be 2,000 men.[9] In response, the conservative magazine *Focus* published on the cover of the 9 January 2016 issue a cropped image of a blond, white woman, covered with black handprints.[10] The same day, the liberal newspaper *Die Süddeutsche Zeitung* published a silhouette image of a black hand reaching up between a pair of white, female legs.[11] Concern about widespread violence against all women is warranted and should be addressed by the left and the right, but as Beverly Weber points out, the images published by these news sources replicate "discourses of shame and violation of the white, European woman,"[12] and reduce all men of Colour to predators.

In her 2018 monograph, *White Rebels in Black*, Priscilla Layne contrasts anti-Black stereotypes with the self-assertion of Black masculinity in texts by white and Black men in Germany. She explores first how some white authors created "rebellious white male protagonists [who] use black popular culture as a vehicle to allow them to step out of their (white) shells and behave in a manner that mainstream society considered oppositional to conventional German cultural practices."[13] While white men find liberation in this move, Layne argues, ultimately they posit Blackness "as always already outside of German culture and in opposition to German culture, foreclosing the possibility of being both black and German."[14] From there, Layne turns to texts by "African American and black German artists who take issue with white Germans' fantasies about blackness"[15] while working to break free of stereotypes and to define and express Black masculinity on their own terms. This results in a more varied and individualized picture of what it means to be a Black man in Germany.

Within the context of the present volume, Layne's work raises questions of how German-speaking *women* depict Black masculinity, and of the extent to which they render Black men visible or invisible. Do their texts use Black male characters as surfaces onto which they project stereotypes? Do their texts objectify, sexualize, or in any way "Other" their male, Black characters? Or do they challenge stereotypes and individualize Black men?

One set of answers to these questions can be found in two texts by Yoko Tawada. Her short story, "The Shadow Man" (1998)[16] offers a fictionalized account of the life of Enlightenment philosopher Anton Wilhelm Amo (c. 1703–c.1759), the first Black man to receive a PhD from a German university in 1734. In that same story, she references the American popstar Michael Jackson (1958–2009), who later appears as a minor character in her 2014 novel, *Etüden im Schnee* (*Memoirs of a Polar Bear*).[17] The first part of this paper will offer support for the contention that "The Shadow Man" employs a range of strategies to make Amo visible as a unique human being and simultaneously dissects the societal processes by which he was emasculated, made invisible, and erased from history. The second part will argue that, by depicting the Black, male body in animalistic and sexual terms, "The Shadow Man" and *Etüden* (*Memoirs*) nonetheless participate in what Ronald Jackson refers to as "scripting the Black body."[18] In this way, the texts end up undoing some of the work they have done to make Black men visible as individual human beings.

Among scholars and book critics alike, Yoko Tawada is a highly regarded, and one could also say beloved, author. Her work is held up as transnational,[19] multilingual,[20] and marked by globality.[21] She is a "German-speaking" writer who currently resides in Berlin, but Japanese is her first language and she retains her Japanese citizenship. Critics note that her characters inhabit spaces between national, gender, and even species identities.[22] Yasemin Yildiz considers the author's writing emblematic of "the post-monolingual condition."[23] Indeed, some of Tawada's works appeared first in Japanese, others appeared first in German. She wrote *Tabi o suru hadaka no me* (2004) and *Das nackte Auge* (2004) as two different manuscripts at the same time, one in Japanese and one in German. She wrote *Yuki No Renshūsei* (*The Snow Apprentice*) in 2011.

Her own German translation of it appeared in 2014 as *Etüden im Schnee* (*Etudes in Snow*), and Susan Bernofsky entitled her English translation *Memoirs of a Polar Bear*.[24] Tawada's work not only helps us to reconsider our understanding of "German" literature and Germanness but also offers a welcome opportunity to connect German studies with the questions of global and transnational studies.

Such a burnished reputation can be a burden for author and scholar alike, however. On the one hand, it can mean that we scholars assign the task of representing diversity to Tawada and other writers of Colour, thereby relieving white German authors of the responsibility of representing diversity and engaging with issues such as racism and xenophobia. On the other hand, it can be easy to assume that a Japanese, German-speaking, and German-writing author can and will always authentically represent Otherness because of their own status as Other within German society. Yet being a Person of Colour does not automatically exclude one from perpetuating stereotypes. For this reason, as Ibram X. Kendi advises, we should read all books from an "antiracist critical eye" to "protect ourselves from unknowingly consuming a book's hard to parse racist ideas." Kendi continues:

> this isn't just about books. How we read old and new books is no different from how we read society, past and present. We must read all characters – living and dead, fictional and real – with respect and not diminish them, or allow them to be diminished because of the color of their skin. At the same time, we cannot allow racism to be diminished and overlooked in literature, in policy, in power.[25]

The aim of this paper is to show how, even when literary texts demonstrate evidence of respect for their characters, they can simultaneously fall back on stereotypes that have been in global circulation for centuries.

"The Shadow Man" divides Amo's story into seven chapters. We see the protagonist being taken away from his native land as a seven-year-old, being given as a "gift" to the Duke of Braunschweig at the age of ten, pursuing an education, studying philosophy in Halle in 1727, completing his PhD, receiving an appointment at the university in Jena, only to then return full of disillusionment to his place of birth. Interwoven with Amo's story is a second narrative strand, set in the present, that recounts the story of a Japanese exchange student, Tamao, who has come to Wölfenbüttel to study philosophy and experiences racism there. Each of the first six chapters begins with a scene from Amo's life and then abruptly switches to a scene from Tamao's life that echoes what has happened to Amo. In this way, the story weaves together the stories of two men of different racial backgrounds living at two very different times but sharing the status of racialized outsider.

The parts of "The Shadow Man" that deal with Amo adhere closely to biographical accounts of the historical individual and demonstrate engagement with his extant writings. For the most part, the text avoids generalizations. It strives to make its protagonist visible by intentionally using his name, by giving him a strong emotional presence, by making his suffering palpable, and drawing him as a character with agency. Naming plays a key role here. Although the characters with whom Amo interacts in Europe refer to him by the European name given to him, and although Amo himself sometimes forgets his birth name, "The Shadow Man" insists on referring to its protagonist with the name given to him by his birth family, "Amo." The reader is encouraged to do the same, thereby naming him in a manner that honours the family and land from which he comes. At the same time, the narration employs indirect interior monologue and attributes few direct quotes to Amo, most of which have to do with his philosophical writing. This strategy allows the reader to experience events through Amo's perspective, while maintaining a distance to the first person that reminds us of the impossibility of walking in his footsteps.

The narrative further individualizes Amo by giving him a forceful emotional presence. We see this already in the opening scene describing his reaction to the arrival of a slave ship on the shore of his homeland: "The world was turning upside down and the elders didn't speak, their hips moving sluggishly. Amo watched them, burning with frustration. This was his first memory."[26] Amo's fury and sense of vertigo are made palpable. The narrative then imagines his sensory responses to his abduction. A seven-year-old from the west coast of Africa would not have had words for the sugar and wine with which a Dutch captor lures him onto a ship bound for Europe, the same one on which – Amo realizes much later – his relatives are packed together to be sold as slaves. We therefore read of the boy tasting a "pristine powder … so sweet a pain darted through his chin,"[27] and seeing "a blood-colored drink that felt so cool going down before sending him into a dreamy haze."[28] A few pages later, the story employs synesthesia to express the effect that hearing the word "book" for the first time has on Amo: it "sounded so delicious that Amo immediately began to yearn for one."[29] This use of poetic language and stylistic devices in the depiction of Amo renders him a nuanced and multidimensional character.

The individualization of Amo necessarily involves making his suffering visible. In a close reading of the South African setting of Tawada's short story "Bioscope of the Night," Jeremy Redlich argues that Tawada's representations and interrogations of "skin color, race, racial performativity, and the ideological power of whiteness"[30] point to the ways in which the Black-white binary is constructed, but then ultimately "undercut the fixity and reliability of racial difference."[31] "The Shadow Man," in contrast, is much more about the power that the ideology of whiteness and the resulting shame about his Blackness exert over Amo. It shows us in detail that survival, for Amo, requires dissociation: a "discontinuity in the normal integration of consciousness, memory, identity, emotion, perception, body representation, motor control, and behavior."[32] In psychological terms, dissociation may be brought on by a traumatic event, but it is also a way of coping with the devastating effects of trauma.

When he is young, the symbol of the mirror signals a split in Amo's sense of self. After servants dress him in European finery, the boy that Amo sees in the mirror seems to be a "ghost"[33] whom he considers "beautiful"[34] and whom he watches grow older. His new European name leads to an awareness that those around him do not know who he is, which gives rise to further dissociation: "To everyone here he was Anton. But a name other people used was merely something given from the outside – it had nothing to do with your real self. Amo felt sure he once had a name, although try as he might, he couldn't remember it."[35] While the narrative honours Amo by connecting him to his birth name, Amo himself has lost that sense of connection.

Trauma psychiatrists have found evidence that "dissociation is associated with a remarkable avoidance of self-perception" to the extent that one's "own face might be considered a trigger for traumatic memories."[36] Amo seeks to escape not only his past but also recognition of his difference in the present. He therefore comes to the self-preserving conclusion that, to avoid harm, he must pretend to forget where he is from and to act as if he is one of the Europeans. As he grows older, Amo turns away from mirrors, which continue to reveal his Blackness, and immerses himself in his studies.

The things Amo tries to forget find a way to return. While Amo spends his days studying philosophy, his memories and even past sensory perceptions surface in his dreams. "The stench of rotting flesh,"[37] of which he must have been aware on the ship that transported him to Europe, comes to him in a dream about "Bad Spirits hurling people into the sea."[38] The night after he receives his doctorate, he dreams of being tied and bound to a tree by "vaguely familiar men ... With the tips of quill pens they stabbed the insides of his elbows, his thighs, his chest."[39] No matter how much education Amo acquires, he senses deep down that he will continue to be subjected to the anti-Blackness of his colleagues. And although Amo wishes to escape his past, his dreams bring back to him the trauma of being taken from his place of birth, the pain inflicted by the daily racism he experiences, and the fear of being found out as someone whose family members either were alive as slaves or had been cast dead into the sea.

In addition to seeing Amo's pain, we see him as an Enlightenment intellectual. The scholarship and the life of the mind that Amo pursues during the day do provide some respite from his fears. They also allow him to assert his humanity and agency in terms understandable to those around him. Against the colonial logic that asserts that only Europeans possessed the "rationality and souls that are ordained by God,"[40] Amo insists firmly on the existence of his soul. Notably, the dissertation written by the historical Amo agrees with Descartes's assertion of a mind-body dualism, but criticizes Descartes's contention that the mind – and with it the soul – is capable of feeling sensation. Kwasi Wiredu posits that Amo's opposition to Descartes might be due to the influence of "the concept of mind implicit in the language and thought of the Akans, the ethnic group among which he was born."[41] According to this Akan concept, "the feeling of a sensation does not fall within the domain of the mental," and Wiredu contends that "the non-sensate conception of mind was a kind of 'cultural survival' in Amo's psyche."[42]

"The Shadow Man" does not focus on cultural survival but rather presents Amo's understanding of the soul as both intellectual tool and strategy for psychic survival. Amo conceives of his soul as an "invisible mass of power that was always very near him."[43] He believes that his soul helps him to work through problems and motivates him towards a purpose, even though his teachers and students – individuals not accustomed to attributing souls to Black people – find his ideas uncanny and cannot believe he came up with them himself.[44] The text hints here at an eighteenth-century form of the "exclusionary incorporation"[45] to which Partridge refers in his article about Black men in post-unification Berlin: Amo is tolerated because he is exotically interesting, but his outsider status remains intact.

It would appear that Amo's soul protects him, at least during the daytime, from the pain caused by his difference: "'The soul itself does not suffer,' wrote Amo."[46] During the day, Amo is able to learn and read and think like any of the white Europeans around him, with the result that "even the stones that people threw could not injure his soul ... his soul would always travel with him. It had been with him since his childhood."[47] Yet Amo's soul cannot keep him safe from racism or from the feelings of shame and guilt that racism produces in him. Beverly Weber has argued that those possibilities of fluidity – of "living in imagined border spaces (produced by both geographic and linguistic borders), and through the act of constant and ongoing translation" – that are available to many characters in Tawada's oeuvre – remain unavailable to Amo.[48] In "The Shadow Man," this fluidity is hindered by the intermingling of guilt about what he was not able to do and shame about who he thinks he is.

W.E.B. Du Bois wrote in 1933, "we are still ashamed of ourselves and are thus estopped from valid objection when white folks are ashamed to call us human."[49] Ralph Ellison repeatedly depicts his eponymous Invisible Man as being ashamed of his Southern roots and connections to Black people he considers less educated than himself. David Leverenz tells us that today, "Many African Americans as well as many light-skinned Americans still presume that white means honor and black means shame."[50] "The Shadow Man" transports the reader back to the Enlightenment – the period that saw the beginnings of racial categorization – to examine how the shaming of a Black man might have worked in a German context.

Amo's sense of guilt arises from not having been able to help his family members on the ship. He understands his nightmares to be the result of his soul leaving him at night, which leaves him vulnerable to his memories. His dreams reveal that he was transported to Europe on a slave ship and that he survived while the rest of his family did not. They remind him that he was unable to save his relatives from the sharks to which some were thrown.

In waking life, Amo's sense of shame about his difference from the white people around him leads him to deny this history, for he fears that any association with others on the ship would cause him to lose his status in society. In 1729, the historical Amo wrote a no longer extant dissertation on the rights of Blacks in Europe entitled *Dissertatio inauguralis de iure maurorum in Europa* (Dissertation on the legal status of Moors in Europe), in which he used the Latin root of the oldest German term referring to Black people, the same term used to describe him in Johann Heinrich Zedler's lexicon.[51] In contrast, the Amo of "The Shadow Man" is so afraid to contemplate this issue aloud that the question, "'Are black people on a slave ship human beings?' stay[s] on the tip of Amo's tongue."[52] He can neither object to the way that whites view and treat Blacks nor argue for the legal rights of the latter.

Amo is plagued by the guilt arising from his dreams and the shame he feels on a daily basis. At the same time, white Europeans limit his autonomy so that he is never able to achieve the *Mündigkeit* – or ability to speak for himself – that Kant would later consider prerequisite for the enlightened individual.[53] Although initially angry at his relatives for failing to resist the "Bad Spirits," or white people, he quickly finds that he must submit both his body and his identity to those same "Spirits." On the ship to Europe, he is forced to sleep pressed against the "Heer" – the Dutch word can mean ship's captain or master – who takes him onboard, "like a baby animal huddled against his mother."[54] After Amo is beaten when he tries to explore the ship, the Heer declares that Amo is safe only "because I've chosen you."[55] Amo must call his new patrons "father" and submit to a new name, at least in public. When his last sponsor, Professor Ludwig, dies, Amo no longer has the protection that he still requires as an adult. As a result, his sense of dissociation is exacerbated so that, even in his waking hours, he senses his soul is no longer in him but following "not far behind."[56]

In contrast to the white men who assert their power over Amo through forced patronage, white women do so by sexualizing him. An ocean away, American whites, both male and female, were sexualizing and perpetrating sexual violence against enslaved Black men,[57] while abolitionist texts were eroticizing them.[58] Upon his arrival in northern Europe, the boy Amo is put in the care of white women who secretly fondle his buttocks and genitals. As an adult, after he assumes his teaching position at the university of Jena, women continue to fetishize his skin colour and sexual organs, quizzing his servant, Margarete, "about what Amo ate, whether his whole body was black, the size of his penis."[59]

Despite the fact that Amo is teaching at a university and can hold his own with the thinkers of his day, white Europeans do not grant him equal standing as a human being and as a man. This creates an ever greater disconnect between Amo's soul and his body. The connection between the two is completely severed when he falls in love with a woman who is both white and above his station. After he fails in an attempt to deliver a note to her, he is shamed because "the whole town was talking about how he had tried to attack the young lady." Indicating that Amo can no longer maintain any semblance of integrated humanity, "his soul was about to set out on a long journey away from the land of the Bad Spirits."[60]

The story of Amo's love is the sole focus of the seventh chapter of "The Shadow Man." We do not hear again about Tamao. At the end of the chapter, Amo leaves Europe for Africa filled with shame. The writings by the historical figure are mostly forgotten until the twentieth century. What remains in the "Shadow Man" version of Amo's story is a travelling puppet-drama created by "a shadowy figure named Hans,"[61] an apparent allusion to the satirical and often bawdy *Hanswurst* theatre tradition.

The play in "The Shadow Man" presents Amo as an escaped lion trying to seduce a young woman: "a huge tongue drooped wantonly from the lion's mouth like a banana."[62] One could interpret the obvious symbol of a flaccid penis as a reminder of the white fear – which will move to the foreground in the German territories as German colonization progresses, in Germany in the aftermath of the First World War, and in the US throughout slavery and beyond – that Black men are a sexual danger to white women. The only way that German society is willing to allow Amo a presence is through emasculation and dehumanization.

We have seen how, as a narrative, "The Shadow Man" humanizes and individualizes Amo – it imagines his story in order to make him visible – while simultaneously showing how white Europe dehumanized him by making him both invisible and hyper-visible. Yet there are moments when the story's descriptions of Black men zero in, in ways that are reductive, on what Ronald Jackson describes as "visible racial markers or corporeal zones."[63] In the remainder of essay, I would like to explore those passages in "The Shadow Man," as well as in *Etüden im Schnee* (*Memoirs of a Polar Bear*), that racialize and eroticize their Black male characters. We see this in depictions of Amo's body, in a comparison of chapter 7 to the historical version of the puppet play to which it alludes, and in the references to Michael Jackson. Consciously using her standpoint as an East Asian, female author with Japanese citizenship who writes and publishes in Japanese, German, and English, Tawada writes against ethno-nationalism and challenges Eurocentrism. Nevertheless, there are points where these two texts both fall back on and demonstrate the global reach of anti-Black stereotypes.

Side by side with empathetic and individualizing depictions of Amo, there are passages in "The Shadow Man" that racialize and eroticize his body. Descriptions of "the ebony smoothness"[64] of Amo's chest and his "black and shiny skin"[65] encourage the reader to marvel along with the Dutch maids at the young boy's appearance. The reader observes with the servant girl, Margarethe, who works for Amo until he departs for Africa, that "Amo's bottom was round and hard, and moved as if it had a life of its own."[66] For all the ways that it reminds the reader of the harm done to Blacks by colonization, "The Shadow Man" simultaneously engages with the trope of the sexualized Black male.

With this in mind, the puppet-show account in "The Shadow Man" of Amo's love story reads differently, especially after considering a collection of satirical poems from 1749 by Johann Ernst Philippi, writing under the pseudonym of M. Leberecht Ehrenhold. In the latter, we find an exchange, in the form of two extended poems, between Amo[67] and a woman named Mademoiselle Astrine.[68] The accounts in this collection are intended to be humorous renderings of academic life. The lyrical "I" of the first poem refers to himself as "Rosantes." He complains bitterly that Venus and her son Cupid have turned his love away from him, and he expresses the wish that they will return her to him. In the following poem, Astrine tells Rosantes that his skin colour makes a return impossible.

These poems, which are overly sentimental and engage in anti-Black racism, will most likely not strike the modern reader as funny. Philippi's contemporaries may not have been impressed either: the *Allgemeine deutsche Biographie* describes Philippi as someone who wrote "tactless occasional poems," and whose life was "a chain of ill-advised pranks that ultimately revealed traces of madness."[69] Those contemporaries will, however, most likely have associated the term that the poems use to describe Amo, "Moor," with the same negative connotations with which the term had been associated since the Middle Ages,[70] and therefore will have understood why they were expected to laugh.

The intended humour is suggested by the title of the first poem: "A gallant declaration of love from Mr. M. Amo of Jena, an educated Moor, to Miss Astrine, a beautiful brunette." One traditional mode of humour is incongruity or unexpected contrast, and the assumption was that the eighteenth-century white reader would find a love letter written to a white woman by a Black man funny. The eighteenth-century reader might also laugh when "Astrine" tells "Rosantes" that Venus told her in a dream: "A Moor is something unknown to the German maiden," a sentence that contrasts Blackness with virginity. We see in this eighteenth-century document, then, the prohibition against the mixing of races that would gain a pseudo-scientific foundation over the course of the next two centuries.

While these poems provide evidence of a long history of racism in Europe, we find in them neither a salacious puppet drama nor the comparisons of Amo to a wild beast nor the reduction of him to his genitalia that we see in "The Shadow Man." This comparison between the writing of Tawada and that of Philippi, whose work Tawada may or may not know, reveals overt twenty-first-century sexualization of a Black man. Like other fictional works based on historical individuals and events, "The Shadow Man" strives to reimagine Amo and the time in which he lived. It is honest in its recognition that we can never know exactly what happened. And as observed above, imagining the *Hanswurst* play is a way of criticizing the mistreatment and misrepresentation of Blacks in Europe. Yet by ending with reference to this play, "The Shadow Man" also makes the decision to allow the troubled intellectual whom it takes such pains to individualize, to disappear behind a sexualized stereotype.

Through the figure of Michael Jackson, this engagement with anti-Black stereotypes occurs again in the Tamao sections that alternate with

Making the Invisible Visible? 143

the sections about Amo in the first six chapters of "The Shadow Man." The inhabitants of Wölfenbüttel seem not to know what to make of the Japanese student in their midst. A man who appears to be the town drunk, Manfred, upon hearing that Tamao is studying philosophy, comments that he must be "one of Amo's descendants."[71] This comment points to the inability of Manfred – as a stand-in for "the white German" – to distinguish between the physical features of the peoples of West Africa and East Asia, while at the same time establishing a connection between Amo and Tamao as racialized Others. As the story shifts back and forth between narrative strands, it strives to continue to draw these connections, but they leave the reader thinking that the experiences of the two characters are not all that comparable. Once he realizes that the rest of his family was sold into slavery, Amo begins having nightmares; Tamao is nervous because he is convinced others do not take him seriously. Like Amo, Tamao is judged by his appearance rather than by his intellectual abilities, and he finds "it unbearable that people here saw him not as a student in the philosophy department, but above all as a Japanese."[72] This does not, however, inspire in Tamao sympathy for or identification with Amo. Once Tamao learns who Amo is, he cannot "forgive Manfred for calling him that name."[73] Situating himself within a hierarchy of race and skin colour, Tamao chafes at the racism of the white Germans but exhibits his own racist attitudes towards Black people. The meaning here is slippery. Certainly, the story appears to be poking fun at Tamao's fragile sense of his own masculinity while critiquing his anti-Blackness. Tamao is meant to be a humorous character. The result, however, is that Black masculinity shifts to become representative of absolute Otherness.

This shift is cemented when Michael Jackson is brought into the story. Visiting the German professor who has sponsored his visit, Tamao worries that he has made a fool of himself when, trying to make polite conversation, he says that he likes the music of Richard Wagner. The reasons for this are unclear. Perhaps he is merely insecure. When Tamao quickly adds "But I like Michael Jackson, too,"[74] it does not make the situation any better, because now he feels that he will be judged as superficial.

We then learn through indirect interior monologue just how much Tamao identifies with the pop star:

When he watched Michael Jackson's videos, every cell in Tamao's body started to seethe; he even felt his appearance begin to change. His friends all said plastic surgery was in bad taste. But didn't everyone harbor a secret desire for a new face? ... He told himself that fretting over one's appearance was a job for women. But deep down, doesn't every man who lacks confidence in his looks yearn for that moment when the Beast turns into a handsome young man?[75]

This passage contains multiple layers of associations: Michael Jackson's purported desire to change his appearance relates both to Tamao's distancing of himself from Amo's Blackness and to Tamao's identification with Jackson's plastic surgery. Tamao's connection of plastic surgery to the fairy tale of "Beauty and the Beast" associates Blackness with that which is animalistic and whiteness with that which is beautiful.

This chain of associations directs the reader back to Amo's interactions with his servant Margarethe, both of whom, as the story tells us, move differently from the stiff-legged, rigid-hipped professors at the university, so much so, that Amo wonders if the professors "were of the same species as himself."[76] A story that aims to rewrite a Black man and his positive cultural contributions into a fictional history cannot avoid, it would appear, reinscribing stereotypes: Amo becomes connected with Michael Jackson. Instead of consistently unpacking the ways that stereotypes render Amo invisible, the narration here accepts the tired stereotype that all Black people can dance.

Michael Jackson appears again in the third chapter of Tawada's novel *Etüden im Schnee* (*Memoirs of a Polar Bear*), which focuses on Knut, the iconic polar bear cub born in 2006 who was rejected by his mother at the Berlin Zoological Garden and then cared for by his zookeeper. As with "The Shadow Man," chapters in the novel reimagine historical events. The relationship between Knut and his keeper comes to an end when Knut accidentally injures the latter, forcing their inevitable separation. Knut is left quite alone with questions about who he is and where he came from. When he is around three years old, Knut encounters, and for a short time is watched over by, a man who appears first out of nowhere and then out of a television set. The man introduces himself as Michael, and allusions to his appearance and biography suggest he is the ghost of Michael Jackson, who died in 2009.

Michael offers comfort by telling Knut their stories are similar. Like Knut, Michael was famous when he was young but then fell out of favour with the public. In direct response to Knut's question about why the public condemns his mother Toska for not mothering her cub, and in indirect response to the criticism of his own plastic surgeries, Michael explains, "Human beings hate everything that is unnatural … They think that bears must remain bears. It is the same way some people think that the lower classes must remain poor. They would consider anything else unnatural."[77]

As is the case with the depiction of Amo in "The Shadow Man," depictions of both Knut and Michael in *Etüden im Schnee* are deeply empathetic. Michael is also fetishized and eroticized, however. He is depicted as catlike and sensual.[78] In an allusion to rumors that Jackson was bleaching his skin or wearing excessive make-up to mask vitiligo – a skin condition caused when pigment-producing skin cells stop functioning – Michael jokes about his fascination with Knut's white fur. He alludes to an attraction to children.[79] All of this is delivered with Tawada's signature humour and lightness of touch, yet the result is that the only Black man in the text becomes representative of a sexy freakishness.

"The Shadow Man" and *Memoirs of a Polar Bear* both strive to make invisible individuals visible and to address the ways that identity is produced when "bodies ... have been assigned social meanings."[80] At the same time, they participate in this assignation of meaning by racializing their Black characters, a sleight of hand that leads to diminishment and erasure, not only of the individual contours of Amo, but of Black men in general. This is not an argument that Tawada or any author should avoid representing "the Other." Rather, it is a reminder of the global reach of anti-Black stereotypes, and of the need for continual self-questioning when engaging with difference. Moreover, acknowledgment of these moments of slippage in literary works helps us to see them in our own lives as well so that remain both vigilant and humble.

NOTES

1 Ralph Ellison, *Invisible Man* (1947, repr., New York: Vintage, 1995), 3.
2 Anderson Franklin describes invisibility as a "a psychological experience wherein the person feels that his or her personal identity and ability are undermined by racism in a myriad of interpersonal circumstances." Anderson J. Franklin, "Invisibility Syndrome and Racial Identity Development in Psychotherapy and Counseling African American Men," *The Counseling Psychologist* 27, no. 6 (1999): 761.
3 W.E.B. Du Bois, "Strivings of the Negro People," *The Atlantic*, August 1897, https://www.theatlantic.com/magazine/archive/1897/08/strivings-of-the-negro-people/305446/.
4 Silke Hackenesch, "'Hergestellt unter ausschließlicher Verwendung von Kakaobohnen deutscher Kolonien': On Representations of Chocolate Consumption as a Colonial Endeavor," *Rethinking Black German Studies: Approaches, Interventions and Histories*, ed. Tiffany N. Florvil and Vanessa D. Plumly (New York: Peter Lang, 2018), 51.

5 Julia Roos, "Women's Rights, Nationalist Anxiety, and the 'Moral' Agenda in the Early Weimar Republic: Revisiting the 'Black Horror' Campaign against France's African Occupation Troops," *Central European History* 42, no. 3 (2009): 479.
6 Tina Campt, *Other Germans: Black Germans and the Politics of Race, Gender, and Memory in the Third Reich* (Ann Arbor: University of Michigan, 2003), 35.
7 Campt, *Other Germans*, 28.
8 Damani J. Partridge, *Hypersexuality and Headscarves: Race, Sex, and Citizenship in the New Germany* (Bloomington: Indiana University Press, 2012), 91.
9 Georg Mascolo and Britta von der Heide, "1200 Frauen wurden Opfer von Silvester-Gewalt," *Süddeutsche Zeitung*, 10 July 2016, https://www.sueddeutsche.de/politik/uebergriffe-in-koeln-1200-frauen-wurden-opfer-von-silvester-gewalt-1.3072064.
10 "Frauen klagen an: Sind wir tolerant oder noch blind?," *Focus*, 9 January 2016, https://www.focus.de/politik/focus-titel-die-nacht-der-schande_id_5198275.html.
11 "Auf Armlänge. Was tun mit den Männern, die Frauen sexuell belästigen?" *Süddeutsche Zeitung*, 9 January 2016, www.süddeutsche.de. The image is no longer available online. It appeared in vol. 72, week 1, no. 6, title page.
12 Beverly Weber, "'We Must Talk About Cologne': Race, Gender, and Reconfigurations of 'Europe,'" *German Politics and Society* 34, no. 4 (2016): 69.
13 Priscilla Layne, *White Rebels in Black: German Appropriation of Black Popular Culture* (Ann Arbor: University of Michigan Press, 2018), 2.
14 Layne, *White Rebels in Black*.
15 Layne, *White Rebels in Black*.
16 Yoko Tawada, "The Shadow Man," *Facing the Bridge*, trans. Margaret Mitsutani (New York: New Directions, 2007), 1–48. I will be citing from this English version that was translated from the original Japanese.
17 Yoko Tawada, *Etüden im Schnee* (Tübingen: Konkursbuch, 2014).
18 Ronald L. Jackson, *Scripting the Black Masculine Body: Identity, Discourse, and Racial Politics in Popular Media* (Albany: State University of New York Press, 2006), 11.
19 Caroline Rupprecht, "Haunted Spaces: History and Architecture in Yoko Tawada," *South Central Review* 33, no. 3 (Fall 2016): 122.
20 Marjorie Perloff, "Language in Migration: Multilingualism and Exophonic Writing in the New Poetics," *Textual Practice* 24, no. 4 (2010): 725–48.
21 Kathrin Maurer, "Im Zwischenraum der Sprachen: Globalität in den Texten Yoko Tawadas," *Globalisierung und Gegenwartsliteratur: Konstellationen, Konzepte, Perspektiven*, ed. Wilhelm Amann, Georg Mein, and Rolf Parr (Heidelberg: Synchron, 2010), 328.
22 Doug Slaymaker, "Introduction," *Tawada Yoko: On Writing and Rewriting*, ed. Doug Slaymaker (Lanham, MD: Lexington Books, 2020), vii.

23 Yasemin Yildiz, *Beyond the Mother Tongue: The Postmonolingual Condition* (New York: Fordham University Press, 2012).
24 Yoko Tawada, *Memoirs of a Polar Bear*, trans. Susan Bernofsky (New York: New Directions, 2016).
25 "Ibram X. Kendi Likes to Read at Bedtime," By the Book, *New York Times*, 25 February 2021, https://www.nytimes.com/2021/02/25/books/review/ibram-x-kendi-by-the-book-interview.html.
26 Tawada, "Shadow Man," 4.
27 Tawada, "Shadow Man," 5.
28 Tawada, "Shadow Man," 5.
29 Tawada, "Shadow Man," 12.
30 Jeremy Redlich, "Representations of Public Spaces and the Construction of Race in Yoko Tawada's 'Bioskoop der Nacht,'" *The German Quarterly* 90, no. 2 (Spring 2017): 210.
31 Redlich, "Representations of Public Spaces," 210.
32 *The Diagnostic and Statistical Manual of Mental Disorders*, 5th ed. (Arlington, VA: American Psychiatric Association, 2013), 291.
33 Tawada, "Shadow Man," 8.
34 Tawada, "Shadow Man," 8.
35 Tawada, "Shadow Man," 13.
36 Eva Schäflein, Heribert C. Sattel, Ulrike Schmidt, and Martin Sack, "The Enemy in the Mirror: Self-Perception-Induced Stress Results in Dissociation of Psychological and Physiological Responses in Patients with Dissociative Disorder," *European Journal of Psychotraumatology* 9, sup. 3 (2018): 15.
37 Tawada, "Shadow Man," 6.
38 Tawada, "Shadow Man," 22.
39 Tawada, "Shadow Man," 14.
40 Tshepo Lephakga, "The History of the Conquering of the Being of Africans through Land Dispossession, Epistemicide and Proselytisation" *Studia Historiae Ecclesiasticae* 41, no. 2 (2015): 157. http://dx.doi.org/10.17159/2412-4265/2015/300.
41 Kwasi Wiredu, "Amo's Critique of Descartes' Philosophy of Mind," *A Companion to African Philosophy*, ed. Kwasi Wiredu (Oxford: Blackwell, 2004), 204.
42 Wiredu, "Amo's Critique," 205.
43 Tawada, "Shadow Man," 24.
44 Tawada, "Shadow Man," 25.
45 Partridge, *Hypersexuality and Headscarves*.
46 Tawada, "Shadow Man," 32.
47 Tawada, "Shadow Man," 33.
48 Beverly Weber, "Precarious Intimacies: Yoko Tawada's Europe," *Critical Ethnic Studies* 1, no. 2 (Fall 2015): 63–4.

49 W.E.B. Du Bois, "On Being Ashamed of Oneself: An Essay on Race Pride," *The Crisis* 40, no. 9 (September 1933): 199.
50 David Leverenz, *Honor Bound: Race and Shame in America* (New Brunswick, NJ: Rutgers University Press, 2012), 2.
51 Johann Heinrich Zedler, *Grosses vollständiges Universal-Lexikon* (Halle and Leipzig, 1732–54; repr. Graz, 1964), 65:1369, https://daten.digitale-sammlungen.de/bsb00000427/images/index.html?id=00000427&groesser=&fip=193.174.98.30&no=&seite=696.
52 Tawada, "Shadow Man" 28.
53 Immanuel Kant, "Beantwortung der Frage: Was ist Aufklärung?" (Königsberg in Preußen, 1784; Project Gutenberg), accessed 26 January 2021, https://www.projekt-gutenberg.org/kant/aufklae/aufkl003.html.
54 Tawada, "Shadow Man," 5.
55 Tawada, "Shadow Man," 6.
56 Tawada, "Shadow Man," 38.
57 Thomas A. Foster, *Rethinking Rufus: Sexual Violations of Enslaved Men* (Athens: University of Georgia Press, 2019), 3.
58 John Saillant, "The Black Body Erotic and the Republican Body Politic, 1790–1820," *Journal of the History of Sexuality* 5, no. 3 (1995): 405.
59 Tawada, "Shadow Man," 43.
60 Tawada, "Shadow Man," 47.
61 Tawada, "Shadow Man," 47.
62 Tawada, "Shadow Man," 48
63 Jackson, *Scripting the Black Masculine Body*, 15.
64 Tawada, "Shadow Man," 7
65 Tawada, "Shadow Man," 8.
66 Tawada, "Shadow Man," 42.
67 Johann Ernst Philippi, "Herrn M. Amo, eines gelehrten Mohren, galanter Liebes-Antrag an eine schöne Brünette, Madem. Astrine," *Belustigende Academische Schaubühne. Auf welcher die, auf Universitäten im Schwange gehende Tugenden und Laster in sieben Auftritten poetisch abgeschildert werden* (Frankfurt and Leipzig: Cöthen, in der Cörnerischen Buchhandlung, 1749), 2. Auftritt, 10–14.
68 Johann Ernst Philippi, "Der Mademoiselle Astrine Parodische Antwort auf vorstehendes Gedichte [sic] eines verliebten Mohrens," *Belustigende Academische Schaubühne. Auf welcher die, auf Universitäten im Schwange gehende Tugenden und Laster in sieben Auftritten poetisch abgeschildert werden* (Frankfurt and Leipzig: Cöthen, in der Cörnerischen Buchhandlung, 1749), 2. Auftritt, 15–19.
69 Berthold Litzmann, "Philippi, Johann Ernst," *Allgemeine Deutsche Biographie* (Leipzig: Duncker and Humblot, 1888), 26:76–8, https://www.deutsche-biographie.de.
70 Susan Arndt and Ulrike Hamann, "Mohr_in," in *Wie Rassismus aus Wörtern spricht: (K)Erben des Kolonialismus im wissensarchiv deutsche Sprache: ein*

kritisches Nachschlagewerk, ed. Susan Arndt and Nadja Ofuatey-Alazard (Münster: Unrast, 2019), 649–53.
71 Tawada, "Shadow Man," 9.
72 Tawada, "Shadow Man," 29.
73 Tawada, "Shadow Man," 29.
74 Tawada, "Shadow Man," 18.
75 Tawada, "Shadow Man," 18–19.
76 Tawada, "Shadow Man," 42.
77 Tawada, *Memoirs*, 244.
78 Tawada, *Memoirs*, 238.
79 Tawada, *Memoirs*, 246.
80 Jackson, *Scripting the Black Masculine Body*, 12.

SECTION III

White Settler Colonialism and Its Legacies

7 German Cultural Superiority and Racial Hierarchy in Gabriele Reuter's *Glück und Geld*

DAVID TINGEY

Near the end of Gabriele Reuter's novel, *Glück und Geld: ein Roman aus dem heutigen Egypten* (Happiness and money: a novel from today's Egypt, 1888),[1] a pastor, his wife, and their children are at their home in Thüringen awaiting the arrival of a guest from afar. The Frau Pastorin had invited Madame Octavia Riviotti, one of the novel's two protagonists, a young German widow whom she had met in Egypt, to join her family for Christmas. Their youngest daughter, Tabea, can hardly wait for "die Fremde" (the foreign woman) whom the children have never met:

> "Hui!" rief Tabea mit blitzenden Augen und schüttelte ihren flachsblonden Krauskopf, "wie ich mich freue!" – "Nicht wahr," fragte sie ihre Mutter geheimnisvoll, "Frau Riviotti ist doch schwarz?"
> Die Pastorin hielt entsetzt ... inne.
> "Wie kommst du auf diese tolle Idee?"
> "Na," sagte Tabea keck, "sie kommt doch aus Afrika! Da wohnen doch die Mohren!"
>
> ("Wow!" exclaimed Tabea with flashing eyes, and shook her flaxen head of curls, "I am so excited!" – "It's true, right" she asked her mother mysteriously, "Frau Riviotti is black?"
> The pastor's wife stopped, aghast.
> "Where did you get that crazy idea?"
> "Well," said Tabea without embarrassment, "she comes from Africa, of course! That's where the Moors live!")[2]

To her great initial disappointment, Tabea learns that her mother's African friend is white and German. A few hours after meeting Madame Riviotti, she confesses to her brothers, "sie hätte es viel hübscher gefunden, wenn Frau Riviotti schwarz wäre und solche rothe Jacke trüge, wie die Frau in der Löwenbude auf dem Jahrmarkt" (it would have been much more enjoyable for her if Madame Riviotti were black and wore the same kind of red jacket as the woman in the lion cage at the annual town fair).³ Despite this disappointment, Tabea is the first of the children to befriend their guest. An attitude of both real wonder and cultural superiority are reflected in the girl's mistake.

While this is not a paper about centring or demarginalizing Black characters in a novel that could have focused on them, it does examine a few references to Sub-Saharan Africans, because their depictions support a nationalist idea of German cultural superiority over Egypt and Africa. This novel takes place largely in Egypt, where unofficial colonies of Germans and Western Europeans, non-Egyptian Levantines, native Arabic-speaking Egyptians, and Sub-Saharan Africans subsisted under the semi-autonomous Ottoman Khedive, or viceroy. The setting in Egypt establishes a hierarchy of races, even if Reuter believes she is treating the native Egyptians and Sub-Saharan Africans with sympathy.

Recalling Edward Said's concept of Orientalism, Achill Mbembe suggests that the idea of Africa is necessary to the identity of the West. Africa is "that something invented," which the West uses to construct its world and against which the West defines itself in contradistinction.⁴ Vumbi Yoka Mudimbe adds to this the notion of the "idea of Africa" in contrast to the actual place and people.⁵ Egypt held a unique position in the nineteenth century European imagination. While it belonged largely to the African continent, it was viewed as separate from Africa. The Greeks already saw Alexandria as more European than African. Later, many Europeans adopted this same view, largely because Egypt was seen as a land with culture and history, while Sub-Saharan Africa was thought to be primitive and without culture.⁶ Katharine Machnik notes this long-held distinction between "White Africa" and "Black Africa," and observes that this type of European thinking about Sub-Saharan Africa as underdeveloped and without history elevated European countries and culture, while legitimizing the transatlantic slave trade and colonial ambitions.⁷

The novel's portrayals of Germans and Germany on the one hand, and of Levantines, Egyptians, and Africans on the other, are largely Orientalist in Edward Said's sense. Indeed, while describing in her autobiography a scene she witnessed daily from her school window in Alexandria, Reuter uses the very language Said characterizes as Orientalist: "Primitive," "ancient," "simple," "natural."⁸ This depiction portrays a Muslim family sympathetically, but likewise reinforces "dogmatic views of 'the Oriental' as a kind of ideal, unchanging abstraction."[9] These paternalist, culturally nationalist, "Orientalist" attitudes, described by Said decades after the publication of *Glück und Geld*, are already present in Reuter's first novel.

This chapter explores how *Glück und Geld* engages in a Eurocentric manner with Egypt and Africa. As I examine the representations of Germans in Ottoman Egypt, German researchers and their view of Africa, the non-Egyptian Levantines, and Sub-Saharan Africans, I will show that Egypt acts as an ideological vehicle that sets up a hierarchy of people with Germans and Europeans at the top, and Black Africans at the bottom. Reuter uses Egypt as a foil to Germany, and champions Germans and German culture as superior to Ismail Pasha's Egypt in the mid-nineteenth century.[10] *Glück und Geld* reveals a narrative that takes for granted, and thus helps to perpetuate, a sense of German cultural superiority vis-à-vis Egypt and Africa.

Ottoman Egypt: Germans and Native Egyptians under Ismail Pasha

Reuter presents in the novel an Egypt that is "[ein] Zwitterding von Barbarei und Kultur" (a hermaphroditic blend of barbarism and culture), that is, two opposites in one;[11] both modern and decaying, with luxury and riches on the one hand, "Schuld und Elend" (debt and squalor) on the other;[12] a site of hypocrisy with the illusion of prosperity; a place where men come to earn a fortune, but where those who act with honesty are crushed by those who do not. This Egypt is Ismail Pasha's state as portrayed by Reuter. The novel's first sentence sets up Egypt, in particular the Alexandria of Reuter's childhood, as a threshold between "civilized" Europe and the "uncivilized," "wild" interior of Africa. The narrator characterizes the Mediterranean city as "den Übergang von moderner Kultur zu der phantastischen Gestaltung orientalisches Lebens und zu einer von beiden unberührten Wildniß [sic]" (the transition from modern culture to the fantastical embodiment of Oriental life and to a wilderness unspoiled by both).[13] That is, as a somewhat Europeanized modern Egyptian city, Alexandria stands both as a doorway between civilized Europe and a fantasy presentation of the Orient, and as a gate to an untouched Sub-Saharan Black Africa.

Reuter's first published novel, *Glück und Geld: ein Roman aus dem heutigen Ägypten*, aims to entertain German readers with descriptions of an exotic land and people, and is based in part on Reuter's personal observations. One of the most prominent writers at the turn of the last century, Reuter was born in 1859 in Ottoman-era Egypt during the rule of the famed Khedive of Egypt, Ismail Pasha. She was best known for her groundbreaking novel *Aus guter Familie: Leidensgeschichte eines*

Mädchens, published in 1895. Reuter lived in Alexandria with her four brothers and her German parents into her early teen years while her father ran a successful import-export business until his death.

The mention of Egypt in the title of the novel was certainly meant to attract a German readership that was becoming increasingly interested in the Orient and Africa. The plot centres on Octavia, who chooses money and luxury – which she mistakes for happiness – over love, when she marries a wealthy Ottoman businessman, a Levantine from Smyrna (in modern-day Turkey). Like Reuter, Octavia is the daughter of a German merchant family that lives in an unofficial colony of Germans among other Europeans and Egyptian Levantines. These groups are portrayed against the backdrop of the native Egyptian people who enter the story more as a concept than as real living, breathing characters. The narrator discusses them sympathetically as a people oppressed by the Ottoman ruling class, yet still in the service of the idea of German and European cultural superiority. After trials, sacrifices, and an increasingly unhappy marriage, Octavia eventually returns to Wulfhart, the man she had rejected years earlier, a German professor of antiquities whom she met in Alexandria. She ultimately finds happiness once she renounces the opulence and wealth of her Levantine husband and their extravagant upper-class social circle, abandons the parallel "Trug und Schein" (deceit and sham) of Ismail Pasha's Ottoman Egypt, and embraces the traditional values of Protestant Germany. Indeed, the narrator links Octavia first to the Egypt of Ismail Pasha, including its extravagance, decadence, superficiality, and lack of moral clarity, then to the Egyptian people who are victims of the Ottoman ruling class, and finally to Germany, when she chooses to return to the German homeland she has never seen and marry the German professor. Octavia finds a redemptive, happy ending in Germany as she frees herself from the grasp of her Ottoman husband and awakens to her Germanness after a long period of frustration and sorrow in Egypt, just as the narrator hopes the Egyptian people will find redemption in self-determination after Ismail Pasha's reign.

The narrator attempts to provide a realistic glimpse into 1860s and 1870s Egypt by connecting historical events and people to her plot, including the conflicts among England, France, and the Ottoman Empire.[14] Reuter's novel takes place during Ismail's reign (1863–79), but it was published in 1888, with the benefit of hindsight after Ismail was removed from power by the Ottoman sultan under pressure from the British and French governments. Ismail attempted to modernize and Europeanize Egypt, but he incurred heavy debts for the native Egyptians through the construction of the Suez Canal, the building of the Gezirah

Palace, and war with Ethiopia.[15] In the chapter of her autobiography titled "Orientbilder" (Images of the Orient), Reuter observes that Ismail was a marked improvement over his predecessor, during whose reign of cruelty harsh public punishments and a lack of electricity in the streets were the norm.[16] Yet, while she praises these advancements, Reuter contrasts the cheap, superficial modernity of the Potemkin village–like cities with the slow-paced and authentic lifestyle of the old Orient.[17] Although the city streets look like those of a modern European city, they still retain the typical figures one would expect in an "Oriental" city.[18] The novel refers to this fake reality as "Trug und Schein" (deceit and sham).

The narrator's description of the mashup of cultures is not as straightforward as it might first appear. While she criticizes the falseness of Ismail's new modern city, she seems to see nothing wrong with the poverty of the Egyptian people there, but in fact praises them for their simple and traditional life, as if life on the streets were traditional, rather than the product of sheer need. She speaks of the people in the patronizing manner described by Said: this "Völkchen der arabischen Eselbuben, Taschenspieler und Märchenerzähler," this (adorable little nation of Arab donkey-boys, street conjurers, storytellers) live their cheerful lives in their tattered clothing in front of the fashion and jewelry shops for the wealthy and the Europeans.[19] Although she intends to extol the Egyptian Arabs and their non-European lifestyle, she also belittles them from the point of view of a citizen who contrasts her own perceived "culturally superior civilization" with this more "primitive" one.

Germany's Desire for Empire: The German Researchers and Their View of Africans

Germans were interested in descriptions of Egypt and Africa, and many of these portrayals, such as Reuter's, represented Egyptians and Africans in an Orientalist manner. Dirk Göttsche observes "the growing fascination in German-speaking Europe with the exploration of hitherto unknown territories overseas." He notes also that geographical and anthropological societies sponsored "academically trained explorers," who "played a significant part in mapping the African interior, capturing the imagination of the German and European public, while also paving the way for later colonial rule."[20] He notes further that by the 1850s, such "colonial exploration, exotic African cultures, and European adventures in the African interior" had become prominent themes both in academic periodicals and in the popular "family journals," including *Unterhaltungen am häuslichen Herd*, *Die Gartenlaube*, *Über Land und Meer*, and *Westermanns Monatshefte*, thus transforming the popular print media of the late nineteenth century into "agents of Eurocentric cultural globalization." Göttsche's study clarifies the connection between German nationalism and identity and the colonialist project.[21]

By the second half the nineteenth century, German fascination with the foreign peoples of the colonial world manifested itself in "human zoos" that entertained German audiences with examples of the so-called "primitive" and "exotic" races from Africa and other places.[22] Pascal Blanchard, Bruno Bancel, Gilles Boëtsch, Éric Deroo, and Sandrine Lemaire argue that these "spectacularizations" of exotic races, that is, the public exhibition of dark-skinned "Others," which had already begun in the early nineteenth century, not only explain the formation of racial stereotypes, but also play a central role in the construction of European identity.[23] Western identity is constructed in contrast to the savage, primitive, exotic Other: "The world order was divided into exhibited peoples on the one hand and spectators at the exhibition on the other."[24] Sebastian Conrad argues that such displays were another important forum for the German colonial imagination: "These ethnographic shows presented the Germans as masters of the world, and as benevolent civilizers in the colonies. They also brought home the message to the German audience that there were natural hierarchies of races and peoples, and suggested the social order in Germany, with its class and gender differences, be regarded as natural."[25]

This assumed hierarchy of races with Germans at the top is in play when the narrator mentions in passing the human zoo that so fascinated the young German child at the end of the novel. The narrator could have depicted the child's excitement at the pending visit of her mother's "African" friend and still conveyed the perhaps understandable childlike and innocent confusion that Octavia would be a "Moor" without the child's memory of the African woman in the cage. This detail seems to be very deliberate. The reason for the inclusion of this unnecessary detail is the same as the reason for the human zoos themselves. The message: we can capture and display these Others as if they were dangerous and wild animals whom we have subdued. We are a little afraid of them, but fascinated at the same time, just as with zoo animals. We civilized Germans are superior to these exotic, uncivilized primitives. We are a great nation.

Likewise, the narrator reveals an Orientalist attitude when depicting the German researchers in Egypt. The characterization of Ismail Pasha's assistance to the German researchers both advances the plot and reinforces the cultural and racial hierarchy at work in the novel. The story begins by introducing Professor Wulfhart, who is part of a German expedition to the African interior. The Khedive himself is hosting the members of the expedition in the Ras-el-Tin Palace as they prepare for their trip into the unknown interior:

> Ismail Pasha bewirthete dort in seiner üppigen Weise die Mitglieder einer Expedition, die sich neu gebildet hatte, um zur Lösung jenes großen Räthsels beizutragen, welches die Gelehrten um so mächtiger anzieht, je mehr Schwierigkeiten und Gefahren es ihren Bemühungen entgegenstellt: die Erforschung Inner-Afrikas.[26]

(Ismael Pasha hosted there in his extravagant manner the members of an expedition that had recently been formed for the purpose of contributing to the solving of that great mystery that attracted the scholars that much more powerfully, the more difficulties and dangers stood in the way of their efforts: the exploration of Inner Africa.)

The reader learns that the expedition has come to Alexandria to secure supplies and, they hope, to obtain protection and financial assistance for their enterprise. At first, the Khedive's government appears enthusiastic, but the expedition's progress has stalled. The delay has already lasted weeks and has no end in sight.

Wulfhart is happy that the delay has allowed him to meet Octavia, "ehe ich an den Nilquellen bei den Negerkönigen gänzlich verwildere" ("before I sink completely to the level of a wild brute among the N-word kings at the sources of the Nile").[27] The narrator has already called the interior of Africa a "Wildniß" (wilderness, or the wild)[28] and Wulfhart has observed that the Sub-Saharan Africans he sees in Alexandria are "wild"[29] – thus, Reuter's use of the N-word next to the German "verwildern" suggests that the kings and their people are akin to savage animals or uncivilized sub-humans whom the Germans can study, capture, and tame, and to whom they can bring civilization and culture. While Wulfhart seems to be speaking lightheartedly, the verb may suggest a possible danger of reverting to a wild state after having been civilized. Reuter presents Egypt matter-of-factly as the jumping-off point for the culturally imperialistic German researchers of Black Africa, enabled by their Ottoman benefactors.

In the meantime, according to the narrator, Ismail Pasha offers these honoured guests of the German consul every comfort: "Er betrachtete sich vollständig als ihr Wirth und suchte ihnen von seiner Hofhaltung und Regierung einen glänzenden Begriff zu geben. Von allen Seiten beeiferte man sich in der europäischen Kolonie, seinem Beispiel zu folgen" (He considered himself completely to be their host and sought to give them a glittering impression of his holding of court and his government. Everyone worked zealously to follow his lead in the European colony).[30] The Khedive celebrates the presence of the European explorers with fireworks. A German consulate is situated in Alexandria to support the interests of just such German-led scientific expeditions and the growing number of German merchants living and operating in Egypt, such as Octavia's family.[31]

These passages are revealing for several reasons. The narrator does not question the purpose of the expedition nor the colonialist idea behind it. Nor does she question the Khedive's role in outfitting the European researchers and granting permission to explore the African interior. The narrative criticizes only the inconvenience to the Germans. Wulfhart and the other German researchers are portrayed positively. In fact, the Khedive's behaviour towards the Germans suggests that he views them as superior to himself. The narrator suggests that the exploration of the African interior is a positive project in the name of science, and gives no thought to the cultural chauvinism behind such a project. The Pasha's support of the expedition does not indicate the people's permission to map the interior or to search for and remove ancient artefacts or to observe Sub-Saharan African peoples. The Egyptian people are under the rule of a foreign, albeit semi-autonomous, power whose approval of and support for the Europeans and their scientific expeditions may not coincide with that of the government's native subjects or of those various African peoples beyond the borders of Egypt. While these elements add to the novel's realistic historical background and provide a critical view of Ismail's regime, about which Reuter's German audience was eager to hear and read, the narrative takes for granted a hierarchy of peoples, with the Germans at the top, followed by the Khedive's Turkish government, with the native Egyptians further down, and the Sub-Saharan Africans at the bottom. It suggests further that the German scientists are perhaps not as welcome in Egypt as they believe they are.

Characterization of Levantines

Another group described in the novel in a condescending manner is the people of the Levant. The Levantines as a group within Reuter's hierarchy overlap with the Turkish ruling class and the native Egyptians. While some Levantines are poor and live on the streets, and others are extravagantly wealthy, such as the Khedive and Octavia's husband, none are enslaved or otherwise in servitude, as the Sub-Saharan Africans are. The term "Levant" comes from the French word *lever*, "to rise," and refers to the place where the sun rises, that is, the East. The geographical area of the Levant, the eastern Mediterranean region from

German Cultural Superiority in Reuter's *Glück und Geld* 161

Greece to Egypt, received this designation based on its geographical position vis-à-vis Europe, that is, based on a Eurocentric perspective.

The narrative introduces a particular family into the story for one main reason: to depict negatively the Levantines who live in Alexandria and set them in contrast to the German readers. The narrator describes the Stolzenfels family as newly rich. Baron von Stolzenfels had recently secured a financial deal that lifted them from among the ranks of the poor: Stolzenfels, a German nobleman and former soldier, did not have the same misgivings about unprincipled business dealings as Werther, Octavia's father, who is his neighbour and fellow German merchant. While the family is now rich, the narrator finds fault with their new apartment: "[Das Gemach zeigte] einen vollständigen Mangel der hunderterlei Kleinigkeiten: Bilder, Bücher, Nippsachen, die wir gewöhnt sind, als Vervollständigung einer eleganten Einrichtung zu betrachten" ([The chamber revealed] a complete absence of the hundred and one odds and ends – pictures, books, knick-knacks – which we are accustomed to considering to be the completion of an elegant furnishing).[32] The "we" in this sentence appears to be the narrator and her German middle-class reader. Furthermore, the narrator adds the following comment regarding the baroness: "Die großen Brillantenohrgehänge stimmten schlecht zu der ungekämmten Frisur" (The large diamond drop earrings were a bad fit for her unkempt hairdo).[33] The baroness, a native speaker of Arabic, has bad taste – a hallmark of the so-called newly rich. The middle-class German readership is expected to recognize the baroness's bad taste. The contrast is implied: A German wife would have decorated her home with taste, and therefore is superior to the Oriental wife.

The next sentence explains the characterization of Frau von Stolzenfels in a matter-of-fact way: "Die Baronin war eben eine Levantinerin" (The Baroness was, after all, a Levantine).[34] The narrator characterizes the Levantines negatively over the next couple of paragraphs before proceeding with the description of the Stolzenfels family:

> Es ist eine eigenthümliche Menschensorte, diese Levantiner, die den Handelsstädten des Orients ihr spezifisches Gepräge verleihen. Aus einem Gemisch der Völkerschaften zusammengesetzt, die um das Mittelländische Meer herrschen und hausen, scheinen sie von ihnen Allen nur die Schwächen geerbt zu haben. Ihr Charakter bildet eine wahre Musterkarte von Nationalfehlern, unter denen die Tugenden nur wie zufällig verlorene Goldkörner vorkommen ... [35]

(It is a peculiar type of people, these Levantines, who impart their specific imprint on the trading towns of the Orient. Consisting of a composite of nationalities that rule and reside around the Mediterranean Sea, they appear to have inherited from all of them only their weaknesses. Their character constitutes a veritable pattern card of national faults, among which the virtues appear only rarely, like randomly lost grains of gold ...)

The narrator continues, listing the different nationalities that make up the people of the Levant and outlining the characteristics of the men (tenacious, sophisticated, clever, successful by any means necessary, passionate, easy-going, petty, spiteful, cruel), followed by those of the women (indolent, idle, unclean, ignorant, good-natured, with a lustre of French elegance and a hint of classical beauty).[36] This characterization of the supposedly stereotypical "national faults" of the Levantine people allows the German readers to view themselves positively in contrast to these "Others." It is noteworthy that Octavia is not prejudicial against Levantines: her confidant is the Levantine baroness and she marries a Levantine man. There appears to be some ironic distance between the protagonist on the one hand and the narrator and her German readers on the other. Despite the irony, the narrator depicts the Alexandrian Levantines as inferior to the Germans.

Sub-Saharan Africans: Wild, Ornamental

The Black Africans are portrayed at the bottom of the hierarchy of peoples. While Reuter may not have focused in her novel on Sub-Saharan Africa or Africans, she does bring to the reader's attention the Black African woman on display in the cage in the German town, the poor denizens of the street, and the protagonist's uniformed African soldier-servant-youth. I'll discuss the African guards of the Khedive's palace in the next section. In these occurrences, the Sub-Saharan Africans are depicted either as wild, captured, tamed, and/or ornamental. The narrator appears to use "Neger" for dark-skinned or Black Sub-Saharan Africans, and "Levantiner" or "Araber" for lighter-skinned Egyptians of Middle Eastern or North African descent.[37] The pastor's daughter uses the word "Mohren" (Moors). Susan Arndt observes that while "Mohr" most often refers to any person from North or Sub-Saharan Africa, the term "Neger" is meant to be derogatory and suggests a direct connection to colonialism and slavery.[38] Its use in the mid- to late nineteenth century may have been commonplace, but it reinforces imperialist, racist, and Eurocentric attitudes. The narrative function of these Sub-Saharan Africans may appear to be simply an attempt to paint a realistic-looking narrative picture of the exotic for Reuter's German audience. However, the effect of these appearances of Black Africans reinforces the supposed cultural superiority of Germans over these "Others" in the same way as the unnecessary mention of the African woman in the human zoo in Germany.

The novel's first several pages present a picture of the racial and ethnic plurality that made up Egypt and especially Alexandria. The narrative contrasts the German researchers, the government of Ismail Pasha, and the Egyptian "Volk" in Alexandria as observed by Wulfhart. From his point of view, the narrator describes the ragged, homeless people who come out at night to marvel at the Pasha's fireworks in honour of his German guests: native Arabs, Greeks, Maltese, Italians, and "manche wilde Gestalt, der das Kainszeichen des Verbrechens auf der Stirn stand" (many a wild figure on whose brow the mark of Cain's crime stood), that is, Black Sub-Saharan Africans.[39] This instance is the first and one of the few mentions of Black Africans in the novel. The German professor does not think of the people of Levantine heritage as wild figures, although he characterizes them and the Sub-Saharan Africans together as "die wunderlichsten Gestalten" (the most peculiar figures). He identifies the Sub-Saharan Africans as wild and cursed with dark skin because of a forefather's crime (according to traditional Christian interpretations of the Old Testament). This description sets up the hierarchy of cultures from the novel's beginning.

Another example of this use of a Black African to paint a realistic-looking picture of the exotic while taking for granted and reinforcing the inferiority of Sub-Saharan Africa occurs in the first scene after Octavia's wedding to Riviotti.[40] Octavia's servant-guard appears only briefly, but he speaks: he reminds her that a visitor is coming. He had been attending Octavia after she had fallen asleep in a rocking chair in her new home. The servant wears the Egyptian national uniform. Octavia calls him by his name: Abdallah. The narrator calls him "den Negerknaben" (N-word lad). The presence of this Black servant, dressed in his ceremonial military garb, serves to demonstrate the level of wealth and extravagance that Octavia has attained as Madame Riviotti: The young servant "steht nun in seinem egyptischen Nationalkostüm, elegant und farbenprächtig, wie Alles in ihrer Umgebung, vor ihr" (stands now before her in his Egyptian national uniform elegantly and in a blaze of colour, as was everything in her surroundings).[41] Octavia speaks to the young Abdallah at least in part in French. Later, when Octavia arrives home, Abdallah "flog wie ein schöner, bunter Panther herbei" (flew around like a beautiful, colourful panther).[42] In the latter instance, she appreciates his eager service to her, and he basks in the influence of her grateful smile. He is beautiful and swift, but is also a black animal, akin to a pet. He is a wild, dangerous animal who has been tamed and domesticated.

Octavia has a Sub-Saharan African youth as her personal servant because she has married up into the uppermost class of Egypt. Monsieur Riviotti has Sub-Saharan servants, just as Ismail Pasha has Sub-Saharan servants. The narrator does not inform the reader how Abdallah came to be employed by or in servitude to the Riviotti household or whether he is there by choice. The presence of a Sub-Saharan servant-guard is meant to communicate to the German reader not only Octavia's greatly elevated wealth and social status, but also the position of the Black Africans as servants, inferior to the Europeans and Ottomans. The animalization of the Black characters shows them to the German reader to be wild, dangerous, exotic, but also able to be tamed. Only Black Africans are uniformed, tamed, ceremonial guard-servants. This use of Black Africans as ornamental occurs on a larger scale at Ismail's palace.

Gezirah Palace: The Hollowness of Ismail and the Hierarchy of Races

Reuter uses one especially important section of *Glück und Geld* to advance Octavia's story, but more significantly for this paper, to put on display the novel's racial and cultural hierarchy. Here the narrator presents the superiority of the Europeans; criticizes the extravagance of the Khedive and the hollow foundation upon which the modernization of Egypt was built; sympathizes with the "good" Egyptian people under Turkish rule; and puts Black Africans on display. This scene takes place at an extravagant party at Ismail's new Gezirah Palace. Octavia, a guest at the party, chooses here her old, wealthy suitor over the younger, much more modest, clearly more sympathetic and, by implication, appropriate, Wulfhart. They, too, were guests at this celebration of the German expedition members. In her autobiography, Reuter remembers a visit to the castle, when her parents were invited to attend a party to celebrate the castle's opening, just prior to the grand opening of the Suez Canal. She notes that Ismail had built it as a residence for the French Empress Eugénie.[43] Ismail used a German decorator because he wanted the castle to look European for her.[44] The guests at the grand opening were Europeans.

The narrator criticizes Ismail Pasha and explains to her readers Egypt's precarious position during his reign. The narrative links the Khedive, the building of the expensive, extravagant palace, Octavia's Levantine husband, and the deception and illusion of much of the modernization, which is the source of the great national debt. Both Ismail and Riviotti are Ottoman Levantines in Egypt, part of the upper class that has come to its wealth and power through ruthless means. The

Khedive taxes the Egyptians unscrupulously to pay for his extravagant projects and lifestyle, which leads eventually to bankruptcy and a takeover by the British; the Levantine merchant acts in a similarly amoral manner and takes every financial advantage, even when it leads others to ruin. The narrator observes that Ismail is not a prince whose self-image is built on the foundation of history and tradition, as a European prince – or as genuine Egyptians – would be. Instead, he resembles

> einem reich gewordenen Finanzier, welcher ängstlich bedacht ist, die Welt mit seinen Schätzen zu blenden, damit sie vergesse, dass der Boden unter seinen Füßen morsch und hohl ist; der in tollem Uebermuthe versucht, es den Mächtigeren gleich zu tun, ja sie zu überbieten und am Ende nichts damit erreicht, als ihren Spott.[45]

> (a newly rich financier who is anxiously intent on dazzling the world with his treasures, so that they will forget that the ground under his feet is rotten and hollow; who in his mad arrogance tries to do as the more powerful ones do, indeed, to outdo them, but in the end achieves nothing but their derision.)

She characterizes the Khedive as simply another newly rich businessman, of which there were many in Egypt, including Riviotti.[46] Ismail attempts to hide the hollow foundation of his power and wealth. Outwardly, Egypt appears modern and European; but below the deceptive surface lurk bankruptcy, financial ruin, and misery. His strategy is to blind the Europeans to the country's poverty and debt by promoting superficial signs of wealth and success.

Not accidentally, this scene in which the narrator criticizes Ismail is the scene during which Octavia chooses the rich Levantine merchant as her husband. Like most of the unscrupulous European and Levantine merchants, she chooses the quick way to wealth – Octavia's father remains the novel's lone exception. In this way, she is perhaps just as unscrupulous as her fiancé, the Khedive, and most of the businessmen in Egypt. They sacrifice genuineness and human understanding for the facade of happiness based in wealth, luxury, and power. The narrative links Octavia's Turkish fiancé to the Turkish Khedive through their unscrupulous behaviour.

Of the palace itself, the narrator explains that the Khedive wasted millions on the grandiose structure; soon after his ouster, the new foreign government ignored it and let it fall into disrepair. It was soon forgotten.[47] The Gezirah Palace is one of the best examples of the title's message. Like Octavia in her choice of husbands, Ismail tried to find a personal or national happiness through extravagant spending. In a sense, he enters a risky marriage contract with his debtors, England and France. He has to incur great debt to fund the extravagant palace, but then it remains in use only a short while. Octavia makes a similar discovery in her marriage to Riviotti. In the end, however, Octavia has the opportunity to undo her mistake by choosing the German husband she had spurned.

The narrator pauses to express sympathy for the "good people" of Egypt. She explains that England and France would soon hereafter halt their mutual hostilities to cooperate in driving Ismail from power, "fort von dem guten Volke, das sich so geduldig den letzten Piaster aus der Tasche ziehen ließ, wenn Hoheit die Laune hatte, einer italienischen Sängerin oder einem fremden Schriftsteller mit goldenem Regen zu lohnen, damit sein königlicher Name in Druckerschwarz verherrlicht werde" (away from the good people that so uncomplainingly allowed the last farthing to be pulled from their pockets, when His Highness decided on a whim to shower an Italian singer or a foreign author with gold, so that his royal name would be glorified in printer's ink).[48] Here the Egyptians are the good people who cannot refuse to pay the tax that benefits their ruler. The narrator calls the people "good" again in the next sentence, adds two new adjectives, and states that the Egyptians would not have been able to rid themselves of the Khedive without the help of the two European powers: "Das gute heruntergekommene, armselige Volk hätte niemals Miene gemacht, sich seines Peinigers zu entledigen, wenn es nicht durch fremde Hilfe förmlich dazu gezwungen wäre" (The good, down-and-out, miserable people would never have been ready to rid themselves of their tormenter, had they not been positively compelled to do it through foreign assistance).[49] Ismail and the Ottomans are not "Egypt." Ismail is Egypt's tormenter. The narrator suggests that the Egyptians deserve sympathy, but the attitude is again paternalistic, even as she tries to express solidarity with them: the Egyptian people are good, but they are helpless without the assistance of the Western Europeans. This paternalistic attitude says again for the German reader: Germany and the West are superior to the good, but helpless, Egyptian people.

The narrative continues with a description of the entrance to the palace that reinforces a clear cultural ranking. The Khedive has caused the soldiers to be arranged in an ornamental formation on the stairs. The soldiers are dressed in special uniforms that are a cross between French and Prussian uniforms, including bearskin busbies and armour: "Dazu nahmen sich die Negergesichter wunderbarlich aus" (Together with these [uniforms], the black N-word faces had a marvellous contrasting effect).[50] In other words, just as with Octavia's Sub-Saharan African servant, the Black Sub-Saharan African soldiers at the palace are intended as decoration, to add a sense of realism and exoticism for the German audiences – Ismail's and Reuter's. The author means for the description of the Black faces in contrast to the colourful uniforms to be positive. She thinks they look striking. However, Octavia beholds them with both wonder and condescension. Their presence as ornaments and as soldier-servants of the Khedive reminds the German reader that the Ottoman Turks have colonized Egypt and allowed a semi-autonomous foreign viceroy to rule over the native Egyptian people. It validates a sense of cultural hierarchy that sets the Ottomans above the Egyptian people and Black Sub-Saharan Africans. Germany and the West are above all of them.

Reuter is writing for her target audience: middle-class Germany. The Germans who enjoyed the travelling "human zoos" would also be interested in the depiction of the uniformed Sub-Saharan African soldiers guarding a palace at which the Ottoman ruler hosts his European guests. The Ottoman Khedive tries to please his European guests, and uses ornamental soldier-servant Black Africans to impress them. The cultural and racial hierarchy is unmistakable.

Conclusions: Octavia, Egypt, and Germany

The narrative links Octavia to the Egyptian people under the dominion of the Ottoman Khedive. The Egypt of the novel, Octavia's Egypt, becomes increasingly a place of illusion, deception, and death, a place from which she flees and to which she has no desire to return.[51] The dreams of her youth and their so-called fulfilment in her marriage to the wealthy Ottoman were "Trug und Schein" (deceit and sham), a phrase appearing numerous times in the novel's second half as Octavia becomes increasingly aware of her husband's ruthlessness. This happiness was a sham happiness, a cheap falseness, just as the Khedive Ismail's superficial boulevards and palace were a sham civilization. Octavia is now able to see both the promised personal happiness in marriage to the wealthy Levantine and Ismail's modern, extravagant Egypt as an illusion; their ruin was just under the surface.[52] The good fortune Octavia received through her marriage to Riviotti was hollow and unfulfilling. The narrator links Egypt's fate and future to Octavia' fate and future. Both are ruled by the colonial Ottomans, whose reign is built on deception and the outward signs of success instead of genuineness and authenticity. When Octavia's husband dies, he writes her out of his will and deprives her of her considerable inherited wealth if she ever remarries; she will be left to fend for herself. Similarly, once the Pasha's rule collapses, it will leave the "good" people of Egypt to fend for themselves, to find their way under Ismail's crushing debt. The novel suggests that once the Egyptian people can be rid of the Turkish ruler, the debt he incurred, and the misleading illusion of superficial prosperity, they might have a hopeful but as yet unwritten future: "Ob Land und Volk die Kraft haben wird, verjüngt und gereinigt sich eine neue Zukunft zu schaffen – wer kann es sagen?" (Whether the country and people will have the power, rejuvenated and cleansed, to create a new future for themselves – who can say?)[53] In her depiction of Octavia's future, the narrator points to an optimistic future for Egypt.

Octavia finds happiness, home, and redemption in Germany. The choice between the two husbands sets up a contrast between Germany and Ottoman Egypt, in which Germany is authentic, good, and superior, while Egypt is superficial, immoral, and exotic; in which the German husband is moral, modest, and virtuous, while the Ottoman-Egyptian husband is merciless, self-centred, and material. While she remains faithful to her unloved first husband until his death, she abandons the notion that happiness is money. She finds authenticity and happiness in her turn away from the falseness of the Pasha's Egypt and towards her Christian (German) faith, her new German husband, and her Germanness.

Despite Reuter's enthusiasm for and sympathy with the diverse peoples of Egypt, her narrator speaks of them in a condescending, paternalistic manner. This patronizing portrayal of the Egyptian people – the Levantines, the native Egyptians, and the few Sub-Saharan Africans – is written as if such attitudes are widely held and agreed upon by her German middle-class readers. The author's culturally racist and nationalist message is unmistakable: Germans are superior to the Ottomans, the Levantines, and the Egyptian people, who are in turn portrayed as superior to the Sub-Saharan Africans. This is a significant finding about an author who is known best in the field of feminist German studies for the feminist qualities of her works. Her assertion of the rights of women in later works does not necessarily preclude her from expressing paternalistic and culturally racist attitudes towards Others.

NOTES

1 Gabriele Reuter, *Glück und Geld: ein Roman aus dem heutigen Egypten* (Leipzig: Wilhelm Friedrich, 1888). All translations are my own.
2 Reuter, *Glück und Geld*, 256.
3 Reuter, *Glück und Geld*, 256.

4 Achille Mbembe, *On the Postcolony* (Berkeley: University of California Press, 2001), 2, https://hdl.handle.net/2027/heb.02640.
5 V.Y. Mudimbe, *The Idea of Africa* (Bloomington: Indiana University Press, 1994), 41.
6 See Olufemi Taiwo, "Exorcising Hegel's Ghost: Africa's Challenge to Philosophy," *African Studies Quarterly* 1, no. 4 (1998): 3–16.
7 Katharine Machnik, "Schwarzafrika," in *Afrika und die deutsche Sprache: ein kritisches Nachschlagewerk*, ed. Susan Arndt and Antje Hornscheidt (Münster: Unrast, 2018), 204.
8 Gabriele Reuter, *Vom Kinde zum Menschen: die Geschichte meiner Jugend* (Berlin: S. Fischer, 1921), 85. All translations are my own.
9 Edward Said, *Orientalism* (London: Routledge and Kegan Paul, 1978), 24.
10 Reuter's ongoing interest in German colonists and in using the non-European world as a foil in order to show Germany's cultural superiority manifests itself again in her second novel, *Kolonistenvolk* (The colonists) (Berlin: S. Fischer, 1889). See David Tingey, "Seductive and Destructive: Argentina in Gabriele Reuter's *Kolonistenvolk* (1889)," in *Sophie Discovers Amerika: German-Speaking Women Write the New World*, ed. Rob McFarland and Michelle Stott James (Rochester, NY: Camden House, 2014), 102–10.
11 Reuter, *Glück und Geld*, 228.
12 Reuter, *Glück und Geld*, 11.
13 Reuter, *Glück und Geld*, 3.
14 Reuter, *Glück und Geld*, 100.
15 Fawaz A. Gerges, "Egypt's 'Liberal Age,'" in *Making the Arab World: Nasser, Qutb, and the Clash That Shaped the Middle East* (Princeton: Princeton University Press, 2018), 37–8, https://doi.org/10.2307/j.ctvc7728b. See also "What Ismail Pasha Did for Egypt," *Scientific American* 41, no. 6 (9 August 1879), 89, https://www.jstor.org/stable/10.2307/26071482.
16 Reuter, *Vom Kinde*, 83. See also "What Ismail Pasha Did for Egypt."
17 Reuter, *Vom Kinde*, 83.
18 Reuter, *Vom Kinde*, 83.
19 Reuter, *Vom Kinde*, 83.
20 Dirk Göttsche, *Remembering Africa: The Rediscovery of Colonialism in Contemporary German Literature* (Rochester, NY: Camden House, 2013), 47.
21 Göttsche, *Remembering Africa*, 47–9.
22 Göttsche, *Remembering Africa*, 48.
23 Pascal Blanchard, Bruno Bancel, Gilles Boëtsch, Éric Deroo, and Sandrine Lemaire, "Human Zoos: The Greatest Exotic Shows in the West," in *Human Zoos: Science and Spectacle in the Age of Colonial Empires*, ed. Pascal Blanchard, Nicolas Bancel, Gilles Boëtsch, Éric Deroo, Sandrine Lemaire, and Charles Forsdick, trans. Teresa Bridgeman (Liverpool: Liverpool University Press, 2008), 1–49.
24 Blanchard, Bancel, Boëtsch, Deroo, and Lemaire, "Human Zoos," 6.

25 Sebastian Conrad, *German Colonialism: A Short History*, trans. Sorcha O'Hagan (Cambridge: Cambridge University Press, 2011), 140. Originally published as *Deutsche Kolonialgeschichte* (Munich: C.H. Beck, 2008).
26 Reuter, *Glück und Geld*, 4.
27 Reuter, *Glück und Geld*, 56.
28 Reuter, *Glück und Geld*, 3.
29 Reuter, *Glück und Geld*, 8.
30 Reuter, *Glück und Geld*, 5.
31 Reuter, *Glück und Geld*, 110.
32 Reuter, *Glück und Geld*, 42.
33 Reuter, *Glück und Geld*, 43.
34 Reuter, *Glück und Geld*, 43.
35 Reuter, *Glück und Geld*, 43.
36 Reuter, *Glück und Geld*, 43–4.
37 Reuter, *Glück und Geld*, 56.
38 Susan Arndt, "Neger_in," in *Wie Rassismus aus Wörtern spricht: (K)erben des Kolonialismus im Wissensarchive deutsche Sprache: ein kritisches Nachschlagewerk*, ed. Susan Arndt and Nadja Ofuatey-Alazard (Münster: Unrast, 2019), 653–4.
39 Reuter, *Glück und Geld*, 8.
40 Reuter, *Glück und Geld*, 129.
41 Reuter, *Glück und Geld*, 129.
42 Reuter, *Glück und Geld*, 174.
43 Reuter, *Vom Kinde*, 104; Reuter, *Glück und Geld*, 99; "Ernst Keil's Nachfolger," *Die Gartenlaube* (Leipzig, 1882), 644, updated 15 December 2020, https://de.wikisource.org/w/index.php?title=Seite:Die_Gartenlaube_(1882)_644.jpg&oldid=-.
44 Reuter, *Vom Kinde*, 104.
45 Reuter, *Glück und Geld*, 98–9.
46 Reuter, *Glück und Geld*, 99–100.
47 Reuter, *Glück und Geld*, 99.
48 Reuter, *Glück und Geld*, 100.
49 Reuter, *Glück und Geld*, 100.
50 Reuter, *Glück und Geld*, 99.
51 Reuter, *Glück und Geld*, 257 and 281.
52 Reuter, *Glück und Geld*, 227–8.
53 Reuter, *Glück und Geld*, 228.

8 The Black Slave Martyr Re-imagined for Christian Missions in Colonial Africa: Maria Theresa Ledóchowska's *Zaïda* (1889)

CINDY PATEY BREWER AND ELIZABETH MOYE-WEAVER

In the history of anti-slavery literature, no work of fact or fiction has had a broader or longer-lasting impact on the collective memories of Europe and North America than the sentimental reform novel *Uncle Tom's Cabin* (1852) by Harriet Beecher Stowe.[1] Furthermore, there is no hero quite so enshrined and transmuted as Uncle Tom himself. Even today, the name "Uncle Tom" persists in popular culture, albeit as a slur used by Black people to refer to an exceedingly servile Black person.[2] The hero in Stowe's novel is certainly good-natured and acquiescing, but he is also brave and defiant. Uncle Tom resists his cruel master and is tortured to death for not revealing the location of escaped slaves. In the nineteenth century, *Uncle Tom's Cabin* sold more copies internationally than any other book with the exception of the Bible.[3] In the same year as its initial publication, fourteen German translations appeared on the market.[4] A decade later, more than half a million copies were sold in Germany alone.[5] By then, the United States was at war over slavery. According to legend, President Lincoln greeted Stowe in 1862 with the words, "so you are the little woman who wrote the book that started this great war."[6] Though the Lincoln quote is entirely apocryphal, this legend's persistence in over a century of Stowe scholarship attests to something more fundamental: the desire to believe that a work of literature can move a nation, right social wrongs, and change the course of history.

This very idea inspired the twenty-eight-year-old Maria Theresa Ledóchowska (1863–1922) to pick up her pen and follow in Stowe's footsteps. In 1888, she read a London anti-slavery speech by Cardinal Charles Lavigerie (1825–92). She describes the impact of his speech as follows:

> Ein Satz in dieser Rede entschied meinen Beruf: Ich las darin Folgendes: Mögen die Frauen und Mädchen Europas, welche Talent zum Schreiben haben,

es wohl bedenken, dass es der Roman einer Frau war – Onkel Tom's Hütte – welcher die Veranlassung gab zur Aufhebung der Sclaverei in Amerika.[7]

(One sentence in this speech decided my calling: I read the following: May the women and girls of Europe who have a talent for writing consider that it was a novel by a woman – *Uncle Tom's Cabin* – that gave rise to the abolition of slavery in America.)

From this point forward, Ledóchowska dedicated her life to fight slavery and free Africans from what she perceived as "doppelte Knechtschaft ..., gefesselt an Leib und Seele" (double subjugation, chained in body and soul).[8] By the time of Lavigerie's 1888 speech, slavery in the Americas had ended, but the slave trade in Africa persisted into the first decade of the new century until it was gradually replaced by wage labour economies. Ledóchowska became a venerated anti-slavery advocate for Africa.[9] She lectured all over Europe, drumming up support for the cause, and founding a new religious order, the St. Petrus Claver-Sodalität, named after the Jesuit priest and patron saint of enslaved peoples. During her lifetime, Ledóchowska wrote nine full-length dramas, several children's stories, and countless brochures, essays, and magazine articles advocating Christian involvement in Africa. Her works have been published in German, Polish, Czech, Slovene, Hungarian, French, Italian, and English. At the time of her death in 1922, she was revered by Catholics worldwide as "Africa's Mother" and, in 1975, she was beatified by Pope Paul VI.[10] The religious order she founded is still active today with thirty-three convents in nineteen countries.

Ledóchowska's zeal for Christianity and human rights led to the 1889 publication of *Zaïda, das Negermädchen*, the first of six anti-slavery dramas written over her lifetime. *Zaïda* debuted that same spring in the Salzburg Stadttheater.[11] The purpose of this chapter is to situate this unusual drama within contemporary European discourses on slavery, race, religion, and gender. While *Uncle Tom's Cabin* remained the dominant narrative on race and Christianity, Ledóchowska's drama moves beyond Stowe to challenge a variety of racial and gender tropes including the figure of Uncle Tom himself, enshrined in the European mind as the ultimate Black Christian slave hero. Ledóchowska does this by leaning heavily on a long tradition of hagiographic tales of saints and martyrs for the faith.

Uncle Tom's Transatlantic Transformations

There is no question that Ledóchowska was inspired by Stowe. While traditional Christianity sometimes justified slavery as a curse inflicted by God upon the descendants of Ham,[12] for Ledóchowska and Stowe, the Bible constituted the ultimate repudiation of the institution, but ironically also the justification for European intervention in Africa. At the end of *Uncle Tom's Cabin*, Stowe sends Eliza and George Harris to Africa to help "roll the tide of civilization and Christianity along its shores."[13] Ledóchowska's vision was the same. Though Stowe was Calvinist and Ledóchowska Catholic, the two writers shared the same missionary zeal and a common anti-slavery message, arguing for the humanity of Black races on the basis of their potential for spiritual depth and saint-like devotion to Christian beliefs. Like the African American hero Uncle Tom, Ledóchowska's African heroine, Zaïda, proves her Christian worthiness via an act of supreme self-sacrifice, surrendering herself to torture and death for the sake of others. However, Zaïda is not simply a feminine version of the original Uncle Tom, she is a heroine for a new age.

By 1889, when Zaïda debuts on stage, Uncle Tom had undergone countless transformations in the collective European imagination.[14] By this point, he bore little resemblance to the heroic character that originally captivated readers in 1852. Uncle Tom had been staged in dramas, comedies, minstrel shows, and operas. His image had been appropriated, stereotyped, marketed, and sold as art, dishes, toys, and trinkets.[15] As a particularly dynamic artefact of global cultural mobility,[16] Uncle Tom travelled through time and space to be enshrined in new contexts. In Germany's colonial era, Uncle Tom was transplanted onto foreign landscapes and redeployed in fantasies of colonized Africa.[17] Some of these ubiquitous iterations of Uncle Tom even turned traitor to the anti-slavery cause, suggesting that African peoples are happiest under the paternalistic care of "benevolent" slave owners.[18]

Within this commodified and contradictory tangle of discourses about race, religion, slavery, and Europe's colonization of Africa, Ledóchowska's *Zaïda* might be seen as a gendered reimagining of the heroic Christian slave of antebellum America now projected onto Africa as a modern mission fantasy. Her character recalls the bravery of the original Uncle Tom but challenges his passivity. A rarity among colonial writers of her day, Ledóchowska humanized her Black characters, challenged dominant discourses on race and gender, and created a role model for Christian women's activism. All of this led to real human rights improvements. Yet, in spite of her dedication to the cause, we must acknowledge that Ledóchowska never fully escaped the project of whiteness, measuring the worthiness of her Black heroes and heroines on the basis of European cultural standards. Karen Sánchez-Eppler says it best: "The problem of antislavery fiction is that the very effort to depict goodness in black involves the obliteration of blackness."[19]

Indeed, in the final analysis, the heroine of Ledóchowska's hagiographic anti-slavery drama only achieves sainthood by rejecting her African cultural heritage.

Black Characters in European Colonial and Mission Narratives

Black characters like Zaïda were unheard of within mainstream German-language colonial literature published in the time period encompassing Europe's "scramble for Africa" and Germany's corresponding colonial period (1884–1918). During these decades, German-speaking writers produced vast amounts of literature about Africa – colonial reports, magazine articles, memoirs, and novels – all populated by white colonialist heroes and heroines.[20] These narratives reinforced racial perspectives that justified European political and economic power and fortified the boundaries of difference. Black characters, if they appeared at all, were relegated to the roles of devious villains, ignorant savages, or mere props in the exotic African landscape.[21] Even Stowe's Black heroes had diminished to "projective justification of German colonial intentions."[22] In short, in the cultural imagination of colonial-minded Germany (and perhaps the rest of Europe), Black African heroes were virtually non-existent.

While colonial and mission literature shared a penchant for the cliché and a general belief in European superiority, mission literature offered more perspectives on racial difference. Contrary to what some scholars have postulated, missionaries did not simply reproduce the values of the colonizer.[23] Many mission narratives are marked by tension between loyalty to the missionary's European origins and dedication to their vulnerable African congregations, thus producing a mix of perspectives about Africa and its people. Some mission narratives, like the extensive personal letters of Protestant Sophie Schröder, who lived with her missionary husband in South West Africa from 1863 to 1895, focus entirely on the white population of missionaries, their trials and travels, but never once mention an African native by name. Schröder focuses on what she sees as the brutality and atrocities of the natives and never sees their humanity.[24] Another Protestant missionary wife, Hedwig Irle, who lived in the same territories as Schröder from 1890 to 1903, used her published memoirs to introduce her readers to many native Africans by name and recount the details of their lives and cultures. Her narratives emphasize the fundamental humanity of native Africans and contrast this with the brutality and atrocities of European settlers and colonial soldiers.[25] Some mission texts tackle the question of race directly, such as Frieda Pfinzner's 1912 children's story

"Eine afrikanische Prinzessin" (An African princess). This story, with its initially racist white characters and its courageous and clever Black heroine, teaches children and adults, "dass der Wert eines Menschen nicht in seiner Hautfarbe steckt" (that the worth of a human being is not measured by their skin colour).[26] This great disparity of views among mission-minded authors complicates simple paradigms for understanding colonial mission texts.

Representations of Race and Religion in Ledóchowska's Works

Ledóchowska's writing is particularly interesting in this regard, because her views of Africa and its native peoples were shaped entirely by second-hand accounts in newspapers, books, magazines, and letters. Four of her plays – *Zaïda* (1889), *Ein Freiheitlicher am Kongo* (A free man in the Congo, 1910), *Von Hütte zu Hütte* (From hut to hut, 1912), and *Die Prinzessin von Uganda* (The princess of Uganda, 1915) – are set in Africa.[27] Though she dedicated her life to raising funds for the Catholic missions in Africa, Ledóchowska's poor health prevented her from ever travelling there. Thus, her dramas are products of her imagination, works of fiction in a setting entirely unfamiliar to her. Given the racist rhetoric of her day, her belief in the spiritual potential of Black peoples is all the more remarkable.

All of her narratives depict a polarized world view that pits good against evil, and, for Ledóchowska, these lines tend to pass along religious rather than racial divides. Ledóchowska vilifies Muslims, Jews, and even Protestants,[28] but praises the potential of Black Africans. Admittedly, her frequent use of the term "N*" is jarring, and its racist impact undeniable, contradicting the otherwise inclusive message of her writings. However, Ledóchowska's usage of the word does not suggest an exclusionary intent, aligning with the definition in the 1890 *Meyers Konversations-Lexikon* referring to African people with Black skin.[29] Of the twenty-seven instances on stage, the term only assumes an intentionally malicious tone when employed by the villains, who pair it with words like "blöd" (stupid), "einfältig" (simpleminded), or "mein" (my). The latter is particularly offensive to Zaïda, who insists she will belong to no one. While Ledóchowska's works are in no way free of racist notions, the final scene of the play calls on the audience to fight for the "Menschenrechte" (human rights) of Black Africans,[30] thus reinforcing an inclusionary intent. For Ledóchowska, Black rights are *human* rights.

Taken as a whole, Ledóchowska's African plays share a surprisingly egalitarian representation of the morality of white and Black races. Looking at the four plays, we note that the various villains are

Black Africans and white Europeans in roughly equal numbers. They are both Black and white slave traders, "uncivilized" Black cannibals, "civilized" but scheming white Protestants, Black Protestant converts bent on rape, and, most corrupt of all, white colonial officers exploiting Africans for political power and material gain. Ledóchowska casts these white colonial officials as metaphorical rapists in her play *Prinzessin von Uganda*.[31] Ledóchowska's heroes are also Black and white in equal measure, but the greatest heroes and lead characters are Black and almost always female. Ledóchowska presents these women to her European audience as saints and reinforces these ideas by adopting narrative hallmarks of the traditional hagiography. *Zaïda*, in particular, leans so heavily on the classic tales of saints that it appears as a modern version of a medieval mystery play, functioning as a dramatized catechism for Christian behaviour.

The Hagiographic Tradition of Mission Narratives

Foreign missions, where Christian fervour met Indigenous resistance, were a prime arena for the emergence of hagiographic narratives, the popularity of which spans centuries. Mission literature of the most mundane varieties is sprinkled with inspirational death narratives. Many have generic titles, such as "Ein erbaulicher Tod" (An uplifting death) or "Ein schöner Tod" (A beautiful death). The most common plot involves a European man who departs from home to declare God's word in hostile lands and meets a martyr's fate.[32] Such narratives reinforced established ideas about European cultural and racial superiority. Alternatively, the inspirational deaths of saintly non-European native converts, though less common, could do the opposite.

A proportionally small number of hagiographic narratives in mission literature describe deaths of African converts and attribute to them the postmortem intercessory potential of saints. For example, one missionary in Africa reported the death of a Black Christian girl as follows:

> Nach einer Nacht der quälendsten Schmerzen, starb die kindliche Dulderin wie eine kleine Heilige ... dessen tief erbaulicher Tod uns so gewaltigen Eindruck gemacht ... Im Himmel wird uns dieses reine Seelchen gewiß allen eine mächtige Fürsprecherin sein.[33]

> (After a night of the most excruciating pains, the childlike silent sufferer died like a little saint ... whose deeply edifying death made such a tremendous impression on us ... In heaven this pure little soul will certainly be a mighty advocate for all of us.)

In describing this death, the writer stacks the superlatives one after another. The girl's torturous suffering, her quiet unperturbed endurance, the profound effect on those present, and the authoritative pronouncement of her role in heaven leave no room for the reader to doubt.

It seems evident, in spite of the conservatism of religious institutions, that the colonial encounter itself could challenge beliefs about the spiritual potential of other races. As Allan Greer notes:

> Given the well-documented tendencies of colonialist writing, not to mention the fundamental presumptuousness of the missionary enterprise, it is hardly surprising to find these texts objectifying natives. More remarkable is the contrary tendency. Hesitantly at first, the Catholic chroniclers ... began to recognize some native Christians as complete spiritual subjects and even contemplate the prospect of genuine cross-cultural holiness.[34]

The re-evaluation of other races as complete subjects with the potential for exemplary spiritual achievement was more likely to occur by way of an actual encounter, where proximity and interaction with the Other contest facile categorizations and expose cultural hypocrisy.

Tom and Zaïda within a Gendered Hagiographic Tradition

Though their stories are fiction, Stowe and Ledóchowska created for their audiences a virtual encounter with exemplary African saints, Black heroes conjured from the pages of an American novel or summoned into three dimensions on the European stage. For Uncle Tom, the path to holiness is simple and one that is more typical of women who tend to become saints by virtue of quiet (private) abnegation and deep contemplation.[35] He is depicted as one bound to home, hearth, and family and who spends every spare moment contemplating the Bible. Following the New Testament admonition to love one's enemy, Tom poses no threat to his white masters, hoping, instead, to win them for Christ. At the moment of death, as in all classic tales of Christian martyrs, Tom appears as one transfigured.[36]

Given that fiction allows for all possible narrative paths, we may ask why Stowe would craft Uncle Tom as a martyr of the more "feminine" variety. The answer seems simple enough. The 1850 census reports over three million Black slaves living in the United States. The prospect of freeing them raised concerns about social unrest and violence. Stowe needed to reassure her audience that such concerns were unfounded. As such, neither Tom, nor any of the Black characters in her novel, could appear as particularly threatening. The Black slave hero of Stowe's American novel had to be a pacifist or risk undermining the anti-slavery agenda.

Forty years later, at the height of the "scramble for Africa," Europe constituted an entirely different context for the emergence of the Black slave heroine in Ledóchowska's anti-slavery drama. The Black population in Europe is so small as to be virtually non-existent. But, with eyes on their fledgling colonies in Africa, Germany and the rest of Europe were concerned about maintaining control over Black populations. Furthermore, though slavery had been abolished in the United States, German-speaking visitors had almost nothing positive to report about race relations there.[37] As Heike Paul points out, "descriptions of the American South ... implicitly connect to developments in the African colony."[38] In this context, Uncle Tom only seems good-natured and docile *because* he is enslaved. Paul concludes that "in this ideological climate the continuation or even 'revival' of forms of human bondage and forced labor could easily be defended and legitimized."[39]

Ledóchowska's new Black slave martyr acknowledges European fears of racial unrest and simultaneously offers an alternative to slavery. However, unlike Uncle Tom, whose character remains uniformly faithful, giving rise to the stereotype of a submissive and good-natured Black man, Zaïda is not a docile Black character conveniently crafted to dispel white fears of racial unrest. Instead, Zaïda is a complicated and modern woman, caught between her cultural sense of duty and her desire to have a meaningful impact on the world around her. She is a multidimensional individual marked by her hopes, fears, and inner conflict. She is ambitious, proud, intractable, fraught by temptation, and uncertain of her path forward. As such, Zaïda represents a potential threat to European power in Africa, albeit one that, as the youthful Ledóchowska imagines, is ameliorated by her sincere acceptance of Christianity.

Ledóchowska leads her heroine through the entire gamut of trials reserved for the saintliest of Christian martyrs in the hagiographic tradition; however, in a surprising inversion of the traditional gender paradigms, Zaïda pursues a man's path to holiness, departing from hearth and home to enter the public arena and die a martyr's death. While stock ingredients in hagiographic tales vary slightly from tradition to tradition, what follows is a synthesized list of the most common steps on a man's narrative path to sainthood:[40] 1. The protagonist learns the ways of God; 2. The protagonist experiences communion with the divine by way of visions or premonitions; 3. The protagonist rejects the worldly values of luxury, vanity, sex, and power; 4. The protagonist is captured; 5. The protagonist experiences a miraculous escape or intervention; 6. The protagonist willingly chooses death; 7. The protagonist is tortured and proves himself impervious to provocation or pain; 8. The protagonist is killed. Death (at once also a denial of death) is the apex of the saint's life. The narrative marks the martyr's passing with an overt indication of saintliness. This may manifest as physical transfiguration of the protagonist's countenance, or it may be marked by a more mundane but authoritative declaration of holiness. This formulaic narrative structure of hagiographic texts is a function of the genre itself. Writers of sacred biographies focused on demonstrating that the religious hero in question met the classic criteria for sainthood, and they did this by establishing similarity to other canonized saints.[41] It is important to note that the tales of saints may not include all the steps outlined here, nor do they appear in this exact order. However, in Ledóchowska's play, Zaïda does not miss a single one.

Zaïda as a Modern Woman

Zaïda's "masculine" route to holiness is perhaps indicative of Ledóchowska's desire to depict a modern woman, who, like Ledóchowska herself, does not shy away from public engagement and who yearns for more than the domestic confinement allotted by her culture. When Zaïda first appears on stage, she stands apart. Other African girls tease her for having ridiculously high expectations for her life. Unlike the peaceable Uncle Tom, Zaïda is complicated, aspiring, and proud. Already in Act One, she is tempted by the flirtations of the evil African king Kaduna, who offers her the fulfilment of all worldly desires: vanity, luxury, power, and sex. He promises to make Zaïda his wife and queen, if she will join her mother, the sorceress Rasorina, in putting a curse on the mission station, thereby making it vulnerable to attack. She is drawn into a plot that involves deception, sorcery, kidnapping, attempted murder, and slavery. Zaïda's initial behaviour fulfils the audience's cultural expectation that Black Africans pose a tangible and immediate threat to Europeans in the colonies. But these expectations are challenged as Zaïda undergoes a spiritual transformation.

Zaïda embarks on the path to sainthood soon after she infiltrates the mission as a spy and saboteur. There she is tutored (however reluctantly) in the faith. Initially she acts antagonistically towards Christians, but she finds herself attracted to the peaceable ways of believers. As the second step towards sainthood, she communes with the Virgin Mary in her dreams. Her vision awakens a burning passion she describes as so "heiß und innig" (hot and intimate)[42] as to surpass any worldly love, including love for her own mother. This is the first time

Zaïda articulates a tension between her loyalty to her biological family and her new-found religious inclinations.

Zaïda rejects the prospect of marrying Kaduna, thus casting aside all worldly allures and taking the third step towards sainthood. Zaïda's explanation to her disappointed mother asserts that the African girls at the mission have no expectations of royalty, and yet they are "glücklicher, als ich es bin, jemals es sein werde" (happier than I am or ever will be).[43] Zaïda ends this monologue with an outright declaration that she will not participate in any plot that could harm Europeans. This particular scene directly addresses Europe's racial anxiety. Conversion is touted as the ultimate alternative to slavery, mitigating fears of unrest in the colonies.

At this point, Zaïda's path to sainthood intersects with a subset of hagiographic stories chronicling the martyrdom of virgins. Karen Winstead explains that a virgin martyr must surrender more than just worldly aspirations, she must also reject her parents and their social expectations. The virgin martyr resists "parental authority to pursue an alternate destiny."[44] This involves refusing to "consort with men by marrying them or having sexual intercourse."[45] For Zaïda, rejecting her mother for Christianity would also include rejecting her entire cultural upbringing: in essence, her very Blackness. Rasorina, who can imagine nothing worse for her daughter than the prospect of converting to Christianity, puts pressure on Zaïda to change her mind about marrying Kaduna. She insists that Zaïda's refusal to comply would ensure death or slavery for both of them. Because Zaïda loves her mother, she vacillates.

The next two steps on the path to holiness involve Zaïda's capture and the miraculous intervention that allows her to escape. Zaïda has already spurned Kaduna before she realizes he never intended to marry her. Before she can escape, she is bound and sold to slave traders. After praying to the Virgin, Zaïda is miraculously rescued and returns to the mission station, now besieged by Kaduna and his slave-trading allies. The colonial troops are coming to the rescue but may not arrive in time. The slave traders demand that Zaïda be handed over to be killed as a warning to other rebellious slaves.

Zaïda as Martyr and Role Model

An important aspect of a hagiographic martyr narrative is that the saint must die willingly. Unlike Uncle Tom, who has death thrust upon him, Zaïda makes her choice freely. In order to delay the attack on the mission station, she sneaks out and surrenders to the astonished slave traders. The evildoers put her in chains and tie her to the stake.

Zaïda's torture and death, the final two steps on the path to sainthood, are not portrayed on stage, but rather described by a native convert who is watching from atop the walls surrounding the station:

> In Ketten haben sie Zaïda geworfen – schnell wird ein hoher Holzstoß aufgerichtet – unter wildem Hohngeschrei wird das Mädchen hingezerrt – jetzt zünden sie den Holzstoß an – die Flammen belecken schon des Opfers Füße ... Zaïdas Kleider hat das Feuer ergriffen – noch steht sie aufrecht – wie verklärt blickt sie gen Himmel – jetzt schlagen die Flammen über ihr Haupt – sie sinkt um – es ist um sie geschehen![46]

> (They have thrown Zaïda in chains – a high pile of wood is being quickly raised – the girl is dragged among wild shouts of scorn – now they are lighting the pile of wood – the flames are already licking the victim's feet ... Zaïda's clothes have caught fire – she is still standing upright – as though transfigured, she looks towards heaven – now the flames are breaking over her head – she is falling over – she is done for!)

These words are punctuated by gasps of horror from the mission inhabitants and by her mother's screams. The description of Zaïda's death emphasizes the relevant aspects of the hagiographic narrative. She is impervious to both provocation and pain. She offers no resistance. She does not cry out. Instead, she remains standing, looking towards heaven.

In Zaïda's death scene, Ledóchowska presents her as a Christ figure and bridge to salvation. She is described as one "transfigured."[47] The significance of this word would not have been lost on Ledóchowska's Catholic audience. Thomas Aquinas considered the transfiguration to be Christ's greatest miracle.[48] Christians understood the transfiguration as a merging of the temporal and the eternal, Christ himself forming a bridge between heaven and earth and thus revealing the glorious perfection of the afterlife.[49] Before his crucifixion and death, Jesus appeared transfigured on a mountaintop. St. Matthew writes that his face "did shine as the sun and his raiment was white as the light."[50] Even before she collapses, Zaïda's transfigured appearance indicates her unity with the divine and her saintly role in the afterlife. Zaïda literally shines. Just as Christ's raiment burned with light, Zaïda's clothing burns with fire. She becomes a veritable pillar of light that hastens the European troops onward to the rescue. They are too late to save Zaïda, but her death ensures the salvation of the mission and its inhabitants.

In the final scene, Zaïda is declared a saint or saviour no fewer than five times. The leader of the colonial troops explains that Zaïda's pyre inspired their march. The missionary replies that Zaïda was a literal guiding light: "Wie gnädig nahm der Herr ihr Opfer auf! Sie wollt' uns retten – und wird zur Fackel, die unsern Rettern leuchtet!" (How graciously the Lord received her sacrifice! She wanted to save us – and became the torch that lit the way for our rescuers!)[51] He declares that she is now a saint in heaven: "Um eine Heilige ist der Himmel reicher!" (Heaven has become one saint richer!)[52] Finally, he names Zaïda "euer Anwalt vor Gottes Thron" (your intercessor before God's throne), emphasizing her role as a spiritual (not just physical) saviour.[53] Thus concludes a whole series of authoritative declarations of holiness, each attesting that a Black African slave can be a saint of the highest order.

Zaïda defies cultural stereotypes for both race and gender. She is not just a rational moral subject. She is not just clever or brave. She is not just a woman defying social expectations and willfully pursuing a path in the public sphere. Zaïda is a Black character fully worthy of Christian emulation, living up to the highest (Catholic) standards of sacrifice and holiness. In this way, Ledóchowska dispels the fears of her audience. Any threat to Europeans perceived in the Blackness of Zaïda's skin is fully ameliorated by a religious devotion that is equal to the greatest of Christian heroes.

Qualifications and Limitations of Ledóchowska's Egalitarian Perspective

However, Ledóchowska's rather egalitarian view of the potential of Black peoples must be qualified. Even though Ledóchowska constructs her Black heroine as an exemplary and complete spiritual subject, as a whole, the play constitutes a convenient colonial fantasy that rejects Black culture and institutions.[54] Esaïe Djomo's analysis of Ledóchowska's *Zaïda* focuses on the representation of Kaduna as a symbol for native leadership that is entirely reprehensible. As Djomo notes, "with this concentration of negative character traits, Ledóchowska presents the ruler's loss of power as self-inflicted."[55] Ledóchowska's drama delegitimizes native African leadership from the start and practically insists that European colonial forces intervene.

The Catholic missions, on the other hand, are constructed as entirely benevolent, a veritable bulwark against the evils of slavery and other European vices. Unlike other colonial fantasies, where the battles are waged over the possession of land and natural resources, Ledóchowska imagines a battle over the possession of the Africans themselves. Kaduna wants to enslave them. The missionaries want to convert them. One Catholic mission strategy depicted in the play is the practice of taking in African children to raise in Christian villages. Ledóchowska imagines African parents recognizing the value of such a transaction and readily unburdening themselves of "superfluous children."[56] This depiction of Africans casually casting aside their children reinforces racist notions that Africans do not feel as deeply for their children, nor do African parents have anything of value to offer them. While the audience may feel some sympathy for Zaïda's grieving mother, the narrative logic of Ledóchowska's play demands that she, as the prime conveyor of Black culture, convert or die. Distraught over Zaïda's death, Rasorina kills herself. For the Catholic missions, the Black mother must be supplanted by a white Christian "mother" (represented by Catholic missionaries) who will raise Africa's children to accept Europe's "superior" codes of conduct and faith values, thus obliterating their cultural Blackness.[57] Indeed, Christian missionaries of all denominations during the colonial era seemed to accept the idea that Africa's original religions possessed nothing of spiritual value, a position endorsed by the 1910 World Missionary Conference in Edinburgh.[58]

As the final element in Ledóchowska's colonial mission fantasy, the European colonial forces are depicted as partners in the anti-slavery effort and fully aligned with the Christian missionary agenda. Ledóchowska's colonial troops come when summoned and share in the vision of Zaïda as saint and saviour. The idea that colonial forces and Christian missionaries would work hand in hand to bring "civilization" and Christianity to Africa is, perhaps, Ledóchowska's most naive projection. The works of a mature Ledóchowska depict a more nuanced understanding of European intervention in Africa, including some biting critiques. Ledochowka's 1905 lecture, *Ein Hilfswerk für Afrika*, contains a particularly caustic rebuke of colonial actions in Africa. In response to the assertion that one would do better to leave Black Africans alone, Ledóchowska distinguishes between political and religious influence:

Ja, da muß man eben unterscheiden, *wer* die Neger in Ruhe lassen soll. Wenn gewisse Herren Europäer nach Afrika ziehen, nur um dort die Neger zu knechten, ihnen das Beispiel der Sittenlosigkeit zu geben, als die Herren des Landes sich einzusetzen und den armen Negern die "Wohltaten" der Steuern aufzubürden, dann wären die Neger freilich besser in Ruhe gelassen.

(Here we must discern *who* should leave the Black Africans in peace. When certain Europeans move to Africa only to subjugate the Black inhabitants there, to give them an example of depravity, to install themselves as the lords of the land, and to impose on the poor Africans the "benefits" of taxes, then the Africans would certainly be better off if left in peace.)[59]

As is evident in this statement made sixteen years after the publication of *Zaïda*, Ledóchowska's views of colonial politics change significantly as she comes to recognize the physical, moral, and economic threats posed by European rule in Africa.

Missionizing Her European Audience

In 1889, as she first set out to fight slavery, Ledóchowska may have been young and inexperienced regarding colonial oppression, but she did not shy away from criticizing her European audience for their sins of complacency. In the final scene of the play, the priest does something surprising. The stage instructions indicate that he should take a few steps forward and speak directly to the European audience. He addresses them as the inhabitants of "*this* dark part of the world" and refers to them as "slaves" who need to be liberated:

> Und auch ihr, dieses dunkeln [*sic*] Erdtheils Bewohner, die ihr ach! noch in Sclavenketten schmachtet! Preist sie mit uns! Der Erlösung Stunde – nimmer ist sie fern! denn auch für euch ist Zaïda gestorben! Sie selbst ist nun euer Anwalt vor Gottes Thron. Ihr Andenken aber, es wirbt euch auf Erden Freunde und Befreier, so dass Europa aufsteht wie ein Mann zum heil'gen Kampfe für Religion und Menschenrecht!

> (And you *also*, you inhabitants of *this* dark part of the world, who, alas, still languish in slave chains! Praise her with us! The hour of redemption – it is never far away! Because Zaïda died *for you too*! She herself is now your advocate before God's throne. Her memory will solicit for you friends and liberators on earth, such that Europe will stand up like a man and engage in the holy battle for religion and human rights!)[60]

Europe, as Ledóchowska sees it, is also enslaved and in need of redemption. Liberation, she asserts, will come by way of remembering the Black slaves of Africa (both literal and figurative), thus linking the spiritual fates of Europe and Africa. She calls upon Europeans to stand up, shake off their own chains, and become Christian soldiers for human rights, suggesting that failure to do so puts their eternal souls in peril.

The idea that Europeans are also "slaves" on a "dark continent" strikes us as a bold metaphor. It places Black Africans on equal footing with Ledóchowska's white audience and suggests that Europe is no better off in terms of spiritual enlightenment. In the final words of the play, Africa and Europe, Black and white, bond and free are all conflated into one group that is languishing in chains and in need of redemption. However surprising, this idea was not a great stretch of the European cultural imagination of Ledóchowska's day. At the peak of European enthusiasm for missionary work abroad, some Christian organizations turned their attention away from the "äußere Mission" (outer mission) overseas to focus on the "innere Mission" (inner Mission) on the home front with the goal of (re)converting the unbelievers of Europe.[61] Metaphors used to discuss the missions abroad were also used to discuss missionizing efforts at home, such that Europe was seen in some missionary circles as another "dark continent" inhabited by "uncivilized heathens."

Ledóchowska fully embraced the idea that Europeans were in danger of losing the faith and becoming "Neu-Heiden" (new heathens)[62] and yet, she was different from contemporary inner-mission advocates who targeted the inner-city and rural poor. Ledóchowska focused her missionizing efforts and social criticism on members of the European middle and upper class, those with adequate means and time to attend the theatre. In some of her later plays, Ledóchowska skewered wealthy Europeans for their greed, vanity, and lack of empathy.[63] She saw the world in which slavery was politically and socially sanctioned (or ignored) as a world that was fundamentally sick. Europe's spiritual maladies were colonial vices: luxury, vanity, and power. Significantly, it is these very vices that first tempt Zaïda into participating in the exploitation of her people.

The solution to these maladies, however, is not embodied in the passivity of a good-natured and unprotesting Christian martyr like Uncle Tom. Instead Ledóchowska puts forward her own fictional saint, one strong enough to subvert gender norms and challenge racial prejudice. Her choice of genre, though conservative, lends itself surprisingly well to narratives of social disruption. Speaking of the hagiographic tradition, Allan Greer notes, "the stories of saintly lives deserve examination in their own right as sites where notions of gender difference and racial hierarchy were enunciated, qualified, challenged, and inverted."[64] Thus the hagiographic form can be an effective platform for promoting social change and recruiting like-minded and forward-thinking believers. Late nineteenth-century Europe, as Ledóchowska saw it, needed bold heroines.

Zaïda's more masculine path to sainthood is an especially important aspect of the heroic role model Ledóchowska envisioned. She called upon European women to abandon their social and political passivity, to defy cultural and parental expectations, and to lead in the pursuit of human rights for Africa. While men certainly played a significant role in the Christian missions, the fundraising organizations in Europe were primarily in the hands of women.[65] Ledóchowska ultimately led an international army of women following the call to arms against slavery. In fact, Ledóchowska believed that fighting slavery would be the key to saving Europe's own soul. In 1892, Ledóchowska quoted Bishop Armand Josef von Gernoble, saying: "Durch Afrika wird Europa selbst, das kranke Europa, echt christlich und gesund" (Through Africa, Europe itself, sick Europe, will become truly Christian and healthy).[66]

Ledóchowska spent the rest of her life pursuing this end, giving up marriage and the luxury of her aristocratic upbringing to enter the public arena as a writer, publicist, and religious leader. Though Ledóchowska's writings are now obscure, and none achieved the popularity of *Uncle Tom's Cabin*, she has secured her place in history alongside Stowe as a formidable anti-slavery advocate. While she embraced beliefs of Christian religious and cultural superiority that were ultimately destructive to Black cultural identity, Ledóchowska nevertheless envisioned racial equality that presaged a modern understanding. While some of her contemporaries were still debating whether Black peoples had souls, and even sympathetic Black characters in colonial literature faded into the background, Ledóchowska kept her Black heroine front and centre. Ledóchowska imagined Black saints like unto Christ himself, brave African women serving as role models for a European audience, encouraging them to venture boldly into the public sphere and take up the cause of human rights in Africa.

NOTES

1 Harriet Beecher Stowe, *Uncle Tom's Cabin: Authoritative Text, Backgrounds and Contexts, Criticism*, ed. Elizabeth Ammons (New York: W.W. Norton, 1994).
2 Jo-Ann Morgan, *Uncle Tom's Cabin as Visual Culture* (Columbia: University of Missouri Press, 2007), 21–2.
3 Kathryn Kish Sklar, "Chronology," in *Harriet Beecher Stowe: Three Novels* (New York: Library of America, 1982), 1471.
4 Grace Edith Maclean, Uncle Tom's Cabin *in Germany* (New York: D. Appleton and Co., 1910).
5 Harry Birdoff, *The World's Greatest Hit:* Uncle Tom's Cabin (New York: S.F. Vanni, 1947), 179–80.
6 Daniel R. Vollaro, "Lincoln, Stowe, and the 'Little Woman/Great War' Story: The Making, and Breaking, of a Great American Anecdote," *Journal of the Abraham Lincoln Association* 30, no. 1 (Winter 2009): 18–34.
7 Maria Theresa Ledóchowska, *Die Antisklaverei-Bewegung und die St. Petrus Claver-Sodalität* (Salzburg: St. Petrus Claver-Sodalität, 1900), 5. All translations are our own.

8 Maria Theresa Ledóchowska [Alexander Halka, pseud.], *Was geht das uns an? Gedanken und Erwägungen über das Werk der Antisclaverei und die katholische Missionsthätigkeit in Afrika* (Salzburg: Anton Pustet, 1892), 3.
9 See Vera Brantl, "Zwischen Anti-Sklaveri und Bekehrung: Die Missionsideologie der Gräfin Ledóchowska" (master's thesis, Universität Wien, 2010).
10 For more information, see the following biographies: Valeria Bielak, *The Servant of God: Mary Theresa Countess Ledóchowska, Founder of the Sodality of Saint Peter Claver* (Saint Paul, MN: The Sodality of St. Peter Claver, 1940); Mary Theresa Walzer, *Two Open Hands Ready to Give: The Life and Works of Blessed Mary Theresa Ledóchowska* (Saint Paul, MN: Missionary Sisters of St. Peter Claver, 1978); Maria Winowska, *Das Geheimnis der Maria Theresia Ledóchowska: Leben und Werk der seligen "Mutter der Schwarzen"* (Aschaffenburg: Pattloch, 1977).
11 Ledóchowska, *Die Antisklaverei-Bewegung*, 4.
12 See David M. Goldenberg, *The Curse of Ham: Race and Slavery in Early Judaism, Christianity, and Islam* (Princeton: Princeton University Press, 2003).
13 Stowe, *Uncle Tom's Cabin*, 375.
14 Maclean, *Uncle Tom's Cabin in Germany*.
15 Sarah Meer, *Uncle Tom Mania: Slavery, Minstrelsy, and Transatlantic Culture in the 1850s* (Athens: University of Georgia Press, 2005), 1–2.
16 See Stephen Greenblatt, "Cultural Moblity: An Introduction," in *Cultural Mobility: A Manifesto*, ed. Stephen Greenblatt (Cambridge: Cambridge University Press, 2010), 1–23.
17 Heike Paul, "Cultural Mobility between Boston and Berlin: How Germans Have Read and Reread Narratives of American Slavery," in Greenblatt, *Cultural Mobility*, 145.
18 Paul, "Cultural Mobility," 135, 140–5.
19 Karen Sánchez-Eppler, "Bodily Bonds: The Intersecting Rhetorics of Feminism and Abolition," in *The Culture of Sentiment: Race, Gender, and Sentimentality in Nineteenth-Century America*, ed. Shirley Samuels (New York: Oxford University Press, 1992), 102.
20 For discussions of white colonialist heroines, see Gallagher and Daffner in this volume.
21 See Tingey and Muellner in this volume.
22 Paul, "Cultural Mobility," 141.
23 See Jeremy Best, *Heavenly Fatherland: German Missionary Culture and Globalization in the Age of Empire* (Toronto: University of Toronto Press, 2021); Irving Hexham, "Violating Missionary Culture: The Tyranny of Theory and the Ethics of Historical Research," in *Mission und Gewalt: der Umgang christlicher Missionen mit Gewalt und die Ausbreitung des Christentums in Afrika und Asien in der Zeit von 1792 bis 1918/19*, ed. Ulrich van der Heyden and Jürgen Becher (Stuttgart: Steiner, 2000), 193–206.

24 Sophie Schröder, *In fernen Welten: Briefe einer deutschen Missionarsfrau in die Heimat*, n.d.
25 See Cindy Patey Brewer, "Christian Love and Other Weapons: The Domestic Heroine of the Multiracial Colonial Mission 'Family' as an Antiwar Icon in Hedwig Irle's Mission Memoirs," in *Women Writing War: From German Colonialism through World War I*, ed. Katharina von Hammerstein, Barbara Kosta, and Julie Shoults (Berlin: De Gruyter, 2018), 57–78.
26 Frieda Pfinzner, *Heidenkinder in Jesu Licht* (Frankfurt am Main: Orient, 1912), 39.
27 Maria Theresa Ledóchowska [Africanus, pseud.], *Zaïda, das Negermädchen* (Salzburg: Matthias Mittermüller, 1889); Maria Theresa Ledóchowska, *Ein Freiheitlicher am Kongo* (Salzburg: St. Petrus Claver-Sodalität, 1910); Maria Theresa Ledóchowska, *Von Hütte zu Hütte* (Salzburg: St. Petrus Claver-Sodalität, 1912); Maria Theresa Ledóchowska, *Die Prinzessin von Uganda* (Salzburg: St. Petrus Claver-Sodalität, 1915).
28 Ledóchowska describes Muslims as "arabische Bluthunde"(Arabic bloodhounds) in *Was geht das uns an?* (49–50). She calls Jews "unsere ärgsten Feinde" (our worst enemies) in *Die Frau im Dienste der afrikanischen Missionen* (Salzburg: St. Petrus Claver-Sodalität, 1916), 17. In her 1915 play, *Prinzessin von Uganda*, European Protestants are among her worst villains.
29 *Meyers Konversations-Lexikon: eine Encyklopädie des allgemeinen Wissens*, 4th ed. (Vienna: Verlag des Bibliographischen Instituts, 1890), 12:39.
30 Ledóchowska, *Zaïda*, 81.
31 Cindy Brewer, "Fantasies of African Conversion: The Construction of Missionary Colonial Desire in the Dramas of a Catholic Nun, Maria Theresa Ledóchowska (1863–1922)," *German Studies Review* 30, no. 3 (October 2007): 563–5.
32 For example, Hermann Wegener, *Opferleben und Opfertod: Kurzgefaßte Lebensbilder berühmter Missionare und Martyrer der neueren Zeit* (Steyl: Missionsdrückerei in Steyl, 1896).
33 *Das Negerkind* (Salzburg: St. Petrus Claver-Sodalität, 1912), 142.
34 Allan Greer, "Colonial Saints: Gender, Race, and Hagiography in New France," *The William and Mary Quarterly* 57, no. 2 (April 2000): 342.
35 Greer, "Colonial Saints," 347.
36 Stowe, *Uncle Tom's Cabin*, 363.
37 Paul, "Cultural Mobility," 141–5.
38 Paul, "Cultural Mobility," 142.
39 Paul, "Cultural Mobility," 144.
40 See Greer, "Colonial Saints," 326–8, 334–5; Vicki L. Hamblin, *Saints at Play: The Performance Features of French Hagiographic Mystery Plays* (Kalamazoo, MI: Medieval Institute Publications, 2012), 4–5; David L. Weaver-Zercher,

Martyrs Mirror: A Social History (Baltimore: Johns Hopkins University Press, 2016), 267; Karen A. Winstead, *Virgin Martyrs: Legends of Sainthood in Late Medieval England* (Ithaca, NY: Cornell University Press, 1997), 5.

41 Hippolyte Delehaye, *The Legends of the Saints: An Introduction to Hagiography* (New York: Longmans, Green and Co., 1907), 12–27, 68–78; Greer, "Colonial Saints," 325.
42 Ledóchowska, *Zaïda*, 28.
43 Ledóchowska, *Zaïda*, 30.
44 Winstead, *Virgin Martyrs*, 50.
45 Winstead, *Virgin Martyrs*, 51.
46 Ledóchowska, *Zaïda*, 78–9.
47 Ledóchowska, *Zaïda*, 79.
48 Nicholas M. Healy, *Thomas Aquinas: Theologian of the Christian Life* (Burlington, VT: Ashgate, 2003), 100.
49 Dorothy A. Lee, *Transfiguration* (New York: Continuum, 2004), 2.
50 Matthew 17:2 (King James Version). See also Mark 9:2–3 and Luke 9:28–36.
51 Ledóchowska, *Zaïda*, 80.
52 Ledóchowska, *Zaïda*, 80.
53 Ledóchowska, *Zaïda*, 81.
54 See Susanne Zantop, *Colonial Fantasies: Conquest, Family, and Nation in Precolonial Germany, 1770–1870* (Durham, NC: Duke University Press, 1997); Brewer, "Fantasies of African Conversion."
55 Esaïe Djomo, "Konstruktion des afrikanischen Machthabers und Putschsimulation im kolonialen Missionsdrama: am Beispiel von Ledóchowskas *Zaïda*," in *Koloniale und postkoloniale Konstruktionen von Afrika und Menschen afrikanischer Herkunft in der deutschen Alltagskultur*, ed. Marianne Bechhaus-Gerst and Sunna Giesecke (Frankfurt am Main: Peter Lang, 2006), 110.
56 Ledóchowska, *Zaïda*, 12.
57 See Susan Thorne, "Missionary-Imperial Feminism," in *Gendered Missions: Women and Men in Missionary Discourse and Practice*, ed. Mary Taylor Huber and Nancy C. Lutkehaus (Ann Arbor: University of Michigan Press, 1999), 55.
58 Kwame Bediako, "Understanding African Theology in the 20th Century," *Themelios* 20, no. 1 (October 1994): 15.
59 Maria Theresa Ledóchowska, *Ein Hilfswerk für Afrika* (Salzburg: St. Petrus Claver-Sodalität, 1905), 20 (emphasis in original).
60 Ledóchowska, *Zaïda*, 81 (emphasis added).
61 Robert McFarland, "Dark Savages in the Vorstadt: Literature, Colonial Discourse and Germany's Innere Mission" (unpublished manuscript, n.d.). McFarland argues that this discursive overlap between the colonial mission and the European metropolis exhibited itself in art, literature,

and architecture throughout Europe. The racial and cultural "Others" in European imperial discourse were also associated with multiple "dark spaces" in the empire, including the urban poor in the dark substrata of the metropolitan environment.

62 Ledóchowska, *Ein Hilfswerk für Afrika*, 22.
63 For example, see Maria Theresa Ledóchowska, *Baronesse Mizzi* (Salzburg: St. Petrus Claver-Sodalität, 1908).
64 Greer, "Colonial Saints," 324.
65 Thorne, "Missionary-Imperial Feminism," 41.
66 Ledóchowska, *Was geht das uns an?*, 23–4.

9 Rethinking the Periphery: Blackness in Eugenie Marlitt's *Im Schillingshof* (1879)

BETH MUELLNER

The oeuvre of nineteenth-century popular romance novelist E. Marlitt – born Frederike Henriette Christiana Eugenie John (1825–87) – provides an excellent case study in the search for African-descended characters in nineteenth-century German women's writing, particularly due to her reputation as a liberal author. Her romances feature heroines in pursuit of happy endings in the face of myriad social, economic, and moral challenges, stories shaped in part by Eugenie John's own biography: with her father's encouragement and Princess Mathilde of Schwarzbach-Sonderhausen's financial support, she initially pursued a singing career that was cut short due to paralysing stage fright and hearing difficulties. She was employed for another eleven years as the princess's social companion until tight finances terminated the arrangement, whereupon Eugenie John reinvented herself as a novelist at age thirty-eight, using the mental fodder of courtly travel and intrigue to bolster her imagination.[1] She never married, but became successful and wealthy as a writer, built a villa for herself and her extended family, and enjoyed an unprecedented, worldwide readership until her death at age sixty-one.

Widely translated, her romance formula perfectly blends domestic, national, and global narratives that extend far beyond the localized world in and around her native region of Thuringia where she lived and worked. Lynne Tatlock notes that her heroines display "delayed gratification, self-possession, and duty," and her stories foreground "family romance in the German provinces and affective communities, where femininity grounded in sentimental domesticity appears to matter deeply."[2] Set against the backdrop of many of Germany's nineteenth-century nation-building events, Marlitt's serialized stories were regularly published in the liberal family magazine *Die Gartenlaube*.[3] Her work is broadly recognized as a central factor in boosting the magazine's circulation to nearly four hundred thousand readers by 1875 (in comparison with the four thousand copies made of daily newspapers), and subsequently reaching nearly a million readers, or roughly 5 per cent of the total German-speaking population, both within and well beyond Germany's borders.[4] Of Marlitt's eight novels, all written within the final two decades of her life, five feature central non-white or racially mixed characters who might be said to reflect the author's global awareness and racial diversity, as Todd Kontje has argued, especially in comparison to the "growing xenophobia, anti-Semitism, and racism of her more conservative contemporaries."[5] Careful analysis of key figures in Marlitt's works shows them to stand for Enlightenment principles of religious tolerance (her anti-Catholicism notwithstanding), economic and social justice, and generosity of spirit.[6]

Despite the oft-blurred identities of her heroines, Blackness is never a central focus of her narratives. Instead, it hovers on the margins to uphold the heroine's humanity and whiteness as necessary features of the European Enlightenment. One such example is the two liberated African American slaves Deborah and Jack found in her 1879 work *Im Schillingshof* (*In the Schillingscourt*), who accompany their former mistress and the novel's heroine, Mercedes de Valmaseda, from the Southern United States to Germany.[7] The only African-descended Black characters in all of Marlitt's stories, the pair labour alongside Mercedes as she transforms from a Creole mistress into a model of true German womanhood. Once this process is complete, Deborah and Jack simply vanish from the narrative. In this chapter, I will explore the marginalization of Black characters in the novel and examine the way they function to uphold whiteness. With their disappearance and Mercedes's eventual embrace of all things German, I analyse how the depiction of the Black characters shifts from reflecting the idea of the Lost Cause to upholding the project of the Enlightenment in Germany. I establish the interplay of the speech and silence of the Black characters as a way of reinforcing the text's participation in this shift. In my exploration of the final erasure of Deborah and Jack from the story as fundamental to the story's outcome, I will demonstrate the way in which the characters of Colour are assimilated into whiteness.

In Marlitt's version of the Enlightenment, humanity has the capacity to learn and grow beyond its own prejudices and biased thinking and behaviour, but anti-Black racism remains lurking under the surface. Thus, Marlitt's racism differs slightly from that of the US's Lost Cause, which was the belief that the plantation system of the South would yield to a superior civilization of enlightened masters working side by side with contented slaves. Marlitt's novel advances its own variant of the structure: instead of remaining in perpetually inferior and degraded coexistence with whites, Marlitt's Black characters function to uphold the myth of white (male) superiority/humanity and disappear once the goal is achieved.

In what follows, I outline the novel's plot and then I take a closer look at the main female characters of Mercedes and Deborah, following Marlitt's focus on women, and consider how they reflect the Lost Cause, as Tatlock has argued.[8] I briefly consider Germany's role in the history of colonialism via postcolonial thinkers Anne McClintock and Susanne Zantop to differentiate racism's history in the US versus in Germany. I then offer a close analysis of Deborah to show how her character visually and verbally functions to uphold whiteness, with the structure of racism revealed most saliently via her (and the text's) silent complicity.[9] Ultimately, the novel "vanishes" its Black and racially mixed characters into the German landscape at the novel's conclusion (using Raymond Stedman's term in reference to Native Americans), a common fate for characters of Colour, whitewashing and blending them into their dominant surroundings.[10] The perspectives of Black Studies scholars Nell Irvin Painter, Zakiyyah Iman Jackson, and E. Patrick Johnson inform my deeper analysis of the novel's marginal characters and help clarify how they function to uphold whiteness. My understanding of race as a constructed identity category rather than a biologically determined marker is reinforced by this scholarship. Painter's book *The History of White People* presents foundational thinking of German scientific and philosophical positions on race and "universal humanity," positions that are reflected (and critiqued to a degree) in Marlitt's prose. In my attempt to understand how the text frames Black identity, Jackson's post-humanist analysis helps me ponder the behaviour of non-human vs. human animals in the text and to consider how "animalistic" behaviour figures in the hierarchy of being. While acknowledging a narrative construct dependent on racism, I also consider E. Patrick Johnson's study of stereotypical Black literary tropes to imagine Deborah's primary function as children's nurse as a place of potential resistance, particularly in the context of her spoken and unspoken communication.

The main narrative revolves around the fates of two families – the parsimonious, bourgeois Wolfram family and the impoverished, aristocratic von Schillings – who are linked through their connected properties, but also through the brief marriage and subsequent divorce of daughter Theresa Wolfram and Major Lucian, the "adopted" son of the von Schillings. The Wolframs, who are greedy, untrustworthy, and fearful of all that is foreign, live on the side of the property that was once a Benedictine cloister with attached barns, a space described as "urdeutsch,"[11] squat, dark, and labyrinth-like. The von Schillings, who appear enlightened, tolerant, and open-minded, live on the side of the cloister's former inn, an airy Italianate mansion that they continuously renovate and improve, adding a winter garden, fountains, and palm trees. A dense and deep hedge-covered wall separates the properties from each other, although secret passages link them. While the Wolframs remain reclusive, secretive, and inaccessible behind a wall, the von Schillings' gated iron fence that allows passersby to glimpse inside permits some porosity with the outside world.[12]

Theresa Wolfram remains at her family's estate with her son Felix after the divorce, whereas Major Lucian leaves for the New World and becomes a rich cotton plantation owner in South Carolina. He marries a wealthy Spanish Floridian and produces a daughter, Mercedes, who becomes Felix's half-sister. Meanwhile, to save his parents from financial and social ruin, Arnold von Schilling agrees to an ill-fated marriage of convenience to the wealthy but unkind Clementine. When Theresa disowns her son Felix for marrying the flighty dancer Lucile Fournier from Berlin, he too leaves for America, but dies with his father defending the South in the Civil War. The year 1868 finds Mercedes journeying to Germany to bring the widow Lucile back and to unite Felix's two children Paula and José with their grandmother Theresa (her aunt), fulfilling her half-brother's dying wish. This endeavour is challenged by the destructive forces of Theresa's brother, the Wolfram patriarch, and his evil son Veit, as well as by Theresa's own stubbornness. Arnold von Schilling welcomes the American group with open arms, unlike his wife Clementine, who leaves in protest for a monastery in Rome. Whereas greed and corruption lead to the Wolframs' demise, the love between the unhappily married German artist Arnold (who ultimately divorces Clementine) and the independent and strong-willed Mercedes fulfils the romance's requisite happy ending.

My focus is ultimately on how Deborah and Jack function on the margins to urge Mercedes onward and to highlight her humanity, and so I introduce them first. Their marginal position is cemented structurally in our first encounter with them, which comes a third of the way into the story. As ex-slaves who represent all that remains after Mercedes loses her father, brother, and the family's cotton plantation in the Civil War, the pair are often presented together with Mercedes as a unified, almost familial unit, and the trio act with a type of innate loyalty to one another. Mercedes's task in Germany is to deliver her quasi-orphaned niece and nephew, Paula and José, to their grandmother. As the children's primary caregivers, Deborah and Jack surface at each point in the narrative in which the white children also appear, but their appearances are equally determined by Mercedes. As a Spanish-German-American, she is clearly described as racially mixed, and seems to occupy a privileged, liminal in-between space, but she ultimately also "vanishes" into whiteness at the end. In this way, the Black characters function to uphold whiteness throughout the entire story. Their purpose aligns with Toni Morrison's claim that Black characters operate to sustain an "ideological dependence on racialism," and that white characters' freedom, pursuits, struggles are "relished more deeply in a cheek-in-jowl existence with the bound and unfree."[13]

A closer examination of Mercedes and her relationship to Deborah and Jack underscores Morrison's point. Mercedes first enters the von Schilling household as a thirteen-year-old via a miniature portrait of her painted on an ivory plaque, sent from America to Felix to reveal that he has a sister.[14] Mercedes's racial Otherness is highlighted repeatedly with references to her such as "Mädchen aus den Tropen" (girl from the tropics),[15] "spanische Baumwollenprinzessin" (Spanish cotton princess),[16] and "Zigeunerin" (gypsy).[17] Her "strange" complexion is underlined as "ein seltsames Colorit, das an die leuchtende hellste Nüance des Bernsteins erinnerte" (the strange colouring resembled the lightest luminescent shade of amber),[18] her "fremdartige Erscheinung in keiner Linie, keiner Farbennüance an germanischen Ursprung denken ließ" (an exotic appearance that recalled neither in form nor hue its German origins).[19] Tatlock emphasizes that "her black and yellow coloring and her affiliation with black African Americans in any case obfuscate her German heritage, emphasizing instead her status as an intruding outsider."[20]

When Mercedes finally arrives at Schillingscourt in person, Marlitt links her visually to Deborah's and Jack's Blackness via her clothing, in her "strenge Schwarz tiefer Trauer – wie eine Statue der Nacht" (severe black of deep mourning ... like a statue of night).[21] In Marlitt's closer focus on the two female characters of this trio, the skin colour of Mercedes and Deborah is contrasted with the anthropomorphized white stone statues at the entrance: "die Hüterinnen der Flurhalle, die Karyatiden mit ihren strengeschnitteten, weißen Steingesichtern" (guardians of the hall, the caryatides, with their sternly cut white stone faces).[22] The statues seem to gaze at Deborah especially, and are described as being shocked by their first glimpse of an "ebenholzschwarzes, krausköpfiges Menschenwesen," (ebony-black, curly-haired human being),[23] as they proclaim: "Eine N* im Schillingshof!" (a Black woman in the Schillingscourt!).[24] Deborah is reduced to physical features that distinguish her from whites, and is presented as an exotic stereotype who is rendered completely passive, as "[d]ie ab- und zugehenden Leute des

Hauses starrten sie an" (the servants, as they came and went, stared at her).[25] The narrator's choice of grammatical structure suggests that she does not even have control of her own smile: *"ihr spielt* ein gutmütiges Lächeln um den dicken, rothlippigen Mund" (a good-natured *smile played around* her thick, red-lipped mouth; my italics).[26] The description also reduces her to static, stereotypical features.

The close association between Mercedes and her former slaves makes clear that the novel "depends precisely on ideas associated with Confederate Nationalism and the Lost Cause movement that were circulating in America," where the myth of solidarity reflects a tragically missed opportunity for slaves and slaveowners to live in peaceful co-existence.[27] So how do we reconcile Marlitt's supposedly liberal attitudes with this narrative? The reception that Harriet Beecher Stowe's novel *Uncle Tom's Cabin* experienced in Germany, as the most popular anti-slavery text of the time, is an interesting case in point. The novel was widely read throughout Germany by the mid 1850s, and it was reviewed regularly in the pages of *Die Gartenlaube*. However, the impact of Stowe's novel was not entirely positive. By 1852, a "typically American" Black person for the German visitor now is no longer the free Black but the good-humored, docile, and child-like Black slave. The cultural mobility of Stowe's novel in the mid-nineteenth century thus – instead of adding complexity and flexibility to the German perception of African Americans – reduces the popular image of Black people in America to a single, highly generalized and – above all – static stereotype.[28]

The structure of slavery as an institution appealed to the authoritarian-minded German and the stable, paternalistic social order of the Kaiserreich, in which "it is not slavery itself, so the argument runs, which is the problem, but the profit-oriented trading and mistreatment of slaves at the hands of immoral and brutal owners that give slavery a bad name."[29] As liberated slaves who choose to remain with their former mistress, Deborah and Jack present a German alternative to the Lost Cause. The reader is led to believe a former slave might begin a new life in Germany working for more humane masters.

To be sure, the erasure of Black characters in Marlitt's works does not reflect Germany's marginal role in the history of the colonization of Africa and/or in the enslavement of Africans. It does, however, reinforce Germany's influential and racist position within the history of the Enlightenment. In the end, the marginalization of Black characters also tells us more about white Germans than about Black people themselves.[30] The publication in 1879 of *Im Schillingshof* came just prior to Germany's late entrance into the "scramble for Africa," a move marked by Bismarck's proclamation of "imperial protection" over the Bremen merchant Lüderitz's territories in South West Africa in 1884.[31] Susanne Zantop argues that Germany's tardiness to the actual landgrab period of Africa (the map of which was carved up at the Berlin Conference in 1884–5) did not make it a lesser player in the production of fantasies of colonial power.[32] In observing other European colonial powers like Britain from the late sixteenth century onwards, Germany had time to develop an imaginary *Spielraum* for its own colonial fantasy, and most importantly, one where German authors could make their German characters out to be "better" colonists. Thus, the history of the Southern US in *Im Schillingshof* stands in opposition to the European – and German – Enlightenment and is presented in a main confrontation between the novel's German hero, Arnold, and the Spanish-German-American Mercedes over the question of Deborah's and Jack's humanity. Because their argument hinges on his reference to slaves as "Menschen" (human beings), Iman Zakiyyah Jackson's questioning of the concept of "universal humanity" is useful: "[t]he more 'the human' declares itself 'universal,' the more it imposes itself and attempts to crowd out correspondence across the fabric of being and competing conceptions of being."[33] Because the Enlightenment's ultimate goal of achieving humanity implies whiteness (and anti-Blackness), it remains inaccessible to the enslaved and colonized, unless, as Jackson suggests, we shake up the definition of what it means to be human. Thus, Arnold's humanity unsurprisingly represents an enlightened Germany, one in which a light-skinned Other in the guise of Mercedes can pass and adapt (and be adopted). Deborah's and Jack's position within the text, on the other hand, shifts accordingly through a reconsideration of their identities along the human-animal spectrum.

Further deconstructing the notion that Marlitt at least leaned towards enlightened, abolitionist principles, Jackson's perspective proves critical. Building on Saidiya Hartman's study of slavery's reliance on the abjection and criminalization of the enslaved people rather than an outright denial of their humanity, Jackson discusses the "conditions under which black people have been *selectively incorporated* into the liberal humanist project. Blackness has been central to, rather than excluded from, liberal humanism: the degraded black body is an essential index for the calculation of degree of humanity and the measure of human progress."[34] Given the histories and characters included in *Im Schillingshof*, Marlitt seems to have followed the debates around slavery and abolition although she did not critique them, as Tatlock points out.[35] After all, as Morrison reminds us, "slave narratives were a nineteenth-century publication boom."[36] As will become evident, Deborah (and

Jack) serve to propel Mercedes into enlightenment and towards humanity, so that she can stand side by side with the enlightened Arnold.

Marlitt's foray into the liberal humanist project is most telling at the moment when Arnold refers to enslaved Africans/African Americans as *humans*, prompting Mercedes to indignantly blurt out "Menschen?!"[37] as if the concept were new and shocking to her. It is at this approaching midpoint in the narrative when European Enlightenment thinking begins to peel away from the Lost Cause as the more progressive stance. Mercedes is in the midst of condemning Germans' ignorance about the Civil War: "Man tanzt blindlings vor dem Götzen 'Humanität,' den der Norden heuchlerisch aufgestellt hat ... Man läßt die weißen Brüder zermalmen und liebkost die schwarzen Race" (They join in the blind dance before the idol "humanity" which the North hypocritically set up; they [i.e., Northerners] allow their white brothers to be crushed and caress the black race).[38] In suggesting that racial betrayal led to the deaths of her father and half-brother in the Civil War, Mercedes reveals a deep identification with Southern whiteness. Arnold counters that breaking chains is hardly a caress.

Reference to her insensitive comment comes up two more times in relatively quick succession at the novel's exact midpoint. The second time, Marlitt uses the subjunctive voice (distancing Mercedes from the description), a key adverbial phrase, and a rhetorical question to suggest that Mercedes's hardened resolve on slavery is evaporating: "man hätte damals glauben müssen, sie habe auch zu jenen raffinirt [sic] grausamen Plantagenherrscherinnen gehört, die das Fleisch ihrer Sclavinnen [sic] als Stecknadelpolster benutzen sollten, *und doch* – kamen die sanften, gütevollen Laute, mit denen Jack und Deborah immer stets und immer angeredet wurden, wirkliche von den stolzen Lippen?" (at the time she might have been taken for one of those cruel mistresses who were said to use their slaves' skin as pincushions, *and yet*, did the gentle kindly accents in which Jack and Deborah were always addressed really come from those proud lips?; my italics).[39] At the third mention of her "vernichtender Ausspruch über die unglückliche N*-race" (annihilating sentence over the entire Black race),[40] Arnold looks to a heavenly intervention to correct Mercedes's bad upbringing. With Arnold's humanity cemented from the beginning, it is only a matter of time before Mercedes finds her own humanity in his proximity, demonstrated especially through her insistence on nursing Deborah when she falls ill.

Deviation from the Lost Cause narrative slowly continues to unfold throughout the narrative. In the strong association that Marlitt repeatedly draws between Mercedes, Deborah, and Jack, the popular notion that whites in the Southern states physically resemble the Blacks and Native Americans among whom they live, given their stronger exposure to sun, is reflected in *Im Schillingshof*. Along these lines of thinking, by extension, the opposite would also seem possible: association with German whiteness would eventually "humanize"/"civilize" Mercedes away from her racially mixed associations with Blackness. German thinkers had long played a prominent role in perpetuating the myth of Anglo Saxon superiority, as Painter outlines in *The History of White People*.[41] In their effort to maintain power, American leaders refused to see the "African-Indian-European mixing occurring right under their noses in [the] eighteenth century," a blind spot of Western philosophical, especially Enlightenment, critiques of humanism.[42]

In *Becoming Human*, Jackson outlines the "racist Enlightenment thought" of David Hume, Georg Wilhelm Friedrich Hegel, Thomas Jefferson, and Immanuel Kant, who followed the Aristotelian concept of humans as animals as well as studies of the natural and geographical world, adopting the belief that different regions of the world produce either inferior or superior humans.[43] Jackson clarifies the concept of dehumanization that emerges from the Enlightenment as "shorthand" for Blackness. She explains that our conception of "universal humanity, a specific 'genre of the human,' is produced by the constitutive abjection of black humanity" ... and that

> blackness is not so much derived *from* a discourse on nonhuman animals – rather the discourse on "the animal" is formed through enslavement and the colonial encounter encompassing *both human and nonhuman* forms of life. Discourses on nonhuman animal and animalized humans are forged through each other, they reflect and retract each other for the purposes of producing an idealized and teleological conception of "the human."[44]

Jackson's critique of Western Enlightenment encourages a rethinking of how hierarchies of humanity have been constructed and instrumentalized, exemplified in her reframing of the "animalization of blackness."[45] While my analysis is far from Jackson's post-humanist concept of plasticity regarding Black humanity, her ideas encourage me to ponder more deeply "the animal potential of the human" or its reverse.[46] In the case of Deborah, who seldom speaks, and whose physicality is emphasized when she does speak, I consider what we might gain in prioritizing other forms of communication over rational/linguistic expression.

Clementine's pet monkey Minka, for example, seems at first to serve as a foreshadowing of the foreign, exotic, and destructive elements of the American entourage that Clementine describes as a "Menschenkarawane" (human caravan) to come.⁴⁷ In the end, the animal truly only mirrors the decadence, the repressed emotions, and the destructive nature of her own white aristocratic "Herrin" (mistress) Clementine, who will adopt savage antics at the novel's end. Minka ultimately reproaches Clementine's uncouth behaviour altogether by breaking the umbrellas and fans that protect its human owner's skin, thus destroying the artificial superiority of whiteness. Another example that challenges the human-animal hierarchy (in which Black characters are frequently viewed as lesser humans) reflects a kind of inverse paradigm. As Mercedes lets go of her plantation-owner past, surrendering the inhumane logic of slavery, her transformation to enlightened thinking is especially visible to her former slaves, who perceive her in this instance as a caged animal: "die beiden Schwarzen sahen in diesen Tagen ihre Dame [an] ... als entbehre die Herrin der gewohnten Sicherheit, als verliere sie für Momente den starken Willen ... im Ausdruck aber ein eingefangener wilder Edelfalke, der mit seinen Flügeln die Käfigstäbe zerschlagen möchte" (the two Blacks often looked at wonder at their mistress nowadays ... losing at times her characteristic strength of will ... but with an expression like that of a captured wild falcon wishing to shatter the bars of its cage with its wings).⁴⁸ Signifying her idealistic aspirations, it is Arnold who unsurprisingly helps liberate Mercedes, while Deborah and Jack merely observe her imprisonment. Might this be read as a small act of defiance? In a closer look at Deborah, more possibilities to read resistance emerge.

Speech and silence become important factors in the way the Black characters are received by the white characters. Despite frequent depiction as passively occupying the liminal spaces of the household, when Deborah is given the opportunity to express herself, her interventions are crucial. Her reactions are almost always first signalled through body language and only later through linguistic communication, however, negatively stereotyping her behaviour as instinctual, impulsive, and animal-like. Still, upon closer inspection, when she does speak, her words are well-timed and logical, often adding a needed dose of reality. In celebration of little José's return to the Schillingshof by the Wolfram's maid (after his traumatic abduction by the evil Veit Wolfram), for example, Deborah "stieß einen Schrei aus und stürtzte mit grotesken Sprüngen und Armbewegungen auf den Knaben zu" (she produced a scream and rushed towards the boy with grotesque leaps and arm movements),⁴⁹ adding a sober if slightly out of breath comment about her own self-preservation: "Konntest überfahren werden, und Jack und Deborah sind nun schuld, haben nicht aufgepaßt, o!" (Could have been run over, and all Jack's and Deborah's fault, weren't paying attention – oh!).[50] Later, when Paula is almost kidnapped by her own mother Lucile (who intends, irresponsibly, to take the child with her to Berlin), we see first Deborah's "runden Augen wurden weit vor Erstaunen und Bestürzung" (round eyes [that] became wide with amazement and consternation), then a "wilder Schrei sprang empor" (wild scream that sprang up),[51] and finally, her yelling "zu Hülfe Jack! Hülfe, sie wollen das Kind stehlen!" (Help Jack, help, they want to steal the child!),[52] the only sentence she is allowed before Lucile grabs her and tries to stuff a cloth into her mouth. While the ability to speak is an undeniable primary signifier of power, if we push against the insistence on linguistic dominance as primary in rational (human) communication, Deborah's impulsive body language and screams (as much as they reduce her to stereotypically described features of Blackness) do suffice to bring desired results: Paula is rescued.

While a Black character's actions ultimately support white power structures, some potential for resistance in the performance thereof still exists, specifically in Deborah's decisive use and withholding of language. When Deborah is first introduced into the narrative, the "Goldkind" (Paula) whom she cares for is described as almost a part of her body, though her Black skin contrasts sharply with Paula's pale, butterfly arms: "ihr kleine(s) Gesicht unter einer niedersinkenden Fluth goldblonder Haare drückte sich fest an die schwarze, feiste Wange" (her small face tucked under a flood of golden blond hair was pressed close against the full Black cheek).[53] Deborah represents a stereotype, "characterized with a broad grin and a shuffle ... the 'happy-go-lucky' slave content with the status quo."[54] But Deborah's care and protection of the children is not unimportant, even if it ultimately serves to uphold the system of white supremacy, because her role also gives her immediate access to important interior spaces in the house. To boot, Deborah's obliging attitude and behaviour can be seen as performance, as survival strategies that mask other motives and behaviours, such as her decisive use and withholding of language.

Marlitt allows Jack and Deborah to speak "ziemlich gutes Deutsch" (pretty good German).[55] However, as Johnson explains:

> Once the domestic learns the necessary "language" and is a trusted subordinate within her employer's home, her visibility decreases, and thus she is able covertly to insert her own language (e.g., black vernacular) and pursue motives that are not necessarily those of her employer. Like the monkey in the "signifying monkey" tales, the domestic bides her time until she finds an opportunity to dupe her employer.[56]

Deborah's and Jack's duping comes as an (ultimately welcome) disruption to the uptight order of the von Schilling household, where they refuse to participate in the gossip of the white servants. Instead, "[d]en Schwarzen ... schien sofort jegliches Verständnis abzugehen, wenn auf die Verhältnisse ihrer Herrschaft jenseits des Meeres angespielt wurde" (the Blacks ... appeared immediately to lose all comprehension in relation to any allusion to the circumstances of their master from across the ocean).[57] Mercedes herself never speaks to the white servants, but offers only brief nods, for which the German servants despise her. In return for their devotion, Mercedes remains loyal to Deborah and Jack in her own way, refusing to be served by anyone but them, and sharply reprimanding the white German sycophant-servant Robert for intruding on Jack's territory.

Deborah withholds information from Mercedes as well, however, building an important narrative tension that also reflects how racism functions, literally (as part of the novel's structure) and socially (for the readers accepting given racist stereotypes in the text). Deborah does not speak about an important incident to Mercedes, but only because she knows (as does the reader) that her words would be futile. As mentioned earlier, despite the separation of the dwellings, a secret passageway maintained by the corrupt old Wolfram allows him to spy on, swindle, and destroy the von Schillings economically: it is he who steals the old Baron von Schilling's plan about the mine.[58] Adam, the von Schillings' oldest and most trusted servant is wrongly accused of spying for Wolfram and commits suicide as a result. His daughter Hannah, who is still employed by the von Schillings, remains convinced of foul play, but has no evidence. Mysterious sounds, misplaced items, and the servants' penchant for ghost stories, many of which Deborah tells, contribute to the belief that Adam's ghost haunts the Schillingscourt in search of retribution.

Despite her marginalization and minimal access to speech, Deborah's role as the nursemaid with access to important interior spaces compounds the mystery of Adam's ghost, a narrative element that could be said to contain some power. After all, she has information that could help Mercedes and Arnold: aside from little José, whose claim to have seen "the terrible man" is attributed to a feverish dream, Deborah is the only other character to witness the elder Wolfram creeping into the house at night, and yet she says nothing. Like José who hides under the covers, her reaction is to throw her apron over her head "um nicht zu sehen" (so that she might not see).[59] Deborah's potential as an insider with keen observational skills thus remains unknown, though perhaps not only due to her Blackness. In a discussion of Sigmund

Freud's elision of the nurse from his Oedipal theory, McClintock points out that "[t]o admit the power and agency of the nurse is to admit that the power of the paternal authority is invented and hence open to change."[60] Thus, as childish as her reaction may appear, Deborah's action is actually logical: she seems aware that it is her identity that prevents her from serving as credible witness. Through depictions of her as animalistic, through stereotypical descriptions of her features, and through her use of speech mainly to tell ghost stories, the narrative renders her unreliable.[61] Thus, it is obvious that the spectre can only be a figment of her imagination and not the very real criminal of the white patriarch, Wolfram. On the other hand, if Mercedes were to ask her outright, as she does on another occasion to which Deborah responds "*sofort mit Bestimmtheit*" (declared instantly that she was sure; my italics),[62] perhaps Deborah would have told Mercedes what she had seen. We will never know. The knowledge about Wolfram that Deborah withholds dupes Mercedes and is thus an important element of narrative tension, but it also a part of the reader's racist expectation of the novel.

Morrison claims that "the habit of ignoring race is understood to be a graceful, even generous, liberal gesture."[63] Considering Marlitt a liberal author, one who gestures towards tolerance in her narratives, we could be lulled into seeing Deborah and Jack slipping off happily, though silently, into the German sunset. In many ways, the main narrative serves to reflect the dangers of moral corruption in the face of an unwillingness to accept change or difference. The Wolfram family succumbs to its own greed and the von Schillings' success ultimately depends on Arnold's generous Enlightenment spirit and openness to change.

As Mercedes's once-fierce independence begins to wane, her dislike of all things Germanic begins to dissolve, and her rediscovery of family leads to her decision to stay in Germany, suggesting her ability to find purchase and blossom in the fertile soil of the new German nation. Mercedes buys a villa on her own, a house that reminded her "nach Stil und Lage an mein niedergebranntes Geburtshaus daheim, und im Sommer kann ich mich leicht der Täuschung hingeben, als sei ich *nicht* auf deutschem Boden" (the villa reminds me, in its style and situation, of my burned-down birthplace back home, and in summer I can easily persuade myself that I am *not* on German soil),[64] its purchase only possible, however, because of her seemingly endless wealth. Its factual basis as reliant on slave labour remains unacknowledged in the text. In ultimately giving the house to Theresa and the children, with whom Deborah and Jack will remain, Mercedes makes the final transition away from any Lost Cause associations and reaches final absolution. She liberates herself ultimately from her American roots when she decides to marry Arnold and promises to be financially supported only by the income from his art. Even her "pale yellow skin" turns to an "incomparable bloom and freshness in the northern air" (blaßgelbe Haut vom nordischen Hauch zu unvergleichlicher Blüthe und Frische)[65] in the process of her full conversion to a German housewife.

With all of this happening in the main story, one might question why we even consider characters on the margins. But without characters on the margins to urge the heroines onward, the "the center cannot hold."[66] Exploring the margins offers more a precise reminder of the systemic racism that prevails to keep People of Colour marginalized, and white readers may begin to comprehend the instrumentalization of Blackness in the Western ideology of the Enlightenment. This may perhaps nudge white readers and writers to make more room at the centre, or to move more willingly towards the margins. Much like the trope of the "magical negro" that perpetually lingers in Hollywood cinema, it is evident that Deborah and Jack function to highlight Mercedes's humanity.[67] In straying from the Lost Cause of the US, the German variant of the Enlightenment that Marlitt offers, however, is no solution. Given the tone set by eighteenth- and nineteenth-century German racial scientists and the pinnacle of racist German ideology during the Holocaust, an equally challenging path for Black people to become visible within Germany and German literature remains.

NOTES

1 Marlitt began to write around 1863, when her first stories were sent to *Die Gartenlaube* anonymously by her brother-in-law.
2 Lynne Tatlock, "The Afterlife of Nineteenth-Century Popular Fiction and the German Imaginary: The Illustrated Collected Novels of E. Marlitt, W. Heimburg, and E. Werner," in *Publishing Culture and the "Reading Nation": German Book History in the Long Nineteenth Century*, ed. Lynne Tatlock (Rochester, NY: Camden House, 2010), 119.
3 Some of these events include the aftermath of the 1848 Revolution (that led to a quarter of a million Germans emigrating to the United States), the Franco-Prussian wars of the 1870s, German unification of 1871, and the period of German colonialism from 1884 to 1919.
4 *Die Gartenlaube* was published in Leipzig, but reader letters from Königsberg, Freiburg, Kiel, and Munich attest to its local reach. Evidence of collections and readers from Austria, Siberia, Peru, Australia, Brazil, and the United States reveal its international readership and influence outside of Germany. Kirsten Belgum, *Popularizing the Nation: Audience, Representation, and the*

Production of Identity in Die Gartenlaube, *1853–1900* (Lincoln: University of Nebraska Press, 1998), 18.
5 Todd Kontje, "Marlitt's World: Domestic Fiction in an Age of Empire," *The German Quarterly* 77, no. 4 (Autumn 2004): 410, https://www.jstor.org/stable/4488702.
6 Kontje describes Marlitt's work as exhibiting a "moderate liberalism" and as offering a vision of "a new class of socially conscious captains of industry who provide for the needs of their workers in a modern capitalism with a human face" ("Marlitt's World," 410, 412). Lynne Tatlock describes *Im Schillingshof* as a novel that "by no means approves of slavery," but it remains "uninterested in interrogating the inhumane system that generated slavery." Lynne Tatlock, "'Family Likenesses': Marlitt's Texts as American Books," in *German Writing, American Reading: Women and the Import of Fiction, 1866–1917* (Columbus: Ohio State University Press, 2012), 74, 75. Kirsten Belgum explains that Marlitt's heroines "manage to save lives (*Goldelse*), expose sinister authorities, be they Jesuit Priests or aristocrats (*Die zweite Frau* [The Second Wife] 1879), and assist the poor and needy (*Im Hause des Kommerzianrates*) ... they frequently take on the task of convincing a skeptical man that an intelligent, rational, outspoken, active, and determined woman is the best partner for an enlightened and moral man." Kirsten Belgum, "E. Marlitt: Narratives of Virtuous Desire," in *A Companion to German Realism, 1848–1900*, ed. Todd Kontje (Rochester, NY: Boydell and Brewer, 2002), 271. Lauren Nossett sees Marlitt's female protagonists as speaking "out against class prejudice, religious fanaticism, and educational barriers." Lauren Nossett, "Bad Mothers and Good Virgins: Gender, Identity, and Maternity in the Novels of E. Marlitt," *Women in German Yearbook* 31 (2015), 28.
7 Eugenie Marlitt, *Im Schillingshof* (Berlin: Holzinger, 2015); Eugenie Marlitt, *In the Schillingscourt: A Romance*, trans. A.L. Wister (Philadelphia: J.P. Lippincott, 1879).
8 Tatlock views the novel as employing "a vocabulary that echoes revisionist apologetics for the Old South in post-Reconstruction America," and it is my view that the vanishing of the Black characters in the story is key to this vocabulary. Tatlock, "Family Likenesses," 76.
9 The "saintly" or "magical" Black character that acts as a "mentor to a questing white hero, who seems to be disconnected from the community that he adores so much, and who often seems to have an uncanny ability to say and do exactly what needs to be said or done in order to keep the story chugging along in the hero's favor" is not leaving the literary or filmic landscape any time soon, as Matt Zoller Seitz, explains in "The Offensive Movie Cliché That Won't Die," *Salon*, 14 September 2010, http://www.salon.com/2010/09/14/magical_negro_trope/.

10 In *Reichsgräfin Gisela* for example, the "Brazilian" Herr Oliviera is none other the younger brother of Theobald Ehrhardt, Bertold, tanned and "Othered" from living many years in South America before returning to Germany. On "vanishing," see Raymond William Stedman, *Shadows of the Indian: Stereotypes in American Culture* (Norman: University of Oklahoma Press, 1982).
11 Marlitt, *Im Schillingshof*, 127.
12 Like the exotic elements in the Atelier (and Wintergarten that includes palm trees and fountains), the activities in the gardens also draw attention, with the children's loud activity, the dog Pirat, and the "N*-sclaven," passing townspeople slow their step and peek inside the iron gates, the foreignness carefully contained. The image conjures up the colonial commodity of the *Völkerschauen*, those public anthropological-zoological displays of ethnic groups that were just entering their heyday in Europe around 1870. Adding to the scene that "immer wieder fesselte" (always riveted) is the children's mother Lucile, whom spectators cannot quite determine as woman or child.
13 As Morrison claims, "There is still much ill-gotten gain to reap from rationalizing power grabs and clutches with inferiority and the ranking of differences. There is still much national solace in continuing dreams of democratic egalitarianism available by hiding class conflict, rage, and impotence in figurations of race. And there is quite a lot of juice to be extracted from plummy reminiscences of 'individualism' and 'freedom' if the tree upon which such fruit hangs is a black population forced to serve as freedom's polar opposite: individualism is foregrounded (and believed in) when its background is stereotypified, enforced dependency. Freedom (to move, to earn, to learn, to be allied with a powerful centre, to narrate the world) can be relished more deeply in a cheek-by-jowl existence with the bound and unfree, the economically oppressed, the marginalized, the silenced." Toni Morrison, *Playing in the Dark: Whiteness and the Literary Imagination* (New York: Random House, 1993), 64.
14 The ivory of the plaque, the trade of which peaked during Africa's colonial period, magnifies the exoticism of Mercedes's image and Arnold's attraction to her.
15 Marlitt, *Im Schillingshof*, 76; Marlitt, *In the Schillingscourt*, 92.
16 Marlitt, *Im Schillingshof*, 108.
17 Marlitt, *Im Schillingshof*, 133; Marlitt, *In the Schillingscourt*, 160.
18 Marlitt, *Im Schillingshof*, 114.
19 Marlitt, *Im Schillingshof*, 119. I will primarily use my own translations of the text (marked by no quotation marks around the English and no page number) instead of A.L. Wister's official English translation, which inserts quite free (and often problematic) interpretations of the text. One example of such is in the translation of "spanische Baumwollprinzessin"

as "haughty plantation princess," to which I thank editor Lisa Hock for drawing my attention. Where the translation is usefully direct, I use Wister's version. In these instances, the English text will appear with quotation marks around it, followed by a page number referring to the translation.

20 Tatlock, "Family Likenesses," 74.
21 Marlitt, *Im Schillingshof*, 108.
22 Marlitt, *Im Schillingshof*, 108. While "Mercedes" as the heroine is mentioned most often, by name in the German digitized text she appears 141 times; "Deborah," referred to both by her name (forty-one times), the descriptor "die Schwarze" (thirty-one times) or "N*-in" (three times), appears a total of seventy-five times. In the English text (Wister translation), "Deborah" appears thirty-four times, "Negress" is mentioned twelve times.
23 Marlitt, *Im Schillingshof*, 108.
24 Marlitt, *Im Schillingshof*, 108. Wister's translations here are especially troubling: ("ebony face, woolly head"), and ("a negress in the Schillingscourt!"). *In the Schillingscourt* (Philadelphia: J.P. Lippincott, 1879), 130. In replacing Marlitt's word "Menschenwesen" for "head," Wister reinforces a dehumanization of the character of Deborah, bypassing the more complex meanings in the word. "Menschenwesen" is like a doubling of the term "human being," where "Mensch" can mean "human" as well as "human being," and "Wesen" means "being," but also refers to deeper, epistemological qualities of a living being as "essence," "nature," or "creature."
25 Marlitt, *Im Schillingshof*, 108; Marlitt, *In the Schillingscourt*, 130.
26 Marlitt, *Im Schillingshof*, 108.
27 Again, the Lost Cause refers to the idea that racial prejudice and slavery were necessary building blocks for the South's ultimate goals for enlightenment. Tatlock, "Family Likenesses," 76.
28 Heike Paul, "Cultural Mobility between Boston and Berlin: How Germans Have Read and Reread Narratives of American Slavery," in *Cultural Mobility: A Manifesto*, ed. Stephan Greenblatt (Cambridge: Cambridge University Press, 2010), 134.
29 Paul, "Cultural Mobility," 135.
30 In her book *White Rebels in Black*, Priscilla Layne asks what knowledge about Blackness is being conveyed when peripheral Black characters or tropes appear in literature by white Germans, and specifically, "how does this knowledge really convey nothing about black people, but rather something about white Germans?" Priscilla Layne, *White Rebels in Black: German Appropriation of Black Popular Culture* (Ann Arbor: University of Michigan Press, 2018), 6.
31 Susanne Zantop, *Colonial Fantasies: Conquest, Family, and Nation in Precolonial Germany, 1770–1870* (Durham, NC: Duke University Press, 1997), 1.

32 German colonies included Deutsch-Ostafrika/Tanzania-Rwanda-Burundi, 1885–1917; Deutsch-Südwestafrika/Namibia and Wituland/Kenya, 1885–90; Deutsch-Westafrika/Cameroon-Togo, 1884–1914.
33 Zakiyya Iman Jackson, *Becoming Human: Matter and Meaning in an Antiblack World* (New York: New York University Press, 2020), 32.
34 Jackson, *Becoming Human*, 46.
35 See Tatlock's comment above, n8.
36 Morrison, *Playing in the Dark*, 50.
37 Marlitt, *Im Schillingshof*, 134.
38 Marlitt, *Im Schillingshof*, 134; Marlitt, *In the Schillingscourt*, 161.
39 Marlitt, *Im Schillingshof*, 168; Marlitt, *In the Schillingscourt*, 201–2.
40 Marlitt, *Im Schillingshof*, 178.
41 Painter discusses German influences beginning with Tacitus's *Germania*, Johann Winckelmann, Germaine de Staël's *De l'Allemagne*, Johann Blumenbach, Christoph Meiners, Franz Boas (in dissent) among others. Thomas Jefferson, for example, insists on projecting an image of eighteenth-century Virginians as idealized specimens of white Saxon purity, despite the daily reminder of his very own "rainbow" family at Monticello (117). Jefferson had seven children with Sally Hemming, a woman he owned as a slave (110). Nell Irvin Painter, *The History of White People* (New York: W.W. Norton, 2010).
42 Painter, *History of White People*, 117.
43 Jackson, *Becoming Human*, 23.
44 Jackson, *Becoming Human*, 23.
45 Jackson, *Becoming Human*, 4.
46 Jackson, *Becoming Human*, 31. Jackson's concept of plasticity "maintains that black(ened) people are not so much as dehumanized as nonhumans or cast as liminal humans nor are black(ened) people framed as animal-like or machine-like, but are cast as sub, supra, and human *simultaneously* and in a manner that puts being in peril because the operations of simultaneously being everything and nothing for an order – human, animal, machine, for instance – constructs black(ened) humanity as the privation and exorbitance of form. Thus the demand placed on black(ened) being is not that of serialized states nor that of the in-between nor partial states but a statelessness that collapses a distinction between the virtual and the actual, abstract potential and situated possibility, whereby the abstraction of blackness is enfleshed via an ongoing process of wrestling form from matter such that raciality's materialization is that of a dematerializing virtuality." Jackson, *Becoming Human*, 35.
47 Marlitt, *Im Schillingshof*, 100. Troublingly again, Wister's translation here leaves the "human" out of "Menschenkarawane" (human caravan).
48 Marlitt, *Im Schillingshof*, 188.
49 Marlitt, *Im Schillingshof*, 153.
50 Marlitt, *Im Schillingshof*, 153.

51 Marlitt, *Im Schillingshof*, 251.
52 Marlitt, *Im Schillingshof*, 252.
53 Marlitt, *Im Schillingshof*, 108. A similar description of Arnold and Paula appears at the end of the story, signalling that Deborah will be replaced: "Noch trug er das Kind, das die Ärmchen um seinen Nacken geschlugen hatte und sein kleines Gesicht so fest an seine gebräunte Wange schmiegte, daß sich die blonden Locken mit seinem Bart mischten." Marlitt, *Im Schillingshof*, 221.
54 E. Patrick Johnson, "'Nevah Had uh Cross Word': Mammy and the Trope of Black Womanhood," *Appropriating Blackness: Performance and the Politics of Authenticity* (Durham, NC: Duke University Press, 2003), 106.
55 Marlitt, *Im Schillinghof*, 125. Wister translates this notably as "quite intelligible German" (150).
56 Johnson, "'Nevah Had uh Cross Word,'" 109.
57 Marlitt, *Im Schillinghof*, 125.
58 He almost succeeds in destroying the von Schilling family a second time when he steals a valuable silver box from Mercedes's room that contains papers giving Arnold legal custody of the children.
59 Marlitt, *Im Schillingshof*, 167; Marlitt, *In the Schillingscourt*, 200.
60 Anne McClintock, *Imperial Leather: Race, Gender and Sexuality in the Colonial Contest* (New York: Routledge, 1995), 93.
61 Lucile also refers to her penchant for telling ghost stories (Marlitt, *Im Schillingshof*, 112).
62 Marlitt, *Im Schillingshof*, 196; Marlitt, *In the Schillingshof*, 234.
63 Morrison, *Playing in the Dark*, 9–10.
64 Marlitt, *Im Schillingshof*, 292.
65 Marlitt, *Im Schillingshof*, 316.
66 From the poem "The Second Coming" by W.B. Yeats (1919), Poets.org, https://poets.org/poem/second-coming.
67 Seitz, "The Offensive Movie Cliché."

10 White Feminism and the Colonial Gaze: Frieda von Bülow's Diaries from German East Africa

CAROLA DAFFNER

In the midst of the infamous "scramble for Africa" during the nineteenth century, Germany's political and intellectual elite became more and more obsessed with the concept of Africa as both a geographical location waiting to be conquered and an imaginary playground with sheer endless opportunities for adventure, discovery, and experimentation. Especially the latter often inspired writers to construct a fictious Africa that had little in common with actual life in the colonies. Instead, the literary depictions frequently served as a way to critique political institutions, economic systems, and traditional values back home. The writer Frieda von Bülow (1857–1909) became one of the main voices in the public perception of Africa, providing both negative and positive associations in her writings. Indeed, the publication of her travel diary from her first trip to German East Africa (June 1887–January 1888), entitled *Reisescizzen and Tagebuchblätter aus Deutsch-Ostafrika*[1] (Travel sketches and diary pages from German East Africa, 1887), caused a veritable "Africa fever"[2] in the German Empire. Many consider her the "founding mother of German colonial literature," a strong, independent, and successful female writer who inspired contemporary colonialists, feminists, and artists alike.[3]

Reading Bülow's writings in the twenty-first century can be challenging, to put it mildly. It is apparent that Bülow was frustrated with the limited opportunities for women during her time and that she saw life in the colonies as a new chance, a life free from the social conventions and restrictions back home. The *Reisescizzen und Tagebuchblätter* are especially relevant, as Katharina von Hammerstein writes in her introduction to their republication in 2012, since they represent the first (white) female voice coming out of the German East African colonies.[4] Bülow's diary is also the only published book by an unmarried German woman who spent time in German East Africa.[5] The poet Rainer Maria

Rilke, intrigued by the primitivism movement and its focus on tribal Africa and Oceania, found her travels fascinating, the psychoanalyst and writer Lou Andreas-Salomé considered her one of her best friends, and Bülow's close circle consisted of several well-known feminists.

At the same time, the alignment of white German women's desire for relative independence and white men's colonial ambitions – both at the expense of Indigenous populations – were (by most whites) not at all perceived as mutually exclusive. White Europeans' claim to hegemony in the colonies represented for many white German women the access to a position of authority impossible to obtain in the motherland. Despite her passionate fight for feminist ideals, Bülow, too, was a radical nationalist throughout her life who strongly believed in the superiority of the white race in general and of Germans in particular. Bülow is also known for her continuous infatuation with the infamous German explorer and ruthless colonialist Carl Peters (1856–1918). As a result, Bülow's writings are full of racist ideology and Orientalist imagery, yet they leave out any real descriptions of colonial acts of cruelty.

While investigating Victorian women travelers in West Africa, Cheryl McEwan wonders if it is possible to "recover the agency of white women without simultaneously erasing the agency of colonized peoples."[6] In her study of British women in colonial spaces, Sara Mills concludes that colonialism always involves violence, injustice, and the appropriation of land. Any studies on gender and colonialism, as Mills stresses, therefore needed to include women's involvement and their exploitation on the basis of white, heterosexual privilege and class.[7] In accordance with McEwan's and Mills's reflections, my study critically analyses the racial demarcation and oppression produced or reaffirmed by Bülow's journal entries under the guise of feminism and female empowerment. Bülow's entries, as I will show, demonstrate what Peggy Piesche has called white people's inability to recognize their own positioning and implication in power.[8] The *Reisescizzen und Tagebuchblätter* advance the very specific struggles of white feminism against conventional gender constraints in Wilhelmine Germany, but they do so by demeaning both the East African space and its local inhabitants.

The first part of my study will provide a brief summary of Bülow's life, with a special focus on her travels to German East Africa, Zanzibar's complicated history as an ethnically diverse region, and the reception of Bülow's work. Close readings in the second part will trace how and why Bülow positions herself as an expert of the East African space. While describing various locations, Bülow frequently uses literary quotations from and cultural references to the European (and specifically German) canon. Doing so allows Bülow to negotiate a place for women in the male-dominated literary canon, yet the constant references to an allegedly exclusive and superior European culture also establish *and* sustain mental borders between the non-white locals and the white colonialists. The third part will demonstrate that Bülow repeats the same racist strategies in her descriptions of other areas along the East African coast. In order to make a case for white women's rights to colonial land, property, and writing, Bülow carelessly overwrites the identities, cultures, and traditions of Black African women. The feminist act of claiming a space for herself heavily relies on markers of cultural and physical differences between white and non-white groups, an aesthetic domination of geographical landscapes and architecture, and the whitewashing of violence in both.

Background and Reception

Born in 1857 as the first of five children to Hugo Baron von Bülow and Clotilde Baroness von Münchhausen, Frieda von Bülow grew up in Berlin and the then Greek city of Smyrna in the Ottoman Empire. Following a time of severe depression, Bülow found a new community in the Gesellschaft für deutsche Kolonisation (Society of German Colonization), led by Carl Peters, with whom Bülow quickly fell in love. Encouraged by Peters, Bülow co-founded the Frauenverein für Krankenpflege in den Kolonien (German Women's Association for Medical Care in the Colonies), with the intention of establishing medical wards in the German colonies and introducing modern methods of nursing and hygiene to the natives.[9] Most importantly, this mission also allowed her, as a single woman, to travel to Africa. In 1887, Bülow started the long journey to German East Africa (today Tanzania), through the Alps and Italy to Egypt and finally, on 16 June 1887, to the island of Zanzibar off the East African coast. A detailed account of this journey can be found in the first part of her *Reisescizzen and Tagebuchblätter aus Deutsch-Ostafrika*.

In the nineteenth century, the Zanzibar Archipelago was widely known as one of the most important trade centres in the Indian Ocean, famous for its spices and the trading of ivory. For centuries, Zanzibar had attracted traders from all over the globe, but the majority who had come and stayed in the decades leading up to the 1880s were from the Indian subcontinent. By the time of Bülow's arrival, a powerful Arab elite had been dominating the Zanzibarian Empire for almost two hundred years, with the current ruler, Sultan Bargash bin Said, in power since 1870. By then, Zanzibar's territory, which at some point had included all of present-day Kenya and several important trading routes, had significantly shrunk in size. When Bülow arrived in 1887, Zanzibar still controlled a ten-nautical-mile strip along the Swahili coast but, starting in 1884, parts of the mainland had been forced under the "protection" of the Society of German Colonization. Headed by the ruthless Carl Peters, the German colonialists had deceived local chiefs into agreeing to give up their lands in exchange for inexpensive gifts.

In the late nineteenth century, many Western visitors (including Bülow herself) compared the "Orientalist" beauty of Zanzibar (especially Stone Town, the old part of Zanzibar City) to the "atmosphere of The Thousand Nights and a Night."[10] Zanzibar's glory, however, came at a horrible price as its trade economy relied heavily on the enslavement of tens of thousands of Black Africans. Black African slaves were not only forced to work on the spice plantations, but Zanzibar's principal port also became a key location for the Indian Ocean slave trade, with thousands of slaves traded every year and many more dying along the way.[11] European colonial powers did not wait long to present themselves as abolitionists and reformers in the spirit of the Western Enlightenment as a justification for taking over.[12] Starting in 1885, the British and the Germans divided the strip along the coast of the mainland between themselves, with the coastal city Dar es Salaam becoming a main centre (and eventually capital) of German East Africa. The British Empire officially abolished Zanzibar's slave trade (but not slavery) in 1876 and, in 1890, Zanzibar became a British "protectorate."

The second part of the *Reisescizzen und Tagebuchblätter* focuses on Bülow's time in Zanzibar, her trips to the mainland, and her infirmary in Dar es Salaam. The entries provide superficial glimpses into Zanzibar's complicated history as a cosmopolitan trading centre, its extensive and ongoing use of slave labour, and the political tensions between the sultan and the colonial powers in the second half of the 1880s. In addition to being invited to social events by the European elite, Bülow also met Arab aristocrats, "Indier" [sic], usually portrayed as a merchant class she elsewhere compares in a derogatory way to Jews, and Black Africans she describes as infantile slaves and lower-class servants. In April of 1888, Bülow reluctantly returned to Europe, following internal arguments with the leadership of the Frauenverein für Krankenpflege in den Kolonien, which had been informed by a fellow nurse of Bülow's love affair with Carl Peters and, in addition, denied her more freedom for her work in Zanzibar. Back home against her will, Bülow decided to continue her work by writing and publishing about her own experiences in Africa. Even though the publication of her diary entries was dedicated to her friends and companions in East Africa, her main goal, as Elke Frederiksen stresses, was to "inform, educate, and entertain a wider public at home, in imperial Prussia."[13] Following the success of her *Reisescizzen und Tagebuchblätter*, Bülow spent the next three years writing and publishing three Africa novels, several novellas, and other prose before she travelled back to East Africa for a second time in 1893–4.

Just like the unmarried protagonists in Lena Haase's later colonial Namibia novels, Bülow used her stay in the colonies to move and act in ways impossible in the German motherland, and this newfound freedom heavily influenced her narratives.[14] Her fictional German East Africa, for example, often mirrored the existing social hierarchies of the empire and, at the same time, provided insight into how Germany *could be*.[15] Bülow's works tend to describe Imperial Germany as a decadent and soft nation, for which Bülow blamed the German elite, the empire's political system, and its capitalist economy. Scholarship on Bülow has also identified the main themes in her oeuvre as radical nationalism, colonialism, and feminism, all of which are represented by Bülow's fictional colonial "Herr*in[nen]*."[16] Yet none of these topics, as Lora Wildenthal underscores, ended up providing a satisfactory answer to Bülow's general dissatisfaction with the limited range of spaces (marriage, nursing, or teaching) available to white German middle-class and aristocratic women in the late nineteenth century.[17] Indeed, several of Bülow's stories repeat feelings of entrapment and social oppression as they were felt by her white female peers.[18] Bülow's *Reisescizzen and Tagebuchblätter* stand out among Bülow's works due to their non-fictional nature. As the titles "Reisescizzen" and "Tagebuchblätter" suggest, Bülow's initial intention was to provide snapshots of Africa – real, spontaneous, and immediate impressions instead of a polished narrative. In von Hammerstein's 2012 edition, the *Reisescizzen* take up about eleven pages whereas the second part, the *Tagebuchblätter*, comes to about 147 pages. The latter are left in their original diaristic form: separate and sometimes daily entries, which start with the exact location and date and go on to summarize the day's activities at varying lengths. As such, Bülow's *Tagebuchblätter* reflect the traditional repetitive form and function of the travel diary as an archive of travel memories.

It quickly becomes obvious that these entries about Bülow's travels to and temporary life in Zanzibar were never meant to remain private reflections. Apart from Bülow's continuous regurgitation of nationalist ideas, her style is marked by confidence and an unconventional lust for adventure in and around the Tanzanian region. The tone, overall, is humorous and entertaining, providing a rich picture of the daily smells, sights, and sounds. Alongside detailed depictions of Zanzibar's landscape or lighthearted complaints about bugs or a lack of hygiene in the colonies, Bülow's entries frequently include famous literary quotations and intertextual references specifically designed for a German audience, from Shakespeare to Schiller. In the following, I trace how Bülow uses these literary quotations and cultural references in order to establish mental borders between the non-white locals and the white colonialists.

Racism and the Colonial Conquest

In her assumed role as objective observer and expert on East Africa, Bülow uses the space of her diary to construct a specific idea of Zanzibar and its surrounding regions for her German audience. The entries not only negotiate her own spatial constraints back home but are also designed to justify the colonial conquest by looking at the East African landscapes through a colonial lens with distinct references to Europe's alleged cultural superiority. In Bülow's narrative, East Africa and Imperial Europe often appear as opposites yet descriptions of both of those places remain more imaginary than connected with the realities. Again and again, the entries juxtapose African poverty and dirt, "tasteless" buildings, exoticized religious practices, and hypersexualized fantasies of the harem with descriptions of little European enclaves, signifying culture, purity, and strength. In an entry from 19 June 1887, for example, Bülow describes Zanzibar City as follows: "Mitten in Neger-Armseligkeit, indischen von Unsauberkeit strotzenden Kramläden und arabischen Schutthaufen sieht man auf einmal ein Stück England vor sich mit seiner blanken in voll entfalteter Blüte stehender Kultur" (In the midst of N.-poverty, Indian shops teeming with filth and Arab heaps of rubble, you suddenly see before you a piece of England with its gleaming culture bursting into bloom).[19] Bülow not only expresses admiration for the British colonialists who were able to change Arabic buildings into "heitere englische 'cottages'" (cheerful English "cottages")[20] but is also overjoyed when the European colonialists rename the sultan's tower "Weihnachtsbaum" (Christmas tree).[21]

In her description, Bülow superimposes an imaginary Eurocentric, Christian architecture and its (implied here: superior and noble) culture onto the (implied here: inferior) Zanzibarian space. Particularly Bülow's heavy use of noun modifiers semantically marginalizes and excludes the ethnically diverse population in the archive of the diary: Black Africans here are associated with poverty, Indian settlers with filth, and African Arabs with rubble. Especially the compound noun "Neger-Armseligkeit" (N.-poverty) stands out. All Black Africans, as we are made to believe through this visual combination, were equally poor. Bülow's interest in pointing this out, however, is not a charitable one nor in support of the abolitionist cause. In line with Susan Arndt's argument in *Afrika und die deutsche Sprache*, we can instead see that the use of the derogatory ethnic slur "Neger" in a German compound noun has an especially colonial connotation. In the German colonial empire, the term was often used in connection with other nouns as a way to emphasize the alleged lack of culture of Black Africans and to highlight what colonialists argued to be their "natural servant status." The connection of Blackness and poverty started to appear in many German idioms and phrases in the nineteenth century and continued to be used in the twentieth and twenty-first centuries.[22]

In the midst of the East African space, the English appear like a blooming flower, organically beautifying, renewing, and culturally elevating the space while Africans, Indians, and Arabs, as Bülow implies though her discriminatory language, would only destroy it. By tying the Zanzibarian landscape semantically to European culture, Bülow, in turn, mentally removes and separates the non-white locals from the land. Images of "cheerful English cottages" and "Christmas trees" support the colonial narrative of white Christian virtue and privilege, further preparing the audience at home for the appropriation of land and property. In the following weeks, Bülow continues to construct an imaginary East African space in her diary, overwriting any poverty or injustice that she sees with tropes from German Romanticism and images from an Orientalist fairy-tale world, inspired by her love for the stories of *One Thousand and One Nights*.[23] By relying heavily on cultural references to racially demarcate the local population, Bülow's entries confirm the prevalent belief in both German nationalism and nineteenth-century colonial discourse that it was "Europe's task" (and Germany's in particular) to civilize the planet through its superior reason and culture.[24]

On 20 June 1887, for example, Bülow describes a big tournament in Zanzibar in honour of the golden jubilee of Victoria, Queen of England and Empress of India. The entire "beau monde Zanzibars"[25] had come to the festival grounds, as Bülow recounts. Zanzibar's "beau monde" here specifically refers to the colonial elite and not to the locals: representatives from different European governments, including those of Germany, England, France, Italy, Portugal, and Belgium, but also from the USA. In addition to European trading companies and other businesses, missionaries, and royal armies, the audience also includes rich Indian and Persian traders. Bülow classifies the latter two groups as "lower" and "other" through specific descriptions of their outward appearances: while the Persians appear in Bülow's description as sullen and strange, with glasses and tall hats, the Indians are characterized by their immediate company: "in goldleuchtenden Seidenfetzen eingewickelten Weiber und Kinder" (women and children wrapped in shimmering golden silken tatters).[26] In her emphasis on the Indian women and their "shimmering tatters," Bülow once more associates Indians with cheap, tasteless ware (similar to the earlier description of "Indian shops teeming with filth") and here, in addition, with the female non-white body, implying softness and weakness.[27] Again and again, Bülow returns to a lack of strength and what she considers culture in her descriptions of the non-white participants, as contrast to an imagined European superiority.

One of the highlights of the celebration is a race between English sailors and the sultan's soldiers. In her summary of the event, Bülow employs stereotypically racist tropes of the Black Africans as primitive and backward. Whereas the Blacks started running without thinking, like a "Grüppchen flüchtiger Antilopen" (small group of fleeing antelopes),[28] the English, as Bülow emphasizes, kept a moderate pace from the beginning and were able to win this way. In the middle of the description, Bülow inserts a quote from Friedrich Schiller's ballad "Die Kraniche des Ibykus" ("The Cranes of Ibykus," 1797): "Wer kennt [original: zählt] die Völker, zählt [original: nennt] die Namen, die gastlich hier zusammen kamen?!" (Who knows [counts] the nations, who counts [knows] the names, of all who there together came?!).[29] Schiller's famous ballad, a story about the power of poetry, criticizes the social conditions of the time and envisions a society led by the people instead of an absolute ruler. The uniting factor here is not only poetry or art, but also the shared hatred of "[d]en schwarzen Täter" (black culprit), the murderer of the poet Ibycus.

In Bülow's description, the imaginary community consists of a number of different upper-class (and implied: culturally educated) representatives from different Western countries, led by Germany in first place. The African runners are reduced to inferior animals, they are denied their own voice, critical thinking skills, or appreciation of culture. Instead, their alleged inability to plan ahead highlights the ability of the Europeans to do exactly that: the Black bodies of the sultan's soldiers (just as the bodies of the Indian wives) become projection screens for racist prejudices and myths of Black inferiority, justifying Europe's and also, more specifically, Germany's colonial appropriation.

The two diary entries overwrite both Zanzibar and the bodies of the non-white locals, semantically replacing them with references to European architecture (see the image of English cottages), objects (see the comparison to Christmas trees), reason (see the moderate pace of the white runners), culture (see the Schiller quote), and, finally, masculinity (see the image of Indian women wrapped in tatters). The reason for doing so is twofold, as it not only supports Carl Peters's goals of colonial conquest, but also allows Bülow to prepare the German readers back home for her desire to be respected as a writer. The following section will demonstrate that Bülow uses similar strategies of distinguishing between her idea of German culture and her racialized and racist notions of Zanzibarians to make a case for German women's writing.

The White Female Hero

In constructing a German claim to the East African space, Bülow continuously links images of hegemonic masculinity, white supremacy, and European culture to the African land, with Carl Peters representing all three. This version of the German claim to African colonies, however, not only excludes men and women of Colour[30] but also leaves out white women, hereby undermining Bülow's own goals of being a writer and a landowner. Sara Mills confirms a similar contradiction in the writings of colonial women writers in general. In her study on colonial British women writers, Mills stresses the complexity of the role of gender in mapping colonial space and subjectivity: "The adventurer role is thus problematic for colonial British women writers because of its association with national masculine subjectivities, and this sometimes results in fissures within women's writing when elements of this stereotype are included in texts. Occasionally, nineteenth-century women travel writers assumed these narrative positions only to mock them or to subvert them."[31] Indeed, similar moments of subversion also appear in the travel entries, as Bülow, fighting for the rights of German women, rewrites herself as a national male adventure hero.

In the middle of a long entry for 19 August 1887, for example, we find Bülow sitting on the *Barawa*, a steamboat provided by the sultan for Carl Peters's exploratory tour of different ports along the East African coast. In this particular entry, Bülow describes the port of Lindi, a city south of Zanzibar (today in south-eastern Tanzania), but suddenly inserts part of a verse from Theodor Fontane's ballad "Die Brück' am Tay" ("The Bridge by the Tay," 1880):

> Am folgenden Tage gelangten wir in den vielgepriesenen Hafen von Lindi. Die Formen der Küste und der waldigen Berge rings um die tiefeinschneidende Bucht bieten allerdings ein schönes Landschaftsbild. Es ist nur tot, denn "das Gebild von Menschenhand fehlt." Dem Menschen hat es Gott verliehen, der schönen Natur den Stempel seines bewußt strebenden

Geistes aufzudrücken; das drängt sich dem Beschauer dieser ostafrikanischen Landschaften immer wieder auf. Sie tragen Reichtum und blühendes Leben in sich verschlossen und scheinen erwartungsvoll dem Herrn der Erde entgegenzusehen, daß er die edlen Keime aus dem langen Schlaf erwecke und an's Licht ziehe.[32]

(The following day we arrived in the much-lauded port of Lindi. The forms of the coastline and the wooded mountains around the deep-cutting bay offer a beautiful landscape indeed. Only it is dead, because "it lacks formation by human hand." God gave man the power to impress the stamp of his consciously striving spirit on the beautiful nature; that is something that continually imposes itself onto the viewers of these East African landscapes. They carry wealth and flourishing life locked within themselves and seem to eagerly await the Lord of the Earth who will awaken the noble buds from the long sleep and draw them to the light.)

Instead of showing the violence in the colonies, the Lindi region appears here as a beautiful and wild space without buildings, reminiscent of images featured in modern European "primitive" art. Unmistakably written from the point of view of a male colonialist conqueror, Bülow uses Fontane's poem to insert a German claim to the landscape into the text. Evoking images of the fairy tale of Sleeping Beauty, Lindi's unbelievable wealth and fertility remain asleep or even dead since, as implied here, none of the natives were able to see its true potential. The feminized space, as Bülow further stresses, is pregnant with possibility, waiting to receive *her* German lord and his "Gebild von Menschenhand," his active shaping (*Bildung*) of her primitive form.

To a certain extent, Bülow's entries demonstrate a confident appropriation of the established male-dominated German canon as a source of *Bildung*, or self-cultivation. She too, as the frequent references imply, is part of this distinguished knowledge of "the white Christian man" and could access and use it whenever she saw fit.

In his ballad, however, Fontane had been inspired by a horrible disaster in Scotland in 1879, when the recently built Tay Bridge collapsed during a storm, causing the death of about seventy-five people. As it turned out, the "Gebild von Menschenhand," the bridge, previously celebrated for its design, had several flaws and could not cope with high winds. For Fontane, the disaster triggered a larger reflection about the powers of nature and technological hubris in the age of industrialization.[33] In Bülow's travel journal, Fontane's quotation not only appears out of context but also completely devoid of its original message. At first sight, this misinterpretation is rather confusing and should come as a surprise to readers, given Bülow's strong belief in feminist ideals. After all, her misuse of the quote in the context of colonial politics (a rather transparent attempt to connect the African landscape with German "culture") reaffirms the exact traditional gender dichotomy against which Bülow is supposedly fighting: Fontane's quotation is used to show that a passive and uncivilized feminine vessel is in need of an active and civilized masculine force. At the same time, the passage confirms the aforementioned ambivalence in Bülow's writings since her act of misremembering the correct context and meaning of Fontane's quote contradicts the diary's primary function as a stabilizing archive and, instead, points to different modes of remembering. The passage is therefore relevant in that it narrates and interprets Fontane's canonical story about the Tay Bridge differently. Bülow's imaginary appropriation of the East African space holds within itself a realization that the past is not a fixed entity but is continually reread, rewritten, and reconstructed for a newly imagined future.

Bülow continues to undermine the traditional narrative position of the classical male adventure hero again later in the same letter. Reminiscent of what Katharina von Hammerstein has called the "monarch-of-all-I-survey" attitude in Bülow's writings,[34] the scene describes the act of looking and the written recording of *what* is being looked at as an act of objectification, appropriation, and domination. Again, East Africa appears as a feminine, passive vessel but here the space resists its active shaping by a colonialist hand. This time, the sultan's ship arrives at the banks of the Indian Ocean island community of Kilwa Kisiwani. While still on the steamboat, Bülow as well as two other travelers, Baron St. Paul and Dr. Kling, try to sketch the coast from their different positions on the boat. However, the boat keeps moving back and forth in the wind, causing the coast to constantly appear differently:

> Baron St. Paul, Dr. Kling und ich versuchten vom Schiffe aus die Küste, deren waldige Ufer sich rechts und links wie Kulissen voreinander schoben, zu scizzieren; aber da der Wind unser Schiff an der Ankerkette in fortwährender Drehung erhielt, unser Modell sich also beständig verschob, wollte das Zeichnen nicht recht gelingen.[35]

> (From the ship, Baron St. Paul, Dr. King, and I attempted to sketch the coast, whose wooded shores thrust themselves right and left against each other like stage backdrops; but as the wind held our ship in constant rotation at the anchor chain, so our subject constantly shifted, our drawing would not quite succeed.)

The passage combines several ambivalent moments, symbolizing Bülow's own position as one of shifting back and forth between progressive feminism and the restrictions of the traditional nineteenth-century notions of a woman's place. The act of sketching, of course, emphasizes the privileged position of power, assumed expertise in the African space, and "cultural chauvinism" of the Europeans during the colonial period, "when white German researchers traveled to Africa to study 'primitive' peoples."[36] Bülow stresses at the same time that, despite the failed attempts to capture the space, she still had "Achtung […] vor den Talenten meiner verehrten Reisegefährten" (respect for the talents of my esteemed travelling companions),[37] implying that her own sketch was far worse than that of her male companions.

The tension between gender constraints and white women acting as agents in colonies points to the complexity and wide variety of women's roles in the colonies.[38] Just as in the Fontane passage above, Bülow uses the East African space to reflect on her own position in relation to her male companions. Her awareness regarding her inferior status anticipates several observations which Bülow lays out about ten years after the publication of the *Reisescizzen*. In an essay called "Männerurtheil über Frauendichtung" (Men's judgment on women's poetry) published in the German social-democratic weekly *Die Zukunft* (The future) on 7 January 1899, Bülow publicly discusses her realization that contemporary women's writing was almost exclusively reviewed by male reviewers and that texts by female authors were always evaluated based on their similarities to male authors.[39] Women, as Bülow goes on, often accepted this behaviour because for so long men had taken on the roles of teachers and masters in the history of German literature and women had taken on the role of the shy student who merely imitated these male masters.[40] Currently, however, women writers were trying to find their own ways, a specifically feminine form of writing, which often would be met with criticism and harsh judgment from their former male teachers and masters. Bülow closes her essay with the urgent plea to women writers to believe in themselves and to be themselves instead of imitating the work of male authors.

In her journal entry, Bülow anticipates these thoughts by projecting them onto the act of sketching the island of the Kilwa Kisiwani community. The island here functions not only as an aesthetic object but is also turned into a landscape to be surveyed, claimed, and named by *both* white men and white women. After landing on the coast, the three colonial explorers – the two men *and* Bülow – are finally able to metaphorically conquer the space by focusing on a Portuguese ruin on a cliff:

Während wir die malerische Ruine von allen Seiten betrachteten, photographierten und scizzierten, versammelten sich die Dorfbewohner um uns, und ich fand mich plötzlich ganz umringt von den Mädchen des Ortes. Ich hatte eine gelbe Blume abgepflückt. Die jungen Mädchen, die sich ersichtlich bewogen fühlten die Honeurs ihrer Küste zu machen, bedeuteten mir durch Worte und Zeichen, ich möchte die Blume fortwerfen. Dieselbe sei nichts wert, den sie habe keinen Duft. Sie gaben mir dafür einige süßduftende aber stiellose Jasminblüten.[41]

(While we observed, photographed, and sketched the picturesque ruin from all sides, the villagers gathered around us, and I suddenly found myself surrounded by local girls. I had plucked a yellow flower. The young girls who clearly felt moved to do the honours on behalf of their coast signalled to me through words and signs that I might want to throw away the flower. It would be worth nothing, since it had no fragrance. In its place, they gave me some sweet-scented but stemless jasmine blossoms.)

In accordance with the colonial belief in a European cultural conquest, the scene again superimposes a reference to Germany's cultural memory onto the East African land. Bülow's description of the Portuguese ruin strongly alludes to typical settings in the stories of German Romanticism, with the reference to a yellow flower bringing to mind Novalis's famous "blue flower" in his fragment *Heinrich von Ofterdingen* (1800). Just as in *Heinrich von Ofterdingen*, the flower on this East African island appears in connection to a young woman. Unlike in Novalis's story, however, in which the blue flower becomes synonymous with longing and inspiration for the male poet, the young Indigenous women in Bülow's narrative, in a strange twist, tell her to throw away the flower and take theirs instead. Symbolizing Bülow's wish to leave the male-dominated canon behind, the sweet-scented but stemless jasmine blossoms suggest a new, free, and confident feminine form of writing.

As previously mentioned, Bülow's description demonstrates what Peggy Piesche called a tendency of white people to be oblivious to their own implication in power structures.[42] Despite describing what at first appears like a moment of mutual understanding between herself and the local women, Bülow uses both the East African space as well as the Black female bodies to advance the very specific struggles of white feminism against conventional gender constraints in Wilhelmine Germany. In Bülow's entry, the young Black women, just as the Black runners in the earlier entry, appear as peripheral fictional characters without individual features, names, or voices, overwritten by a German, white-centric literary setting. Bülow's description not only reaffirms her ignorance of the local cultures but also exposes, ultimately, her indifference to non-white experiences.

Conclusion

Frieda von Bülow's main goal of being a landowner in Africa inspired her to narratively reinvent herself as a male hero and to place herself in aesthetic positions of colonial power, on par with her male peers. As passionate supporter and defender of women's rights, Bülow presented herself proudly in traditionally masculine roles, as an explorer, surveyor, and expert on the East African space. Just as we see in accounts of other women settlers in South West and East Africa, however, descriptions of the non-white population remain fiercely racist, with Bülow reducing local men and women to ignorant, mute servants or exotic curiosities, devoid of any ethnic distinctions or individual personalities. Relying on markers of superiority and inferiority rooted in biological and cultural racism, Bülow further removes the local population semantically from the East African land by continuously relying on assumptions to set up the racial hierarchy of her text: the assumptions that non-white locals could not regenerate and appreciate the land, that they could not reason and think strategically, and that they could not appreciate high culture. In addition, Bülow's rebellious self-staging as a white hero, landowner, and writer relies heavily on the reduction and appropriation of the Black female body. All encounters, including moments of non-verbal communication with the female members of the Kilwa Kisiwani community, again and again reveal Bülow's ignorance and ultimately her disinterest in the ethnically and culturally diverse East African population. Bülow's confident justifications of her rightful presence as a white woman in both German East Africa and in German literature were truly novel for her time. But her unreflective appropriation of the colonial gaze, enhanced further by the popularity of the *Reisescizzen* in the Wilhelmine Empire, helped support and legitimize the violence, cruelty, and injustice of the colonialist period, from the humiliation, expropriation, and forced labour all the way to the torture and genocide of Black Africans.

NOTES

1 All translations are my own.
2 Monika Czernin, *"Jenes herrliche Gefühl der Freiheit": Frieda von Bülow und die Sehnsucht nach Afrika* (Berlin: List, 2008), 145.

3 Friederike Eigler, "Engendering German Nationalism: Gender and Race in Frieda von Bülow's Colonial Writings," in *The Imperialist Imagination: German Colonialism and Its Legacy*, ed. Sara Friedrichsmeyer, Sara Lennox, and Susanne Zantop (Ann Arbor: University of Michigan Press, 1998), 69.
4 Katharina von Hammerstein, "' … ein segenspendendes Werk zur Ehre der deutschen Nation.' Vorschlag einer Lesart von Frieda von Bülows national-kolonialistischen Aufzeichnungen aus Deutsch-Ostafrika," in Frieda von Bülow, *Reisescizzen und Tagebuchblätter aus Deutsch-Ostafrika*, ed. Katharina von Hammerstein (Berlin: trafo, 2012), 13.
5 Diana Miryong Nattermann, *Pursuing Whiteness in the Colonies: Private Memories from the Congo Freestate and German East Africa (1884–1914)* (Münster: Waxmann, 2018), 153.
6 Cheryl McEwan, *Gender, Geography and Empire: Victorian Women Travellers in West Africa* (London: Ashgate, 2000), 176.
7 Sara Mills, *Gender and Colonial Space* (Manchester: Manchester University Press, 2005), 12.
8 Peggy Piesche and Sara Lennox, "Epilogue. Of Epistemologies and Positionalities: A Conversation, Berlin, October 21, 2014," in *Remapping Black Germany: New Perspectives on Afro-German History, Politics, and Culture*, ed. Sara Lennox (Amherst: University of Massachusetts Press, 2016), 276.
9 See Elke Frederiksen, "Journeys across Continents – Writing across Borders: From Europe to Africa – from Africa to Europe," in *"Wenn sie das Wort Ich gebraucht": Festschrift für Barbara Becker-Cantarino*, ed. John Pustejovsky and Jacqueline Vansant (Amsterdam: Rodopi, 2013), 255–6.
10 See n21 below. For a more detailed account of the history of Zanzibar's empire see William Harold Ingrams classic text *Zanzibar, Its History and Its People* (1931; repr., London: Routledge, 1967). The quotation here is from Ingram's preface in *Zanzibar, Its History, and Its People*, 5.
11 See John Donnelly Fage and William Tordoff, *A History of Africa*, 4th ed. (London: Routledge, 2001), 258.
12 See Peter N. Stearns, *Human Rights in World History* (London: Routledge, 2012), 103–4.
13 Frederiksen, "Journeys across Continents," 257.
14 See Maureen Gallagher's article in this volume on Lena Haase's *Raggys Fahrt nach Südwest* (Raggy's journey to South West, 1910) and *Um Scholle und Leben* (For land and life, 1927) by Lydia Höpker. Both feature unmarried protagonists who travel to Namibia under colonial rule, which, as Gallagher demonstrates, allows them to defy traditional gender roles and opens up completely new narrative possibilities. European colonists, as Russell Berman stresses, often regarded Africa as a playground where they could perform and experiment with different identity and gender structures. See also Russell A. Berman, *Enlightenment or Empire: Colonial*

Discourse in German Culture (Lincoln: University of Nebraska Press, 2007), 172.
15 See Joachim Warmbold, *Germania in Africa: Germany's Colonial Literature* (New York: Peter Lang, 1988), 63.
16 Katharina von Hammerstein, "'Rasse' ist Trumpf und sticht Geschlecht: Konstruktionen kolonialer Männlichkeiten in ausgewählten Werken von Frieda von Bülow," in *Frauenphantasien: der imaginierte Mann im Werk von Film- und Buchautorinnen*, ed. Renate Möhrmann (Stuttgart: Alfred Kröner, 2014), 276.
17 Lora Wildenthal, *German Women for Empire, 1884–1945* (Durham, NC: Duke University Press, 2001), 54.
18 Nicholas Saul, for example, sees in Bülow's prose text "Sie und Er" (She and he, 1899) a radical utopian design of gender equality, inspired by feminist pioneer Sophia Goudstikker. See Nicholas Saul, "' … Das normale Weib gehört der Zukunft': Evolutionism and the New Woman in Leopold von Sacher-Masoch, Frieda von Bülow and Lou Andreas-Salomé," *German Life and Letters* 67, no. 4 (2014): 564.
19 Frieda von Bülow, *Reisescizzen und Tagebuchblätter aus Deutsch-Ostafrika*, ed. Katharina von Hammerstein (Berlin: trafo, 2012), 81. All following quotations from the primary text are from this edition.
20 Bülow, *Reisescizzen und Tagebuchblätter*, 81.
21 Bülow, *Reisescizzen und Tagebuchblätter*, 85.
22 Susan Arndt, *Afrika und die deutsche Sprache: ein kritisches Nachschlagewerk* (Münster: Unrast, 2004), 187.
23 See for example, Bülow's entry from 26 June 1887: "Ich habe als Kind mit Vorliebe die Märchen von tausend und einer Nacht durchblättert, die mein Vater in einer vier Foliobände starken Prachtausgabe mit unzähligen Illustrationen besaß. Jetzt scheint mir diese orientalische Märchenwelt vor meinen Augen lebendig geworden, so oft ich Gelegenheit habe, nachts die Gassen zu durchwandern" (As a child I delighted in leafing through the fairy tales of *The Thousand and One Nights*, which my father owned in a four-volume luxury folio edition with countless illustrations. This oriental fairy-tale world now seems to come alive before my eyes whenever I have the opportunity to wander through the alleyways at night). Bülow, *Reisescizzen und Tagebuchblätter*, 92.
24 Dirk Göttsche, *Remembering Africa: The Rediscovery of Colonialism in Contemporary German Literature* (Rochester, NY: Camden House, 2013), 46.
25 Bülow, *Reisescizzen und Tagebuchblätter*, 97.
26 Bülow, *Reisescizzen und Tagebuchblätter*, 97.
27 Bülow repeats the connection between Zanzibar's Indian population and weakness in a later entry from 26 June 1887 in which she directly compares the features of the local "Indier" [sic] to "Weichlichkeit" (softness). Bülow, *Reisescizzen und Tagebuchblätter*, 94.

28 Bülow, *Reisescizzen und Tagebuchblätter*, 97.
29 Bülow, *Reisescizzen und Tagebuchblätter*, 97.
30 See Priscilla Layne, *White Rebels in Black: German Appropriation of Black Popular Culture* (Ann Arbor: University of Michigan Press, 2018), 20: "If hegemonic masculinity is on the side of reason, then men of color, who for centuries have been considered *irrational*, are automatically not included."
31 Mills, *Gender and Colonial Space*, 60.
32 Bülow, *Reisescizzen und Tagebuchblätter*, 144–5.
33 See Katharina von Hammerstein in Bülow, *Reisescizzen und Tagebuchblätter*, 144n170.
34 A familiar narrative position in colonial travel writing, as introduced by Mary Louise Pratt in *Imperial Eyes: Travel Writing and Transculturation* (London: Routledge, 2008), 201, quoted in Katharina von Hammerstein, "'Imperial Eyes': Visuality, Gaze and Racial Differentiation in Texts and Images around 1900," *Colloquia Germanica* 43, no. 4 (2010): 298.
35 Bülow, *Reisescizzen und Tagebuchblätter*, 135.
36 Layne, *White Rebels in Black*, 7.
37 Bülow, *Reisescizzen und Tagebuchblätter*, 135.
38 See Mills, *Gender and Colonial Space*, 68.
39 Frieda Freiin von Bülow, "'Männerurtheil über Frauendichtung.' Aus: 'Die Zukunft,' Jg. 7, 1898/99, Bd. 26, S. 26–29," in *Literarische Manifeste der Jahrhundertwende, 1890–1910*, ed. Erich Ruprecht and Dieter Bänsch (Stuttgart: J.B. Metzler, 1970), 562.
40 Bülow, "Männerurtheil über Frauendichtung," 563.
41 Bülow, *Reisescizzen und Tagebuchblätter*, 137.
42 Piesche and Lennox, "Epilogue."

11 Single White Female: Independent Women and Colonial Knowledge Production in German Colonial Fiction

MAUREEN O. GALLAGHER

In this essay I examine two colonial novels written by women – *Raggys Fahrt nach Südwest* (Raggy's journey to South West) by Lena Haase (1910) and *Um Scholle und Leben* (For land and life) by Lydia Höpker (1927) – that feature unmarried protagonists who travel to Namibia[1] under German colonial rule and demonstrate the narrative possibilities open to single women in German colonial fiction set in Africa. Both authors write heroines who defy traditional gender norms, enacting white female authority in colonial spaces and going beyond the relatively narrow possibilities envisioned for them by colonial authorities who sought to recruit white women to serve primarily as wives, mothers, and housekeepers in Namibia. These characters benefit from white supremacist hierarchies and participate in the exploitation and subjugation of Indigenous peoples. They assemble knowledge and experiences to aid colonial efforts, thereby producing colonial knowledge. The heroines Raggy Warden and Fräulein Imhoff embody some aspects of what Lora Wildenthal has called the "ideal of the independent woman farmer."[2] Travelling to a colonial space grants white German women a kind of precarious privilege. They are, to a certain extent, freed of the rigid gender roles and expectations of the German metropole while also given status over Indigenous men and women. They are granted – temporarily – an independent, self-sufficient female colonial existence distinct from white men, where they participate in adventure and exploration and become co-producers of colonial knowledge. This privilege is precarious because in the end both novels present narratives of failed or frustrated desire where there is ultimately an inability to reconcile singleness with the biopolitical ideals of German colonialism.

Race, Gender, and Privilege in German Colonialism

As Germany's only settler colony, Namibia captured special attention from colonial officials and the public as efforts were made to Germanize the space, and it consequently became a contested border of "civilization." Much attention was paid in particular to questions of race, gender, and respectability.[3] George Mosse argues that respectability "served to legitimize and define the middle classes as against the lower classes and the aristocracy,"[4] and the control of sexual behaviour lies at the heart of this bourgeois morality, an endeavour that relies on gendered assumptions.[5] Anne McClintock has further shown how ideals of domesticity and "gender dynamics were, from the outset, fundamental to the securing and maintenance of the imperial enterprise."[6] White women, as the bearers of Germanness and the only means to propagate white families in the colonies, came to be seen as central to the project of making German South West Africa *German*, as both Katharina Walgenbach and Lora Wildenthal have shown.[7] As Wildenthal notes, "women's ability to sustain racial purity was the basis for their political participation in colonialism."[8] German colonial organizations sent single white women abroad to marry white male settlers and ensure the growth of white German families in the colonies.

Colonial literature reflects these biopolitical ideals of the centrality of white women and their reproductive capacity to colonial efforts. Ezra Tawil has argued that frontier literature relies "on a set of ideas about kinship – desire, courtship, and the formation of families – that an emergent middle class had embraced as universal. These fictions naturalized race by articulating it to a discourse of gender which had already acquired the power to speak the truth about human identity."[9] German colonial literature set in Namibia can be seen as a similar kind of frontier fiction that both reflects the ascendency of the nuclear family as the ideal model for settler life in the colonies and seeks to regulate desire as legitimate only between married white settlers. Key to both of these functions is the figure of the white German woman. In an essay on Höpker's colonial novels, Jill Suzanne Smith notes this gender division, arguing that it fell to white women, as the complements of white male explorers and conquerors, "to domesticate the wild African landscape, its farms, and its people. As arbiters of domesticity and respectability, these 'white women' proclaimed their moral and racial superiority over the African natives."[10]

White women were therefore the antidote to the perceived problem of white men marrying or entering into sexual relationships with native women. Vron Ware has argued that "gender played a crucial role in organizing ideas of 'race' and 'civilization,' and women were involved in many different ways in the expansion and maintenance of the Empire."[11] Their gendered function of regulating race and civilization in colonial spaces granted white women a particular privilege and offered them a limited way out of the restrictive gender norms of Wilhelmine society. In an essay on German colonial memoirs, Marcia Klotz asks "What Do White Women Want?" and notes that the development of a racial hierarchy had "empowering consequences for women, opening up new avenues for women's political agency and expressions of erotic desire."[12] In her study of the woman figure in British colonial literature, Jenny Sharpe similarly argues that women "negotiate for power within a finite range of gender roles that constitute the cultural norm."[13] Sharpe further argues, "We need a critical model that can accommodate, on the one hand, female power and desire, and, on the other, gender restrictions and sexual subordination."[14] In the German case, the empowerment tentatively granted to white women in colonial spaces was predominantly centred on their traditional gender roles as wives and mothers. A less explored question in scholarship is what this empowerment looked like for single white women, both in their portrayal in fiction and in the lived experiences of settler women as documented in colonial memoir.

This essay thus offers an exploration of how single white women fit into the German colonial imaginary. The two works of fiction under consideration here offer portrayals of female independence in German colonial Africa that mirror non-fiction portrayals in many ways but ultimately present the difficulty of reconciling female independence with the gendered expectations of German colonialism. For the heroines of these two novels, Namibia offers not only freedom but also a new understanding of their roles and responsibilities as white women, and these authors portray colonial Africa as a site both of white female power and desire and of gender restriction and sexual subordination.

These novels largely break with the dominant colonialist discourse of the importance of marriage and child-rearing. German American Hannelore Warden, known by her nickname Raggy, the heroine of Haase's *Raggys Fahrt nach Südwest*, is in some ways an anti-heroine, with the novel showing colonial scepticism.[15] Driven by boredom, Raggy flees her strict patrician relatives in Hamburg to visit friends in Namibia. She freely drinks, smokes, flirts, gambles, shoots weapons, and hunts, paying little mind to what others think of her. Eventually a broken engagement and failed relationship drive Raggy back to Hamburg at the end of the novel, presumably for a life of bourgeois respectability.

Like Raggy, Fräulein Imhoff, the heroine of Höpker's *Um Scholle und Leben* who is never given a first name, values adventure and resolves not to marry because "man noch so viele Abenteuer erleben konnte" (one could have so many adventures) as a single woman that would be impossible for a housewife and mother.[16] She initially travels to Namibia to keep house for two single white men and goes on to lease her own farm after turning down several marriage proposals. She is an entrepreneurial woman who values her independence and only marries in the closing pages of the novel, doing so in a way that shows "her freedom to select her own life partner."[17]

Clara Brockmann: A Case Study in Single Womanhood and Non-fiction Writing in Namibia

Before looking more closely at colonial fiction, I would like to briefly discuss the life and writings of Clara Brockmann as a case study in single white women forging independent lives in Namibia under German colonial rule.[18] Brockmann immigrated to Namibia in 1907 with the intention of becoming a writer, doing secretarial work for the civil service in Windhoek and writing two non-fiction texts about the German colony: *Die deutsche Frau in Südwestafrika: ein Beitrag zur Frauenfrage in unseren Kolonien* (The German woman in South West Africa: a contribution to the woman question in our colonies, 1910) and *Briefe eines deutschen Mädchens aus Südwest* (Letters from a German girl from South West, 1912).[19] Non-fiction writing by German authors in Namibia like Brockmann offers a contrast to the fictional portrayals of single white female heroines discussed in this essay. In reality, Namibia offered a chance for a select few white German women to forge independent lives as single, divorced, or widowed women, like Margarete von Eckenbrecher or Helene von Falkenhausen, who both wrote memoirs about their experiences. Carola Daffner's analysis of Frieda von Bülow's diaries from Tanzania (German East Africa) in this volume shows a similar dynamic at work. Scholars have noted the "narrative exclusion of men" that was common in this woman-centred genre.[20] In contrast, Höpker's and Haase's novels show the limitations of the German colonial imaginary in picturing white women in roles other than that of wife and mother.

In her writing, Brockmann unabashedly claims a place for unmarried women in the German colonies. In *Die deutsche Frau in Südwestafrika* Brockmann makes use of colonialist rhetoric to ground her argument for an expanded role for white women in the colony. She calls work in the colonies a "nationale Pflict" (national duty) and notes that anyone interested in working on the "Kulturaufgaben" (cultural mission) in

Namibia and possessing a "Willen zur Arbeit" (will to work) will find "ein reiches Feld der Tätigkeit" (a rich field of action).[21] In the first half of the work she outlines possible roles for white women in the colonies, from wife of a farmer, missionary, merchant, or civil servant, to teacher, hotel cook, tailor, nurse, and farmhand. These roles stretch across social classes and offer a diverse picture of possibilities for married and single white women in the colonies; Brockmann even portrays a lesbian couple working as farmhands while saving to buy their own farm.[22]

Through her use of the non-fiction form and depiction of the daily life of Germans in the colonies, Brockmann claims female authority and presents white women as important sources of firsthand knowledge of Germany's colonies, with particular expertise in managing a home, understanding Indigenous peoples, and solving problems. The title of her second work – *Briefe eines deutschen Mädchens aus Südwest* – underscores the importance of single women in particular as sources of knowledge. At this time, it was common to use the word "Mädchen" (girl) to refer to any unmarried woman, regardless of age. The broad range of topics she discusses in this work – including geography, agriculture, zoology, Christianity, water management, jobs for women, clothing and fashion, and the diamond fields – shows that Brockmann's deployment of her marital status does not signal naivety or inexperience but instead knowledge and authority. As a white woman she can write about a greater range of topics than a white man, covering both the public and domestic spheres, and as an unmarried woman her range of experiences is much broader than that of a married woman more tied to the home, allowing her to, as she argues in the foreword, capture "das eigentliche, alltägliche Leben" (the real daily life) including the "Sitten und Gewohnheiten" (manners and morals) that she feels are missing from other colonialist texts.[23] Overall, Brockmann offers a portrayal of colonial Namibia as a space where single and married white women can lead relatively free and independent lives and where both groups make an important contribution to the colony. Like Brockmann, Haase and Höpker portray single white women as sources of knowledge and authority in colonial spaces, but neither work is able to offer a convincing image of enduring female independence in colonial spaces.

Claiming Authority and Producing Colonial Knowledge

In line with Brockmann's writing, the authors of *Um Scholle und Leben* and *Raggys Fahrt nach Südwest* construct their heroines as producers of colonial knowledge in Namibia, thereby writing white women a greater role in the management and success of the colonial enterprise than that traditionally granted in German colonial rhetoric. Raggy and Fräulein Imhoff both awaken to the privileges of their status as white women after travelling to Namibia, which offers these young, single women new possibilities to transform and reinvent themselves.[24] In colonial Africa, each of these characters claims a distinctly female authority within the German colonial racial hierarchy and engages in the production and co-creation of white knowledge about the colony, its Indigenous peoples, and settler populations.

In these novels, Africa serves as a site of transformation for white women. Like other contemporary girl heroines,[25] Raggy is described as "wild," "stolz," and "trotzig" (wild, haughty, and defiant) and a "Wildfang" (tomboy), but unlike most girl heroines, her taming seems partial, incomplete, or unsuccessful. Raggy consents to an engagement with German officer Hanns von Reberg only because she imagines she will enjoy a "freies, wildes Farmerleben" (free, wild farmer life) in colonial Namibia.[26] The major change Raggy undergoes is in her attitude towards other colonialist women, from dismissive to appreciative of women and their role in bringing German culture to colonial Namibia. Her journey to Namibia also helps her emerge from a depression following the death of her father, who had been described as the only person capable of taming her,[27] and she finds joy engaging in domestic labour – helping her friend Kläre Hartwig on the Hartwig family farm with milking, making cheese, working in the garden, slaughtering hogs, and making sausage – alongside what she terms her "Abenteuer" (adventures), which generally take the form of solo hunting trips.

Fräulein Imhoff's arrival in colonial Namibia awakens her to a sense of authority as a white woman. Although she has no experience in farm work, she confidently asserts her knowledge and experience in order to impress the native servants: "Eine weiße Missis, die nicht alles kann, hat verlorenes Spiel bei den Eingeborenen" (A white mistress who can't do everything is playing a losing game with the natives).[28] She thus pretends a confidence and authority she does not initially feel in order to maintain her privileged status as a white woman. This sentiment, which gives the first chapter its title, "Eine weiße Missis muss alles können" (A white mistress must be able to do everything),[29] summarizes the racial dynamic in which she finds herself in Namibia. Throughout the course of the novel she grows into this feigned confidence, as she turns down marriage proposals and embraces her entrepreneurial spirit to in turn sell goods to the Herero, make cheese, bake bread, and engage in other ventures to fund her dream of owning her own farm, which she dubs "mein eigenes Reich" (my own empire) before ultimately marrying her neighbour and having a child.[30] By the end of the novel she even positions herself as an expert in the management of Indigenous household help, vocally criticizing British policies and drawing on her authority as a white German woman who manages a household.

Both Raggy and Fräulein Imhoff exhibit a particular kind of white colonial authority that relies on the subjugation of Indigenous peoples. The practice of this authority allows these heroines to become co-producers of white colonial knowledge and participate in the cultural process of colonial rule. Nicholas B. Dirks writes in the foreword to Bernard S. Cohn's *Colonialism and Its Forms of Knowledge*, "colonialism was itself a cultural project of control. Colonial knowledge both enabled conquest and was produced by it; in certain important ways, knowledge was what colonialism was all about."[31] Höpker and Haase, like Brockmann, intentionally write white girls and women into this process of colonial knowledge production. Both novels are peppered with facts, stories, and anecdotes that contribute to a colonial knowledge base that justifies German rule in Namibia. These heroines gain a greater understanding of the German colony, its landscape, resources, and peoples through travel, "adventures," and managing a farm or household. Seemingly, the ability of white women to cross from the public to the domestic sphere and back gives them a unique insight into the colony, its development, and management, and each heroine acquires colonial knowledge in a distinct way.

Raggy, with her self-confident independence, relishes being away from white civilization and surrounded by people she believes are only there to serve her: "Raggy war beinahe ein bisschen verkaffert, sie sehnte sich gar nicht nach einer größeren Gesellschaft weißer Menschen zurück. In Ihrer Einöde, unter den Pferden und Hottentotten, die ihr alle freiwillig dienten, fühlte sie sich unendlich behaglich. Hier war sie unumschränkte Herrin" (Raggy had almost gone native; she no longer wished herself back in the company of white people. In her solitude, among the horses and Hottentots, who all freely served her, she felt endlessly comfortable. Here she was the absolute sovereign).[32] The term "verkaffern" was generally applied to white men who married or entered relationships with Indigenous women; Haase's use of the term seems ironic and absent the sense of racial degeneration otherwise associated with the word.[33] Instead it reinforces Raggy's affinity for the colony as embodying an "ungebundene, beschauliche Leben" (unbound, introspective life) that she finds more appealing than the constraints of metropolitan Germany.[34]

Nonetheless, the use of racializing terms and the depiction of Indigenous servants as animalistic – Raggy's servant Eisib looks at her "mit den Blicken eines treuen Hundes" (with the gaze of a loyal dog) and sleeps at her feet[35] – serves to normalize white rule in Africa. Throughout the novel, Haase repeatedly deploys the discourse of "civilization," a term that "serves in its usage to negatively demarcate other societies from Western societies that are confirmed as the norm. To this day this concept is used to legitimize Western values and above all Western claims to power."[36] Raggy may find "uncivilized" Namibia more appealing, but the language used is still embedded in colonialist rhetoric that helps construct a racial hierarchy dominated by white Europeans like her.

Fräulein Imhoff's contribution to the colonial knowledge base is largely in the domestic sphere. In keeping house for others and later running her own farm, she collects knowledge about racial relations and the management of the Indigenous peoples of Namibia. Höpker's autobiographical novel mirrors non-fiction works like those of Brockmann in its description and evaluations of the Indigenous peoples and their capacity to work and be trained to accept German authority.[37] These descriptions are suffused with white supremacist ideologies that place the Indigenous people of Namibia far below white Germans in the hierarchy:

> Ich versuchte, der Kaffernseele etwas beizukommen, denn anfangs ist man noch so gutgläubig, bei diesen Eingeborenen eine Seele zu suchen; ein ganz aussichtsloses Beginnen, da die Eingeborenen in Südwestafrika auf einer recht niederen Stufe der Gesittung stehen und mit wenigen Ausnahmen weder Dankbarkeit noch Anhänglichkeit lernen. Am höchsten stehen noch die Ovambos.[38]

> (I attempted to get the better of the Kaffir soul – in the beginning one is credulous enough to look for a soul among these natives – a totally futile beginning because the natives of South West Africa remain at a very low level of civilization and, with few exceptions, can learn neither gratitude nor attachment. At the highest level stand the Ovambos.)

This portrayal of Namibians serves to reduce the complexity of Indigenous life in the colony to a hierarchy of who is most of use to Germans. Fräulein Imhoff takes each individual as an accurate representation of their nation and evaluates their worth based on their perceived subservience, loyalty, willingness to work, and usefulness. Creating a hierarchy among the Indigenous peoples of Namibia was an effective strategy of control. According to Arndt and Hornscheidt, "This model corresponds to a typical colonial practice ... of securing power and domination (by a minority) by pitting different African cultures against one another by giving some partial privileges that were denied to others."[39] Höpker's "domestication" of this colonial racial ideology serves as an example of the gendered deployment of colonial knowledge production in colonial novels.

Fräulein Imhoff's domestic role gives her access to native informants, and she uses the information that she learns to further support the colonialist racial hierarchy. Descriptions of native dress and customs are offered in a mocking tone. For example, after Fräulein Imhoff reacts with shock to her servant Kanakawi modifying her teeth according to local custom, telling her, "du bist wohl übergeschnappt" (you've gone mad), Kanakawi's response is repeated in indirect discourse: "Doch stolz erwiderte sie, sie sei Omuherero und dies das Merkmal ihrer Nation" (But she replied haughtily that she is an Omuherero and this is the mark of her nation).[40] The repetition of Kanakawi's words in indirect discourse is an Othering strategy that reinforces Fräulein Imhoff's own status and authority. These anecdotes serve as bits of local colour that reinforce colonial racial hierarchies by presenting Indigenous people as naive, illogical, closer to nature, and childlike, and Germans as more advanced, rational, and able to govern.

By contrast, the types of colonial knowledge Raggy assembles differ. Raggy pays little attention to the native people, with Haase marginalizing their presence, as this passage demonstrates:

> Auf dem Platz herrschte reges Leben. Einige große Planwagen, die berühmten südafrikanischen "Treckwagen," standen umher, dazwischen liefen wild aussehende, braun gebrannte Frachtfahrer, Hottentotten mit ihren malerischen Kopftüchern oder Filzen mit der Straußenfeder, Hereros, etwas mangelhaft bekleidet, Hunde, brüllende Ochsen und Bockies herum. Ein Gewirr von deutschen, englischen und holländischen und hottentottischen Rufen ertönte durcheinander.[41]

> (The square was abuzz with activity. Several large covered wagons, the famous southern African "trek wagons," stood there, around which ran wild-looking, tanned cargo drivers, Hottentots with their picturesque headscarves or felt hats with ostrich feathers, scantily clad Herero, dogs, lowing oxen, and goats. A confused jumble of calls in German, English, Dutch, and Hottentot resounded.)

In this description, the Herero and Nama are described alongside and equivalent to dogs, oxen, and other animals. The value to German colonial effort of the various Indigenous peoples for their ability to work or submit to German authority – otherwise such a prominent part of colonial literature – rarely rates a mention in this novel. However, descriptions of other white inhabitants of Namibia serve to reinforce the

German colonial hierarchy, such as when Haase contrasts a messy, dirty Boer house with the "meticulous order and cleanliness" of the white German Emsch family and their "deutschen Gutshof" (German estate), offering a racialized contrast between white German culture and that of the Boer, the Dutch or Afrikaans speaking descendants of Dutch settlers in southern Africa.[42] Like in Höpker's novel, these contrasting examples reinforce white supremacist hierarchies that present Germans as more civilized and therefore worthy of ruling over the other inhabitants of Namibia.

The relative invisibility of Indigenous people in Haase's novel serves as a contrast to the emphasis on critiquing white settlers for the failure of both white men and white women to conform to the proscribed sexual morality of German colonial rhetoric. For example, Raggy's friend Kläre blames Frau Emsch for the birth of "ein Baby mit blondem Haar" (a blonde-haired baby) to one of the family's Indigenous servants, telling Raggy that Frau Emsch should have been more attentive to her husband's sexual needs: "Warum ist sie immer so kalt und abstoßend gegen ihn?! Da ist's doch kein Wunder, bei diesem gesunden, kräftigen Mann, wenn nachher solche Sachen passieren" (Why is she always so cold and repellent towards him?! With him being such a healthy, strong man, it's no wonder that such things happen).[43] White women, brought to Namibia as a solution to the perceived problem of miscegenation, are expected to be sexually available to and to police the sexual morality of their husbands. Here we see the reproductive politics of German colonialism on display, embodied in the person of a frigid white woman who wants to return to Germany instead of fulfilling her proper role in the colonies by serving as a sexual object for white German men and discouraging or preventing cross-racial sexual relationships.[44]

Single heroine Raggy, who is secretly engaged but reluctant to marry and who speaks mockingly of the idea of colonialism at the outset of the novel, learns to appreciate the role of white women in the German colonial enterprise but remains seemingly unwilling to take on this role herself. During her initial journey, she discusses *Kolonialpolitik* with the white male passengers on the ship and claims she is travelling to Namibia because she is sick of civilization.[45] After spending time there she shows a change of heart, defending white German women against her friend Dahlmann, who derides them for importing German culture wholesale without attempting to adapt to fit local circumstances. He mockingly refers to white German women as "Kulturträgerinnen" (culture-bearers) but Raggy defends this role passionately, noting they have not had it easy and "Jedenfalls bringt die deutsche Frau erst wahres Deutschtum in ein Land" (In any event it is the German woman that finally brings true Germandom to a country).[46] While Raggy's methods of acquiring colonial knowledge and the kinds of information she collects differ from those of Fräulein Imhoff, both heroines convey the unique importance of white women to the civilizing mission of German colonialism.

Violence and Colonial Knowledge

For both heroines, the exercise of authority and acquisition of colonial knowledge is tied not only to power and control, but to violence, demonstrating the centrality of violence to German colonial rule. As David Kenosian notes, "The story of German colonialism in Southwest Africa must be understood within the context of the history of violence as a political praxis."[47] Like the white girl heroines who wield weapons in their own defence during the German-Herero Colonial War,[48] Raggy and Fräulein Imhoff do not hesitate to carry and use guns for hunting and self-defence. While Fräulein Imhoff directly participates in colonial regimes of violence by using corporal punishment against her staff, Raggy must defend herself against rapacious white male settlers who threaten her sexual purity.

Höpker's novel, with its focus on the racial management of the German colony, emphasizes the need for violence as a means of control. Set during the final years of German rule in Namibia, it narrates the colony's military loss during the First World War. Fräulein Imhoff laments British rules forbidding the beating or whipping of Indigenous peoples: "Es war ein Elend mit den Eingeborenen. Sie waren unbotmäßig und faul, aber man konnte nichts dagegen machen. Prügelstrafen waren verboten; die neue Regierung verkündete, dass die Schwarzen gleiches Recht wie die Weißen hätten" (It was a misery with the natives. They were insubordinate and lazy and one couldn't do anything about it. Corporal punishment was forbidden, and the new government proclaimed that Blacks had the same rights as whites).[49] Linguistically, the use of the subjunctive here calls into question the fundamental equality of Black and white people. In spite of the frequent laments about how unmanageable the Indigenous people became once they could no longer be beaten into submission, the novel nonetheless contains several incidents of white settlers hitting or physically punishing people with no repercussions, showing that the Indigenous inhabitants had failed to achieve equal rights and freedom from violence under British rule. Here Höpker draws on the trope of Germans as superior colonizers, which she ties explicitly to regimes of violence: corporal punishment is presented as a necessary management strategy, with the Germans who are willing to use it superior to the British who ostensibly forbid it.

While *Um Scholle und Leben* emphasizes the need to protect white interests by controlling Indigenous people through violence, *Raggys Fahrt nach Südwest* presents white men as more dangerous to Raggy than Namibia's native inhabitants. The title of the novel, which calls to mind Gustav Frenssen's well-known novel about the German colonial wars in Namibia, *Peter Moors Fahrt nach Südwest* (1906), is ironic. Though Raggy fetishizes guns and violence and laments that she arrives in Namibia only after the war, her time there is peaceful. When it finally appears as if Raggy will get her oft-repeated wish of seeing an uprising, expectations are undermined. Upon arriving at a watering hole where she anticipates meeting an armed group of Herero, Raggy instead finds a friendly if wary group of Nama, who, in spite of their "Verbrecherphysiognomien" (criminal physiognomies), share their coffee with her and prove to be "Gemütsmenschen" (good-natured people).[50] Raggy only encounters danger in colonial Namibia at the hands of a white man who tries to assault her. Raggy accepts his invitation for a moonlit horseback ride, and naively misunderstanding the man's intentions, must fight him off and escape by riding into the ocean. This experience is one of the only times in the novel that the otherwise fearless heroine experiences fear: "Sie sah an seinen Augen, dass er zu allem fähig war. Das war Gefahr!" (She saw in his eyes that he was capable of anything. This was danger!).[51] In this Haase undermines reader expectations, as scenes of violent conflict and sexual threats against white women by Black men were common tropes in colonial literature;[52] instead Haase posits that the true dangers for white women in Namibia are the white male settlers.[53]

Höpker's conventional colonial rhetoric, with its call for corporal punishment in the management of the Indigenous workforce, is contrasted with Haase's depiction of dangerous white men. However, in both novels, the logic of colonial violence goes unchallenged. White characters have an ultimate right to exercise violence in defence of white homes and white bodies.

Unhappy Endings, or the Narrative Impossibility of Staying Single in a Colonial Novel

In contrast to Brockmann's portrayal of the possibilities for white women to contribute to German colonialism outside of the married state, Höpker's and Haase's novels both ultimately explore the limits of single womanhood in the colonial imaginary. Both works, with their independent single heroines, challenge many aspects of colonialist rhetoric that valued white women only for their reproductive and sexual potential. Ultimately, however, neither heroine is able to maintain her happy independent life in Namibia.

While Raggy and Fräulein Imhoff both embrace the privilege and authority granted to them as white German women, they are nonetheless limited by gender expectations, particularly in regard to marriage. *Um Scholle und Leben* offers a traditional happy ending in the marriage of Fräulein Imhoff to her friend and neighbour Rolf Witte. Narratively, this is the logical ending to a story set during the end of German colonial rule. The child born to the couple stands as a testament to the continued German presence in Namibia and the potential for a white future there, shown in the novel's closing words, uttered by Fräulein Imhoff to her young son: "Um Dich nur wagte ich die weite Fahrt!" (It was only on your account that I risked the long journey!).[54]

However, in light of the repeated emphasis on the heroine's independence and the number of marriage proposals she declines throughout the novel, this abrupt change of heart at the conclusion of the novel strikes a discordant note, implying that it is ultimately impossible for a single white woman to flourish long term in a colonial space. The engagement is also clouded with violence. After Rolf and Fräulein Imhoff share a passionate kiss, Rolf grabs her by the throat and declares, "Schwör's, dass du meine Frau werden willst, oder ich erwürge dich!" (Swear that you'll be my wife or I'll wring your neck!).[55] Though the scene is played for laughs – a comedic, almost slapstick commentary on Fräulein Imhoff's obstinacy – it nonetheless reinforces the colonial logic of the novel that white women are weaker than and subservient to white men and best suited to be wives and mothers.

Throughout *Raggys Fahrt nach Südwest*, the heroine challenges conventional gender roles, but her inability to conform to gender expectations leads to dysfunctional relationships and her unhappy return to Hamburg in the novel's final chapters. John Noyes has described the novel as a story of how colonialism "fails to reproduce its requisite attitudes in certain individuals," with Raggy serving as a prototypical example of a white woman without the correct colonialist attitude.[56] Her flippant attitude towards colonialism and traditional gender roles plagues her throughout the novel. Raggy's engagement to German military officer Hanns is troubled from the start, with Raggy disinterested in marriage, hoping only that a marriage in "unziviliziertem" (uncivilized) Namibia will offer a more appealing kind of marriage than the "enge, städtische Verhältnisse" (narrow, city circumstances) of metropolitan Germany.[57] After their arrival, Hanns is subjected to a court martial proceeding for his alleged behaviour with Raggy on board the ship. Raggy is frustrated that the freedom she experiences in Namibia is curtailed by gossip, conventional morality, and small-mindedness. She nonetheless maintains her engagement out of an almost masculine sense of honour, even after realizing she doesn't truly love him, until Hanns chooses to break the engagement to further his career.[58]

Haase subverts the tropes of colonial romance when Raggy, released from her unhappy engagement, fails to successfully start a relationship with the man she is actually attracted to, a much older colonial war hero with a notorious reputation, Captain Warnow. Like the case of Nazi colonial heroine Wiete discussed in Julia Gruber's chapter in this volume, Haase ultimately denies her heroine a happy ending. The strong emotions Raggy feels for Warnow do not lead her towards marriage, reproduction, and a happy ending like in Höpker's novel, but instead weaken her physically and mentally. She initially tries to suppress her attraction to Warnow and resolves to return to Germany after a fall from a horse and a resulting life-threatening fever. On the boat, Raggy encounters Warnow, who has also fallen ill and is returning to Europe. After studiously avoiding each other for most of the journey, they finally embrace and kiss during a celebration just past the Canary Islands, but the expected ending to the colonial romance never materializes. When Warnow attempts to manoeuvre Raggy into his cabin, she reacts with "wildem Trotz" (wild defiance) and refuses to submit to him.[59]

Noyes reads this as evidence of Raggy's sexual non-conformity: "Where we thought we would see successful settlers conceiving little colonists, we find two prototypes of fin de siècle sexual malfunction – the brutal woman and the masochistic man."[60] Raggy has expressed fears that she and Warnow are "zu wild und zügellos auf beiden Seiten" (too wild and dissolute on both sides) for happiness in marriage, and she further seems ultimately unable or unwilling to submit to a man, remaining as full of "Trotz" (defiance) as at the beginning of the novel.[61] At the same time, the novel's conclusion finds her prepared to marry her cousin Fred, now the head of the family after her uncle's sudden death, implying there is something about the colonial war hero in particular that makes her unable or unwilling to submit. For Noyes this is her acknowledgment of the "Unmöglichkeit der Geschlechter-Ideologie des Kolonialismus" (impossibility of the gender ideology of colonialism).[62] However, I read it as a nod to the heroine's ultimate *submission* to conventional bourgeois ideals of marriage and sexual morality otherwise at odds with her seemingly libertine behaviour. Throughout the novel Raggy freely and openly flirts and engages in behaviours that are traditionally coded as masculine. She also regularly turns down advances by men, even fleeing on horseback into the ocean to escape unwelcome sexual advances. She admits her life in Africa was "frei und wild" (free and wild) but she was nonetheless "untadelig in ihrer Ehre" (unimpeachable in her honour).[63] She turns from Warnow only when he has manoeuvred her to his open cabin door, refusing to enter in spite of her "rätselhafte Wünsche" (baffling desires) and feelings of "reine, tiefe Liebe" (pure, deep love).[64] What she stubbornly rejects is a sexual liaison outside of marriage, and here again, the novel's critique is not of Raggy for failing to adapt to colonial ideals but of the white men around her.

I read *Raggys Fahrt nach Südwest* as expressing a deep scepticism towards colonial reproductive politics. Haase is critical not of white women like Raggy but of white men who fail to adhere to the colonialist ideal of sexual relationships and reproduction only within their own race and while married. Haase deprives the reader of a conventional ending to a colonial novel, with the heroine able to return to Namibia as the wife of a German officer, to raise children and ensure a German future there. Ultimately, this is not a failure of Raggy to submit to colonialist ideology but another failure of white German men to adhere to the reproductive politics of German colonialism.[65] As different as *Raggys Fahrt nach Südwest* and *Um Scholle and Leben* are, both Haase's sceptical colonial novel and Höpker's pro-colonial novel end with their heroines abandoning their single lives in colonial Africa.

The answer to the question posed by Marcia Klotz, "What do white women want?" is, according to these colonial novels, independence, authority, privilege, adventure, and to be of use to the German colonial project on their own terms. Haase and Höpker construct their single white female heroines as independent and active participants in German colonialism in Africa, equal to but distinct from men. In Namibia they are awakened to the knowledge of their whiteness and the privilege it brings, and they contribute to the formation of a white colonial knowledge base through their observations of the Indigenous people, the management of households, farms, and laborers, and colonial policies. Both craft self-sufficient lives for themselves in German colonial Africa that ultimately prove to be unsustainable. The desire for an independent existence comes into conflict with a colonialist ideology that calls for white women to serve as the symbolic border guards of race, nation, and respectability solely in their roles as wives and mothers.

NOTES

1 Though during colonial rule the country was known as German South West Africa – and is called such in the texts – I choose instead to attempt to break the colonial logic and use contemporary terminology to refer to the country of Namibia and its inhabitants unless I am quoting directly.

2. Lora Wildenthal, "'She Is the Victor': Bourgeois Women, Nationalist Identities and the Ideal of the Independent Woman Farmer in German Southwest Africa," in *Society, Culture, and the State in Germany, 1870–1930*, ed. Geoff Eley (Ann Arbor: University of Michigan Press, 1996), 371–95.
3. For a further discussion of race and respectability politics, see Kira Thurman's work on Black singers such as Josephine Baker and Marian Anderson and their reception in Central Europe: "Blackness and Classical Music in the Age of the Black Horror on the Rhine Campaign," in *Singing Like Germans: Black Musicians in the Land of Bach, Beethoven, and Brahms* (Ithaca, NY: Cornell University Press, 2021), 97–133.
4. George L. Mosse, *Nationalism and Sexuality: Respectability and Abnormal Sexuality in Modern Europe* (New York: Fertig, 1985), 9.
5. For an excellent discussion of how this relates to German girls and nationalism in this period, see Jennifer Askey, *Good Girls, Good Germans: Girls' Education and Emotional Nationalism in Wilhelminian Germany* (Rochester, NY: Camden House, 2013), 12–14.
6. Anne McClintock, *Imperial Leather: Race, Gender, and Sexuality in the Colonial Contest* (London: Routledge, 1995), 7.
7. Katharina Walgenbach, *"Die weiße Frau als Trägerin deutscher Kultur": koloniale Diskurse über Geschlecht, "Rasse" und Klasse im Kaiserreich* (Frankfurt: Campus, 2006); and Lora Wildenthal, *German Women for Empire, 1884–1945* (Durham, NC: Duke University Press, 2001).
8. Wildenthal, *German Women for Empire*, 6.
9. Ezra F. Tawil, "Domestic Frontier Romance, or, How the Sentimental Heroine Became White," *Novel: A Forum on Fiction* 32, no. 1 (Autumn 1998): 101.
10. Jill Suzanne Smith, "A Female Old Shatterhand? Colonial Heroes and Heroines in Lydia Höpker's Tales of Southwest Africa," *Women in German Yearbook* 19 (2003): 142.
11. Vron Ware, *Beyond the Pale: White Women, Racism, and History* (London: Verso, 2015), 34.
12. Marcia Klotz, "Memoirs from a German Colony: What Do White Women Want?" in *Eroticism and Containment: Notes from the Flood Plain*, ed. Carol Siegel and Ann M. Kibbey (New York: New York University Press, 1994), 154–87.
13. Jenny Sharpe, *Allegories of Empire: The Figure of Woman in the Colonial Text* (Minneapolis: University of Minnesota Press, 1993), 10
14. Sharpe, *Allegories*, 12.
15. Lene Haase, *Raggys Fahrt nach Südwest* (Berlin: Egon Fleischel, 1910).
16. Lydia Höpker, *Um Scholle und Leben: Schicksale einer deutschen Farmerin in Südwest-Afrika* (Minden: Köhler, 1927), 62. All translations from German are my own.
17. Smith, "Female Old Shatterhand," 144.

18 For a more extensive discussion of Brockmann, see Wildenthal, "She Is the Victor," and Klotz, "Memoirs."
19 For the biographical information on Clara Brockmann I am indebted to the work of Lora Wildenthal. See "She Is the Victor."
20 Smith, "Female Old Shatterhand," 142. See also Klotz, "Memoirs," and Wildenthal, "She Is the Victor."
21 Clara Brockmann, *Die Deutsche Frau in Südwestafrika: ein Beitrag zur Frauenfrage in unseren Kolonien* (Berlin: Mittler, 1910), 64–5.
22 Brockmann, *Deutsche Frau*, 38–41.
23 Clara Brockmann, *Briefe eines deutschen Mädchens aus Südwest* (Berlin: Mittler, 1912), v.
24 Compare this with Klotz's discussion of colonial memoir and its contribution "to the development of a racial discourse in Wilhelmine culture that allowed women to think of themselves not simply as women, but as *white* women." Klotz, "Memoirs," 154.
25 See my article on colonial novels with girl protagonists: Maureen Gallagher, "Fragile Whiteness: Women in German Colonial Fiction, 1900–1913," *Women in German Yearbook* 32 (2016): 111–37.
26 Haase, *Raggys Fahrt*, 89.
27 Haase, *Raggys Fahrt*, 24.
28 Höpker, *Scholle und Leben*, 5.
29 Höpker, *Scholle und Leben*, 5.
30 Höpker, *Scholle und Leben*, 145.
31 Nicholas B. Dirks, foreword to *Colonialism and its Forms of Knowledge: The British in India*, by Bernard S. Cohn (Princeton, NJ: Princeton University Press, 1996), ix.
32 Haase, *Raggys Fahrt*, 364.
33 Susan Arndt and Antje Hornscheidt, eds., *Afrika und die deutsche Sprache: ein kritisches Nachschlagewerk* (Münster: Unrast, 2018), 92.
34 Haase, *Raggys Fahrt*, 298.
35 Haase, *Raggys Fahrt*, 293.
36 Arndt and Hornscheidt, *Afrika und die deutsche Sprache*, 220–1.
37 See Wildenthal, "She Is the Victor," and Klotz, "Memoirs," 176–7.
38 Höpker, *Scholle und Leben*, 15.
39 Arndt and Hornscheidt, *Afrika und die deutsche Sprache*, 150.
40 Höpker, *Scholle und Leben*, 79.
41 Haase, *Raggys Fahrt*, 220.
42 Haase, *Raggys Fahrt*, 261.
43 Haase, *Raggys Fahrt*, 263.
44 Haase's condemnation of the white wife rather than her husband, and the lack of detail surrounding the nature of the relationship between Herr Emsch and his servant, reflects the general sexual permissiveness granted

to white men in the colonies, as documented by Daniel J. Walther, "Sex, Race and Empire: White Male Sexuality and the 'Other' in Germany's Colonies, 1894–1914," *German Studies Review* 33, no. 1 (February 2010): 45–71. Interracial relationships between white men and Black women were common; rape and assault were frequent and rarely punished, as seen, for example, in the case of Louisa Kamana, wife of the son of Chief Zacharias, who was murdered after refusing the "sexual advances" of a German settler. The settler was initially acquitted and ultimately sentenced to three years in prison after an appeal. Benjamin Madley, "Patterns of Frontier Genocide 1803–1910: The Aboriginal Tasmanians, the Yuki of California, and the Herero of Namibia," *Journal of Genocide Research* 6, no. 2 (2004): 183–4.

45 Haase, *Raggys Fahrt*, 15–20.
46 Haase, *Raggys Fahrt*, 174.
47 David Kenosian, "The Colonial Body Politic: Desire and Violence in the Works of Gustav Frenssen and Hans Grimm," *Monatshefte* 89, no. 2 (Summer 1997): 182. See also Helmut Bley, *South-West Africa under German Rule* (later reprinted as *Namibia under German Rule*), trans. Hugh Ridley (London: Heinemann, 1971).
48 Gallagher, "Fragile Whiteness."
49 Höpker, *Scholle und Leben*, 120.
50 Haase, *Raggys Fahrt*, 294–5.
51 Haase, *Raggys Fahrt*, 200.
52 Gallagher, "Fragile Whiteness"; Krista O'Donnell, "The Colonial Woman Question: Gender, National Identity, and Empire in the German Colonial Society Female Immigration Program" (PhD diss., SUNY Binghamton, 1996).
53 This seems to conform with historical circumstances, as the Herero largely spared German women and children during the colonial wars. See Klotz, "Memoirs," 159.
54 Höpker, *Scholle und Leben*, 219.
55 Höpker, *Scholle und Leben*, 214.
56 John K. Noyes, "Imperialist Man, Civilizing Woman, and the European Male Masochist," in *The Mastery of Submission: Inventions of Masochism* (Ithaca, NY: Cornell University Press, 1997), 124.
57 Haase, *Raggys Fahrt*, 89.
58 Haase, *Raggys Fahrt*, 313–15. Her cousin Freddy asks if she feels "yearning" (*Sehnsucht*) for him and she admits she does not but maintains: "jedenfalls habe ich dem Hanns mein Ehrenwort gegeben … und das breche ich nicht" (In any case I gave Hanns my word of honor … and I'm not breaking that).
59 Haase, *Raggys Fahrt*, 400.

60 Noyes, "Imperialist Man," 123.
61 Haase, *Raggys Fahrt*, 383.
62 John K. Noyes, "Geschlechter, Mobilität und der Kulturtransfer: Lene Haases Roman *Raggys Fahrt nach Südwest*," in *Phantasiereiche: zur Kulturgeschichte des deutschen Kolonialismus*, ed. Birthe Kundrus (Frankfurt: Campus, 2003), 227.
63 Haase, *Raggys Fahrt*, 389.
64 Haase, *Raggys Fahrt*, 399.
65 Another literary example of this trope is the 1905 novel *Alfreds Frauen* (Alfred's wives) by Hanna Christaller which features a colonist in Togo who commits suicide when his white wife discovers he has fathered a child with a Black woman, as discussed in Gallagher, "Fragile Whiteness." See Klotz, "Memoirs," 155–6 for a discussion of how some colonialists (and later scholars) portray women in the colonies as a disruption to male sexual freedom.

12 Colonial Propaganda Fiction: Else Steup's *Backfisch*[1] Novels from the 1930s

JULIA K. GRUBER

The propagandist's purpose is to make one set of people forget that certain other sets of people are human.
          Aldous Huxley, "Words and Behaviour," *The Olive Tree* (1936)

Introduction

In 2016, I visited the exhibition "German Colonialism: Fragments Past and Present" in the German Historical Museum in Berlin.[2] At the entrance, Walter von Ruckteschell's *Kilimandscharo*, a painting of the magnificent snow-covered mountain soaring high over the dark, blue-green jungle in East Africa, set the tone, which focused on the European colonialists' exotic desires.[3] The exhibition featured objects taken from the office of the last governor of today's Namibia,[4] Heinrich Schnee: ivory, daggers, busts, and fans. After his return to Germany in 1918, and as president of the Deutsche Kolonialgesellschaft (German Colonial Society), Schnee served as one of fifteen trustees on the governing board of a colonial school – a curious institution, since the Treaty of Versailles had officially ended German colonialism after the First World War.

Both Ruckteschell and Schnee were racist, colonial stakeholders. A century later, their perspective and their objects still served to exhibit German colonialism in the most prominent German history museum in the country. One sensed the authority with which German colonialists had staked their claims to African and South Asian soil, and how confidently they had asserted their dominance over the Indigenous peoples. The exhibit highlighted the – mostly male – colonizers' perspective. It barely problematized the experience of the colonized, and largely ignored the participation of German women in colonialism. The museum's curators appeared committed to perpetuating the male colonizer's white gaze and his colonial authority, as well as the colonial propagandist's dehumanizing program.

This essay examines the two museum objects among more than five hundred that stood out for me, namely the two *Backfisch* novels *Wiete will nach Afrika* (Wiete wants to go to Africa, 1936) and *Wiete erlebt Afrika: ein junges Mädchen bei deutschen Farmern* (Wiete experiences Africa: a young girl among German farmers, 1938) by Elisabeth (Else) Steup (1881–1942). Looking at these books under the glass case, I wondered: why were they included in an exhibition on German colonialism, and what was the motivation behind a young German woman's wish to experience Africa in the 1930s? This essay explores these questions first by contextualizing Steup's *Backfisch* novels in historical terms as literary products that mirror the complicated interplay of precolonial times, the colonial period, the First World War, the Weimar Republic, and the National Socialist period. Secondly, I will use literary analysis to uncover what is ideologically at stake in these texts by asking how Steup's *Backfisch* novels clarify the role of gender in the German colonial identity promoted by colonialists, how they reflect white German women's emancipation and their commitment to colonialism, and how they portray Africa, Africans, and Germans. Keeping the Huxley quote in the epigraph in mind, the essay sheds light on colonial propaganda, the so-called colonial woman question, and the plight of the African people during and after German colonialism.[5]

Keeping Colonialism Alive: Colonial Politics, Pedagogy, and Literature without German Colonies

Between 1884 and 1899, German colonies were established in Africa, North-East China, and the Pacific.[6] Namibia, where Steup's Wiete novels are mostly set, was a colony of the German Empire from 1884 until 1915, though Germany did not officially recognize the loss of this territory until the 1919 Treaty of Versailles. The terms of the treaty required that Germany pay financial reparations, disarm, lose territory, and give up all its overseas colonies. The Allies maintained that Germany had to surrender the colonies due to its alleged excessive brutality towards its colonial subjects. From a German colonialist's perspective, however, the country's greatest effort as a colonial power had been to "civilize" the Indigenous inhabitants and to teach them to "work hard."[7] The word "shame" (*Schande*) in the "Treaty of Shame" (*Schandvertrag*), as the Treaty of Versailles was called by those Germans who had embraced colonialism, did not refer to any emotion they might have felt about having harmed the African people, but instead to the "shameful" actions of the Allied Forces, who had dared to "steal" the colonies.

German colonialists soon found that their stance was best represented by the Nationalsozialistische Deutsche Arbeiterpartei or NSDAP (National Socialist German Workers' Party). As early as 1920, when the party was founded, its program demanded colonies for the settlement of Germany's surplus population. This led colonialists to pledge support for Hitler.[8] However, Hitler's position on winning back the colonies was not clear-cut. While he had initially spoken about the irreplaceable loss of the colonies,[9] he dismissed the goal of regaining them in the first paragraph of *Mein Kampf* (1925). In the chapter on foreign policy, he writes: "Insbesondere aber sind wir nicht der Schutzpolizist der bekannten 'armen, kleinen Völker,' sondern Soldaten unseres eigenen" (In particular, we are not the protection police for the well-known "poor, little nations," but soldiers of our own).[10] Hitler's apparent disinterest in the former African colonies clashed with initiatives such as the human zoos featuring people from Africa as well as Black actors staging African life. Between 1935 and 1940, Afro-German actors hired by the Deutsche Arbeitsfront (German Labor Front)[11] toured through Germany to spread the colonial mission among Germans.[12] The actors portrayed "loyal former protégés" (treue ehemalige Schutzbefohlene)[13] and were presented as living proof of Germany's aptitude as a colonial power.[14]

This myth of Germany as a protective colonial authority continued to be popular during the Third Reich. The idea that Germany still had a right to the colonies was also communicated to German children and youth via pedagogy and literature, so that they, too, could develop a colonial mindset from a young age. Third Reich colonial literature was as much a colonial fantasy as that produced by German authors before and during the times Germany had in fact had authority over colonies.[15] As Susanne Zantop has shown, in colonial fantasies of the seventeenth and eighteenth centuries, German writers had "imagined colonial scenarios that allowed them to identify with the role of the colonizer."[16] Thus, even before Germany had become a colonial power, "Germans were creating a colonial universe of their own and inserted themselves into it as better colonists."[17] Zantop proposes that "it was precisely the lack of actual colonialism that created a pervasive desire for colonial possessions and a sense of entitlement to such possessions in the minds of many Germans."[18] Apparently, the colonial fantasizing continued after Germany had lost its colonies.

Viewed today as misleading and fantastical, depictions of Germans in Africa produced during the Third Reich served a clear didactic function. They pointed to the success of heroic German men and industrious German women in the colonies. Both were depicted as having to prove themselves daily and under duress. According to Norbert Hopster, the

Nazis' insistence that literature be an imitation of "real life" did not mean literature was intended to serve as an authentic representation of colonialism, rather it was expected to provide an ideal reality.[19] Consequently, the literature that emerged was mostly propaganda. Many of these texts – reports, memoirs, and autobiographies – combine fictional elements and factual descriptions. Only a few titles were written specifically for women and girls, among them Else Steup's *Backfisch* novels about Wiete's preparatory education in a colonial school for women and her experiences in Africa.[20] At the centre of the Wiete novels is the so-called colonial woman question, i.e., the way in which women and gender issues were raised and debated by various social and political actors at the end of the colonial period.

The Colonial Woman Question

In the 1880s, women's involvement in the colonial endeavour was initially neither intended nor welcomed. Although some women showed interest in participating, male-dominated colonial politics generally considered the colonies too dangerous for women: the harsh climate, military struggles, and the strenuous everyday life served to dissuade women from going overseas. In many texts written about the colonies, women's presence in the colonies is reduced to their role as reproductive forces and thus as victims of male power politics.[21] After the First World War, when German colonialists attempted to turn Namibia into a German settler community, the position on German women's participation changed rather drastically. Relationships between German soldiers and African women were now increasingly considered a threat to the white race and the absence of white women in the white settlements was considered the main reason for it. The Colonial Woman Question addressed this issue and energized women's involvement in managing the German settlements in Africa.

Before German women started travelling to the colonies in significant numbers, there were connections between the German women's movement and German colonial efforts. Hedwig Heyl, the chairwoman of the Deutschkolonialer Frauenbund (Women's League of the German Colonial Society), one of the private colonial associations that promoted colonialism and played an important role in governing the colonies, was also an active women's rights activist. In 1911, the Women's League of the German Colonial Society joined the Bund Deutscher Frauenvereine or BDF (Federation of German Women's Associations), which was founded in 1894 as an umbrella organization of the women's civil rights feminist movement and existed until the Nazis seized power in 1933. The decades-long commitment of these organizations' members explains why the idea of German colonialism lingered and why German women volunteered to emigrate to the former colonies long after the colonies had ceased to exist.

From its founding in 1907 until 1914, the Deutschkolonialer Frauenbund grew to almost nineteen thousand members and received up to fifty requests daily from women interested in migrating overseas. It organized the outward voyages of 561 German women to the colonies and reported about their lives in the weekly magazine *Kolonie und Heimat*.[22] It also promoted the recruitment of young women to the colonial school in Rendsburg, which opened in 1927. It joined the Witzenhausen Colonial School for men, which had been founded in 1899.[23] Both schools were operating until 1944.

Else Steup's Wiete books appear to be promotional material written for the school in Rendsburg. After the First World War, it served as an institution of colonial education in a Germany without an overseas empire. According to Willeke Sandler, colonialists aimed to reclaim the lost overseas territories and to support those Germans who had chosen to stay in Africa after colonialism had officially ended.[24] Although the number of German settlers in the former African colonies had dropped after the First World War, it rose again to fourteen thousand over the course of the 1920s.[25] Since colonialists no longer had administrative control, their focus became cultural support. The women's school in Rendsburg supported this mission with a focus on the role and responsibilities of women. As an early prospectus declared, "the Germanness of the settler territories stands and falls with the worth of the women living there."[26] In 1929, the federal government took over 90 per cent of the financing, which, as Lora Wildenthal explains, "may have contributed to the rapid Nazification of the school in 1933."[27]

Students were to be selected from "the 'most racially sound' (erbtüchtigsten) German girls and women. National political instruction, genetics, eugenics (*Erbgesundheitslehre*), race science (*Rassenkunde*), Germandom abroad, 'colonial questions,' and after 1940, 'Eastern questions' appeared in the curriculum."[28] The curriculum consisted of six main areas: history, civics, ethnography, business training, natural sciences, agricultural economics, and foreign languages.[29] While English was mandatory, learning Swahili or Malay, which would have enabled students to communicate with Indigenous peoples, was the only optional subject. Willeke Sandler points out that "it is doubtful that the young women mastered all these skills."[30] In 1940, the prospectus stated: "We would much rather that they overcome the traditional prejudice that girls are not fit for such things, and that they gain the confidence to help themselves in case of emergencies."[31]

The young women who attended the school were equipped with determination as much as skill, and thus embodied the idea of female independence. While it contradicted the Nazi dictum of the "brave" German woman as wife and mother, it also differed from the independence represented by the (mythical) New Woman of the Weimar Republic.[32] After graduation – over a thousand young women graduated from Rendsburg between 1927 and 1944 – the women were supposed to go overseas expecting to do more than just be a mother and housewife. They were prepared to perform work outside of the prescribed spaces and roles for women. However, as shown in Steup's second Wiete book, that does not mean that women were expected to do any of this work once they arrived in the former colonies. On the contrary, they were often told to have the Indigenous people do the heavy lifting. According to Sandler, the capabilities and mastery of skills of a colonial school graduate were racially defined and used to create racial hierarchies.[33] She notes that the school's prospectus did not discuss the graduates' relationship with colonial populations, but students, who called themselves *Kolomädels* (colonial girls), described the school as "the African colony in Europe."[34] A publication dedicated to reporting about the school and its students even used the German N-word to refer to the white women, thus suggesting that the education they received in Germany prior to going to Africa would turn them into Africans.[35]

The Wiete books were part of a continued effort to promote German life in the former colonies. Steup's *Backfisch* novels are thinly veiled propaganda that encouraged young German women to become settlers abroad. While they are a testimony to the short period of German colonialism, they were also written against the backdrop of German colonialists' fiery commitment to regain authority over the former colonies. They showcased colonialism's continued role in German political, cultural, and economic life, and its place in the curricula of colonial schools. In terms of historical representation, Steup's novels and the photographs in them reveal and convey a false sense of colonial power at a time when Germany no longer had colonial authority. They fulfilled their propagandistic function to keep colonialism alive while highlighting the role German women played as settlers in the former colonies. Finally, they embraced the racist agenda of the National Socialist regime.

Else Steup and the Weitzenberg Estate

Born in 1881 in Northeim, Lower Saxony, Else Steup worked as a governess in England and France and later became a journalist and author. During the First World War, she was the editor of a newspaper, the *Leipziger Illustrierten Zeitung*. After 1914, she was employed by the Lektorat zur Deutschen Gesellschaft für Auslandsbuchhandel (German Society for Foreign Booktrade). From 1920 onward, she also headed the Gesellschaft für kolonialer Fortschritt (Society for Colonial Progress) in Berlin. She died in Berlin in 1942.

It is likely that for the Wiete novels, Steup relied on her stepsister Louise's personal experience in Africa, although Louise is not specifically mentioned. According to Lore Wildenthal, Louise Weitzenberg (nee Steup) was a member of the founding committee of the Women's League of the German Colonial Society.[36] She was married to Arno Weitzenberg, a Leutnant der Pioniere (lieutenant of the pioneers).[37] In 1904, Arno served in the Schutztruppe Deutsch-Südwestafrika (protection forces of Namibia). Ten years later, he participated in the First World War efforts there. After leaving the army, Weitzenberg, together with Carl Hagenbeck,[38] founded an ostrich farm in Namibia's Swakop River Valley. The farm flooded and was destroyed in 1917.[39] Both the ostrich farm as well as the flood are mentioned in the second Wiete book.

During my research for this essay, I stumbled upon photographs on Facebook of what used to be the Weitzenberg estate in Namibia, the place where Else Steup's stepsister Louise and her family had lived in the early 1900s. The no longer available Steup ancestry page notes that in 1984, the remains of the estate were named a National Monument of Namibia. In a report issued by the Museum Development and Monument Services of the United Nations Institute for Namibia, the site is described as follows: "The ruins are in the most dilapidated state, but still remain a great fascination for the *uninhibited visitor* who is merely interested in its historical background."[40] By the time the fictional Wiete, who can be considered an "uninhibited" visitor, arrives in the 1930s, the Steups had long left the estate. Like many German settlers, Arno Weitzenberg had been expatriated and was living in Germany.[41] His wife Louise "died aged 70 in June 1943, after 28 years of austerity in the internment on the plantation Kassibo near Rukoba in [today's] Burundi."[42]

In the second Wiete novel, *Wiete erlebt Afrika*, Wiete tours a deserted farm. Her friend Sven points at places on the ground where a vegetable garden and flowers had once grown. He shares with Wiete that he has seen many of such ruins and heard many of the tragic stories behind them: "Der Mann fiel irgendwo im Busch, und die Frau wurde von den Eingeborenen erschlagen" (The man died somewhere in the bush and the woman was slain by Indigenous people).[43] According to numerous sources, among them Lora Wildenthal, colonial women rarely suffered violence at the hands of Africans. Rather, most of these violent incidents were instead products of the German colonial imagination.[44]

Sven's description of the house resembles the Weitzenberg ruin described and depicted above, the farmhouse where Else Steup's sister had lived during colonial times. Sven remembers being horrified by what he saw and reports that one could see remnants of the previous owners, among them the garden's beautiful design and the house with the open porch. Sven tells Wiete that he could not help but think of the woman who had given those rooms and the surroundings of the house comfort and beauty. He imagines her as lively and warm and as someone who had lost everything.[45] Sven's description of the dilapidated farmhouse seems to convey the idea that if only young German women like Wiete lived there again, the comfort and beauty would return.

In the Wiete books, Steup mentions neither the expatriation of Germans after the First World War, nor the fact that some, like her stepsister, were interned by the Allies, nor that there were exiled Jewish Germans trying to survive as farmers in Namibia.[46] Instead, the focus of Steup's novels is on promoting a colonial life to young German women, as though there were still a dire need for them in the former German colonies.

Wiete will nach Afrika (Wiete Wants to Go to Africa)

Steup's first Wiete book, *Wiete will nach Afrika*, introduces spoiled, opinionated, young Wiete who is tricked by her brother Immo and his friend Götz into attending the Colonial School for Women in Rendsburg. Immo, who runs a cocoa farm in Africa, complains to Götz about Wiete's superficial, selfish behaviour. Her obsession with clothes, make-up, fun-filled days, and other earthly pleasures seem to describe what Immo might have heard abroad about the "New Woman." "Heartless" and "superficial"[47] little Wiete does not live up to Immo's expectations. His impression of Wiete as a fashion doll and self-absorbed brat upends his fantasy of taking her to his African farm.

Götz offers to convince Wiete to enrol in the "Kolo-Schule," a place that will remove all the flimflam in her head, and turn her into an industrious colonist and a good comrade. To achieve this, the young men decide – over Wiete's head – that she must leave the familiar space of her home and shed the behaviour of a modern woman. Wiete is made to believe that the school is a place for wealthy young women. She is shown pictures of females preparing meals and working hard, but no one tells her that those women are the students themselves. Based on a misinterpretation of the school and a lie, Wiete agrees to apply. Once there, Wiete – out of pride – acts as though she is not surprised by what she finds, i.e., a hefty curriculum and hard-working women, as opposed to a more leisurely approach to learning and plenty of opportunities for networking. She adapts to the daily schedule, meets the challenges of the curriculum, and quickly internalizes the school's propaganda, which prepares her for her African adventure.

Boarding schools feature prominently in *Backfisch* novels. Whereas they are fictional places in those novels, the boarding school in Steup's books existed in real life. To underline the authenticity of the material, *Wiete will nach Africa* features sixteen black-and-white photographs that depict actual students at the school.[48] They show anonymous women performing many of the activities listed in the school's curriculum. The photographs signal that this is not an entirely made-up story and thereby convey authenticity. Looking at the photographs, the reader is invited to identify Wiete and the other students, even though none of the photographs explicitly refer to any of the characters mentioned in the text. The lack of identification projects an impersonal, documentary touch. The disconnect between the fictional text, i.e., the *Backfisch* plot, and the photographs (authentic, promotional material) creates a disorienting effect. Steup's texts merge the conventions of *Backfisch* literature with the expectations that Nazi-approved literature be functional and authentic. The reader is thereby encouraged to mature alongside Wiete and to imagine a similar path to hers.

Wiete erlebt Afrika (Wiete Experiences Africa)

According to Albert Memmi, colonial racism is built from three major ideological components: "One, the gulf between the culture of the colonialist and the colonized; two, the exploitation of these differences for the benefit of the colonialist; three, the use of these supposed differences as standards of absolute fact."[49] All three of these components materialize in Steup's second Wiete book. In it, Steup constructs white colonial authority through racist depictions of colonized Black people.

In *Wiete erlebt Afrika*, readers accompany Wiete as she travels with her friends through Africa and visits farms in the former German colonies. While most of the narrative space is taken up by descriptions of white German settlers, Black people feature more prominently in the photographs. In these pictures, they are reduced to the status of extras and are shown facilitating the life of the colonizers by carrying out the hard labour. While the narrative focuses on the gaze of a white woman on the experience of white settlers in Africa, the impact of white Germans on Africans remains at the margins and can only be gleaned by studying the text and the photographs more closely. The twenty-four black-and-white illustrations help create a myth about the life of German settlers in Africa.[50] They are not dated, and so the reader is left to assume that the pictures depict places and people Wiete encounters during her trip to Africa, sometime between the late 1920s and the mid-1930s. However, the pictures might have been taken at an earlier time when Germany still had colonial authority, i.e., when Steup's stepsister and her husband were running the ostrich farm in Namibia. The use of photographs dating back to actual colonial times in a text written in the 1930s mirrors Germany's nostalgic treatment of its colonial past.

The pictures show random white settlers and Africans, all but one remaining unnamed. While the white settlers stand in front of their European-looking homes, ride horses, host other white visitors or, in the case of women, perform light work (feeding ducks, stirring pots, petting a newborn lamb), the African people in most of the pictures are involved in hard labour, such as harvesting, carrying large bundles, and scrubbing laundry in large containers. According to Susan Sontag, "to photograph is to appropriate the thing photographed,"[51] and "to photograph people is to violate them, by seeing them as they never see themselves by having knowledge of them they can never have; it turns people into objects that can be symbolically possessed."[52] For the colonizers, the photographs serve to validate their authority over the colonized, to "make real what one is experiencing."[53] From the perspective of the colonized, the camera "intrudes, trespasses, distorts, exploits and assassinates."[54]

All the photographs of nameless Black people in *Wiete erlebt Afrika* convey Sontag's view of photography as an authoritative force. For example, a photograph showing two African women watching over a toddler is subtitled: "Diese altmodische Tracht ist noch heute bei den Eingeborenen üblich" (This old-fashioned costume is still common among the Indigenous people today).[55] Wiete adds a more thorough description of the Victorian-era clothes, which were introduced by early German settlers,[56] in a letter: "Die eingeborenen Mädchen tragen eine drollige Tracht: hochgeschlossene Kattunkleider mit langen dichtgekrausten Röcken, enger Taille – sie sind sehr gut gewachsen – und dann so komische hohe Kopfbedeckungen" (The Black girls wear a silly costume: high-necked calicos with tightly ruffled skirts, tight waist – they have slender figures – and then the funny headwear.)[57] Another photograph depicting an African male who wears an apron while carefully drying the dishes with a hand towel is subtitled: "Das Mädchen für alles" (The girl for everything),[58] thus mocking the man by questioning his masculinity for doing "women's work." Wiete's descriptions of Africans are limited to their appearance and focused on their labour. In the subtitles of two photographs showing a group of Africans during a harvest and a man carrying a large bundle of grass, Wiete overlooks the people altogether and instead describes what is being harvested: "Sisalernte auf einer großen Pflanzung in Ostafrika. Die fleischigen Blätter liefern eine feste und geschmeidige Spinnfaser" (Sisal harvest on a big farm in East Africa. The meaty leaves deliver a strong and smooth fibre).[59]

Only one Black man, the foreman Menjenje on the farm of Wiete's friend's father, is identified by name. On her first stop in Africa, Wiete learns that white settlers must show Africans respect or they will not respect their "Aubaas" (derived from Hebrew and Arabic "Abass," meaning "stern father"), i.e., the white settler: "Die Eingeborenen waren willig und folgsam, solange sie Respekt hatten. Fehlte der, oder fühlten sie sich überlegen, dann wurden sie unverschämt" (The Indigenous people were willing and obedient as long as they were shown respect. If it was not shown to them or they felt they had the upper hand, they became shameless).[60]

Specific examples of how white settlers show respect to Africans are not provided, but the reader learns of a negative example: a young German man named Quaske is said to treat the Indigenous people disrespectfully. When they make fun of him, he points a rifle at Menjenje who then threatens to file charges against Quaske. This infuriates the white farmer, who wants to avoid trouble with the authorities. Wiete, who earlier had witnessed Mejenje steal jackals, confronts him. Wiete sits straight on her horse and looks down at the man. Sitting on her high horse literally gives Wiete the authority to mingle in Menjenje's affairs. Since Wiete most likely skipped the optional African language lessons in Rendsburg, the entire conversation apparently takes place in German. She informs Menjenje that Quaske has left and assures him that everything is going to be fine. Menjenje, however, reminds Wiete that Quaske had pointed a rifle at him: "Das darf er nicht" (He is not allowed to do that), he insists.[61] Wiete explains that one is also not allowed to steal jackals. Consequently, Wiete and the foreman strike a deal. Wiete will not report him for stealing and in return, Menjenje will not report Quaske to the authorities. The white family is relieved, but also puzzled when Menjenje does not ask for permission to report the incident: "Sie konnten sich das nicht recht erklären, denn sie wussten wie gern die Schwarzen zum Magistrat liefen, wenn sie etwas anzeigen konnten" (They could not figure it out because they knew that the Blacks loved to run to the magistrate to report something whenever they could).[62] Wiete, who has not been in Africa for long and who is only a visitor, has confidently and successfully used her authority as a white woman to intimidate and blackmail an African man to keep him from reporting a reportable offence committed by a white man. Being threatened at gunpoint is compared to stealing an animal. The fact that the Africans seem to report offences to the authorities regularly indicates that they feel the need to protect themselves. They are neither protected nor respected by the German settlers.

After Wiete has arrived at her brother's farm, Immo asks her to take care of the house and urges her to "handle" his "boys." The fact that Immo infantilizes his workers by calling them "boys" reveals what E.S. Grogan and A.H. Sharp have referred to as the colonizer's "good sound system of compulsory labor that would transform the 'African child races' from useless and generous brutes into useful beings."[63] In the German colonizer's mind, Africans' "performance" can only improve by serving the colonizers. Cleanliness and efficiency are mentioned as German qualities that Africans lack and need to be taught: "Nun sind die Eingeborenen sicher geschickt, und man kann ihnen auch Sauberkeit beibringen. Sie sind meistens von sich aus schon sauberer als man denkt, aber sie kennen das europäische Arbeitstempo nicht und wollen auch nichts davon wissen." (The Indigenous people are certainly skillful, and one can teach them cleanliness. Most of the time, they are already cleaner than one thinks, but they do not know the European efficiency and speed, and they also do not want to know anything about it.)[64] Wiete does not have to be convinced. As a graduate of a colonial school, she has been prepared to accept the differences between colonizers and colonized as absolute facts. She reassures her brother and mockingly refers to his workers as "Perlen" (pearls),[65] the German word for an effective German housekeeper.

According to Albert Memmi, "the colonialist stresses those things which keep him separate, rather than emphasizing that which might contribute to the foundation of a joint community":[66]

> In those differences, the colonized is always degraded and the colonialist finds justification for rejecting his subjects. Nothing could better justify the colonizer's privileged position than his industry, and nothing could better justify the colonized's destitution than his indolence [justifying ideology]. The mythical portrait of the colonized therefore includes an unbelievable laziness, and that of the colonizer, a virtuous taste for action.[67]

Wiete has come to Africa fully prepared to take this kind of "virtuous action." However, she soon discovers that the opportunities for meaningful actions are limited. These limitations are explained to her by her brother:

> Ja, kleine Wiete, und dabei vergehen auch die dummen Gedanken wenn man sich beschäftigen kann. Frauen, die das nicht können, passen nicht

hierher. Sieh, vieles was sie zu Hause oder in Südwest tun, wird ihnen hier durch die Boys abgenommen. Körperlich arbeiten können sie nicht bei der Hitze. [...] Aber die Beaufsichtigung der Boys füllt den Tag nicht aus, und wenn sie sich dann nicht beschäftigen können, werden sie unzufrieden und nervös und für den Mann eine Plage.[68]

(Yes, little Wiete, and that is how the silly thoughts pass, when one knows how to keep busy. Women, who cannot do that, do not fit in here. Look, many things that they do at home or in South West, are taken care of by the Boys. They cannot physically work because of the heat. [...] But looking after the Boys does not take all day, and when they cannot occupy themselves, they become dissatisfied and nervous, and a nuisance for the man.)

Immo elucidates that it is fine to sow and plant a little, but he does not want Wiete to work too hard in the sun: "Ich beschränke mich auch mehr auf Anleitung und Aufsicht" (I also limit my efforts to instruction and supervision).[69] Immo's work ethic does not reflect the industrious German settler, as he is typically portrayed in colonial literature. "Ihr müsst euch daran gewöhnen, die Schwarzen arbeiten zu lassen" (You have to get used to letting the Africans work),[70] Immo repeatedly explains, as he relies on the colonizers' established view that Black bodies are more physically able than white ones to carry out hard labour under the hot African sun.

Colonial Propaganda Fiction

Fueled by pro-colonialist Nazi propaganda, Steup's books centre on a white woman's fantasy of what Africa and Black culture is, but mostly what it is not, seen through her white gaze: a "civilized," cultured place like Germany. Steup makes a case for her protagonist's right to participate in the colonial endeavour by moving her to the centre of the narrative, while the setting (Africa) and its inhabitants (Africans) are moved to the margins.

Africa remained a colonial setting in German minds, a place where young white women like Wiete were told they could "weave together feminine independence [and] German nationalism [...]."[71] As the Wiete books show, however, they often found that this promise could not be fulfilled. Sarah Henneböhl's concluding remark in her analysis of Stefanie Zweig's autofictional accounts of her childhood in Kenya about the two memory discourses – the Holocaust and the history of colonialism – seemingly being "at war with each other" also rings true for Steup's colonial propaganda fiction. The Wiete books cling to a colonial time that no longer existed at a time when Germany was preparing to go to war with the rest of the world.

Wiete erlebt Afrika seems to offer a fictional account of a young woman visiting German farmers, but its references to specific events make what is told seem historically authentic. For example, Else Steup's brother-in-law's ostrich farm is mentioned in a conversation between Wiete and her friends. Götz, who repeatedly provokes Wiete with patronizing comments about women and their focus on their appearance, laments women's negative impact on the German colonial economy: "Wieviel Unheil ist schon durch die Eitelkeit der Frauen und ihren wechselnden Modelaunen entstanden. Hier im ganzen Lande blühte die Straußenzucht, bis die Mode sich plötzlich änderte." (How much harm has been done by the vanity of women and their ever-changing fashion quirks. All over the country, ostrich farming was thriving until the fashion sense suddenly changed.)[72] Wiete, who never finds herself short of an answer, admonishes Götz and accuses men of ruining the continent with their greed and passion for hunting:

> Wo sind die Tausende von Elefanten geblieben die früher die Ebenen von Südwest bevölkerten, die Büffelherden in den Prärien Amerikas und überhaupt der Wildreichtum in allen Erdteilen? Ihr habt wirklich keinen Grund, euch zu beschweren. Habsucht und Jagdleidenschaft der Männer haben mehr Unheil angerichtet als die Eitelkeit der Frauen.[73]

> (Where did the thousands of elephants go that used to roam the plains of South West, the buffalo herds in the American prairie, the wildlife in all parts of the world? You really should not complain. Men's greed and passion for hunting have done much more harm than the vanity of women.)

This passage is somewhat surprising as it reveals Steup's knowledge about the negative effects of colonialism and her – albeit weak – emancipatory stance. The passage indicates that her protagonist Wiete is well aware of the destruction and harm colonialism has brought upon not only Africa, but also other parts of the world that white men have conquered.

In the end, Wiete experiences Africa as a place that is not suitable for everyone, including herself. Wiete is portrayed as a woman equipped with what it takes to succeed in Africa, i.e., she knows how to delegate the most strenuous work to Black people. However, the education she has received in the colonial school for women proves insufficient in the end. In typical *Backfisch* novels of the period, the woman would have happily accepted a marriage proposal. A conventional *Backfisch* novel set in Africa would have ended with the protagonist running a spotless German household in the African wilderness, bearing many children, tending to her lush garden, and shielding her husband from sexual relations with Black women. But in the somewhat surprising end, Wiete decides that she is neither ready to commit to a life in Africa, nor to getting married. She tells Götz that because he lied to her about the colonial school, she has not been her authentic self with him either. Wiete's behaviour towards Götz – throughout the second book she pretends that she is still the spoiled woman he had met in Germany – undercuts the otherwise authoritative colonial voice. Wiete's behaviour seems to undermine expectations, which contradicts the dictum of the *Backfisch* plot in which the young woman typically exceeds everyone's expectations in the end.[74] I interpret the tensions between the self-determination of the (failed) female colonial hero Wiete as Steup's quiet nod to female self-autonomy, a rejection of her stepsister's choice of life in the colonies, and of the Nazis' ideas of femininity in general. It is tempting to speculate that Wiete's rebellious, opinionated, and questioning nature, as well as the unusual ending might have been the main reason why Nazi critics did not recommend Steup's books warmly, but instead described them as merely "geeignet" (appropriate).[75]

German Colonialism Revisited

Four years after the exhibition on German colonialism in the German Historical Museum on 15 November 2020, which marked the 136th anniversary of the start of the Berlin Africa Conference, the project "Dekoloniale Memory Culture in the City" convened the Dekoloniale Berlin Africa Conference. The opening event was streamed live from the project space at Wilhelmstraße 92 in Berlin-Mitte, between the former sites of the Reich Chancellery and the Foreign Office where nineteen white men – delegates of the European powers, the USA, and the Ottoman Empire – had met in 1884 to discuss the colonial future of Africa. For the opening event, the conference organizers had invited an anti-colonial panel consisting of nineteen women of African descent to discuss the effects of colonialism on their lives and livelihoods.[76] According to the organizers, the five-year project will focus on a change of perspective in postcolonial memory culture: "Instead of colonial-racist stakeholders, from now on the victims and opponents of colonial racism and exploitation will receive attention and appreciation."[77]

The Dekoloniale Project does what the 2016 exhibition on German colonialism in the German Historical Museum and Else Steup's Wiete novels largely did not do: by giving nineteen Women of Colour the floor, the project shifts the attention to the colonized. The Dekoloniale, too, reflects on the role of gender in colonialism and on the portrayal of Africa, Africans, and Germans, but instead of participating in the white gaze, we are invited to see what is presented through the eyes of Black people, especially Black women. Whereas the exhibition "German Colonialism: Fragments Past and Present" in the German Historical Museum and Steup's *Backfisch* novels served the propagandist's purpose to dehumanize, the purpose of the Dekoloniale and the message delivered by the nineteen women of African descent is to remind us that all "sets of people" are human.

NOTES

1 The *Backfisch* novel typically focuses on a single teenager protagonist in a boarding school environment and the short but essential period of transformation from girlhood to womanhood.
2 "Deutscher Kolonialismus: Fragmente seiner Geschichte und Gegenwart," Deutsches Historisches Museum, 14 October 16–14 May 2017, 2024, https://www.dhm.de/ausstellungen/archiv/2016/deutscher-kolonialismus/.
3 Ruckteschell's young adult book *Heia Safari* (Leipzig: Koehler, 1920) helped render German colonialism into a myth.
4 Throughout this essay I will use the contemporary terminology to refer to the former colonies, unless quoting directly. During colonial rule Heinrich Schnee reigned over what was known as "German East Africa" (*Ostafrika*), a German colony in the African Great Lakes region, which included present-day Burundi, Rwanda, the Tanzania mainland, and the Kionga Triangle, a small region later incorporated into Mozambique. "German South West Africa" (*Südwestafrika*) was a colony of the German Empire from 1884 until 1915. Unless otherwise indicated, all translations are my own.
5 Working with this material has led me to reflect on my own position as a white European woman. It has forced me to confront the ways in which I had internalized the discourses of racism and colonialism, and how that internalization had impacted my perspective. How am I, a white European woman, to interpret a white European woman's colonial fantasy of a female protagonist's experience and depiction of Africa and the African people without putting her, i.e., the white woman, front and centre in my own work? I thank the editors for nudging me to decolonialize my thinking, reading, and writing. I am especially grateful to Maureen Gallagher, Beth Muellner, Jon Jonakin, and the two anonymous readers for reading and commenting on early drafts and to Lisabeth Hock for providing edits and suggestions for the final version.
6 Attempts at colonization by some German states had been made in preceding centuries, but chancellor Otto von Bismarck had refused the idea of a colonial empire until 1884. Germany claimed much of the remaining uncolonized

areas of Africa and built the third-largest colonial empire at the time, after the British and French. The German colonial empire included parts of several African countries, including parts of present-day Burundi, Rwanda, Tanzania, Namibia, Cameroon, Gabon, Congo, Central African Republic, Chad, Nigeria, Togo, Ghana, as well as northeastern New Guinea, Samoa, and numerous Micronesian islands.

7   Sara Lennox, "Postcolonial Writing in Germany," *The Cambridge History of Postcolonial Literature*, ed. Ato Quayson (Cambridge: Cambridge University Press, 2012), 620.
8   Winfried Speitkamp, *Deutsche Kolonialgeschichte* (Stuttgart: Reclam, 2005), 169.
9   Christian Hartmann, ed. *Mein Kampf: eine kritische Edition*, by Adolf Hitler (Munich: Institut für Zeitgeschichte, 2016), 1:432.
10 Adolf Hitler, *Mein Kampf* (Munich: Zentralverlag der NSDAP, 1925), 741, http://www.dedokwerker.nl/copy/mein_kampf_de.pdf.
11 The German Labour Front (Deutsche Arbeitsfront, DAF) was the National Socialist trade union organization which replaced the various trade unions of the Weimar Republic after Adolf Hitler's rise to power.
12 Karsten Linne, *Deutschland jenseits des Äquators? Die NS-Kolonialplanungen für Afrika* (Berlin: Links Verlag, 2008), 44–5, 77.
13 Whereas the English/French term "protégés" suggests that people are (to be) protected, the German *Schutzbefohlene*, which is derived from the verb "befehlen" (to command) conveys the idea that people were ordered to place themselves under protection; "protection forces" (*Schutztruppe*), and "protectorates" (*Schutzgebiete*; the term preferred by Otto von Bismarck for colonies) are euphemistic expressions initially coined to authorize German colonialism under the pretence that Germans had come to Africa to "protect" Africans.
14 Susann Lewerenz, "'Basthütten am Kolonial-Mal': die 'Deutsche Afrika-Schau' (1935–1940)," in *Kolonialismus hierzulande: eine Spurensuche in Deutschland*, ed. Ulrich van der Heyden and Joachim Zeller (Erfurt: Sutton, 2007), 432–8.
15 See Carola Daffner's and Maureen Gallagher's essays in this volume.
16 Susanne Zantop, *Colonial Fantasies: Conquest, Family, and Nation in Precolonial Germany, 1770–1870* (Durham, NC: Duke University Press, 1997), 6.
17 Zantop, *Colonial Fantasies*, 6–7.
18 Zantop, *Colonial Fantasies*, 7.
19 Norbert Hopster, "II.4 Kolonien," in *Kinder- und Jugendliteratur 1933–1945: ein Handbuch*, ed. Norbert Hopster, Petra Josting, and Joachim Neuhaus (Stuttgart: J.B. Metzler, 2002), 2:333–4.
20 Popular books for young women published around the same time such as Senta Dinglreiter's *Deutsche Frau in Afrika* (German woman in Africa, 1940), Christine Holstein's *Deutsche Frau in Südwest* (German woman in South

West, 1937), and Else Frobenius's *Das Mädchen mit dem Pferde* (The girl with the horse, 1941) lament the loss and plunder of the German colonies. They also emphasize, as Dinglreiter's novel's title *Wann kommen die Deutschen endlich wieder?* (When will the Germans finally return?, 1940) suggests, that the former colonies in their current state needed Germans.

21 The work of Martha Mamozai, Katharina Walgenbach, Lora Wildenthal, and Anette Dietrich provides important research results on colonial women's engagement.

22 Katharina Walgenbach, *"Die weiße Frau als Trägerin deutscher Kultur": koloniale Diskurse über Geschlecht, "Rasse" und Klasse im Kaiserreich* (Frankfurt am Main: Campus, 2005), 88.

23 The Deutsche Kolonialschule für Landwirtschaft, Handel und Gewerbe (German Colonial School for Agriculture, Trade, and Industry, also called the Tropenschule, or Tropical School) was founded to train people in agriculture for resettlement in Germany's colonies. The successor institution today is a satellite campus of the University of Kassel, which includes a greenhouse complex dedicated to tropical crops (Gewächshaus für tropische Nutzpflanzen).

24 Willeke Sandler, "Colonial Education in the Third Reich: The Witzenhausen Colonial School and the Rendsburg Colonial School for Women," *Central European History* 49, no. 2 (June 2016): 184.

25 Sandler, "Colonial Education," 185.

26 Untitled prospectus of the Koloniale Frauenschule Rendsburg, DVII 942 1–160, quoted in Sandler, "Colonial Education," 185.

27 Lora Wildenthal, *German Women for Empire, 1884–1945* (Durham, NC: Duke University Press, 2001), 197.

28 Sandler explains that during the Second World War, male students were drafted into military service, whereas female students contributed to the war effort in factory work and as settlement advisers, who "secured" the Germanness of occupied eastern Europe. Sandler, "Colonial Education," 187.

29 Sandler, "Colonial Education," 190.

30 Sandler, "Colonial Education," 190.

31 StR, KFR, DVII 942 161–350, "Mitteilungsblatt Juni 1940," quoted in Sandler, "Colonial Education," 192.

32 According to Wildenthal, "the New Woman was politically enfranchised and economically and sexually independent. Free of family responsibilities she embraced consumerism and entertainment and lived for herself" (*German Women*, 194).

33 Sandler, "Colonial Education," 192.

34 13StR, KFR, DVII 942 Lose Blätter, "Kolozeitung" 1944; Lotte Jacobi, "Ein Tag bei den Kolonegern"; Die Frau und die Kolonien 2 (1 February 1933): 16–18, quoted in Sandler, "Colonial Education," 200.

35 Sandler, "Colonial Education," 200.
36 Wildenthal, *German Women*, 204.
37 This information can be found on a web forum: "Thema: Farm Weitzenberg im Swakoptal – Infos gesucht!," Namibia-Forum, last updated 29 April 2014, https://www.namibia-forum.ch/forum/11-diverses/282594-farm-weitzenberg-im-swakoptal-infos-gesucht.html.
38 Carl Hagenbeck (1844–1913) was an internationally known German animal dealer and trainer. He created the prototype for open-air zoos.
39 According to the no longer available ancestry website, Arno Steup served as first lieutenant in the Second Field Regiment of the *Schutztruppe* in 1904. He was then major of the *Schutztruppe* in Tanganyika. In 1910, while stationed in Germany, he quit and left the military. His adventures with ostrich farming began in the Swakopmund district. He joined the forces again during the mobilization in Namibia in 1914. After 1926, he is listed as a citizen of Bremen.
40 N.A. Mudoga, Museum Development and Monument Services: United Nations Institute for Namibia, UNESCO Digital Library, https://unesdoc.unesco.org/ark:/48223/pf0000062181, 17.
41 I was not able to retrieve more information about Arno Weitzenberg's expatriation.
42 Similarly, I was not able to find out more about Louise's life in Africa except for the information provided on the ancestry page. I found it intriguing that she stayed in Africa while her husband returned to Germany.
43 Else Steup, *Wiete erlebt Afrika. Ein junges Mädchen bei deutschen Farmern* (Berlin: Deutscher Verlag, 1938), 33.
44 Wildenthal, *German Women*, 186–7.
45 Steup, *Wiete erlebt Afrika*, 33–4.
46 See Sarah Henneböhl's essay in this volume.
47 Else Steup, *Wiete will nach Afrika* (Berlin: Deutscher Verlag, 1939), 9.
48 The sixteen photographs were taken by Max Ehlert, Heno Mauritius, Saebens Worpswede, and Scherl-Bilderdienst, all photographers based in Berlin.
49 Albert Memmi, *The Colonizer and the Colonized*, introd. Jean Paul Sartre, expanded ed. (Boston: Beacon, 1965), 71.
50 The twenty four photographs were provided by Bildervertrieb Schröder, Berlin. Deutsche Kolonialgesellschaft, Berlin (Eva McLean and Nora von Steinmeister), Photo Koester, Windhut; Ilse Steinhoff, Berlin; Else Steup, Berlin. See Steup, *Wiete erlebt Afrika*, 244.
51 Susan Sontag, *On Photography* (New York: Farrar, Straus and Giroux, 1977), 4.
52 Sontag, *On Photography*, 15.
53 Sontag, *On Photography*, 19.
54 Sontag, *On Photography*, 13.
55 Steup, *Wiete erlebt Afrika*, between pages 124 and 125.

56 According to this article, Herero women still wear these dresses today as a sign of pride and cultural heritage: Emily Wither, "The Namibian Women Who Dress like Victorians," CNN, 22 October 2012, https://www.cnn.com/2011/11/03/world/africa/namibia-victorian-fashion/index.html.
57 Steup, *Wiete erlebt Afrika*, 107.
58 Steup, *Wiete erlebt Afrika*, between pages 124 and 125.
59 Steup, *Wiete erlebt Afrika*, between pages 204 and 205.
60 Steup, *Wiete erlebt* Afrika, 131.
61 Steup, *Wiete erlebt* Afrika, 133.
62 Steup, *Wiete erlebt* Afrika, 132–5.
63 E.S. Grogan and A.H. Sharp, *From the Cape to Cairo: The First Traverse of Africa from South to North* (London: Hurst and Blackett, 1900), 243.
64 Grogan and Sharp, *From the Cape to Cairo*, 193.
65 Steup, *Wiete will nach Afrika*, 193.
66 Memmi, *Colonizer*, 71.
67 Memmi, *Colonizer*, 71.
68 Steup, *Wiete will nach Afrika*, 217.
69 Steup, *Wiete will nach Afrika*, 179.
70 Steup, *Wiete will nach Afrika*, 179.
71 Wildenthal, *German Women*, 196.
72 Steup, *Wiete will nach Afrika*, 31.
73 Steup, *Wiete will nach Afrika*, 31.
74 I owe this observation to Maureen Gallagher.
75 Recommendations of the Deutscher Verlag Berlin at the end of *Wiete erlebt Afrika*.
76 Dekoloniale Memory Culture in the City is a joint project of Berlin Postkolonial e.V., Each One Teach One - EOTO e.V., Initiative Schwarze Menschen in Deutschland - ISD-Bund e.V. (Initiative of Black People in Germany) and the Stadtmuseum Berlin Foundation. The Landesnetzwerk Berliner Entwicklungspolitischer Ratschlag - BER e.V. (National Network Berlin Development Policy Advice) supports the project as a partner. In addition, the project organizers closely cooperate with the Deutsche Technikmuseum Berlin (German Technology Museum Berlin) and the Berlin district museums in Treptow-Köpenick, Friedrichshain-Kreuzberg, Charlottenburg-Wilmersdorf and Berlin-Mitte. The project is sponsored by the Berlin Senate Department for Culture and Europe and the German Federal Cultural Foundation. "About Us: Dekoloniale Memory Culture in the City," Dekoloniale, https://www.dekoloniale.de/en/about.
77 "Dekoloniale – was bleibt?!": Kurator*innen-Führungen, 23.11.2024, 13:00Uhr, Berlin, Dekoloniale, https://www.dekoloniale.de/de.

13 Perspectives on Namibia by Contemporary White German-Speaking Women Authors[1]

LORELY FRENCH

A sign reading "All Lives Matter" in a restaurant window in the Namibian coastal city of Swakopmund created an uproar in July 2020.[2] The murder of George Floyd in the United States and Black people by police in Namibia and other African countries prompted an opinion piece in *The Namibian* on 17 July 2020.[3] These incidents demonstrate how 2020 Black Lives Matter/BLM actions and protests in the US have sparked offshoots in a country with a colonial history of murder, torture, and oppression. From 1894 to 1915, German *"Schutztruppe"* – a term literally meaning the "protection troop" established to "protect their territory" but also a euphemism paternalistically and falsely assuming that the tribes needed protection from each other – occupied then "South West Africa." From 1904 to 1908, these imperialist forces waged violent genocidal acts against the Ovaherero, Damara, Ovambo, and Nama peoples.[4] For over a century, statues, plaques, buildings, street names, and memorials have commemorated this colonial rule. On 28 May 2021, Germany's foreign minister Heiko Maas officially recognized Germany's colonial actions as genocide and announced an agreement to fund projects worth over a billion euros. The abrupt media announcement, the arbitrary amount of funding, and the stipulation that the funds be used for reconstruction and development projects and not for reparations per se caused many to assert that the gesture was not enough.[5] Amid and in opposition to reminders of their torturous past and half-hearted apologies, the many diverse peoples of postcolonial Namibia envision a history honouring heroes' and victims' actions while condemning perpetrators' violence. For example, several streets are being renamed after prominent leaders of the many ethnic groups in Namibia, and demands that skulls and bones used for "anthropological research" during colonial times be returned from Germany to Namibia have, at least partially, been met. Connections between Namibia and the BLM movement thus belong to the larger persistent struggle against pervasive settler colonialism and white supremacy.

Omnipresent memorialization of settler colonialism countered by the struggles of the diverse ethnic groups in Namibia to create their own postcolonial narrative also gives cause for reflection on the complex and multifarious web of the "koloniale HERRschaft" (colonial MASTERhood/LORDship) that has shaped perspectives on Africa. The gendered emphasis on "HERR" (MASTER/LORD) here is a conscious one. Research has made inroads into investigating the significance of gender in the lived experiences and memories of colonial violence.[6] Identifying male imperialist authorities provokes questions about the role of white women. Certainly, white women have been both complicit and active in fostering an "imperialist imagination" in Germany.[7] Essays by Carola Daffner, Maureen Gallagher, Julia K. Gruber, and Sarah Henneböhl in this volume examine the diverse perspectives and actions of colonial-era German women. My essay moves into contemporary times and analyses perspectives in three writings by white, German-speaking women who are living or have lived in Namibia. I specifically examine how and if these authors confront wrongdoings under settler colonialism and constructively criticize vestiges of white supremacy and settler colonialism at the intersection of gender, politics, economics, history, and literature.

My choice of works is, admittedly, selective, and stems from a particular context and time frame in my own life as a professor and scholar, namely before and after my research sojourn in summer 2018 in Namibia. In preparation for that journey, I read several books, short stories, and scholarly articles by German-speaking authors, including *Hauptsache Windhoek*, edited by Silvia Schlettwein and Erika von Wietersheim (2013); Anna Mandus's *Licht und Schatten in Namibia: Alltag in einem Traumland* (2016); and Hannah Schreckenbach's *Sehnsuchsland Namibia* (2017).[8] I initially read these books to trace German colonialism as portrayed by German speakers. In hindsight, I recognize my uncritical eye towards gleaning colonial mindsets and racism in these works. After travelling through Namibia while observing colonial monuments countered by efforts of ethnic groups to insert themselves into their own history, and then following the impact of the BLM movement in Namibia – a country with a postcolonial minority white presence – I realized that I needed to re-examine these works closely from what Peggy Piesche calls a "critical white perspective." Such a perspective would discern how much white authors recognize and assess the colonial power's lingering impact on Namibia's history and cultures.[9] Additionally, that perspective would acknowledge our positionality as white women and, as Piesche asserts: "would mean that they [here I would use 'we' to refer to myself as well] would finally look at their [our] complicity in whiteness."[10]

Besides being published by white German-speaking women while travelling and/or living in Namibia, all three publications came out within four years, and thus provide important twenty-first-century viewpoints on Namibia decades after independence and during a period of relative political stability. *Hauptsache Windhoek* was supported by the Goethe-Institut Namibia in Windhoek; both *Licht und Schatten in Namibia* and *Sehnsuchtsland Namibia* appeared with the Palmato publishing house in Germany. In fact, Palmato serves as a common thread for the women writers: Erika von Wietersheim – one of the editors of *Hauptsache Windhoek* – also published her *Guten Morgen Namibia! Eine Farm, eine Schule und unser Weg von der Apartheid zur Unabhängigkeit* with Palmato in 2019, and Silvia Schlettwein – the other editor – translated *Licht und Schatten in Namibia* into English and published her book *Katima: eine Kindheit in Namibia* with Palmato in 2021. In analysing the publications with a critical lens, I ask how the authors have confronted colonialism and white supremacy as the country has undergone visible struggles against memorializing imperialist occupation. Moreover, when I contextualize these works through further theoretical readings, Dirk Göttsche's observations in his book *Remembering Africa* regarding literary works – mostly historical fiction – about Namibia became relevant; he remarks that literary works tend to normalize and mainstream the "postcolonial gaze,"[11] to move "beyond postcolonial politics," and "to combine explicit criticism of colonial conditions with a return to the excitement of colonial adventure in exotic terrain and colonial myths of personal liberation, fulfillment, and achievement in colonial space."[12]

To be clear, the works I examine are neither literary historical fiction nor scholarly studies such as those published by the Basler Afrika Bibliographien, the Namibia Wissenschaftliche Gesellschaft, or the University of Namibia (UNAM) Press. Palmato – named after the unusual, web-footed, translucent Palmato gecko (*Pachydactylus rangei*) that is highly adapted to the harsh, sandy, rocky Namibian desert regions – was founded in 2015 to focus on themes from Africa, and particularly Namibia and Ghana. Palmato's founding editor, Felizitas Peters, aims to have the books be informative, entertaining, high quality, and indicative of the perspective of outsiders on Namibia.[13] The works attempt to engage a wide range of intellectually curious readers to discover further the history, geographical areas, peoples, cultures, and current concerns in Namibia. At the same time, they target a German-speaking audience with the desire and means to travel to Namibia. Therefore, the critical white perspective must ask how these publications support the tourism industry which, as research shows, presents problems for local peoples, including exoticization, exploitation of natural resources, endangerment of local flora and fauna, and commoditization that dilutes and destroys local cultures.[14]

First, some demographic background and definitions are necessary. Approximately twenty thousand people of German descent reside in Namibia; within the country's total population of around 2.5 million, approximately one per cent of Namibian households speak German as a main language.[15] They identify themselves as *Deutschnamibier* (German Namibians) in contrast to *Deutschländer* (Germans from Germany). Some also still refer to themselves and others as *Südwester* (South Westerner) or *Südwesterdeutsche* (South West German), with no critical reflection on the history of violence and white supremacy embedded in that colonial term. In many cases, "Deutschnamibier" refers to a native German-speaker – in contrast to the national language of English; the other main colonial language, Afrikaans; and the many languages spoken by the native inhabitants, such as Oshiwambo, Khoekhoegowab, and Otjiherero. "Deutschnamibier" can also designate a person as white, as opposed to the majority of inhabitants composed of diverse Black populations. Many "Deutschnamibier" belong to the fifth generation after colonial times, and there are now sixth- and seventh-generation "Deutschnamibier." The German-speaking Black South West Africa People's Organization (SWAPO) fighters' children who grew up as foster children in the German Democratic Republic (GDR) and then returned to Namibia also speak German, but must clearly be distinguished historically, culturally, ethnically, and socially from the white "Deutschnamibier" who descend from white German colonial settlers and still own much of the land in Namibia.[16] The melding of cultures and languages makes determining the exact linguistic and ethnic identities of "Deutschnamibier" statistically difficult, although the majority most likely are white. Groups of mostly white "Deutschnamibier" still maintain their heritage through organizations and activities. Their influence manifests itself in the above-mentioned public memorialization of German imperial presence and in the presence of cafes, bakeries, restaurants, the supermarket chain Spar, and the active Goethe-Institut, which published *Hauptsache Windhoek*.

Hauptsache Windhoek contains almost three dozen stories and poems by German-speaking Namibians who grew up in Windhoek, where German schools, churches, markets, and newspapers existed earlier. The book thus offers an apt introduction to the remaining traces of German colonialism. The co-editor Erika [Falk] von Wietersheim was born in 1952 in

Lüderitzbucht, Namibia. After studying *Germanistik*, social anthropology, and mathematics at the University of Cape Town, she returned to southern Namibia to help run and then take over her then in-laws' farm. While tending to the farm, she began educating the families of the Black farmhands and engaging with issues related to education and land reform. After giving up the farm, she worked as an editor and journalist in Namibia and Europe and authored five books. The other co-editor of *Hauptsache Windhoek*, Sylvia Schlettwein, was born in 1975 in Omaruru in the central Erongo region of Namibia, known for its annual festival at which the Ovaherero commemorate their past chiefs. She writes, translates, and edits short fiction and poetry in English, German, and Afrikaans.

While the book includes biographies of the two editors and photographer, Christine Skowskmi, biographies of the edition's other contributors are missing. Hence, readers cannot judge whether themes or perspectives that surface fall along colour lines. However, the first-person narrator in the first story, "Mein Windhoek-Spaziergang durch die Kinderzeit" (My Windhoek-walk through childhood times) by Ingrid Kubisch, reveals that she is white, as the places she visits as a child in Windhoek were built and frequented by German-speaking white people.[17] Leaving the reader to assume that the narrator is white signals white privilege in a country where narratives of white colonial power still surface as the norm. In the story, the adjective "*deutsch*" (German) implicitly indicates white people, as when the narrator describes being born with her twin in the Elisabethhaus: "Da wurden alle deutschen Kinder geboren" (All German children were born there).[18] The twin birth caused a sensation. The narrator invokes a stereotypical cultural clash – that of native women wanting to steal babies from the white colonizers – when she comments on the Ovaherero women standing in front of the hospital door and trying to convince her mother to give them one of the twins.[19]

Here and in many other childhood reminiscences, the narrator lacks reflective self-criticism when portraying what she sees as a clear demarcation between white and tribal peoples' values and customs. At one point, the narrator's aunt Eva asks the narrator to bring her "*Hottentottenpopos*," the name given to green and brown Lithops plants. The offensive name "Hottentot" derives from the highly sexualized image of members of the Khoi people – referencing the clicks in their language – whose buttocks (in German *Popos*) were objectified in European human zoos in nineteenth-century Europe.[20] Instead of critically questioning this offensive colonial meaning, the narrator launches into what she considers cute childhood associations. She talks about the neighbour's young boy gardener who identifies himself as a Hottentott – "'*Fritz die Hotnot*,' sagt er immer. Ich kann seinen Popo nicht so direkt sehen, da ist ja seine Hose drüber. Ich kann mir aber nicht vorstellen, dass der so aussieht wie diese *Hottentottenpopos*. Auf jeden Fall nicht grün. Sicher braun" ("Fritz the Hotnot," he always says. I can't exactly see his buttocks, his pants are always covering them. But I can just imagine that they look exactly like these *Hottentottenbuttocks*. In any case, not green. Surely brown).[21] Just as Saartje Baartmann was exhibited in Europe in the early 1800s, dehumanized and compared to an animal, the "Hottentot" here is compared to a plant from a Eurocentric perspective that ridicules and exaggerates their anatomy and sexuality.

Other anecdotes and comments depict childhood innocence without critical reflection. In the section "Ein schwarzes Kind!" (A Black child) the narrator declares "Ich hab' ein Kaffernkind gesehen!" (I saw a Kaffir child).[22] During South African apartheid, right-wing white people used the word consciously to offend and demean Black Africans; thus, the word is currently banned in South Africa.[23] Instead of apologizing for or criticizing her racism, the author defends her usage and invokes her childhood innocence. The word *Kaffer*, she states, was a South African word used in everyday speech in the 1950s and 1960s.[24] She then makes whites the victims of apartheid injustice, disregarding the harm inflicted on Black people "Die *Apartheid* hat auch den weißen Kindern insofern Unrecht getan, dass sie ihre schwarzen Altersgenossen nicht kennen lernen durften" (The apartheid also did white children a disfavour by not allowing them to get to know their Black peers).[25]

The matter-of-factness that normalizes colonial influence and justifies racism occurs repeatedly. After attending mass at the *Christuskirche*, the family rides around town, passing the controversial *Reiterdenkmal* (equestrian monument), an homage to the colonial forces who fought against the Ovaherero and Nama, which has in reality been removed in 2013. She writes in admiration: "Der Reiter ist für mich so ein schöner Mann, edel und gut – ich nenne ihn heimlich *Old Schatterhand* und er reitet auf dem edlen Hengst, Hatatila, den Winnetou ihm geschenkt hat" (The equestrian is such a handsome man, noble and good – I secretly call him "Old Schatterhand," and he rides on his noble stallion, Hatatila, that Winnetou had given him).[26] The story displays a deep-seated nostalgia for and identification with colonial rule. By invoking the German author Karl May's nineteenth-century racist Winnetou texts of cowboys and Native Americans in the American West, she pejoratively and dangerously maintains hierarchies of the conquerors and the conquered with no regard for Namibia's historical, geographic, social, or cultural contexts. Telling this story from childhood remembrances without commenting on the racism behind words, expressions, and actions does not address the colonial mentality that still exists. Whether in the minds of a child or an adult, consistent use of such imagery without reflection constitutes racism.[27]

While I cannot examine all of *Hauptsache Windhoek* here, this opening story provides a foray into the colonial mentality fraught with racist perspectives from white authors writing about Namibia. Anna Mandus's biography printed on the cover of her *Licht and Schatten*, which is a collection of essays based on Mandus's own observations while visiting and living in Namibia, belies vestiges of colonial and Eurocentric viewpoints. Born in 1962 in Germany, Mandus lived in the United States and in Asia before returning to Germany to begin a business and start her writing career. Using the imperialist metaphor of conquest, the book jacket describes her going to Africa to "erobern" (conquer) another continent. There she found a partner, "einen waschechten Südwester" (an honest-to-goodness South Westerner), a self-identifying term harking back to the colonial territory "Südwest Afrika" and used by German-speaking settlers. Historically, "Südwester" have espoused an ideology displaying elements of nationalism – not necessarily a political structure, but more a cultural survival of their language, traditions, religion, and way of life.[28]

The first chapter, "Einmal Schwarzwälder Kirschtorte, bitte" ("A piece of Black Forest cake, please"), applies the metaphor of the traditional German layer cake of chocolate cake, whipped cream, cherries, and kirschwasser to Namibia's cultures and peoples. It's clear, the first-person narrator states, that the colours of the cake layers and the whipped cream represent the diversity of Black, white, and brown people in the country. But where, she asks, do the red cherries fit into this metaphor? She suggests they could stand for the blood the people have shed in their long violent history. Instead, she insists, they signify all the beautiful things the country has to offer.[29] She mentions, in this order, the sunsets, landscape, natural resources, animals, cliff formations, and secrets of the desert. She concludes by listing everyday moments that exhilarate, including the evening "Braai" grilling, rugby tournaments, and the colourful dresses and headscarves of the Ovaherero and Nama women.[30] A footnote identifies the Ovaherero and Nama as ethnic groups and describes the Nama emigration from the Cape region in the eighteenth and nineteenth centuries. Critical readers should first ask why she reduces Ovaherero and Nama women to their dress at the end of a running list. Second, they should ask whether the two options – the violent colonial history and the beauty of the land, peoples, cultures – need be mutually exclusive. In choosing this false dichotomy, Mandus privileges the option that would be more attractive to the tourism industry – namely outer appearances – instead of espousing a profounder historical viewpoint.

While Mandus stresses here that peoples' skin colours and dress make Namibia diverse and colourful, the chapter entitled "Glücklich ist ein deutscher Hund" (A German dog is happy) monolithically depicts Black people as criminals. The narrator relates how she and her partner Kurt acquire a Boerboel – a large, South African dog breed – to accompany her on her walks because she is afraid of being robbed by the "Tsotsis," a South African slang word for hoodlums or gang members. Tsotsi culture was seen as having developed particularly in townships populated by Black people; thus, this passage reflects the automatic prejudicial connection between Black people and criminality. Indeed, when the narrator walks along the Avis Dam, a popular nature reserve outside of Windhoek, she discovers that her dog Sanya growls only at Black people. When she relates this reaction to Kurt, he rejoices how they made the right decision in choosing this dog because the narrator will now be safe. After all, he asks, how many whites are going to attack her along the Avis Dam?[31] The narrator does not counter this racist remark, but merely agrees, admitting rather flippantly that she needs to abandon what she identifies as her "German scruples," referring perhaps to the critical perspective she should be conscientiously adopting. Instead, she accepts her dog's behaviour and thereby the racist belief that Black – not white – people are always the attackers.

While Mandus feels she needs to abandon her "German scruples," she by no means abandons her Eurocentric viewpoint when giving advice on the Namibian school curriculum. In the chapter "Der Knabe im Moor" (The boy in the bog), Mandus finds her partner's son reading the poem by the nineteenth-century German author Annette von Droste-Hülshoff, who was born in North Rhine-Westphalia and died in Baden, and wonders why he has not been assigned more relevant texts and authors. She questions whether adolescent pupils who have never seen Germany will be able to relate to the poem, as she surmises that the boggy, foggy November landscape in the poems will be totally foreign to them.[32] Mandus makes clear that she is an avid fan of poetry and that her criticism is not against reading poetry. Instead, she asks whether it would make more sense to read more modern, true-to-life authors.[33]

Mandus does pose a dilemma that all instructors face in these utilitarian times, that is, choosing texts that students might find "relevant" enough to their lives and thus engaging them. But instead of using this criticism as a springboard for suggesting possible contemporary works to reflect the multifarious cultures living in German-speaking countries today, or instead of promoting a critical look at German colonialism in Namibia, she criticizes the school lessons for not preparing students well enough for future jobs in Germany where they would be using the German language. In this same vein, she criticizes the lessons for concentrating too much on Namibian history and culture and not enough on Europe (61). Although she understands why students need to learn Namibia's history, she also asks: "Aber: Reicht es aus, zu wissen, wer Henrik Witbooi und Maherero waren? Kann man dafür Napoleon, Bismarck und Stalin ignorieren? Ganz zu schweigen von Hitler, Willy Brandt und Helmut Kohl?" (But: is it really enough to know who Henrik Witbooi and Maherero were? In exchange, can one really ignore Napoleon, Bismarck, and Stalin? Not to mention Hitler, Willy Brandt, and Helmut Kohl?).[34] She subsequently connects this Eurocentric argument to Black pupils pursuing employment: "Würden nicht auch sie davon profitieren, wenn sie wüssten, welche Länder der Welt demokratisch und welche totalitär regiert sind, oder wie diese Regierungssysteme funktionieren?" (Wouldn't they also profit from knowing which countries in the world were ruled by democracy and which by totalitarianism, or how these systems of government function?).[35] This question invites more questions on the part of the reader who wishes for a more critical, inclusive perspective. Why would learning about white male historical figures help pupils more than learning about Peoples of Colour? Why not add Martin Luther King Jr., May Ayim, Audre Lourde, Nelson Mandela, and Wangari Maathai, for example, to her list of world leaders and cultural icons? Instead of placing the burden and criticism solely on the Namibian educational system, why not demand that the German educational system incorporate more Namibian leaders and value that knowledge for successful careers and diplomatic relations?

When I asked Palmato editor Felizitas Peters in an email about this focus on male leaders, she answered diplomatically and equivocally. She acknowledged the wish that Mandus would have included more women. She explains, however, that including women would have been difficult due to the lack of female political and historical figures in Namibia. But, she states, female independence fighters in Namibia did exist, and were less acknowledged than their male counterparts. Also, the fact that Namibian schools do not teach about international Black artists or politicians "ist ein Thema für sich" (is a subject in and of itself).[36] Peters mentions that possible future publications by Palmato will most likely rectify these weaknesses. As Black Namibian voices emerge, readers hope these promises are fulfilled.

The book's title – *Licht und Schatten* (Light and shadow) – does prepare readers for positive and negative reflections on the country. Yet the subtitle of the book – *Alltag in einem Traumland* (Everyday life in a dreamland) – substantiates Göttsche's observations of recent works that have moved away from postcolonial politics to project an image of colonial adventure and freedom. In general, the chapters in the book create the impression that adventure and freedom belong to white Germans, largely those who visit Namibia in the short or long term, or who take up residence there. Thus, they can live largely with their "imperialist imaginations," exoticizing the country with images of cakes while living out racism through their dogs and Eurocentrism through their suggestions for educational lessons.

The title of Hannah Schreckenbach's book – *Sehnsuchtsland Namibia* (Land of longing Namibia) – exoticizes the country. Born in 1932 in Magdeburg, Germany, Schreckenbach spent twenty-two years living and working as an architect and educator in Ghana, for which she received the German Federal Cross of Merit in 1981. Between 1992 and 2011, Schreckenbach made ten trips to Namibia. She attributes her life-long fascination with the country to her father's own wishes to work as a waterworks engineer in Africa and to his special interest in "Deutsch-Südwestafrika." For Christmas 1944, her father gave her the 1941 children's book, *Die Kinderfarm* (The children's farm) by Ernst Ludwig Cramer, which Schreckenbach managed to save from her house, bombed during the Second World War, but then lost in post-war chaos. She recounts how, through pure circumstance, she found the book in a bookstore's catalogue. During a visit to Namibia in December 2004, she was able to meet Cramer's descendants and to visit the farm.

Using Cramer's book as an inspiration, however, represents, again in Göttsche's words, "a return to the excitement of colonial adventure in exotic terrain and colonial myths of personal liberation, fulfillment, and achievement in colonial space."[37] Simply the 1941 publication date of *Die Kinderfarm* at the height of National Socialism offers a clue to its racist perspectives.[38] The children's book not only idealizes farm life, nature, and the German language, culture, and customs in the former "South West Africa," but also contains blatant racist elements.[39] As Andrée-Jeanne Tötemeyer states, passages in the book describe Black farm hands as "cheeky," "lazy," "dirty," and "smelly."[40] Some of the Black farm hands even acquired names based on these characteristics. Sendine's name, for example, comes from "Ölsardine" (sardines in oil) because, following an Indigenous custom, the woman rubs herself with a red oil to protect herself from the sun: "Für unsere Nasen stinkt dieses Öl," (To our noses, this oil stinks).[41] And the skin colour of some is often attributed to their "dirtiness."[42] In response to my observation about Schreckenbach's nostalgic view of Cramer's racist book, Palmato editor Peters again diplomatically emphasizes the context in which Schreckenbach had originally read the book, namely as a child experiencing fear in a bomb shelter. That, Peters argued, would explain her remembering the work as one that consoled and distracted her as opposed to one that promulgated racism.[43] Peters recommends reading Schreckenbach's book *Herzensheimat Ghana* (Home of the heart Ghana), which reflects a much stronger anti-racist sentiment.[44]

Unfortunately, Schreckenbach takes no critical stance on Cramer's book in *Sehnsuchtsland Namibia*, nor does she inform readers much about colonial atrocities. Only a brief passage recommends that visitors to the Waterberg National Park learn about the horrible history of the area. There, in August 1904, the colonial forces began their genocide of the Ovaherero by pushing thousands of men, women, children, and their cattle into the sandy, dry Omaheke Desert where thousands of them died. She also mentions that many died in the concentration camp in Windhoek.[45] Besides these few passages, her book reveals historical developments largely from a colonial perspective. She visits and comments on the several museums devoted to German colonial artefacts, such as those in Windhoek, Tsumeb, and Swakopmund, but she does not appear to have visited the exhibit in the Independence Museum in Windhoek, which showcases the local tribes' contributions to the area and their fight for independence as told from the perspective of the SWAPO independence movement itself. She merely criticizes the Independence Museum for being "ugly" on the outside.[46]

Schreckenbach uses descriptions of poorer areas of the country populated by Black people to point to what she perceives as lingering problems of poverty and alcohol addiction. The mining town of Tsumeb, for example, is known for its huge mineralized pipe containing ore that was originally mined beginning in 1905 by the Otavi Minen- und Eisenbahn-Gesellschaft (OMEG) for copper, lead, silver, gold, arsenic, and germanium. After visiting the colonial museum in Tsumeb, Schreckenbach writes about driving through the townships and squatter settlements. She describes them as places where mostly unemployed former miners live, creating what she identifies as "slums." These "slums," like the illegal settlements in the Kombat Mine outside Tsumeb, cause problems for the city.[47] Her lamentations about this poverty come across more as a description of the so-called "white man's burden" than a critical look at possible imperialistic roots of that poverty. She includes nothing about the history of the exploitation of Black mine workers by the colonial powers, the economic consequences for the local populations when colonial industries vacate the area, and the responsibilities that such powers should assume. When she revisits in 2003, she finds nothing changed, just as her tainted colonialist viewpoint also has not changed. She continues to comment on the unemployed and the squatters in the town and wishes to see the copper mine in business again instead of suggesting more viable sources of income and assistance for the townspeople.[48]

In general, as an architect and engineer, Schreckenbach relishes what she deems are the architectural "jewels" of the colonial times: the post office in Keetmanshoop;[49] the Swakopmund "Ärztehaus;"[50] the fort in Namutoni;[51] the Immenhof farm from colonial times from Cramer's book;[52] and Fort Sesfontein. Her picture of the tribal peoples and their business endeavours, however, focuses mostly on the poverty of the people, as when she talks about the numerous shops alongside the road[53] and the infamous township of Katutura in Windhoek.[54] She does not describe in detail the roots of the township, whose name in Otjiherero means "the place where we do not want to live." Katutura was originally created in 1961 by a forced removal of the Black population from an area of town that evolved into the richer all-white neighbourhood of Hochland Park. The creation followed years of protests and boycotts by the residents against the relocation and the 1959 massacre by the police during the so-called "Old Location Uprising," which resulted in eleven people dead and forty-four wounded. Schreckenbach has not taken the time to describe this horrible history and to see the evidence of the exploitation of Black labour and the disenfranchisement and uprooting of people as the main causes of poverty.

As with Kubisch's description of "My Windhoek," Schreckenbach's text conveys nostalgia for a past she sees will never return. In all three works I have examined, what the authors do not see and describe becomes as significant as what they observe. They rarely take a critical look at the way in which colonial history still determines the economic, social, and cultural divides in the country. As much as they want to show an appreciation for the beauty, diversity, and complexity of the country and its peoples, they ultimately focus on whites as harbingers of those positive aspects. The authors often fail to acknowledge and recognize cultural racism, which, as defined by Kendi, ends up "creating a cultural standard and imposing a cultural hierarchy among racial groups."[55] They never free themselves from their imperialist imaginations.

In conclusion, I want to mention that since these three works appeared, Palmato has published three more books on Namibia that display more recognition of the need to develop a heightened critical white perspective. First, Anna Mandus's *Licht und Schatten in Namibia 2*, the sequel to her first book, contains her introduction that addresses readers who criticized her first book for reflecting the perspective of a white middle-class female emigrant too much and for omitting perspectives of Black people and the problems of the underprivileged.[56] Mandus promises to rectify this bias and to report more on women, children, and youth in the diverse populations and in various parts of the country, if not in this book then in a possible future project. The book's chapters confront controversial topics such as the change of street names; the high rates of rental and the lack of affordable housing; climate extremes of cold winters and drought; migration of people from farms to the city; the land resettlement program; the twelfth Namibian Women Summit in 2018; and the continuing lack of opportunities for youth. In-depth analysis of the individual chapters would reveal Mandus presenting diverse opinions of Black activists and scholars.

Second, Erika von Wietersheim, in her *Guten Morgen Namibia! Eine Farm, eine Schule und unser Weg von der Apartheid zur Unabhängigkeit* (2019), provides an account of her life while managing the farm in Namibia from 1976 to 1990. Political actions leading up to independence serve as background to her building a farm school and to the political involvement of her white husband, Anton von Wietersheim, who was a SWAPO candidate elected to the National Assembly in 1990.[57] Further examination of this work would demand close textual analysis and explorations into Namibian politics, especially the involvement of whites in the independence movement.

Third, Julia Runge's *Sheeban Queens* presents a photographic exploration of women running "shebeen" bars in townships in Namibia and South Africa.[58] The term "shebeen" is derived from the Irish *sibín* and refers to a kind of makeshift bar selling alcohol without a valid licence. Interspersed with Runge's photographs are quotes from the women, and in the final pages, Runge includes brief stories from the women's lives. An in-depth study of this work, which unfortunately cannot be undertaken within the scope of this essay, would analyze the impact of Runge's white, feminist gaze on the photographic portrayal of Black culture and would pay attention to theories espoused by such Black scholars as Tina Campt and bell hooks.[59] Such a future project would determine whether time, political developments, and increased empowerment of Black people, Indigenous Peoples, and Peoples of Colour in Namibia have contributed to the development of a critical white perspective.[60]

In looking at the three earlier works, I have explored ways in which we whites – authors, scholars, and readers – can move away from the confines of nostalgia, defensiveness, and fantasy towards engaging in a more actual, more Black people/Indigenous Peoples/Peoples of Colour-centred, white-decentered postcolonial narrative. The majority Black population in Namibia lives amid persistent memorials to its colonial past while Black people are making strides to insert themselves into that narrative as positive forces of change. White women authors such as Kubisch, Mandus, Schreckenbach, Schlettwein, and von Wietersheim seem particularly well-equipped to take on this task of critical intervention. Their socio-economic positions, personal family histories, and professional networks have connected them to many facets of life in Namibia, including educational institutions, townships, farms, nature, businesses, writers' groups, languages, architecture, construction projects, families, and social organizations. Publishers such as Palmato are in positions to empower Blackness and demonstrate white critical perspectives through selection of works and editorial processes. We whites still have much work to do.

NOTES

1 Thank you to Pacific University's Elise Elliott International and Intercultural Fund and the Confederation in Oregon for Language Teaching for supporting my research in Namibia; to public-health researchers Kimberly Parsons and Rebecca Schoon for travelling with me; to the German Studies Association seminar participants; and to the editors of this volume – Lisabeth Hock, Michelle James, and Priscilla Layne – for suggestions. Many thanks to Prof. Dr. Keya Mitra for her invaluable help in revising.
2 Frank Steffen, "Aufschrei wegen 'All Lives Matter,'" *Allgemeine Zeitung*, 20 July 2020, https://www.az.com.na/nachrichten/aufschrei-wegen-all-lives-matter-2020-07-20/.
3 Clayton Peel and Anna Hamalwa, "Do Black Lives Matter in Africa?," *The Namibian*, 17 July 2020, https://www.namibian.com.na/do-black-lives-matter-in-africa/. I use the self-identifying term "Black" people to refer to non-white Namibians, at the same time recognizing that Black Namibians are not a monolithic group, but rather comprised of at least fourteen main groups that identify as Black people, Indigenous Peoples, and mixed-race Peoples of Colour.
4 See Jürgen Zimmerer and Joachim Zeller, eds., *Völkermord in Deutsch-Südwestafrika: der Kolonialkrieg (1904–1908) in Namibia und seine Folgen* (Berlin: Links, 2003); and David Olusoga and Casper W. Erichsen, *The Kaiser's Holocaust: Germany's Forgotten Genocide and the Colonial Roots of Nazism* (London: Faber and Faber, 2010). I have decided to use the designation Ovaherero, a term by which the people of this ethnicity call themselves, instead of Herero, a name found often in English and German scholarship, but also one that the German colonizers used.
5 At the time of writing this article, the German Bundestag as a whole has yet to vote on a resolution to issue a formal apology for the genocide. The 2021 agreement between the German and Namibian governments has also not been ratified by the Namibian parliament and has been explicitly rejected by the Ovaherero Traditional Authority and the Nama Traditional Leaders Association due to their exclusion from the negotiation table. In January

2023, the two groups filed a lawsuit against the agreement, claiming it illegally does not provide direct compensation to the victims' descendants. See Claudia Bröll, "Herero und Nama klagen gegen Aussöhnungsabkommen mit Deutschland," *Frankfurter Allgemeine Zeitung*, 20 January 2023, https://www.faz.net/aktuell/politik/ausland/herero-und-nama-klagen-gegen-aussoehnungsabkommen-mit-deutschland-18618710.html.

6 See Molly McCullers, "The 'Truppenspieler Show': Herero Masculinity and the German Colonial Military Aesthetic," in *German Colonialism Revisited: African, Asian, and Oceanic Experiences*, ed. Nina Berman, Klaus Mühlhahn, and Patrice Nganang (Ann Arbor: University of Michigan Press, 2018), 230–1; Marion Wallace and John Kinahan, *A History of Namibia: From the Beginning to 1990* (Auckland Park, South Africa: Jacana Media, 2011), 3; and Saskia Trebling, "Personal fürs Humboldt Forum: wo bleiben die anderen Stimmen?" *monopol: Magazin für Kunst und Leben*, 26 April 2018, https://www.monopol-magazin.de/humboldt-forum-weiss-maennlich-kommentar.

7 See "Introduction," in Sara Pugach, David Pizzo, and Adam Blackler, *After the Imperialist Imagination: Two Decades of Research on Global Germany and Its Legacies* (Oxford: Peter Lang, 2020), 14; and Friederike Eigler, "Engendering German Nationalism: Gender and Race in Frieda von Bülow's Colonial Writings," *The Imperialist Imagination: German Colonialism and Its Legacy*, ed. Sara Friedrichsmeyer, Sara Lennox, and Susanne Zantop (Ann Arbor: University of Michigan Press, 1998), 69–85.

8 Sylvia Schlettwein and Erika von Wietersheim, *Hauptsache Windhoek* (Windhoek: Wordweaver, 2013); Anna Mandus, *Licht und Schatten in Namibia: Alltag in einem Traumland* (Hamburg: Palmato, 2016); Hannah Schreckenbach, *Sehnsuchsland Namibia* (Hamburg: Palmato, 2017). I will cite pages from these editions directly in my essay. All translations from the original German into English are mine, unless otherwise noted.

9 Peggy Piesche and Sara Lennox, "Epilogue. Of Epistemologies and Positionalities: A Conversation, Berlin, October 21, 2014," in *Remapping Black Germany: New Perspectives on Afro-German History, Politics, and Culture*, ed Sara Lennox (Amherst: University of Massachusetts Press, 2016), 274–81.

10 Piesche and Lennox, "Epilogue," 279.

11 Dirk Göttsche, *Remembering Africa: The Rediscovery of Colonialism in Contemporary German Literature* (Rochester, NY: Camden House, 2013), 101. Here Göttsche is quoting from Paul Lützeler, *Der postkoloniale Blick: deutsche Schriftsteller berichten aus der Dritten Welt* (Frankfurt: Suhrkamp, 1997).

12 Göttsche, *Remembering Africa*, 101. I must note that the voices of white women of German heritage are not the only ones that have come out of Namibia; see Stefanie-Layla Aukongo and Peter Hilliges, *Kalungas Kind: meine unglaubliche Reise ins Leben* (Scotts Valley, CA: CreateSpace Independent Publishing Platform, 2014); Lucia Engombe, *Kind Nr. 95: Meine*

deutsch-afrikanische Odyssee (Berlin: Ullstein Verlag, 2004); and Katharina von Hammerstein, "The Herero: Witnessing Germany's 'Other Genocide,'" *Contemporary French and Francophone Studies* 20, no. 2 (2016), 267–86, https://www.tandfonline.com/doi/full/10.1080/17409292.2016.1143742.

13 Felizitas Peters, email message to author, 3 August 2020.

14 See Jarkko Saarinen, "Tourism, Indigenous People, and the Challenge of Development: The Representations of Ovahimbas in Tourism Promotion and Community Perceptions Toward Tourism," *Tourism Analysis* 16, no. 1 (2011): 31–42, https://www.ingentaconnect.com/content/cog/ta/2011/00000016/00000001/art00004; and Anna Shilongo, "Tourism and Commoditization of Traditional Cultures among the Himba People of Namibia," *Edition Consortium Journal of Arts, Humanities and Social Sciences* 2, no. 1 (2020): 187–96, https://editoncpublishing.org/ecpj/index.php/ECJAHSS/article/view/173.

15 "Namibia 2011 Population and Housing Census Main Report," Namibia Statistics Agency, https://nsa.org.na/document/namibia-population-and-housing-census-main-report-2011/.

16 Although their stories differ from each other, Stefanie-Layla Aukongo and Lucia Engombe are two examples of these German-speaking foster children. See n12 above.

17 An article about Ingrid Kubisch, whom I presume to be the same author, includes a picture that identifies her as white: "Vom Roman zu Kurzgeschichte: eine Fabuliererin beim Projekthüpfen," *Allgemeine Zeitung*, 19 August 2005, https://www.az.com.na/nachrichten/vom-roman-zur-kurzgeschichte-eine-fabuliererin-beim-projekthpfen.

18 Ingrid Kubisch, "Mein Windhoek-Spaziergang durch die Kinderzeit," in Schlettwein and Wietersheim, *Hauptsache Windhoek*, 2.

19 Kubisch, "Mein Windhoek," 2.

20 Stefan Göttel, "Hottentotten/Hottentottin," *Afrika und die deutsche Sprache: ein kritisches Nachschlagewerk*, ed. Susan Arndt, Antje Hornscheidt, and Marlene Bauer (Münster: Unrast, 2018), 147–53. Saartje Baartmann, named by colonizers as the "Hottentot Venus," was brought to France in 1810 to be exhibited at fairs and in circuses to represent what colonizers deemed as her wild sexuality and racial inferiority. When she died, she was dissected as part of "scientific investigations" into whether she was an animal or a human.

21 Kubisch, "Mein Windhoek," 3.

22 Kubisch, "Mein Windhoek," 8.

23 Katherine Machnik, "Kaffer/Kafferin," *Afrika und die deutsche Sprache: ein kritisches Nachschlagewerk*, ed. Susan Arndt, Antje Hornscheidt, and Marlene Bauer (Münster: Unrast, 2018), 154–8.

24 Kubisch, "Mein Windhoek," 9.

25 Kubisch, "Mein Windhoek," 9.

26 Kubisch, "Mein Windhoek," 8.
27 See Ibram X. Kendi, *How to Be an Antiracist* (New York: One World, 2019). For an example of a critical perspective, see Friederike Habermann, *Der unsichtbare Tropenhelm: Wie koloniales Denken noch immer unsere Köpfe beherrscht* (Klein Jasedow: ThinkOya, 2013), 54–5. Habermann critically revisits her grandfather's positive assessment of colonial times by illuminating destructive outcomes on the Indigenous peoples.
28 See Klaus Rüdiger and Heribert Weiland, "'Hart wie Kameldornholz': der Weg der Deutschsprachigen von Südwest nach Namibia," *Africa Spectrum* 27, no. 3 (1992): 343–65, https://www.jstor.org/stable/40174603.
29 Mandus, *Licht und Schatten*, 16.
30 Mandus, *Licht und Schatten*, 17.
31 Mandus, *Licht und Schatten*, 84.
32 Mandus, *Licht und Schatten*, 60.
33 Mandus, *Licht und Schatten*, 61.
34 Here Mandus includes the footnote identifying the Ovaherero leader Samuel Maherero and the Nama leader Henrik Witbooi in the fight against the German colonial troops. Mandus, *Licht und Schatten*, 63.
35 Mandus, *Licht und Schatten*, 63.
36 Peters, email message to author.
37 Dirk Göttsche, *Remembering Africa*, 101.
38 Ernst Ludwig Cramer, *Die Kinderfarm* (Potsdam: Rütten and Loening, 1941).
39 For an analysis of colonial literature for children during National Socialism, see Julia Gruber's contribution to this volume.
40 Andrée-Jeanne Tötemeyer, "Desert Survival and Wilderness Adventures: Juvenile Literature for a Young Namibian Nation?" in *Preserving the Landscape of Imagination: Children's Literature in* Africa, ed. Raoul Granqvist and Jürgen Martini (Amsterdam: Rodopi, 1997), 119–36.
41 Cramer, *Die Kinderfarm*, 15.
42 Cramer, *Die Kinderfarm*, 15–16.
43 Peters, email message to author, 3 August 2020.
44 Hannah Schreckenbach, *Herzensheimat Ghana: Erinnerungen an ein Land im Umbruch* (Hamburg: Palmato, 2018). Analysis of this book demands yet another essay with a focus different from mine here on literature about Namibia.
45 Schreckenbach, *Sehnsuchsland Namibia*, 110.
46 Schreckenbach, *Sehnsuchsland Namibia*, 274.
47 Schreckenbach, *Sehnsuchsland Namibia*, 107.
48 Schreckenbach, *Sehnsuchsland Namibia*, 198–9.
49 Schreckenbach, *Sehnsuchsland Namibia*, 164.
50 Schreckenbach, *Sehnsuchsland Namibia*, 173.

51 Schreckenbach, *Sehnsuchsland Namibia*, 191.
52 Schreckenbach, *Sehnsuchsland Namibia*, 279.
53 Schreckenbach, *Sehnsuchsland Namibia*, 228.
54 Schreckenbach, *Sehnsuchsland Namibia*, 239.
55 Kendi, *How to Be an Antiracist*, 81.
56 Anna Mandus, *Licht und Schatten in Namibia 2: mehr vom Alltag in einem Traumland* (Hamburg: Palmato, 2019), 11.
57 Erika von Wietersheim, *Guten Morgen Namibia! Eine Farm, eine Schule und unser Weg von der Apartheid zur Unabhängigkeit* (Hamburg: Palmato, 2019).
58 Julia Runge, *Shebeen Queens: Begegnungen in Namibias Townships/Close Encounters in Namibian Townships* (Hamburg: Palmato, 2020).
59 Tina Campt, *Image Matters: Archive, Photography, and the African Diaspora in Europe* (Durham, NC: Duke University Press, 2012); bell hooks, "is paris burning?," *black looks: race and representation* (New York: Routledge, 2015), 145–56.
60 Additionally, two further books have appeared with Palmato, which deserve tangential mention: Sylvia Schlettwein, *Katima: eine Kindheit in Namibia* (2021) and Frank Gschwender, ed., *Deutschland ist für mich ein Flusspferd/Germany Reminds Me of a Hippopotamus – Nambian Perspectives* (2022). The former contains autobiographical stories about Schlettwein's childhood in Namibia, but includes few if any perspectives on or from groups other than white German-speaking Namibians. The latter is a bilingual (German/English) collection of interviews with diverse peoples from Namibia who are living in Germany, focusing on their perspectives of Germans and life in Germany. A theme that arises in many of the interviews is how little Germans know about their colonial history of Namibia and about Africa in general. Ruusa Shuuya, for example, describes going to a German school that followed the German curriculum, "in which colonial history was hardly featured" (60). Henock Ntinda, when asked what he would like to add to his interview, answers: "I find it very surprising and disturbing how little Germans know about Namibia, and the common colonial past. I have no other explanation but the lacking inclusion in school curricula and the absence of it in public discourse" (87). These observations are telling in light of the way in which the history, cultures, and peoples of Namibia are presented in the books I examine in my essay here.

Index

Abbott, H. Porter, 84, 93
Accra, 57, 64
Ackermann, Rolf, 91–2, 95–6; *Die weiße Jägerin*, 91
Adas Raum, 59
Adelson, Leslie, 37–8, 52
Africa, 24, 38–9, 47, 61–2, 154–5, 162, 258–60; colonial, 241; European power in, 178, 215; "fever," 200; Inner, 159; interior, 157, 160; in literature, 54, 116, 232; "scramble for," 178, 196, 210; South West (Südwest Afrika), 5–6, 174, 197, 223, 224n14, 228, 234, 237, 258, 259, 261n4, 266, 275; tribal, 211. *See also* Berlin Conference of 1884
African Americans, 45, 61
African Diaspora, 3–4, 7–8, 24, 26, 39, 41, 44; in literature, 37, 39. *See also* Black Diaspora
Afrikaans, 269–70
Afrikanerin, Die, 86
"afrikanische Prinzessin, Eine," 175
Afrikanissimo, 73
Afrika und die deutsche Sprache, 15, 19n55, 169n7, 216, 225n22, 243n33, 243n36, 243n39, 281n20, 281n23

Afrodeutsche. *See* Black Germans
Afro-German. *See* Black Germans
Ahlman, Jeffrey S., 65–6
Alagi-yawanna-Kadalie, Angela, 60
Alexandria, 154–6, 159–61, 163
Allgemeine deutsche Biographie, 142
Allies, the, 247, 253
Amo, Wilhelm Anton, 8, 12, 46, 134–45; *Dissertatio inauguralis de iure maurorum in Europa*, 139
Andreas-Salomé, Lou, 211
Angola, 41, 47
Angsotinge, Gervase, 69–70
An Maria Ernestina, 96–7, 99
anti-Blackness, 68–9, 133, 138, 141–3, 145, 183, 197
anti-slavery, 172, 183; literature, 171, 178, 186, 196
Aquinas, Thomas, 181
Arabic, 4–5, 82, 94–5, 154, 161
Arndt, Susan, 85, 162, 216, 234
Augen / AUGEN, 40, 42–3
Aus guter Familie: Leidensgeschichte eines Mädchens, 155–6
autofiction, 53–4
Ayim, May, 7, 57, 60, 274; *Farbe bekennen*, 3, 7, 9, 15n1, 17n27, 19n51

Baartmann, Saartje, 271, 281n20
Backfisch, 247, 249, 251, 254, 259–61, 261n1
Barghash bin Said, Sultan, 88, 102, 212
"Beauty and the Beast," 144
Becoming Human, 199
Berlin, 32, 34, 138, 200, 212, 246, 252; Conference of 1884, 5, 197, 260; Wall, 24, 27, 37
Beyoncé, 25
Bible, 171, 173, 177
biracial, 7, 10
"Bioscope of the Night," 137
Bismarck, Otto von, 88, 196, 261n6, 262n13, 274
Black Diaspora, 39, 60. *See also* African Diaspora
Black female body 223
Black Germans, 7, 23, 24, 25, 34, 38, 248; activism, 9; literature, 54, 57–60, 75n15; women, 9, 34, 61, 70
Black German Studies, 57, 60
Black Lives Matter, 25, 39, 266–7
Black masculinity, 132–4, 138, 140–2, 145
Blackness, 3–4, 24, 44–6, 119, 133, 142, 173, 192, 197, 204, 207n30, 279; in literature 39, 54, 115, 137, 144, 180, 182, 195, 199; and poverty, 216
Black women, 4–11, 24–5, 27, 58, 212, 225, 260–1; in literature, 176, 186, 222; mistreatment of, 61–2, 70, 162
Blaßkiewitz, Sarah, 10, 23–4; DRUCK, 23–5; *Ivie wie Ivie*, 23–4, 26, 28, 30–2; *Sam – Ein Sachse*, 24, 25, 27, 31, 36n3; *Schloss Einstein*, 28–9
"Bridge by the Tay, The," 218, 220
Briefe eines deutschen Mädchens aus Südwest, 230–1
Briefe nach der Heimat, 82, 86, 89–92, 94

British Kenya Colony, 11, 112, 114–15. *See also* Kenya
Brockmann, Clara, 5, 230–1, 233–4, 238; *Briefe eines deutschen Mädchens aus Südwest*, 230–1; *Die deutsche Frau in Südwestafrika: ein Beitrag zur Frauenfrage in unseren Kolonien*, 230
Bruno Nagel Band, 23
Buch, Christoph: *Sansibar Blues*, 91
Bülow, Frieda von, 13, 210–23, 225n23, 230; *Reisescizzen and Tagebuchblätter aus Deutsch-Ostafrika*, 210–14, 221, 223

"Call of Zanzibar," 103, *104*, 105
Campt, Tina, 133, 278
"Can the Subaltern Speak?," 98
capitalism, 44, 67
Castle Einstein, 10, 29. *See also* Blaßkiewitz, Sarah
Christianity, 168, 172–3, 178, 180, 182, 216, 231
Christians, 179, 181
Civil War, the, 194, 198
colonialism, 10, 65, 72, 89–90, 95–6, 99, 121, 141, 162, 211, 222, 249; British, 114–15; German, 158, 174, 193, 196, 213, 227–9, 246–8, 251, 257, 259, 260, 261–2n6; German, in Namibia, 239, 273; impact of, 61, 63; in literature, 46, 85–6, 92, 116, 160, 228, 238, 268; Omani Arab, 99; photography and, 255; settler colonialism, 267; violence and, 237, 238, 267, 269; women and, 236, 249–50, 252
Colonial School for Women in Rendsburg, 250–1, 253, 256, 259
colourism, 33–4, 65
Cramer, Ernst Ludwig, 275–7; *Die Kinderfarm*, 275
"Cranes of Ibykus, The," 217

Daffner, Carola, 13, 230, 267
Dako, Kari, 69–70
Damara people, 266
Darko, Ophelia Amma, 57–63, 67, 69–70, 72–3, 75n12; *Spinnweben*, 58, 60–4, 69–71; *Der verkaufte Traum*, 58, 60, 62, 69–70, 73; *Verirrtes Herze*, 58
"Dekoloniale Memory Culture in the City," 260–1, 265n76
Denkabe, Aloysius, 69–70
deutsche Frau in Südwestafrika: ein Beitrag zur Frauenfrage in unseren Kolonien, Die, 230
Deutschkolonialer Frauenbund, 249–50
Deutschländer, 269
Deutschnamibier, 269
Dissertatio inauguralis de iure maurorum in Europa, 139
Dreckfresser, 24, 31
Dresden, 27, 31
DRUCK, 23–5
Du Bois, W.E.B., 132, 139

Egypt, 12, 153–6, 158, 160–2, 164, 167–8; Arabs in, 157; Ottoman, 155, 159, 166, 212; people from, 157; taxes, 165–6
Ehrenhold, M. Leberecht, 141. *See also* Philippi, Johann Ernst
Ellison, Ralph, 132, 139; *Invisible Man*, 132, 139
England, 65, 156, 166, 197, 214, 251
English, 43, 58–60, 88, 103, 105, 250, 269–70
Enlightenment, 138–9, 192, 196–7, 199, 203–4, 213; European, 198
Eppelsheimer, Natalie, 114, 116
Ernestina, Maria, 96–9
ethnicity, 4, 10
Etüden im Schnee (Yuki No Renshūsei), 134–5, 141, 144–5

Eurocentrism, 141, 275
European identity, 158, 183

Fanti people, 57, 64
Farbe bekennen, 3, 7, 9, 15n1, 17n27, 19n51
female genital mutilation (FGM), 67, 76n35
feminism, 69–70, 210–12, 214, 220–1
First World War, 5–6, 133, 141, 237, 246–7, 249–53
Floyd, George, 15, 25, 265
Focus, 133
Fontane, Theodor, 218–21; "The Bridge by the Tay," 218, 220
Fournier, Lucile, 194, 201
France, 133, 156, 166, 251
Frankfurt Book Fair, 59
Frankfurter Allgemeine Zeitung, 122
Freiheitlicher am Kongo, Ein, 175, 188n27
Frenssen, Gustav: *Peter Moors Fahrt nach Südwest*, 238
Freud, Sigmund, 202–3

Gallagher, Maureen, 13–14, 224n14, 267
Gartenlaube, Die, 191, 196, 204–5n4
gender, 3, 10, 11, 13, 41, 47, 158, 173, 182, 211, 218, 247, 260, 267; colonial ideology, 240; constraints, 13, 211, 221, 222; dichotomy, 220; equality, 66, 67; expectations, 227, 229, 239; identity, 135; inequality, 70; issues, 249; norms, 13, 116, 178, 185, 228, 229; relations, 62, 69; roles, 14, 229; stereotypes, 182, 185, 240; tropes, 173
German colonial fiction, 227, 230
"German Colonialism: Fragments Past and Present" (exhibition), 246, 261

German Democratic Republic (GDR). *See* Germany, East
German East Africa, 93, 210–12, 215, 218–23; in fiction, 214, 216
German Historical Museum, 246, 260–1
Germanistik, 270
German language, 24, 41, 57, 59–60, 98, 132, 135, 171, 192, 270
German literature, 37–9, 204, 223
German readership, 156, 161, 167
German Romanticism, 216, 222
German-speaking women, 3–5, 7–8, 10, 12, 14, 24, 134, 267, 268
German Studies, 60, 73, 135
German Studies Association (GSA), 14–15
Germany, 60–2, 69, 89, 91, 155, 167–8, 194, 196–7, 203, 258, 272; East, 27–8, 31, 44–5, 47, 50–1; Third Reich, 38, 115, 248; unification of, 37, 133; Wilhelmine, 222–3, 229, 243n24
Gezirah Palace, 156, 164–6
Ghana, 57–8, 61–2, 64–70, 268, 275
globalization, 8, 158
Glück und Geld: ein Roman aus dem heutigen Egypten, 153, 155, 164
Gordon, Avery, 83–4, 98
Göttsche, Dirk, 91, 157–8, 268, 274–5
Greer, Allan, 177, 185
Gruber, Julia K., 13–14, 240, 267
Guten Morgen Namibia! Eine Farm, eine Schule und unser Weg von der Apartheid zur Unabhängigkeit, 268, 278

Haase, Lena, 13–14, 214, 227, 229–31, 233–6, 238, 240–1; *Raggys Fahrt nach Südwest*, 227, 229, 231, 238–9, 241
Hagenbeck, Carl, 252, 264n38
Hamburg, 5, 81, 229, 239; City Hall, 97
Hammerstein, Katharina von, 210, 214, 220
Hansing House, 105, *106*
Hauptsache Windhoek, 14, 267–70, 272
Heinrich von Ofterdingen, 222
Henneböhl, Sarah, 258, 267
Herero, 235, 238, 244n53, 265n56
Heritage Walks project, 104–5
Herzensheimat Ghana, 276
Hilfswerk für Afrika, Ein, 183, 189n59, 190n62
Hitler, Adolf, 114, 248, 274
HMJokinen, 96–8; *An Maria Ernestina*, 96–7, 99
Holocaust, 11, 37–8, 112, 114–16, 204; in literature, 121, 258
Höpker, Lydia, 13–14, 227–8, 231, 233–4, 236–8, 240–1; *Um Scholle und Leben*, 227, 230–1, 238–9, 241
Hopster, Norbert, 248–9
Hornscheidt, Antje, 15, 234; *Afrika und die deutsche Sprache*, 15, 19n55, 169n7, 216, 225n22, 243n33, 243n36, 243n39, 281n20, 281n23
human-animal hierarchy, 199–200
human rights, 13, 172–3, 175, 183, 185–6
human zoo, 158, 163, 167, 248, 270
Huxley, Aldous, 246–7
Hypersexuality and Headscarves, 70

Implicated Subject: Beyond Victims and Perpetrators, The, 129n1, 129n10
Im Schillingshof, 13, 191, 196–7, 199
Indigenous peoples, 14, 102, 121, 176, 211, 222, 227, 231–8, 241, 246–7, 250–2, 255–7, 275, 278
Invisible Man, 132, 139
invisibility, 115, 132, 134, 138, 141, 144, 145, 145n2
Iowa International Writers' Workshop, 58
Ishema, Lorna, 24, 33
Ivie wie Ivie, 23–4, 26, 28, 30–2

Jackson, Iman Zakiyyah, 193, 197, 199, 208n46; *Becoming Human*, 199
Jackson, Michael, 8, 12, 134, 141–5
Jackson, Ronald L., 117–19, 123, 134, 141
Jarrett, Gene Andrew, 60–1
Jefferson, Thomas, 199, 208n41, 208n46
John, Eugenie. *See* Marlitt, Eugenie
Johnson, E. Patrick, 193, 201
Judaism, 4, 38, 115, 253

kanga, 94–5, 98
Kant, Immanuel, 139, 199
Katima: eine Kindheit in Namibia, 268
Kendi, Ibram X., 134, 277
Kenya, 112, 115–17, 125, 212, 258. *See also* British Kenya Colony
Keshodkar, Akbar, 84, 100
Khedive, 154–5, 158–60, 162, 164–7
Kilimandscharo, 246
Kilimanjaro, 93
Kilwa Kisiwani, 220–1, 223
Kinderfarm, Die, 275
Kiswahili, 91–6, 98–9, 102–3, 106
Klotz, Marcia, 229, 241
Kolonie und Heimat, 250
Köpsell, Philipp Khabo, 58–60
Kubisch, Ingrid, 270, 277–8; "Mein Windhoek-Spaziergang durch die Kinderzeit," 270, 277
Kuhnke, Jasmina: *Ein Schwarzes Herz*, 59

Lavigerie, Charles, 171–2
Layne, Priscilla, 11, 24, 39–40, 53–4, 133–4; *White Rebels in Black*, 133, 226n30
Ledóchowska, Maria Theresia, 12–13, 171–9, 181–6; "Eine afrikanische Prinzessin," 175; *Ein Freiheitlicher am Kongo*, 175, 188n27; *Ein Hilfswerk für Afrika*, 183, 189n59, 190n62; *Die Prinzessin von Uganda*, 175–6; *Von Hütte zu Hütte*, 175; *Zaïda, das Negermädchen*, 12–13, 172, 175–6, 182
Leipzig, 28, 34
Leipziger Illustrierte Zeitung, 252
Levantines, 154, 156, 160, 162–4
Leverenz, David, 139
Licht und Schatten in Namibia: Alltag in einem Traumland, 267–8, 272, 274
Link, Caroline, 113, 116
Lost Cause, 192–3, 196, 198, 203–4, 207n27

Magdeburg, Germany, 27–8, 275
Maherero, Samuel, 274, 282n34
Majid, Sultan, 95
Mandus, Anna, 267, 272–4, 277–8; *Licht und Schatten in Namibia: Alltag in einem Traumland*, 267–8, 272, 274
Marlitt, Eugenie, 12–13, 191–3, 195–8, 201, 203–4, 204n1, 205n6, 207n22; *Im Schillingshof*, 13, 191, 195, 196–7, 199, 202
martyrdom, 177–8, 180, 185
Mbembe, Achill, 116, 154
McClintock, Anne, 193, 203, 228
Meffire, Samuel, 24, 31
"Mein Windhoek-Spaziergang durch die Kinderzeit," 270, 277
Memmi, Albert, 254, 257
Meyerbeer, Giacomo, 86–7, 89–91; *Die Afrikanerin*, 86
Mills, Sara, 211, 218
missions, 182, 185; foreign, 176; literature, 176; missionaries, 174, 176, 183, 216
"Moor," 142, 153, 158, 162
Morocco, 48–9

Morrison, Toni, 194, 197, 203, 206n13
Mtoni, Zanzibar, 102–3, 105
Muslim ("Mohammedan"), 85, 94

"Nachtrag zu meinen Memoiren," 85–6, 89–90
nackte Auge, Das, 134
Nama people, 235, 238, 266, 271–2
Namibia, 227–39, 241, 241n1, 246–7, 249, 253, 255, 266–73, 275; females in, 274; Goethe-Institut, 268–9; life in, 279; in literature, 277; politics, 278
Namibian, The (newspaper) 266
narratives, hagiographic, 176, 178–9, 176, 180–1
nationalism, 154–5, 158, 168, 211, 214, 216, 258, 272; Confederate Nationalism, 196
National Socialism, 11, 112, 247, 249, 251, 262n11, 275; Nazi dictum, 14, 251; Nazi ideology, 260; Nazi propaganda, 258; Nazis, the, 27, 50, 114, 249
neoliberalism, 47–8
New Woman, 251, 253, 263n32
Nirgendwo in Afrika, 112–17, 119, 121–3, 125, 128; film adaptation, 116
Nirgendwo war Heimat: Mein Leben auf zwei Kontinenten, 112–13, 115, 121–3, 125, *126–7*, 128
Nizwa (magazine), 103
Novalis: *Heinrich von Ofterdingen*, 222
Noyes, John, 239–40

Odamtten, Vincent O., 69, 76–7n50
Oguntoye, Katharina: *Farbe bekennen*, 3, 7, 9, 15n1, 17n27, 19n51,
Okpako, Branwen, 8, 24, 31; *Dreckfresser*, 24, 31
Oman, 81, 103–4
One Thousand and One Nights, 88, 216
Orientalism, 154–5, 157–8, 161, 211, 213

Other; Otherness, 44–5, 49, 54, 63, 117–18, 132, 158, 162–3, 177, 190n61, 195, 197; Black masculinity and, 143; Othering, 47, 89, 235
Otoo, Sharon Dodua, 59–60; *Adas Raum*, 59
Ovaherero people, 266, 270–2, 276, 279n4

Painter, Nell Irvin, 193, 199; *The History of White People*, 193, 199
Palmato publishing house, 268, 274–5, 277, 279, 283n60
Partridge, Damani James, 133, 138; *Hypersexuality and Headscarves*, 70
Pasha, Ismail ,155–60, 162–8
patriarchy, 61–2, 70–1, 116
Person of Colour (POC), 10, 82, 274; BIPOC, 15
Peter Moors Fahrt nach Südwest, 238
Peters, Carl, 211–13, 218
Peters, Felizitas, 268, 274–6
Philippi, Johann Ernst, 141–2
photography, 51, 125, 127, 254–5
Piesche, Peggy, 211, 222, 267–8
Princess Salme, 97, 103; "Princess Salme Promenade," 105, *106*. See also Ruete, Emily
Prinzessin von Uganda, Die, 175–6
privilege, 45, 64, 67, 68, 82, 112–13, 221, 234; male, 69, 76–7n50, 236; white, 10, 12, 48, 50, 115, 124, 128, 211, 216, 270; white women's, 3, 14, 227, 229, 232, 239, 241

queer, 38, 71

race, 3–4, 10, 39, 41, 46; families, mixed-race, 6, 33; races, hierarchy of, 158, 167, 185, 223, 229, 232, 234–5, 251, 277
"racial realism," 60–1

racial stereotype, 122, 158, 182
racism, 26–7, 34–6, 60–1, 117, 122–3, 143, 162, 183, 192–3, 217, 223, 271–2; and clothing, 30; colonial, 114–15, 254, 260; effects of, 50, 66, 119, 138; in Europe, 82, 142; function of, 202; global, 10; in literature, 89, 128–9, 135, 142, 168, 175, 203, 275, 277; physical effects of, 33–4; positive, 32–3; structural, 48; systemic, 204; terminology of, 85–6; in United States, 132
Raggys Fahrt nach Südwest, 227, 229, 231, 238–9, 241
Redlich, Jettel, 112–13, 116, 118
Redlich, Walter, 112, 116, 118–19, 125
Reisescizzen and Tagebuchblätter aus Deutsch-Ostafrika, 210–14, 221, 223
Remembering Africa, 268
reproductive politics, 236, 241, 249
Resonanzen (literary festival), 59–60
Reuter, Gabriele, 12, 153–7, 159–60, 162, 164, 167–8; *Aus guter Familie: Leidensgeschichte eines Mädchens*, 155–6; *Glück und Geld: ein Roman aus dem heutigen Egypten*, 12, 153, 155, 164
Rhineland, 6, 133
Riesz, János, 58, 73
Rilke, Rainer Maria, 210–11
Rothberg, Michael, 11; *The Implicated Subject: Beyond Victims and Perpetrators*, 129n1, 129n10
Ruete, Emily, 5, 8, 11, 81–92, 94–7, 97, 98–100; *Briefe nach der Heimat*, 82, 86, 89–92, 94; fictional Ruete character, 92–6, 98; "Nachtrag zu meinen Memoiren," 85–6, 89–90; performances of life story, *101*, 102–5, 107
Ruete, Heinrich, 94–5, 105

Said, Edward, 154–5, 157
Salum, Fatma Khalifa, *104*
Salum, Safia Khalifa, *104*
Sam – Ein Sachse, 24, 25, 27, 31, 36n3
same-sex desire, 70–1
Sandler, Willeke, 250–1
Sansibar Blues, 91
Schiller, Friedrich von: "Cranes of Ibykus, The," 217
Schlettwein, Silvia, 14, 267–8, 270, 278; *Hauptsache Windhoek*, 14, 267–70, 272; *Katima: eine Kindheit in Namibia*, 268
Schmetterling Verlag, 58, 73
Schnee, Heinrich, 246, 261n4
Schreckenbach, Hannah, 267, 275–8; *Herzensheimat Ghana*, 276; *Sehnsuchtsland Namibia*, 267–8, 275–6
Schloss Einstein, 28–9
Schwarzes Herz, Ein, 59
Second World War, 7–8, 263n28, 265
Sehnsuchtsland Namibia, 267–8, 275–6
self, 41–2, 44, 52–3
sexism, 61, 68–9
sexual assault, 133, 140
"Shadow Man, The," 134–5
Sheriff, Abdul, 88, 103–5
skin colour, 44, 48
Skowskmi, Christine, 270
slavery, 45, 60, 67–8, 136, 141, 143, 162, 172, 197, 213; transatlantic slave trade, 154; in United States, 177, 196
Smyrna, 156, 212
Socialism, 47, 51
Society of German Colonization, 212–13, 346
Sons of Sinbad – A History of Oman, 103, *104*
South West Africa People's Organization (SWAPO), 269, 276, 278

Sow, Noah, 114–15
Spinnweben, 58, 60–4, 69–71
Spivak, Gayatri Chakravorty, 82–3, 91–3, 96, 98–9; "Can the Subaltern Speak?," 98
sterilization, 7
Sterne über Sansibar, 91, 95
Steup, Elisabeth, 13–14, 247, 249–51, 253, 254–5, 258–61; *Wiete erlebt Afrika: ein junges Mädchen bei deutschen Farmern*, 247, 249, 252, 254–5, 259; Wiete novels, 240, 249–53, 258, 260; *Wiete will nach Afrika*, 253–4
Stone Town, 102, 104–5, 213
Stowe, Harriet Beecher, 171–4, 177–8, 186, 196; *Uncle Tom's Cabin*, 171–3, 177–80, 185, 186, 196
subject, 40, 52, 60, 177; agency, 51; colonial, 12, 92, 121, 247, 257; German, 86; implicated, 11, 15, 112, 114, 115; moral, 182; position, 42, 81, 82, 84, 96, 99, 100; white, 128. See also Rothberg, Michael
Süddeutsche Zeitung, Die, 133
Suez Canal, 156, 164
Swakopmund, 266, 276–7
Südwester, 269, 272

Tanzania, 81, 91, 95, 97, 212, 230
Tatlock, Lynne, 191, 193, 195, 197, 205n8
1000 Serpentinen Angst, 37–40, 42–3, 46, 50, 57, 59
Tawada, Yoko, 8, 12, 134–7, 139, 141–2, 144–5; "Bioscope of the Night," 137; *Etüden im Schnee (Yuki No Renshūsei)*, 134–5, 141, 144–5; *Das nackte Auge*, 134; "The Shadow Man," 134–45
telos, 38–9, 41
Trappe, Margarete, 92–3, 95
trauma, 46, 51, 52, 137–8
travel, 41–3, 45, 53–4
Turkish German literature, 37–8
Tötemeyer, Andrée-Jeanne, 275

Um Scholle und Leben, 227, 230–1, 238–9, 241
Uncle Tom's Cabin, 171–3, 177–80, 185, 186, 196
United States of America, 35, 194, 196–7, 260, 266, 272

Verirrtes Herze, 58
verkaufte Traum, Der, 58, 60, 62, 69–70, 73
Versailles, Treaty of, 6, 246–7
Virgin Mary, 179–80
Von Hütte zu Hütte, 175
Vosseler, Nicole C., 91–6, 98; *Sterne über Sansibar*, 91, 95

Wagner, Richard, 143
Wainaina, Binyavanga, 83, 94, 128
Walgenbach, Katharina, 228
Weber, Beverly, 133, 138–9
Weimar Republic, 247, 251
weiße Jägerin, Die, 91
Weitzenberg, Arno, 252, 264n39
Weitzenberg, Louise (nee Steup), 252–3
Wenzel, Olivia, 10, 37–40, 42–5, 57–8, 52–7, 59; *1000 Serpentinen Angst*, 37–40, 42–3, 46, 50, 57, 59
Western world, 40–1
whiteness, 39, 44, 47, 62, 65, 118, 137, 192–3, 195, 197, 200; critical perspective, 14, 267; feminism and, 3, 278; German, 199; Southern, 198
white privilege, 48, 50, 115, 123, 128, 232, 239, 241, 270. See also privilege
White Rebels in Black, 133, 226n30

white supremacy, 6, 60, 62, 64–5, 201, 218, 227, 234, 236, 267–9
whitewashing, 193, 212
white women, 4, 12, 211, 218, 221, 228–33, 236, 238, 247
Wiete erlebt Afrika: ein junges Mädchen bei deutschen Farmern, 247, 249, 252, 254–5, 259
Wiete novels, 240, 249–53, 258, 260
Wiete will nach Afrika, 253–4
Wietersheim, Erika von, 267–70, 278; *Guten Morgen Namibia! Eine Farm, eine Schule und unser Weg von der Apartheid zur Unabhängigkeit*, 268, 278; *Hauptsache Windhoek*, 14, 267–70, 272
Wildenthal, Lora, 214, 227–8, 250–2
Windhoek, 230, 268–70, 273, 276–7
Wirtschaftswunder, 7
Witbooi, Henrik, 274, 282n34
Wölfenbüttel, 135, 143

xenophobia, 135, 193

Yitah, Helen, 69–70

Zaïda, das Negermädchen, 12–13, 172, 175–6, 182
Zak, Louise Allen, 58, 61, 63, 73
Zantop, Susanne, 193, 197, 248
Zanzibar, 81–2, 84, 90–1, 95, 99, 102–3, 107, 211–17; City, 213, 215; Revolution of 1964, 99–100, 103
Zukunft, Die, 221
Zweig, Jettel, 122–4. *See also* Redlich, Jettel
Zweig, Max, 118–19, 125, *127*
Zweig, Stefanie, 11–12, 112–15, 117–18, 121–2, 125, *126*, 127–8, 258; *Nirgendwo in Afrika* (book), 112–17, 119, 121–3, 125, 128; *Nirgendwo in Afrika* (film adaptation), 116; *Nirgendwo war Heimat: Mein Leben auf zwei Kontinenten*, 112–13, 115, 121–3, 125, *126–7*, 128
Zweig, Walter, 119, *120*, 121, 123–5. *See also* Redlich, Walter

German and European Studies

General Editor: James Retallack

1 Emanuel Adler, Beverly Crawford, Federica Bicchi, and Rafaella Del Sarto, *The Convergence of Civilizations: Constructing a Mediterranean Region*
2 James Retallack, *The German Right, 1860–1920: Political Limits of the Authoritarian Imagination*
3 Silvija Jestrovic, *Theatre of Estrangement: Theory, Practice, Ideology*
4 Susan Gross Solomon, ed., *Doing Medicine Together: Germany and Russia between the Wars*
5 Laurence McFalls, ed., *Max Weber's 'Objectivity' Revisited*
6 Robin Ostow, ed., *(Re)Visualizing National History: Museums and National Identities in Europe in the New Millennium*
7 David Blackbourn and James Retallack, eds., *Localism, Landscape, and the Ambiguities of Place: German-Speaking Central Europe, 1860–1930*
8 John Zilcosky, ed., *Writing Travel: The Poetics and Politics of the Modern Journey*
9 Angelica Fenner, *Race under Reconstruction in German Cinema: Robert Stemmle's Toxi*
10 Martina Kessel and Patrick Merziger, eds., *The Politics of Humour: Laughter, Inclusion, and Exclusion in the Twentieth Century*
11 Jeffrey K. Wilson, *The German Forest: Nature, Identity, and the Contestation of a National Symbol, 1871–1914*
12 David G. John, *Bennewitz, Goethe,* Faust: *German and Intercultural Stagings*
13 Jennifer Ruth Hosek, *Sun, Sex, and Socialism: Cuba in the German Imaginary*
14 Steven M. Schroeder, *To Forget It All and Begin Again: Reconciliation in Occupied Germany, 1944–1954*
15 Kenneth S. Calhoon, *Affecting Grace: Theatre, Subject, and the Shakespearean Paradox in German Literature from Lessing to Kleist*
16 Martina Kolb, *Nietzsche, Freud, Benn, and the Azure Spell of Liguria*

17. Hoi-eun Kim, *Doctors of Empire: Medical and Cultural Encounters between Imperial Germany and Meiji Japan*
18. J. Laurence Hare, *Excavating Nations: Archeology, Museums, and the German-Danish Borderlands*
19. Jacques Kornberg, *The Pope's Dilemma: Pius XII Faces Atrocities and Genocide in the Second World War*
20. Patrick O'Neill, *Transforming Kafka: Translation Effects*
21. John K. Noyes, *Herder: Aesthetics against Imperialism*
22. James Retallack, *Germany's Second Reich: Portraits and Pathways*
23. Laurie Marhoefer, *Sex and the Weimar Republic: German Homosexual Emancipation and the Rise of the Nazis*
24. Bettina Brandt and Daniel L. Purdy, eds., *China in the German Enlightenment*
25. Michael Hau, *Performance Anxiety: Sport and Work in Germany from the Empire to Nazism*
26. Celia Applegate, *The Necessity of Music: Variations on a German Theme*
27. Richard J. Golsan and Sarah M. Misemer, eds., *The Trial That Never Ends: Hannah Arendt's* Eichmann in Jerusalem *in Retrospect*
28. Lynne Taylor, *In the Children's Best Interests: Unaccompanied Children in American-Occupied Germany, 1945–1952*
29. Jennifer A. Miller, *Turkish Guest Workers in Germany: Hidden Lives and Contested Borders, 1960s to 1980s*
30. Amy Carney, *Marriage and Fatherhood in the Nazi SS*
31. Michael E. O'Sullivan, *Disruptive Power: Catholic Women, Miracles, and Politics in Modern Germany, 1918–1965*
32. Gabriel N. Finder and Alexander V. Prusin, *Justice behind the Iron Curtain: Nazis on Trial in Communist Poland*
33. Parker Daly Everett, *Urban Transformations: From Liberalism to Corporatism in Greater Berlin, 1871–1933*
34. Melissa Kravetz, *Women Doctors in Weimar and Nazi Germany: Maternalism, Eugenics, and Professional Identity*
35. Javier Samper Vendrell, *The Seduction of Youth: Print Culture and Homosexual Rights in the Weimar Republic*
36. Sebastian Voigt, ed., *Since the Boom: Continuity and Change in the Western Industrialized World after 1970*
37. Olivia Landry, *Theatre of Anger: Radical Transnational Performance in Contemporary Berlin*
38. Jeremy Best, *Heavenly Fatherland: German Missionary Culture and Globalization in the Age of Empire*
39. Svenja Bethke, *Dance on the Razor's Edge: Crime and Punishment in the Nazi Ghettos*
40. Kenneth S. Calhoon, *The Long Century's Long Shadow: Weimar Cinema and the Romantic Modern*

41 Randall Hansen, Achim Saupe, Andreas Wirsching, and Daqing Yang, eds., *Authenticity and Victimhood after the Second World War: Narratives from Europe and East Asia*
42 Rebecca Wittmann, ed., *The Eichmann Trial Reconsidered*
43 Sebastian Huebel, *Fighter, Worker, and Family Man: German-Jewish Men and Their Gendered Experiences in Nazi Germany, 1933–1941*
44 Samuel Clowes Huneke, *States of Liberation: Gay Men between Dictatorship and Democracy in Cold War Germany*
45 Tuska Benes, *The Rebirth of Revelation: German Theology in an Age of Reason and History, 1750–1850*
46 Skye Doney, *The Persistence of the Sacred: German Catholic Pilgrimage, 1832–1937*
47 Matthew Unangst, *Colonial Geography: Race and Space in German East Africa, 1884–1905*
48 Deborah Barton, *Writing and Rewriting the Reich: Women Journalists in the Nazi and Post-war Press*
49 Martin Wagner, *A Stage for Debate: The Political Significance of Vienna's Burgtheater, 1814–1867*
50 Andrea Rottmann, *Queer Lives across the Wall: Desire and Danger in Divided Berlin, 1945–1970*
51 Jeffrey Schneider, *Uniform Fantasies: Soldiers, Sex, and Queer Emancipation in Imperial Germany*
52 Alexandria N. Ruble, *Entangled Emancipation: Women's Rights in Cold War Germany*
53 Johanna Schuster-Craig, *One Word Shapes a Nation: Integration Politics in Germany*
54 Kiran Klaus Patel, ed., *Tangled Transformations: Unifying Germany and Integrating Europe, 1985–1995*
55 Abraham Rubin, *Conversion and Catastrophe in German-Jewish Émigré Autobiography*
56 Ulf Brunnbauer, Philipp Ther, Piotr Filipkowski, Andrew Hodges, Stefano Petrungaro, and Peter Wegenschimmel, *In the Storms of Transformation: Two Shipyards between Socialism and the EU*
57 Alexandra Birch, *Hitler's Twilight of the Gods: Music and the Orchestration of War and Genocide in Europe*
58 Jeffrey Champlin, *Born Again: Romanticism and Fundamentalism*
59 Priscilla Layne, Michelle James, and Lisabeth Hock, eds., *Afrika and Alemania: German-Speaking Women, Africa, and the African Diaspora*